Growing
in
Christian
Morality

Nihil Obstat:
  Rev. William M. Becker, STD
  Censor Librorum
  18 May 1995

Imprimatur:
  †Most Rev. John G. Vlazny, DD
  Bishop of Winona
  18 May 1995

The nihil obstat and imprimatur are official declarations that a book or pamphlet is free of doctrinal or moral error. No implication is contained therein that those who have granted the nihil obstat or imprimatur agree with the contents, opinions, or statements expressed.

The publishing team included Stephan Nagel and Michael Wilt, development editors; Robert Smith, FSC, consulting editor; Rebecca Fairbank, copy editor; Barbara Bartelson, production editor and typesetter; Maurine R. Twait, art director; Penny Koehler, photo researcher; Tim Foley, illustrator; and Alan M. Greenberg, Integrity Indexing, indexer.

The acknowledgments continue on page 301.

Printed in the United States of America

Printing: 9 8 7 6 5 4 3 2 1

Year: 2004 03 02 01 00 99 98 97 96

ISBN 0-88489-387-1

 Genuine recycled paper with 10% post-consumer waste.
Printed with soy-based ink.

Saint Mary's Press
Christian Brothers Publications
Winona, Minnesota

Growing in Christian Morality

by
Julia Ahlers,
Barbara Allaire,
and Carl Koch

Contents

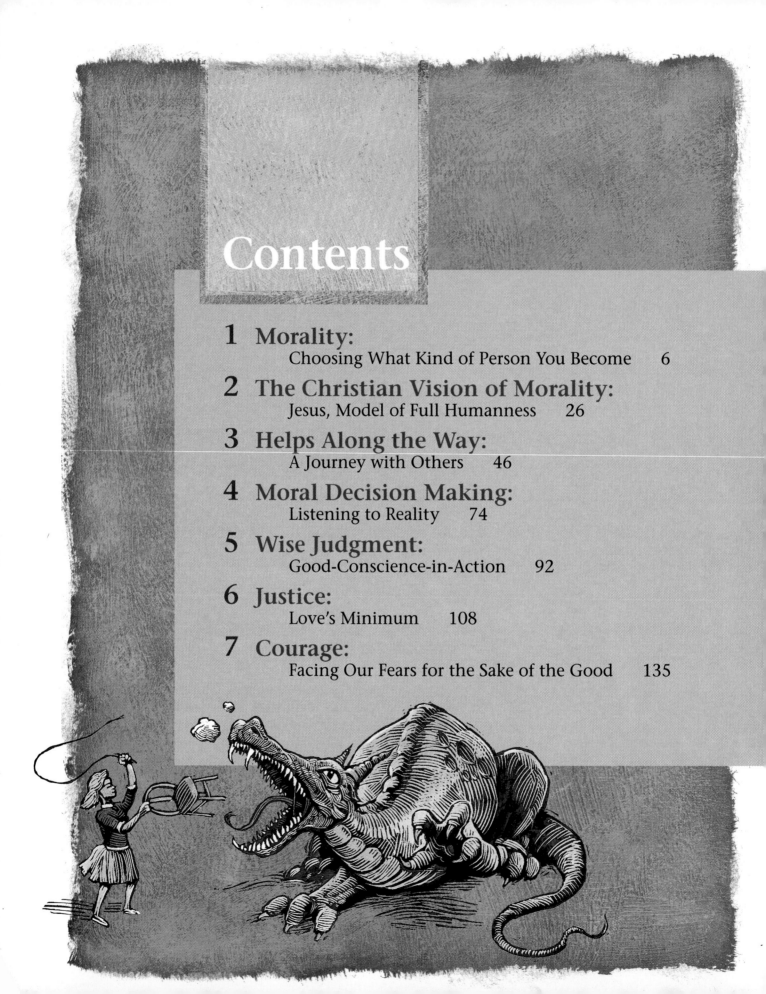

1 **Morality:**
Choosing What Kind of Person You Become   6

2 **The Christian Vision of Morality:**
Jesus, Model of Full Humanness   26

3 **Helps Along the Way:**
A Journey with Others   46

4 **Moral Decision Making:**
Listening to Reality   74

5 **Wise Judgment:**
Good-Conscience-in-Action   92

6 **Justice:**
Love's Minimum   108

7 **Courage:**
Facing Our Fears for the Sake of the Good   135

8 Wholeness:
Toward Strength, Beauty, and Happiness   154

9 Honesty:
Creating Trust   178

10 Respect for Persons:
Looking Again   196

11 Compassion:
Solidarity with Those Who Suffer   214

12 Respect for Creation:
The Earth as God's   228

13 Reverence for Human Life:
Cherishing the Gift   244

14 Peacemaking:
Handling Conflict with Creativity   270

Index   289

1

Morality:
Choosing
What Kind
of Person
You Become

Three Stories, Three Kinds of Choices

Frank, Christine, and Derek

Let's begin this course in morality with three stories that will plunge us into the reality of moral dilemmas that teenagers face today.

Frank's Mess

Frank saw the police car's lights flash in the rearview mirror even before he heard the siren. Panicking, the three other guys in Frank's car started swearing. Harley yelled for Frank to lose the cops, but Frank froze for a moment and then pulled over to the curb. Seconds later, he heard the police yelling for all of them to put their hands where they could be seen. Then, while one officer stayed next to the squad car, the other approached the driver's window. Frank's hands shook, and sweat poured down his face. The evidence convicting the four guys was crammed around them in the car.

In the next few moments, Frank flashed back on how he had gotten into this mess. His mind went over the painful events of recent months. . . .

When Frank's mother told him four months ago that they would be moving from Baltimore to Memphis so she could take a promotion, he could hardly control his anger. Frank's social life had just gotten good. He had finally found a girlfriend, and he even liked his high school. Moving forced him to start all over again, with only two years of school left to win some friends and to feel like he fit in.

Frank entered his new high school in Memphis with about as much enthusiasm as somebody going to have their wisdom teeth pulled. Most of the students seemed like snobs. He missed his girlfriend. Loneliness and boredom finally pushed him to start talking to Harley, a guy who had joked around with him once or twice.

Then Harley invited Frank to go to the last football game of the season with him. At least it was something to do on Friday night. Frank quickly realized that Harley also expected him to drive, because Harley and his two buddies Rick and Dave couldn't get a car.

The game bored Frank and so did the guys, who seemed like jerks to him. But he felt he should pretend he was having fun. Afterward, to "celebrate" the game (their team had lost), Harley told Frank to take them to a liquor store and to buy some beer, because he looked the oldest. A little later, Frank and his three "happy" passengers passed the city zoo.

"Hey," Dave yelled, "let's rip off some of those crazy signs and put them in people's yards!" Frank laughed. The zoo used large, brightly painted signs in the shape of animals to direct people to the different animal areas.

"Yeah, let's go for it. Stop over there, Frank." This time Frank didn't laugh, but when the three guys started shouting at him, he pulled into a parking spot next to a tall fence. In ten minutes, Harley, Dave, and Rick had scaled the zoo fence and returned with three signs—a hippopotamus, a flamingo, and a gorilla. They were too drunk to be quiet. . . .

Frank shook himself out of his flashback when he heard the police officer telling him to get out of the car.

Christine's Fix

Christine and her two friends Lisa and Becky hurried into the cafeteria to get in line for a quick lunch. They glanced over to the Pepsi machine where that new girl was standing, looking uncomfortable. The friends elbowed one another, recalling how the new girl had

unknowingly prompted a ripple of grins and eye rolling when she had walked into homeroom that morning for the first time.

Mrs. Cleary had introduced the new student to the class: "Everybody, this is Monica; she transferred from Central High." Almost everyone had smiled politely at Monica then, but when she had taken her assigned seat in the front row, the smirks had begun again.

Christine, sitting near the back of the room with her friends, had heard them whisper: "Where do you suppose she got those clothes?" "Don't know. . . . Either her grandmother's closet or the Salvation Army reject pile." "Check the hair." "Got it . . . 1980s, definitely."

So now Monica stood by the Pepsi machine, fumbling for change and looking like she didn't want to risk sitting down at a table where she might not be welcome. Lisa, moving quickly through the line with a carton of yogurt, caught up to Christine and Becky and said, "Let's have a little contest to see who can guess what she'll be wearing tomorrow."

Becky, giggling, answered, "No, I think we should try to predict who she'll end up hanging out with here—that'll be more of a challenge!"

Christine liked being in on laughs, but this just did not seem funny. She felt bad for Monica, who was by now seeking out a table where people were leaving. Sure, Monica wasn't dressed in fashion and her hair looked kind of funny, but she didn't deserve to be laughed at.

For a moment, Christine considered saying to her friends, "Don't include me in on your guessing game." But she thought better—why get Lisa and Becky upset with her? So Christine kept quiet, just smiled faintly, and resolved to go and say hello to the new girl when her own friends were not around.

Derek's Conflict

Derek finished up his geometry homework just as the bell for first period rang. He closed his book and prepared to leave for class. Out of the corner of his eye, he noticed his friend Jeff slipping a textbook off a stack of books on the next table. Derek wondered what was going on but kept his mouth shut.

As Derek headed for the door, he heard another friend, Jennifer, asking around nervously, "Has anyone seen my history book? I had it in this stack a minute ago. God, if I lost it! What a bummer! That book's worth twenty-five dollars." Jennifer stared at everyone, suspecting a prank. No one laughed. Most just shrugged their shoulders or shook their head. Jennifer's nervousness turned to anger. Grabbing her other books, she stormed off to the school office.

Derek had seen the whole thing. Now he remembered that Jeff had misplaced his own history book last week and was going to have to pay the school for it if he didn't find it. So Jeff had taken the cheap way out.

Derek wondered what to do. If he told Jennifer that Jeff had taken the book, Jeff would be angry and probably deny it, essentially calling him a liar. But Jennifer needed the book. Why should she end up paying for the book that Jeff lost last week? Well, Derek figured, he could tell Jennifer that Jeff had taken her book but ask her not to let Jeff know how she found out. . . . Nah, he would still get dragged into it. Derek hated these tight situations. Why did he have to get into the middle of this mess? Why couldn't he just pretend he never saw a thing, mind his own business, and forget about it?

But Derek couldn't forget. Jennifer was a friend. So was Jeff, but it wasn't right to say nothing to either of them. Building his courage, Derek caught Jeff by the lockers between classes and told him he had seen him take Jennifer's history book. "Jeff, why don't you just put it on her desk?" Derek suggested. "No one will ever have to know."

"I had to take it, Derek. My dad will kill me if he gets a book bill. You know what he's like."

Jeff was telling the truth, Derek knew. Jeff's dad was always erupting into anger. "We'll figure something out, Jeff. You can borrow my book until then. But Jennifer's a friend, and I'm on the spot here."

Jeff glared at him. "I thought you were *my* friend." He clenched his fists, then turned and stormed off down the hall. **1**

Distinct Approaches to Choices

In your high school years, you face a multitude of moral choices, with any number of pressures attached to each one. You may have seen people your own age thinking and acting much like the characters in the stories that begin this chapter, and you may be able to identify with one or more of the characters. The main character in each story represents a different approach to making choices.

Frank: Loneliness and Insecurity

Frank is driven by a lot of pressures, a key one being his need for acceptance from his peers. He reacts to a difficult period in his life—the move to a new city and a new school—in a natural way: he feels lonely, insecure, and vulnerable. In this emotional state, most of us would do a lot to gain the approval of our new peers—sometimes too much. Even though he is the driver of the car for the evening, Frank is *not* "in the driver's seat"; his peers are. He has surrendered control of his actions, but not his responsibility for their consequences.

1
Think of a situation in your life in which you made a decision similar to Frank's, Christine's, or Derek's. Describe in writing the factors that entered into your decision.

Christine: Integrity and Fear

Christine is more secure and in touch with her emotions than Frank is. Empathizing with the new girl, Christine disapproves of her friends for their sarcastic remarks, and she resolves not to join them in making fun of Monica. We can admire Christine for being in charge of herself and for not participating in hurtful behavior, even though she remains silent with her friends about what they are doing, not daring to make a fool of herself by questioning their ridicule. Christine decides on a *private* course of action—to approach the new girl later and welcome her, but without letting her friends see her friendly gesture. Christine is not yet ready to speak up on Monica's behalf to her friends; she is still fearful of their disapproval. But by choosing not to join in the ridicule, Christine is at least in charge of her own behavior, and she is headed down the road to integrity.

Derek: Courage When the Truth Hurts

Derek's plight is not one to envy. Torn between two friends, it seems that no matter what he does, he will have to be disloyal to one of them—to the friend whose book was stolen or to the friend who stole the book. But, in Derek's mind, the matter does not boil down only to an issue of loyalty, to which friend most deserves his support. (Actually, confronting Jeff may be, in the long run, the most loyal thing Derek could do for him.) Instead, the matter comes down to what is right and fair. Even though Derek feels torn over what to do, he chooses a courageous action—an action that may, however, mean the loss of a friend. 2

Only for Young People?

You have probably seen these three approaches to choosing (Frank's, Christine's, and Derek's) at one time or another in yourself or in other high school students. The fact is, however, that people of all ages—adults as well as teenagers—use a combination of these approaches. Many of us have witnessed forty-year-old Franks operating from their weaknesses and following the crowd. Age does not equal maturity. Certainly a situation like Christine's is familiar to people of various ages, not just to teenagers. We have all, adults included, believed strongly in something but tactfully avoided saying what we believe when we fear our friends would be upset by it. The courage of Derek, too, can be seen in people who choose the right path, suffer for it, and sometimes wonder if they could have found a better way to deal with the situation.

So these approaches characterize not only teenagers but people at many stages of life. In high school, though, you are at a crucial stage of forming your identity; you may not be sure of your values and beliefs yet. Thus, many factors can seem outside your control—peer pressures or feelings or impulses that seem to compel you to do something or that blind you from seeing a situation clearly. Becoming conscious and courageous about our decisions can seem a tough, if not impossible, task. 3

For Review

- Describe the three approaches to choosing represented by Frank, Christine, and Derek.

2
Write a brief inner monolog (self-talk) that Frank, Christine, or Derek might have had in trying to decide what to do.

3
What factors make it difficult for many teenagers to make informed and courageous decisions? List as many as you can.

Backing Up to Define Morality

This course is all about what it means to become morally mature, and before we go any further, it would help to reflect on just what morality is.

What Kinds of Decisions Involve Morality?

Look at the following list of choices. Decide which ones involve a moral decision and which ones are morally neutral—that is, a person would not need to use any moral considerations in deciding on them:

1. whether to go out with friends on a Friday night or stay home ∧
2. whether to lie to avoid being blamed for something that was your fault ⋌
3. whether to go to McDonald's or Burger King for a hamburger ∧
4. whether to have sex before marriage ⋌
5. whether to try out for the softball team ∧
6. whether to sell crack cocaine in your neighborhood for a drug dealer ⋌
7. whether to work weekends and evenings while in high school ⋌
8. whether to have an abortion ⋌
9. which candidate to vote for in an election ⋌

A review of the list shows that the choices are of different types. Some so obviously involve a moral dimension that we have no difficulty identifying them as moral issues—namely, 2, 4, 6, and 8. Other decisions may prompt us to say, "It depends"—1, 5, 7, and 9. Then there is decision 3, which may seem to be empty of any moral content.

Why do most people identify decisions 2, 4, 6, and 8 as moral ones? These decisions clearly are based on a person's values and principles of right

Above, left and right: Dating behaviors obviously involve moral decisions, but what about decisions such as where to buy a meal?

and wrong. Furthermore, these decisions shape the *kind of person* that the decider is becoming. They go to the core of the person. For instance, the decision of whether to lie to avoid being blamed for a mistake points toward becoming a person who is honest or dishonest, trustworthy or untrustworthy.

Morality, then, has to do with the set of values and principles that guide someone's choices about what kind of person he or she is becoming. These values and principles point to the meaning that life has for that person.

Consider the "it depends" choices from the list—1, 5, 7, and 9. Given the definition of morality just stated, those items could potentially involve a *moral* choice. For example, the decision of whether to go out with friends on a Friday night or stay at home could be a moral one, depending on what the friends are planning to do or on whether the individual has to get up at five o'clock the next morning for a track meet. Now think about decision 3. Can you imagine how the choice between McDonald's and Burger King could have a moral dimension? It *is* possible.

The point is that just about any decision can involve morality. We go through countless moral decisions daily, even though we may never have viewed them as having moral dimensions. Our decisions, small as they may seem, shape the kind of person we are now and will become in the future, and they reflect what life's meaning is for us. **4**

Everybody's Got a Morality

Notice that so far we have not referred to morality as "good" behavior and attitudes. Morality includes *all* the values and principles that shape who a person is becoming. Morality is not concerned only with the values and principles considered good by

religious or other "good" people. (We will explore the meaning of *good* later in this chapter.) In the stories at the beginning of this chapter, the main characters were each operating from their own morality, whether admirable or not. In other words, everyone—every individual and every culture—has a morality. Morality is not reserved exclusively for "good" people.

Individuals and Cultures

Two persons may approach the same situation with vastly different moralities, but they are still each operating from *a* morality. The following story illustrates how moralities can differ:

A manager of a chemical company is faced with the fact that his company has made a serious mistake by spilling toxic chemicals into a river. The spill could endanger public health and wildlife. Because the manager operates from a morality whose basic principle is "Do whatever is needed to get ahead," he chooses to cover up any knowledge of the spill so that his job will not be in jeopardy.

A manager of another chemical plant in a similar situation decides to go to public authorities about the spill so that it can be cleaned up as quickly as possible. This manager operates from a morality whose basic principle is "Do whatever is needed for the well-being of others."

Like individuals, cultures have their own moralities, with a variety of moral norms and values— some that seem to benefit human beings and some that do not. Two cultures may have significantly different moral approaches. In a culture where females are not valued as highly as males, it may be socially acceptable for parents to abandon a female infant and allow her to die. In another culture, all life may be held as sacred and all children treated

4
Review your day and record all the decisions you have made since waking up. Which decisions involved a moral dimension?

as gifts to be cherished. Most people would say that both cultures operate according to their own morality but that these moralities are not equally beneficial to human beings.

Different Stages of Life

Individuals, like cultures, can have differing moralities, and individuals, like cultures, can shift from one morality to another over a period of time. Certainly this is true when a person undergoes a dramatic conversion from a life of crime or addiction to a life of responsible, healthy living, or from one religion that is not strict with its members to another that is very strict.

A more typical way that people change their morality over time is by the profound process of growth through the various stages of life.

The morality of childhood. Children obey their parents because they fear punishment, or because they want to please the ones they depend on for love and support. We could say that the basic moral principle for a small child is "Do what your parents tell you to do so that they will be pleased with you."

This morality works and makes perfect sense during childhood because children are not yet capable of making independent decisions about right and wrong. As they grow, children typically develop a sense that rules and laws can be important in themselves, not just because their parents are enforcing them. In fact, children can become legal sticklers: "You can't do it that way; that's not what the rules say!" However, children perceive rules and laws as outside themselves—somebody else's rules for living—and their job as good children is just to follow along.

The morality of mature adulthood. Unlike the morality of childhood, mature adult morality requires judgment based on values that are *within* the person, not imposed from without. The values

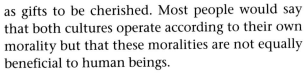

Above, left and right: The profound process of growth changes our morality in dramatic ways.

ically adopt the values of a peer group. Membership in the group offers security and a sense of being somebody. Teenagers may feel that they have "found themselves," when in fact, they have found a group that tells them how to think and act. Actually, this process is typical and normal for younger adolescents. They tend to define themselves almost exclusively through belonging to a peer group and being accepted by their peers.

Usually by their sophomore or junior year of high school, young persons have developed confidence and have begun to trust their own judgments and opinions; thus, their reliance on peers' opinions is not as strong. A student at a midwestern college recalls his high school years:

When I was a freshman in high school, I'd do almost anything to fit in, even if it seemed stupid. I was just trying to be cool, to pump up my ego, which must have been in pretty rough shape. I guess I mistook approval for love, but it's a poor substitute, I must say. Later on, I found out it's okay to be your own person. By junior and senior year of high school, I felt a lot freer to call things as I saw them instead of always looking to someone else to decide for me.

This young adult has described part of the process of transition from the morality of childhood to the morality of mature adulthood. The latter part of adolescence is often characterized by great idealism as young people's moral sensitivities grow, and they become critical of societal values. **5**

Being Critical of the Moralities Around Us

All people are created equal, but not all moralities are. There are beneficial ones and harmful ones, life-giving ones and death-dealing ones, mature

of mature adults are often those that they grew up with—in their family, in their church, or in their ethnic culture. However, now the values are within these individuals, taken on as their own. On the other hand, some of their values might differ from those they learned in their youth. The important thing about maturing morally is that persons have made the values and principles a part of themselves.

The in-between morality of adolescence. Somewhere between the morality of childhood and that of mature adulthood lies the often confusing world of adolescent morality. As young people attempt to move from parent-pleasing behavior and external rules to making choices that come from within themselves, they find an array of peer values to choose from, many of them reinforced by the mass media—advertising, TV shows, magazines, movies, and popular music. To be well liked or even somewhat accepted, teenagers may uncrit-

---

Above: As teenagers move away from parent-pleasing behavior, they find an array of peer values to choose from.

5
Write a "moral development" autobiography, describing the changes you have seen in your own morality as you have grown through the life stages from childhood until now.

How does your experience correspond with the process described in the text?

Universal Rules?

An earlier section of this chapter pointed out that moralities can differ from one society or culture to another. You may wonder if all cultures or religions around the world hold any principles in common—or if there is no universal agreement on any principles.

Although unanimous agreement among all individuals on anything is impossible, we can find consensus on many values and principles among the most

enduring of the world's religions. Because these religions speak for so many of the earth's people and have stood the test of centuries, we can trust that when these religions all share a similar principle, that principle is considered universal.

In fact, many of the values and principles held by Christianity are espoused by the other major faiths as well. Note the Golden Rule as expressed by six world religions:

- *Buddhism.* Hurt not others in ways that you yourself would find hurtful.
- *Hinduism.* Do not do to others what would cause you pain if done to you.
- *Judaism.* What is hateful to you, do not do to others.
- *Taoism.* Regard your neighbor's gain as your own gain and your neighbor's loss as your own loss.
- *Islam.* No one of you is a believer until you desire for your sister or brother that which you desire for yourself.
- *Christianity.* Do to others whatever you would have done to you.

Universal principles that most of the world's people believe in do exist. These principles speak a deep truth about what it means to be human, and they transcend all cultures and religions. How they are applied to everyday life varies, of course, but remarkable consistency in the principles themselves does exist around the world.

Above: In clockwise order from the top, the symbols are Taoist, Islamic, Jewish, and Hindu.

ones and immature ones. It is up to us as we develop into mature adults to be critical of the moralities we find in our pluralistic North American society, in which values and principles often seem to be dished up as options, like a cafeteria-style lunch.

Looking critically at the values of our society does not mean we are being disloyal to it; a critical stance means we are being sensible and living as responsible citizens. In particular, we need to ask ourselves:

- Do some of the values promoted in our society really contribute to the well-being of all people, empowering them and freeing them? Or do they rob people of well-being, power, and freedom?

Some values in our society are among the most noble that humankind has ever known, for example, these beliefs:

- the equality of all persons
- the importance of individual action and initiative
- democracy as the way to govern and make decisions
- equal rights to freedom of speech, religion, the press, assembly, and so on
- the obligation of more fortunate people to help less fortunate people

But in addition to the many positive things we can say about North American values, commentators have pointed to the presence of other values that permeate society through the mass media and other means—values that need to be questioned by all of us. Some of these values even contradict the noble beliefs listed above:

- *Materialism.* The assumption that happiness lies primarily in possessions and a high standard of living

- *Competitiveness and a "me first" attitude.* The assumption that getting ahead and being number one are all-important
- *The "isms"—racism, sexism, ageism.* The assumption that some people and groups are better, more human, and more deserving of rights than others, based on some accidental characteristic like skin color, sex, or age
- *A "quick fix" mentality.* The assumption that the quickest possible escape from problems or pain is the best solution
- *Violence.* The assumption that physical or psychological harm to others is the means to get one's way **6**

Whenever we adopt a critical stance toward societal values, we become more conscious of who we are and what we want out of life. We refuse to follow the noise of the crowd and instead decide to follow another, quieter, inner voice. Henry David Thoreau, a nineteenth-century philosopher and essayist, described this reality with a good piece of advice:

If a man does not keep pace with his companions, perhaps it is because he hears a different drummer. Let him step to the music he hears, however measured or far away. (*Walden,* page 346) **7**

For Review

- What is morality? What kinds of decisions involve morality?
- Describe the morality of childhood, of mature adulthood, and of adolescence.
- What five values in North American society need to be questioned by all of us?

6
Use ads from magazines or newspapers to create a collage that illustrates the negative values listed on this page. Make up a title for your collage.

7
Do some research and write a report on Thoreau's life. In what ways did he march to the rhythm of a "different drummer"? Do you know of a "modern-day Thoreau"—either personally or through the news? Describe him or her.

Which Morality Will Be Mine?

The Kind of Person I Am Becoming

The major moral question that each of us has to answer for ourselves is this:

- **What kind of person am I becoming, and what kind of person do I want to become?**

Morality is about making decisions that shape our character and reflect our understanding of the meaning and purpose of our life. This is about as important as questions get! **8**

Yet, we cannot decide what kind of person we want to become all at one moment or even in a year. We may want to be able to say yes to one direction for our life and no to another in one definite decision. But reality is usually more complicated and less dramatic than that. We answer the crucial question *What kind of person do I want to become?* in thousands of day-to-day, apparently small decisions. Taken together, these decisions create the kind of person we are becoming and will become. The creation of this person is the most important task of anyone's life as a human being.

A wise saying captures this truth:

Plant an act; reap a habit.
Plant a habit; reap a virtue or a vice.
Plant a virtue or a vice; reap a character.
Plant a character; reap a destiny. **9**

As one student says, "Becoming somebody is like becoming a pianist; you have to practice every day until you get good at it."

Unless we become conscious of the significance of our daily choices, we will go through life with

A Few Definitions

A **habit** is a regular pattern of acts.

A **virtue** is a good habit, an inner readiness to accomplish moral good.

A **vice** is a bad habit, an inner readiness to accomplish moral evil.

Character is the combination of our virtues and vices.

Destiny is what finally becomes of us, which depends on the character we build in response to God's help.

8
Write a brief essay answering this question as best you can:
- What kind of person am I becoming, and what kind of person do I want to become?

9
Read a biography of someone who fascinates you, and write about the acts in that person's life that turned into the habits (virtues or vices) that shaped her or his character and destiny.

our eyes closed. A seventeen-year-old girl expresses this reality in the following comment:

We're all so impressionable, you know? Your sense of self, who you are, comes from where you decide to go, what you choose to do, who your friends are, what you buy, things like that. You're surrounding yourself now with what you want to become later.

Turning Points

Looking back on life, we can sometimes identify a significant turning point that set us in a new direction, for example, deciding to hang around with a different group of friends, joining a club or sports team, or breaking up with a boyfriend or girlfriend. Years later, we recognize just how important that decision was in shaping the kind of person we have become. Listen in on a conversation about such a turning point that happened three years ago in Katie's life, when she was twenty-two:

Katie: My life would have been so different if I'd kept up that sick relationship with Phil and never married Josh.

I mean, I would probably be a senior aide in the office of a national politician by now if I'd stayed with Phil. He certainly had all the connections and the experience necessary to groom me for a career in politics. I probably would've been good, too. Even other people besides Phil told me that. And you know, part of me liked that possibility, even though I knew deep down that Phil was no good for me. I liked the idea of being in such a powerful and influential position. I'd also probably have more money and my own house by now!

Ellie: But Katie, think about it. Would you really have been happy? Phil tried to possess you, and you

know it. You said it yourself many times, especially toward the end. It was like you were being swallowed alive.

Katie: You're right. When I think about it, I know I got out of that relationship by the skin of my teeth. A lot of me was already buried when I was going with him; it was like being half-dead. That's why meeting Josh was so incredible. I could be my true self with him, and he never tried to possess me and control me. That weekend when I told Phil to get lost is still so clear in my mind. It was one of the hardest things I've ever done, but I'm so glad I had the guts to do it.

Even now, I'm still recovering parts of myself that got buried when I was with Phil. But I'm truly happy right now, and I'm feeling more like my real self all the time. **10**

What's Good?

As discussed earlier, choosing a morality to live by is highly important in our life. It makes a big difference which set of values and principles we choose to guide our decisions, for some values will lead to our becoming one kind of person, and others will lead to our becoming quite another kind of person.

Most of us want to be *good* persons. We want to be guided by good values, to make good choices, and to live the "good life." Few people deliberately choose evil; usually, evildoing is the product of choices that the individual *thought* were good.

Here are some false assumptions about what is good:

- Good is getting other people to like me or admire me.
- Good is moving up financially.

10
Have you experienced any turning points in your life that required you to make a decision? If so, describe how one of these choices set you in a new direction.

Decisions, Decisions

Life is a series of choices about who we will become.

- Good is making my pain or discomfort go away.
- Good is getting rid of my problems as fast as I can.
- Good is having more control.
- Good is feeling good.
- Good is not getting the blame for something I did.
- Good is making people do what I want them to do.

Can you think of examples of how people can get into big problems because they hold one or more of the above assumptions about what is good for them? **11**

Look at the meaning of *good* in this way: It is good for a thing to be what it is meant to be. For instance, it is good for a rock to be part of the soil; for a tree to put down its roots into the ground, shoot its branches up to the sky, and produce leaves that generate oxygen; for a mountain lion to roam wild and feed itself on its prey; for a hen to scratch the ground, run around pecking for insects, and lay eggs; for an eagle to spread its wings and soar.

Likewise, it is good for a human being to be human, in all that this implies. Morally good actions are those that are in harmony with being a fully human person. In other words, you do good when you act in a way that is truly human—in your relationships with yourself, with other persons, with the earth, and with God.

Maybe you are already asking yourself this question:

- If being good means being fully human, what does it mean to be fully human?

That question has been addressed in one way or another by every major religion and philosophy in the history of humankind. In the next chapter, you will be looking at the Christian response to that question. **12**

This section of the chapter began with a question: What kind of person am I becoming, and what kind of person do I want to become? The way we answer this question for ourselves makes an enormous difference at the personal level.

The effects of a person's character, however, go far beyond that individual's life. Unbelievable as it might seem, what we make of our character in some way touches and affects the whole world, even those parts of it we will never personally see. Doing good on even the smallest scale contributes to the good of the whole human community, just as doing evil contributes to its harm. As the poet Robert Penn Warren expressed it: "The world is like an enormous spiderweb and if you touch it, however lightly, at any point, the vibration ripples to the remotest perimeter." **13**

For Review

- What is the major moral question that each of us has to answer for ourselves?
- What wise saying expresses how day-to-day decisions lead to one's life destiny?
- What makes an action morally good?

11
Select three of these assumptions about what is good, and write down examples of how they can lead to problems.

12
List at least ten characteristics of what you think describes a fully human person. Compare your list with those of others in the class. Which characteristics show up on most lists?

13
Using Warren's idea of the world as a spiderweb, imagine and write about how the vibrations from a good or bad act you do might ripple to "the remotest perimeter"—to the lives of people on the other side of the globe.

Becoming Morally Mature: An Uphill and Downhill Journey

One thing must be clear to us as we go about the business of building our own character: Growing morally is *not* about making no mistakes!

Mistakes will happen to everyone. People who are considered moral giants are not the ones who were perfect all their life. Rather, they are the folks who made mistakes—even big ones that would seem to wreck forever their chances for happiness. But they learned from these mistakes and then went on living as deeper, wiser persons. As a high school junior testifies from his own experience, "Sorrow builds character."

Growing Through Mistakes

An interview with a college English professor offers an illustration of one student's growth through learning from mistakes and problems:

Jerry was the best student in my American literature seminar. On his papers and tests, he got straight *A's*. He was very bright and worked hard. The only thing I couldn't figure out was his silence in class. I mean, he never joined in. I even asked him once about it. He turned red and apologized, but he still didn't talk.

Toward the end of the semester, Jerry started looking awful—messy, sloppy clothes, dirty hair, and tired. I was to the point of asking him what was happening, when he just didn't show up for class. Finally I got a notification from the college counseling center that he had been hospitalized and that I should give him an incomplete. He would be able to make up the work later. I asked a couple of Jerry's friends about him. They finally told me that Jerry was in treatment for alcoholism.

I was shocked. It did explain a lot, but still. Anyway, I sent Jerry a few notes just to reassure him. And after a couple of months, he showed up at my office. He looked great—had lost weight and picked up some color. I didn't want to push him, so the first meeting we just talked about his class work.

Anyway, eventually Jerry told me what had happened. Evidently, when he was a freshman, he felt so lonely and shy that he would have a couple of beers to get himself to talk. It worked, but he couldn't control his drinking. Pretty soon he was drinking regularly; on weekends he'd get wasted. I remember his exact words: "I never realized how much I disliked myself until I was in treatment. I guess I drank so I could overcome my fears."

Crazy—I had seen a bright, competent, cooperative student. All Jerry had seen in himself was a somewhat stocky, freckle-faced, homely guy, too shy and ugly to be popular. He was an ace in the Computer Hackers' Club, but even that made him feel bad because he felt stereotyped as a nerd. You just don't know what's going on with people, I guess.

Holy People Who Had Rocky Starts

You may wonder, Who are some of these moral giants that grew through their mistakes? And exactly what mistakes did they make anyway? Two holy people of the Catholic tradition offer powerful examples to us of the ability to turn one's life around. One is Augustine of Hippo; the other is Dorothy Day.

Augustine of Hippo

Augustine (354–430), born in North Africa, was a brilliant young man. From the time he started going to school, he easily led his class. Yet, at age sixteen, he had to leave school because his father could not pay his tuition; heavy taxes at that time made it impossible. During this year of idleness, Augustine acquired habits that he would later regret and repent of. With a group of wild friends, he went to prostitutes, got drunk, gambled, and led a purposeless life. Returning to school and finishing his studies at eighteen, Augustine then became a teacher. He also took a mistress. Taking a mistress

was not uncommon among non-Christians of the time, but Augustine's mother, Monica, a devout Christian, had tried to raise him in the Christian faith.

Augustine next became a Manichaean, believing that there was one god who created good and another god who created evil, and that therefore, people were not responsible for their sins. Monica could only pray for her son's conversion; he was too brilliant and stubborn to be influenced easily.

Then suddenly, Augustine moved to Rome with his mistress and their young son. A year later, he went to teach in Milan. There he studied the Greek philosopher Plato and was influenced by the wise Bishop Ambrose. Slowly, through the insights of Plato about the reality of spiritual things, the truth of Ambrose's message, and the influence of his mother's love, Augustine began to reform his life—but not without first taking another mistress!

At last, after much dissatisfaction and searching, Augustine was converted to Christianity. Later he became a priest, then a bishop. Today he is regarded as one of the greatest theologians in the church's history and is considered a father of the church.

Dorothy Day

Dorothy Day (1897–1980), like Augustine, had a rocky start. Always a passionate advocate for justice, in her twenties she took up a career in

■
Above: Augustine of Hippo, today considered a great church theologian, lived an idle and corrupt life as a young man.

journalism to further the radical causes she believed in. At that time, she got involved in a fairly "fast" life, becoming a part of the radical Greenwich Village community in New York City.

Casting about for a career, Dorothy entered nursing school but then dropped out a year later because she could not keep up the required discipline of study. She had an unhappy love affair, became pregnant, and had an abortion. Soon afterward, she wed another man, took up heavy drinking, and shortly split up with her husband.

Dorothy had no attraction to organized religion at this point in her life. But, always reflective, she read the Bible, especially the Psalms, while she was in jail. (She had been picked up on suspicion of being "dangerous" and "a communist" because of her social activism.) During this jail time, a fellow prisoner, a prostitute, inspired Dorothy with her gentle kindness and her nearness to God in mind and heart.

Within five years of her jail experience, Dorothy was into a common-law (unofficial) marriage with a man who fathered her daughter—a child that Dorothy wanted very much and that her husband did not. By this time, Dorothy and he were growing apart. The final blow that separated them was Dorothy's decision at age thirty to become a Catholic, a choice that baffled her atheist husband. As biographer Robert Coles recounts, Dorothy once recalled, "I think I realized on the day I was baptized how long I had been waiting for

that moment—all my life" (*Dorothy Day*, page 9).

In fact, Dorothy believed her life had just begun, and in some sense, it had. Dorothy Day went on to turn her radical passion for peace and justice, her career in journalism, and her devotion to Jesus and the Catholic church into a movement. It would change the face of much of North American Catholicism and have an impact on the worldwide church. In 1933, with Peter Maurin, a self-made philosopher and extraordinary man, Dorothy founded the Catholic Worker Movement. The movement consists of a newspaper (which still sells for a penny a copy), houses of hospitality for homeless people and hungry people in communities all over North America, and a strong witness of protest for justice and peace.

Today many people—Catholic and non-Catholic alike—consider Dorothy Day a saint.

Above: Dorothy Day moved beyond a difficult young adulthood to found the Catholic Worker Movement.

What's great and sad at the same time is that it took treatment for alcoholism for Jerry to finally face who he is and start accepting himself. There's a real—I'm not sure if this is the right word—*depth* to him now. I really admire Jerry. He goes to Alcoholics Anonymous and has made some friends there. He's still quiet in class, but he's gotten more involved with other things on campus, like Big Brothers, a group that works with kids from town who need extra attention. There's something else, too: Jerry really seems to listen to other people now. One of the women who knew him before this happened even told me the other day that Jerry is so different, everybody respects him. He may be a resident assistant in a dormitory next year. **14**

Self-esteem as a Factor

A less dramatic, but nevertheless true-to-life, testimony to the ups and downs of moral growth comes from Sheila, a college junior who recalls from her own experience how important a sense of self-esteem is in influencing moral development:

When you're a freshman or sophomore in high school, all you can pay attention to is what people will think of you. Everything you do—even dumb stuff—is decided by how it will make you look to other people.

By the time you get to be a senior, you're used to the people, and they see you a certain way. You just are who you are and you pretty much accept that. Of course, you always struggle with that, I mean feeling a little insecure about your image, but . . .

Anyway, then you go away to college. It's like being in high school again, in a way! I mean, you're around new people, and you want them to see you the way they think you should be, so you have to adjust. You try to impress them for a while. And then, as you get older, you realize it doesn't matter what they think. You know that if you're going to be happy with who you are, then you have to start feeling comfortable with yourself again.

Self-esteem and self-acceptance, as most of us realize, have everything to do with morality and moral growth. If we feel at peace with who we are and not tied up with anxieties about how we are coming across to others, we will be freer to make decisions based on our own values and the needs of a situation, not on our fears and insecurities.

However, as seen in Sheila's description of the transition from high school to college, self-esteem is not a constant in life: it goes up and down. At times we feel on top of the world about ourselves, and at other times we are tied in knots by the negative messages we keep giving ourselves. Getting started in a new situation—like the first year of high school or college—can make us feel vulnerable again. Looking back years later, we may think that we made some pretty screwed-up moral judgments. And maybe we did.

The fact that there is no mistake (except suicide, which is permanent) that we cannot recover from gives us hope. The journey of life will be filled with ups and downs, hills and valleys. We just have to believe that when we are in a valley, the hills are still there waiting for us. **15**

For Review

- How can mistakes enable us to grow morally?
- How is self-esteem related to moral decision making?

14
Interview an adult who is willing to talk about how she or he turned a mistake into an opportunity for growth. Write up a summary of the interview.

15
Draw a diagram of the ups and downs in your self-esteem over the years. Label each peak and valley with a word describing each experience.

What Self-esteem Looks Like

People with poor self-esteem may . . .	People with healthy self-esteem can . . .
1. believe deep down that they are not worth much	1. believe deep down that they are worth a lot
2. be scared of making any mistakes	2. make mistakes and learn from them
3. constantly wish for an "ideal" body	3. accept their body even though it is not perfect
4. stay with activities and interests that are known and safe	4. explore new opportunities and interests in order to grow
5. be unable to accept compliments	5. accept compliments
6. be preoccupied with how they appear to others	6. relate to other people spontaneously
7. either brag a lot and act superior or put themselves down and act inferior	7. be happy with themselves without feeling superior to others
8. either try to dominate others or let themselves be a doormat	8. treat others and themselves with respect
9. engage in self-destructive behavior such as drug abuse or starvation diets	9. take care of themselves physically and emotionally
10. be either defensive to criticism or devastated by it	10. consider criticism a potential means for growth

On to the Journey

In this chapter, we have considered what morality is and noted that everyone has a morality they live by. Some moralities ultimately give life, and others do not. It makes a big difference, then, which morality—which values and principles—we decide to own for ourselves.

This course will present to you the moral vision of Jesus. It will help you consider what Jesus and the Christian tradition have to say about good-ness, about what it means to be fully human. Buying or not buying into that vision, of course, is your choice. No high school course, book, or teacher can make you own something that you do not want to own. But many people believe, with good evidence, that Christian morality points to a path toward true happiness in life if it is taken seriously and owned in a person's depths.

So this course will introduce you to the Christian moral vision, as an attempt to help you find your own path in life, the road to your destiny.

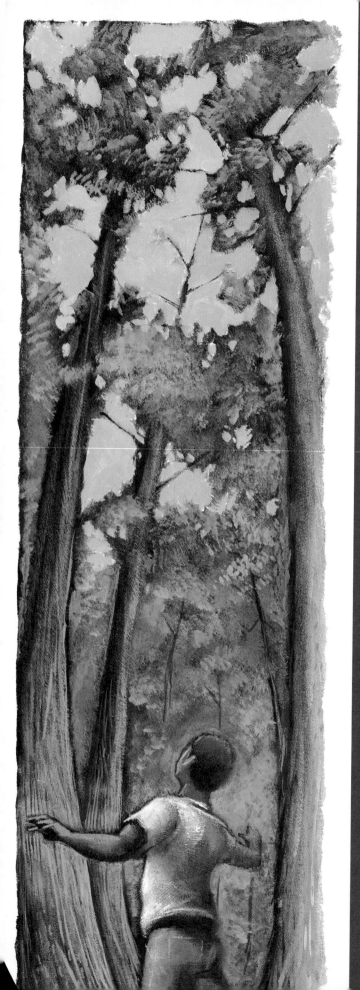

2

The Christian Vision of Morality: Jesus, Model of Full Humanness

CHAPTER 1 pointed out that even though everyone has a morality, which has to do with the values and principles by which they make choices, not all moralities are equal. Some are life-giving and some are not; some moralities are more mature than others.

Chapter 2 introduces the Christian vision of morality, of what it means to be fully human. Much of what Christians hold true about the full potential of our humanness comes from the Bible, culminating in the person of Jesus. Christians believe that Jesus, as the Incarnation of God (God made flesh), was not only fully divine but fully human as well. He is our model of full humanness and therefore of living a morally good life.

Jesus, Simon, and the Woman with the Bad Reputation

An incident from Jesus' life is a helpful place to look for Jesus' vision of goodness, or what it means to be fully human. The following story is based on chapter 7 of Luke's Gospel:

Jesus received an invitation to eat at the house of the Pharisee Simon. The Pharisees had consistently opposed Jesus' teaching, but Jesus wanted the chance to talk with them, hoping that his words and example would change their minds. So he went to the dinner party.

Ordinarily, the host greeted guests by embracing them and by washing the road dust off their feet. Simon did neither for Jesus. Nevertheless, Jesus sat down at the table to eat.

Suddenly, a gasp went through the dining room. A woman had entered uninvited and was standing next to Jesus. Her heavy makeup, hair down to her waist, many rings and bracelets, and red dress marked her as a prostitute. How dare any woman, much less a whore like this one, barge into our gathering! was the thought that flashed across the minds of Simon's guests. Two of the men rose to throw her out, but Jesus signaled them to stop.

Tears streaked the woman's face. She quickly knelt before Jesus and let the tears fall on his feet. Using her long black hair, she started drying the tears away. Jesus sat calmly, gazing at the woman, a tender look lighting his face.

After the woman finished wiping away the dust mingled with her tears, she devoutly kissed Jesus' feet. Then she massaged them with fragrant oil.

Simon, the host, could hardly contain his disgust and anger. He now knew why the other Pharisees despised Jesus. Anyone who would allow himself to be touched by such a sleazy woman must be corrupt himself.

When the woman finished massaging his feet, Jesus dried her tears with the sleeve of his robe and caressed her face with his hand. Then he motioned for her to rise and stand beside him. He had seen the reactions of Simon and the other guests. Their displeasure had silenced the room.

"Simon, answer a question for me."

Warily, Simon nodded.

"Let's say two people owed you money. One owed a thousand dollars, and the other about a hundred. On the due date, they both show up to explain why they cannot pay you back. Instead of getting angry, you cancel the debt for both. Here's the question: Which of these borrowers will be more grateful to you for having cancelled the debt?"

Simon shrugged his shoulders and said, "Obvious-ly, the one owing a thousand. What's the point?" Jesus saw straight through him. Simon grew anxious.

"Right, Simon. Now, look at this woman. She washed my feet and anointed them. She even kissed them with great tenderness. What kind of greeting did you give me? You did not even give me the chance to wash the dust off my feet. Who are you, then, to sneer at this woman? I know she has sinned a lot and has a terrible reputation. But her sins are for-given because in her heart and in her actions, she has shown her love and desire for forgiveness. Simon, your sins may seem small in comparison, but your love is equally small."

Simon was aghast at Jesus' directness.

Then Jesus took the woman's hands and looked into her eyes. "Beloved, your sins are forgiven. Your faith and trust in me is your salvation. Be at peace, and have the strength to turn away from your old ways. Don't let yourself be used anymore. You are worth far more than that—you are God's child."

Jesus embraced the woman, then gently turned her toward the door. Just before she left, she glanced back at him one last time.

"This is an outrage," Simon fumed under his breath. The other men nodded vigorously. One pounded the table.

Shaking his head, Jesus said, "Don't you see, Si-mon? I come as your friend, too. God loves the wom-an *and you.* Can you believe in a God whose love is big enough to take in all of us, even sinners and those whose hearts have hardened into stone?" **1**

Jesus' Actions

We are not told in the Gospel account if Jesus got through to Simon, if Simon's heart ever turned from stone to flesh. What is important about the story is Jesus' manner of acting, not his apparent success or failure:

- Jesus opened himself up to others, even adver-saries, by accepting the dinner invitation to Si-mon's house.
- Jesus dared to pay loving attention to the woman whom the other men scorned, knowing that they would therefore scorn him too.
- Jesus saw what was inside the heart of Simon and the woman; he did not judge them by their appearance or status.
- Jesus spoke the truth to Simon and the woman, even though Simon did not welcome the truth.
- Jesus forgave and affirmed the woman in re-sponse to her trust in him, and he offered love and forgiveness to Simon. **2**

Jesus' actions in this Gospel story are typical of how he lived his everyday life. To Jesus, openness to others, courage, honesty, respect for others, and showing mercy were part of what it meant to be true to himself as fully human. He did not let fear or ridicule get in the way of responding to others in a loving manner.

1
Imagine that you were a guest at Simon's dinner. Write your own journal account of what happened at the dinner.

■
Above: Jesus' love encompasses all persons, especially those cast off or deemed unworthy by society.

2
Imagine that you were the woman who came to Jesus at the dinner. Write down your thoughts after you left Simon's house.

The Challenge to a New Vision of Life

Jesus called both Simon and the woman to a different, fuller vision of life and humanness because he believed in their essential goodness. He asked them to look at their life and their own humanness in a new way. To each of them, Jesus communicated a different challenge:

To Simon the Pharisee. Jesus spoke to Simon's real need, which was to break out of his narrow, stony-hearted life. He tried to tell Simon that being fully human involves much more than living a small, self-concerned existence. Simon believed that life should be orderly, comfortable, and proper. He wanted to determine whom he would associate with; his reputation was at stake. Jesus beckoned Simon to move beyond his fearful, narrow horizons to an open inclusiveness of others—to love even his enemies.

To the woman with the bad reputation. Jesus called the woman to leave behind a way of life that had given her a livelihood but that had been destroying her inner spirit. By welcoming her and affirming her, Jesus was telling the woman that she could trust him and thus find the strength to stop letting herself be used, even though that was the only way she knew how to survive. Jesus invited her to trust in God and in him.

Jesus called Simon and the woman from their false security to a new, but scary, way of being—the way of love. Jesus could call them to love because he himself embodied God's love. Christians believe that God is the source of all love and that Jesus shows us what God's love is like in the flesh. He was living proof that love is possible for human beings. **3**

What Love Is Not

Sometimes people confuse Christian morality with being nice. They think that to be Christian is to act agreeable or pleasant at all times. "Being nice" means going along with others, not upsetting anyone. Of course, being pleasant and cooperative can be wonderful traits in the right situation. However, being nice does not always characterize Christian morality. Love is the bottom line, not niceness. Think about how differently Jesus would have acted at Simon's party if he had been operating from a morality of niceness rather than love. **4**

Contrary to what many people think, the opposite of love is not hate; it is apathy. *Apathy* literally means "without feeling." The opposite of love is indifference, a lack of concern. When we love, we are concerned about others, we care deeply about them, and we act accordingly. Notice, however, that loving or being deeply concerned about the dignity and welfare of others is not the same as liking, or being attracted to, someone. We are called to love even those whom we may not like, as Jesus did.

For Review
- What challenges did Jesus communicate to Simon the Pharisee and the woman with the bad reputation?
- How does "being nice" differ from Christian morality?

3
List some other false securities that Jesus tried to call people away from.

4
Make up a skit to portray what might have happened at the dinner if Jesus had been operating out of niceness rather than love.

Who We Are and Where We Are Going

Created in God's Image

In calling Simon, the woman with the bad reputation, and all human beings to love as God loves, Jesus is reminding us of who we are at our core—children of God. From this standpoint, the Christian vision of humanness is quite astonishing.

The Hebrew Scriptures, in the story of the Creation, tell us very directly that we were created in the image of God, as a reflection of God:

Then God said: "Let us make man in our image, after our likeness. . . ."
God created man in his image;
in the divine image he created him;
male and female he created them.
God blessed them. . . . And so it happened. God looked at everything he had made, and he found it very good. (Genesis 1:26–31)

What an amazing way to begin the Christian story of who we are and where we are going. Human beings could not be more splendid and wonderful than to be made in the image of God, reflecting God's love in the world.

■

Above: The story of Creation tells us who we are—beings made in the image of God, with freedom, power, and responsibility.

As creatures who are made in God's likeness, human beings are given the **freedom** to choose. Unlike other living creatures, human beings, because of their consciousness, can weigh and consider their options and decide among them. They are not completely bound by instinct, genetic heritage, or even previous learning. Besides freedom, God gave human beings the **power** to act on their freely chosen decisions, to have an effect on themselves and the world around them. And with the great gifts of freedom and power, human beings take on **responsibility**, or accountability, for their choices. **5**

The Fall: Believing "Human Is Not Good Enough"

The second part of the story of Genesis, however, tells how our "first parents" got stuck: they believed that being human, being made in God's image, was not good enough! In the familiar account of Adam and Eve in the Garden of Eden, which explains religious truth by way of allegory (or symbolic story), Adam and Eve are said to have wanted something "more." They believed the words of the deceiving serpent, "'No, God knows well that the moment you eat of [the forbidden fruit] your eyes will be opened and you will be like gods'" (Genesis 3:5). Adam and Eve bought the lie that they needed to be something *other,* something supposedly *better,* than they already were—which was marvelous and fundamentally good.

In the story of the Fall, the first humans did not realize that as creatures made in God's image, God was already in them. They did not have to be gods in order to be godlike. By choosing to reject their humanness, they were rejecting a life of grace, a life lived in God's presence.

The Creation allegory describes the plight that human beings throughout history have found themselves in. We do not really believe that at the core we are truly wonderful, truly good. So we try to make ourselves more powerful, "like gods." Sin is a rejection of the inherent goodness of being human, a denial that cuts human beings off from who we really are, from God, and from others. Sin is the refusal to treat ourselves and others as likenesses of God. In the language of Christian theology, this is humanity's *original sin.*

God: Reaching Out to Humanity

The story, however, does not end there. According to the Hebrew Scriptures, God reached out again and again in history to bring people back to a realization of their full potential as humans. You probably know much of the story:

- God fashioned a Chosen People, the Israelites, out of Abraham and Sarah's family.
- In the story of the Exodus, when the people were enslaved in Egypt, God called forth Moses to free them and bring them out of Egypt. On Mount Sinai, Moses received from God the Law, which included rules for the Israelites about how to be human with one another. Then God led them to the Promised Land.
- When the Israelites fell away from the Law, God sent prophets to shake them up and remind them of what it means to be human. The prophet Jeremiah proclaimed that God would write a new covenant of love on their hearts.
- God loved the Israelites through all their sufferings and trials, even when they were mistaken. Moved with compassion, God promised that one day a messiah would come who would usher in a new reign of justice and peace.

5
List five choices you freely made and acted on today. Describe in writing how you are responsible for each of these choices.

Jesus: Taking on Our Humanity

The Christian Testament takes up the story where the Hebrew Scriptures leave off. God, indeed, did send a messiah, God's own son, who took on our humanity. By becoming human, the Word of God made flesh in Jesus shows us what it means to be a fully human being, created in the image of God. Jesus lived among us and shared our human condition in all ways except sin—the refusal to love. He even accepted death so that we might know what it means to live life to the full.

Thus, from the Christian story, you can gather that to be truly, wholly yourself is to be "like God": at the depths of your true self you are a reflection of God. Morality is about getting back to our core—that good center of who we really are as God created us—where we are fully human. Sometimes we take mistaken paths to get there, and we end up farther away. But the restlessness in the human heart is a sign that God is calling us back to communion with God, our true self, and each other. Through Jesus, God is calling us to love. This is who we are and where we are going. **6**

For Review

- What does it mean to say that human beings are "made in God's image"?
- How does the story of Adam and Eve illustrate the rejection of humanness?
- By becoming human, what did the Word of God made flesh in Jesus do for humanity?

"Why Were You Not Zusya?"

A story from the Jewish Hassidic tradition illustrates the point that our destiny is to become no one but ourselves as we are known by God:

> The old rabbi Zusya was the master of a group of disciples. One day he became ill, and within a week he was on his deathbed. His disciples gathered around him to pray the Psalms and comfort him in his dying moments.
>
> As the end drew near, the disciples heard Zusya utter his last words: "In the next world, they will not ask of me, 'Why were you not *Moses?*' They will ask of me, 'Why were you not *Zusya?*'" (Based on a story from the audiotape series *Storytelling*)

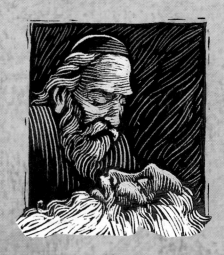

6
On a scale of 1 to 10, identify how much you agree with the following statement. Let 1 represent "I don't agree at all" and let 10 represent "I agree most strongly":

- At the depths of my true self, I am a reflection of God.

In a brief paragraph, explain what might have caused you to answer as you did.

Loved by God
Without Conditions

No Ifs, Ands, or Buts

In our state of brokenness and alienation from our true self, it may seem impossible for humans to embody God's love as Jesus did. Often we may not feel worthy of being loved and therefore are unable to love in return. Part of the Good News of Jesus is that God loves us without any conditions—no ifs, ands, or buts.

God sees beyond our sinfulness to our essential goodness. Receiving love is not a matter of worthiness. We do not have to prove we deserve love, for God created us and all of creation out of love.

Consider this reflection on unconditional love:

Everyone kept telling me to change.

I resented them, and I agreed with them, and I wanted to change, but simply couldn't, no matter how hard I tried.

What hurt the most was that, like the others, my best friend kept insisting that I change. So I felt powerless and trapped.

Then, one day, he said to me, "Don't change. I love you just as you are." . . .

I relaxed. I came alive. And suddenly I changed!

Now I know that I couldn't really change until I found someone who would love me whether I changed or not.

Is this how you love me, God? (De Mello, *The Song of the Bird*, pages 67–68) **7**

A Glimpse of God's Love

We may be told that God loves us without any ifs, ands, or buts. However, it is very hard to grasp that

and believe it in our depths—unless we experience something like unconditional love from other people, as the person in the previous example did. Not even the best parents or the best spouse in the world can love us in the complete way that God does. But, as the First Letter of John from the Christian Testament tells us, when we do love, we are indeed offering each other a glimpse or taste of God's love:

Beloved,
if God so loved us,
we also must love one another.
No one has ever seen God.
Yet, if we love one another,
God remains in us,
and his love is brought to perfection in us.
(1 John 4:11–12)

The following is an account of such a glimpse:

As the jet taxied to the terminal, Max's anxiety grew. He had not seen his sister Rita for years. After he had fled his father's wrath, his own bitterness held him from going back home, even though his father had died two years ago. Rita and he had started writing again, but her letters seemed cautious. Max and Rita had been close when they were younger, but a lot of time had passed.

Rita never condemned his lifestyle, she just never said anything one way or the other. This left Max unsure about her true feelings. The world in which his sister and her family lived was so different from his. She taught in a small, rural elementary school. Her husband, Tom, ran the dairy farm he had inherited from his father. They had two kids, Sally, age eight, and Chad, age six, whom Max had never seen. He wondered how they would react to him.

Snow swirled past the plane's window, bringing with it childhood memories of snowball fights and

---

7
Write about an experience in which you were affected by another person's acceptance or rejection of you.

skating on the backyard rink. But the cold worried Max. His immune system was so weak that the shock of the cold weather might land him in the hospital again. He had spent the last eighteen months in and out of treatment for pneumonia, then bacterial infections that had attacked his intestines, and finally, Kaposi's sarcoma, a form of cancer. The remaining purple welts were covered by his pants legs. He hated for his sister or anyone to see them. But then, Max knew that he was here to die.

When his money had run out and his friends had either died or abandoned him, in a fit of despair Max finally had written to Rita, admitting that he had AIDS and was dying. Could she send him some money? Instead, Rita had suggested that he might be better off back home. Her offer seemed somewhat hesitant, though, leaving Max reluctant to accept it. But his condition was getting worse, and he did want to see her again and, God willing, be accepted. So Max decided to go home.

The plane jerked to a stop. Panic seized Max. Was he crazy to think that Rita and her family would understand? He wondered if he had made a huge mistake in coming home. He never remembered the people of his small hometown as being very open-minded. Word about Max's disease would spread quickly. Would people hassle Rita, Tom, and the kids for bringing him into their home? What if Rita lost her job because of him?

When the last passenger had gotten off the plane, Max dragged himself to his feet, weakened not only by his disease but by his apprehension. He wasn't sure if he had the strength to walk on his own. Staggering slightly, he made it to the front door of the plane. The breeze in the passageway cut through him, but he straightened up the best he could and walked on slowly.

As he turned the corner at the end of the ramp into the terminal, he was breathing hard and concentrating on stepping over the seam. Knots made his stomach lurch.

"Max. Oh, Max."

Looking up, he saw Rita running toward him. Through her tears, she smiled, then threw her arms around him.

"Max. Dear ol' Max. You're home. Thank God, Max." She kissed each of his stubbly cheeks.

As she clutched him, Max noticed Tom standing shyly behind her. The children were each holding on to one of their dad's hands. All three smiled.

When Rita finally released him, Tom stuck out his strong, brown hand. "Glad you made it, Max. We're gonna get a blizzard here!"

Then each of the kids took one of Max's hands. "Hi, Uncle Max. Gee, that's a big plane," Chad said.

Max felt lifted up by their childish wonder and innocent affection. He wiped tears out of his eyes as the kids let go of his hands and ran toward the baggage area. Rita slipped an arm under his. "Come on, let's go home." Max knew now that he was really home and that his passing would be okay.

Max got a taste of God's unconditional love from his sister and her family. Even with his broken body and battered spirit, Max somehow felt whole again. God's love heals our inner wounds, even as we face death and suffering. One of the marvelous things about human love is that it can carry God's love to us and thus bring us closer to realizing the wholeness that was meant for us when we were created. One of the great purposes of families is that its members can communicate to one another a love that is something like God's love. **8**

8

Have you ever experienced love from another person that made you feel whole? This experience of another's love gives you a glimpse of the way God loves you. Complete this sentence by identifying that experience:

• God's love is like _____.

When a Person Doesn't Receive Love

A question may have occurred to you:

• What happens if someone never gets even a taste or a glimpse of God's love from other humans?

After all, in too many families there seems to be little or no love—people constantly hurting one another, not accepting one another, being hostile and violent with one another, letting alcoholism and drug addiction mess up their relationships. Does this mean that the children and the adults in those families will never experience God's love for them?

The answer to this question is not simple. In fact, God's love *is* communicated to people by other people, and if someone has never been loved by another human being, he or she has been truly deprived of life. But this does not mean that God does not love that person. Christian faith tells us that God loves the most forgotten, the despised, and the abandoned ("the widows and the ophans," in the Bible's terms) in the most special way. This means that persons who grow up in a home without love are particularly held in God's care.

But lack of human love in a person's life leaves deep wounds. Such persons have difficulty loving themselves and imagining that they are lovable. Perhaps you know people who have never been loved the way they needed to be. They may come from homes in which there is physical, mental, or sexual abuse; alcoholism or other substance abuse; or in which the parents simply do not have the maturity and the self-love required to give their

■

Above, left and right: God's love is communicated to people by other people. But someone who has been deprived of human love is not forgotten by God; rather, that person is particularly held in God's care.

Witnesses to God's Love for the Forgotten

Mother Teresa of India and her Missionaries of Charity minister to abandoned persons left dying in the streets of Calcutta, taking them in and treating them with the most tender, dignified care, to communicate God's love to them.

The Catholic Worker Movement, founded in the United States in 1933 by Dorothy Day (see pages 22–23) and Peter Maurin, has a similar purpose: to offer hospitality, shelter, and food to the forgotten ones— the homeless, the unemployed, the drifters, the down-and-out.

Such Catholic groups cannot care for *all* the forgotten people in their cities, or even a significant number of them. But these Christians do bear witness to the world that all persons, especially those who are on the margins of society, are precious and beloved in God's sight. In Mother Teresa's words, "'What we are doing is just a drop in the ocean. But if the drop was not in the ocean, I think the ocean would be less because of the missing drop'" (quoted in "Little Things Mean a Lot," *Christopher News Notes*).

children an accepting, secure, consistent environment. After all, maybe the parents themselves came from families that were deprived of love. You yourself might feel a lack of love in your life, and you may suffer the effects in low self-esteem or destructive personality traits. **9**

How does a person recover from the wounds of a life without love? Christian faith tells us that God's love has been made known to us in Jesus. Many people who have been badly hurt by life discover through faith in Jesus that they are loved. The discovery of God's love for them gives them the strength and the self-love to seek out other persons and programs that can help them to heal their wounds—relatives, teachers, counselors, mature friends, priests or ministers, drug treatment programs, and support groups designed for self-help (like Alateen or Adult Children of Alcoholics).

Few people have ever been loved exactly as they needed to be. Yet, by sending us Jesus Christ, God assures us that we can be healed again within ourselves, with each other, and with God. This is the great hope of Christian redemption.

For Review

- What does God's unconditional love for us mean?
- How can human beings experience God's love for them?

■
Above: Mother Teresa visits a young man who is a victim of polio at a home for destitute people operated by the Missionaries of Charity in Manila, the Philippines.

9
Clip out and bring to class a newspaper or magazine article that illustrates the negative effects of being deprived of human love. Write a brief commentary on the article and title it "How Love Could Have Made a Difference."

Responding to Love with Love

The natural response to receiving love is to become a lover. Persons who know they are loved blossom under love's warmth. Even those who have known little love will respond to love in surprising ways. Eddie's story gives an example of this:

Eddie never acted mean, but he always managed to get into trouble. He served detentions with the regularity some people reserve for coffee breaks. Never overtly rebellious, Eddie would simply smirk at the teacher stuck with detention duty for the day. His grades hardly ever crept above C's but never fell below D's. Yet, if asked, most of Eddie's teachers would swear that they saw glimmers of intelligent life in his shining blue eyes.

Eddie bottomed out at the end of his junior year in high school. Late for class one morning, he staggered into the front office. The secretary smelled alcohol on his breath and contacted the vice-principal. When Eddie's parents showed up to take him home, the vice-principal began to understand why Eddie might be drunk at 9:15 a.m. Eddie's father grabbed his son and began yelling at him and shaking him. Eddie's mother stood by passively. She looked embarrassed and fearful.

Describing the scene later, the secretary confided: "Eddie's dad is a huge guy. I mean it, I thought his father was gonna beat him to a pulp right there. You could see Eddie staring at his dad. I think he hates him. And Eddie's mother just stood by, too afraid to intervene."

After his suspension, Eddie finished out the year without getting into more trouble. The vice-principal tried to talk with Eddie occasionally, but the young man just sat and stared at the floor.

Senior year found Eddie back to his pre-suspension self. He returned to school tanned and muscular from his construction job over the summer. The chip on his shoulder seemed to have grown in direct proportion to the growth of his muscles. With his usual sneer, Eddie met the news that he, like all seniors, would have to complete a service project. No one could figure out why he chose to do activities with old people at Ave Maria Nursing Home. Most guessed that he thought he could skip easily.

Then Eddie's teachers started noticing subtle changes in him. A paper would come in neat, organized, and carefully done. Eddie would occasionally set aside his sneer and relax his face. Although his first report card was filled with his normal C's and D's, the second one sported two B's and no D's. Naturally, such changes aroused people's curiosity. Then, when he didn't get sent to detention for two weeks running, quiet murmurings began among the faculty and some of Eddie's classmates. What was going on?

Overhearing some of the faculty musing about Eddie, Sister Jean, the supervisor of the service projects, became curious too. She had to visit the nursing home anyway, so she planned to go at a time when Eddie was scheduled to be there.

When she arrived, Sister Jean toured the facility and visited with the students who were present that day. But she saw no sign of Eddie—perhaps he *was* skipping out of his responsibility. She approached the activities director.

"Eddie Wilson is scheduled to be here today. Did he come in?"

The activities director smiled and nodded. "He's here—never misses a day. Right from the start I knew that guy needed something special—he had such a chip on his shoulder. That smirk, no eye contact—I got Mrs. Hecker on him right away."

"Mrs. Hecker?"

"A tiny old woman with a huge heart. Follow me."

The activities director led Sister Jean down to the end of a corridor. At the last door she motioned for Jean to be silent. Out of the room came Eddie's voice, speaking gently. He was telling the old woman about his girlfriend. Then he stopped.

A frail but enthusiastic voice said: "She sounds wonderful. I'm real glad for you, Eddie. I can tell you two treat each other just right." Then she chuckled a bit and said, "But tell me about school now. I bet you surprised them with those two B's, eh?"

Eddie laughed softly and told Mrs. Hecker about everyone's reaction to his grades. As Sister Jean walked silently away from the room, she knew why Eddie got the B's and why he might be all right from now on.

Mrs. Hecker's love and interest filled a gap in Eddie's life and called forth love and responsibility from him. Like Mrs. Hecker, we can communicate God's love to people—and who does not need to hear that Good News? **10**

The Great Commandment

When Jesus was asked by a Pharisee one day to tell him which commandment of the Jewish Law was the greatest, Jesus answered:

"The first is this: . . .
  'You shall love the Lord your God
  with all your heart,
  with all your soul,
  with all your mind,
  and with all your strength.'
The second is this:
  'You shall love your neighbor as yourself.'
There is no other commandment greater than these."

                           (Mark 12:29–31)

Jesus came from devoutly Jewish roots. The **great commandment of love** was not something that he dreamed up on his own; this teaching was at the heart of the Jewish tradition that had nurtured Jesus from his childhood. Jesus preached the authentic message of Judaism, which later also became the authentic message of Christianity: Love is the highest law, love directed to God, to neighbor, and to self. And although Jesus does not refer to nonhuman creation in the command to love, it was part of the Jewish tradition to care about the welfare of the earth, to be loving stewards of creation. Love is the binding force of all creation.

Keeping the great commandment of love is a response to God's love poured out for us. It is a way to affirm our essential goodness as creatures made in God's image. The great commandment is written by God on our heart. As Jesus made clear on other occasions, all the laws of the Jewish tradition, including the **Ten Commandments**, can be summed up in the one great commandment of love. **11**

Jesus' uniqueness was not that he preached of God's love for all human beings and the response of love required by us. That teaching was already known to good Jews of his time. But Jesus went beyond preaching love to actually embody God's love in his own humanity, to show us in human form what it means to reflect God's love in this world. Thus, Jesus gave us a model of how human beings can love as God does.

The Reign of God

Jesus knew, too, that a community of people who were trying to love as God does could be a beacon or a sign of hope to others in a world that was deprived of love. He once said to his followers:

10
Eddie's life was being changed for the better as a result of Mrs. Hecker's love, but he may not have been aware of the activities director's concern for him. Often love slips by unnoticed, but it still affects us. Write a prayer of thanks to God for persons who are concerned about you without your being aware of their concern.

11
For each of the Ten Commandments, describe in a sentence how that commandment is included under the great commandment of love.

"You are the light of the world. A city set on a mountain cannot be hidden. Nor do [people] light a lamp and then put it under a bushel basket; it is set on a lampstand, where it gives light to all in the house. Just so, your light must shine before others, that they may see your good deeds and glorify your heavenly Father." (Matthew 5:14–16) **12**

Jesus invited his followers to join him in living God's love within the human community. He promised that living a life of love would gradually, ultimately, bring about the Reign of God—that condition of integrity, justice, and peace that people have always yearned for.

In parables like this next one about a mustard seed, Jesus described how the Reign of God would come about from small beginnings in the community:

"The reign of God is like a mustard seed which someone took and sowed in his field. It is the smallest seed of all, yet when full-grown it is the largest of plants. It becomes so big a shrub that the birds of the sky come and build their nests in its branches." (Matthew 13:31–32)

In Jesus' words, "'The reign of God is already in your midst'" (Luke 17:21). However, the Reign of God is not among us completely. It is only here in glimpses. Even intense experiences of love, such as we read in the story of Max and his sister Rita, are only glimpses of the Reign of God that is gradually coming about.

For Review

- What is the natural response to receiving love?
- What is the great commandment of love?
- List the Ten Commandments.

■
Above: The Reign of God is already in our midst, wherever people are living in God's love within the human community.

12
Do you know of a community of people that is a sign of hope to others? If so, write about how this group inspires hope in others.

The Ten Commandments

The Ten Commandments are part of the whole body of laws given to the Israelites after they had escaped from slavery in Egypt and were setting out for the Promised Land.

At Mount Sinai, God promised to take the people as God's own, protecting and caring for them. In exchange, the Israelites had to keep the Law, the rules given by God to help the people survive as a community and live in right relationship with each other and God. This was the Sinai Covenant. The cornerstone of the Covenant was the Ten Commandments.

Today we understand the Ten Commandments as fundamental moral precepts. Yet they are the *minimum* requirements for a life of love. Jesus told his followers not to disregard or forget these commandments but to go way beyond them to fulfill the great commandment of love.

These are the Ten Commandments, from Exodus, chapter 20, in the traditional way they are enumerated by Catholics:

1. "'I, the LORD, am your God. . . . You shall not have other gods besides me.'"
2. "'You shall not take the name of the LORD, your God, in vain.'"
3. "'Remember to keep holy the sabbath day.'"
4. "'Honor your father and your mother.'"
5. "'You shall not kill.'"
6. "'You shall not commit adultery.'"
7. "'You shall not steal.'"
8. "'You shall not bear false witness against your neighbor.'"
9. "'You shall not covet your neighbor's wife.'"
10. "'You shall not covet your neighbor's house.'"

To Live as Jesus Did

In response to the question, *What kind of person do you want to become?* the Christian answer is that persons are called to become fully human, to become persons who reflect God's love in the world. But how do we reflect God's love in our day-to-day life?

Morality was described in chapter 1 as having to do with choices that affect the kind of character we will develop. In the Christian tradition, the response to God's love is to live a life of virtue. The kind of character we develop depends on which virtues we do or do not develop.

Because Jesus lived such a life of virtue, embodying God's love in his full humanness, he is the model for Christian morality. Of course, having Jesus as a model does not force Christians into a mold, so that they all think and act exactly alike. Every person develops a distinct set of talents, traits, interests, and styles of relating to people. Everyone has a particular personality, with a distinctive character. God blesses each person with aptitudes and characteristics that make that person unique.

In Christian theology, there are the theological virtues and the moral virtues.

The Theological Virtues: Faith, Hope, and Love

In the Christian understanding, accepting God's presence in our life means living in faith, hope, and love. These are called the **theological virtues** because they spring from God as gifts and take us to God (*theos,* in Greek).

Most people are familiar with faith, hope, and love at the ordinary, human level:

- *Faith* means having trust in others and being trustworthy and loyal in return.
- *Hope* means expecting that the future is open, that change is possible, and that we can make a difference.
- *Love* means caring for one another, making sacrifices for one another, and rejoicing in one another's companionship.

Without some measure of faith, hope, and love among people, a community cannot function well, if at all. Faith, hope, and love are crucial to life in this ordinary, human sense. **13**

However, the Christian notion of accepting God's presence in our life goes beyond the ordinary human sense: Because of God's presence with us, or grace, we are enabled to respond at a level of faith, hope, and love that we cannot even imagine—a heroic level that can only be appreciated when we see living examples of it.

Faith

Christian faith is the virtue that enables one to trust in God's power to bestow new life. It is a whole new way of seeing reality, an illumination of the mind and heart that gives one a grasp of God's truth, however limited that grasp. It is a surrender of the self to the coming Reign of God.

The following real-life story of Irma Acuna illustrates how the experience of God's grace in our life can build faith:

Irma Acuna's attempt to commit suicide at age forty-one did not end her life. This North Carolina mother of five had recently experienced the breakup of her twenty-year marriage, partly as a result of her alcoholism. Suddenly, Irma found herself permanently blinded from the self-inflicted gunshot wound—but not dead.

In the year following the suicide attempt, on top of her serious problems with alcohol, Irma became addicted to medication prescribed to help her deal with the damage to her face. She wound up in a chemical dependency unit and later in a mental institution. Then she found Alcoholics Anonymous. "Once I was able to get off the drugs, I began to deal with my blindness."

Irma had to rebuild her life. She began to learn braille and other skills to accommodate her lost sight. She also learned to work with her hands—packing and assembling, sewing and riveting. She's proud of the fact that she can now support herself and doesn't have to be on welfare.

Rebuilding her life has meant rebuilding her faith in God as well. During that year of struggle immediately following her suicide attempt, Irma suffered and survived a heart attack. As she recovered from her addiction to drugs and alcohol, Irma realized that God must have wanted her to live. "God wasn't going to take me out. . . ."

In spite of her blindness, Irma has also learned sign language in order to communicate with fellow workers who are deaf, and she uses her fluency in Spanish to help other workers. "You have to help others. . . . I open my heart to people."

Each morning, Irma asks God to give her the strength to do what she has to do that day; every night she thanks God for giving her that day. (Condensed from an article in *National Catholic Reporter*)

Irma Acuna's faith is an active reality. When circumstances were bleak, Irma's faith helped her trust that God would bring light to her darkness. Faith enabled her to understand the reality of God's truth and to commit herself to living a life dedicated to the coming Reign of God.

13
In writing, give an example of how difficult it would be for people to live in community if they lacked either faith, hope, or love at the ordinary, human level.

Hope

Christian hope is the virtue by which one takes responsibility for the future in the expectation that God's Reign will surely come. It is the belief that good ultimately will triumph over evil because Jesus has already won the victory over death. The source of Christian hope is, therefore, the Resurrection—the fact that Jesus was raised from the dead by God.

Charo, a young woman living in Lima, Peru, comes from a desperately poor barrio, or neighborhood, of the city. Charo describes conditions in her barrio and reflects on the need to maintain hope:

"The people of our barrio came here [to the fringes of Lima] from the mountain areas of Peru . . . looking for work and a better future for us. But, for most Peruvians, life is a harsh struggle to survive. . . .

. . . Many houses are only one room . . . often occupied by three or four families. . . . Many homes have no light and no sewers . . . [no] running water at all."

This young woman goes on to tell of the unending poverty, the sickness, the scarcity of food, the unemployment, and the lack of educational opportunities that people in her barrio live with every day. She says that some young people despair and escape from their harsh world through drugs, alcohol, or crime. Others are attracted to groups that advocate violent revolution. Charo is frustrated by the waste of talent and good minds among the young people. They have no hope because society is not offering them a future. She continues:

"Sometimes I feel it is really hopeless. But that's where my faith challenges me. My faith calls me to hope and to work for some changes that will build a more just society.

"To keep my hopes alive, I need to be with people who have faith and hope. . . . Yes, the Gospels are good news for me. Jesus was a young person who knew about work. I think he knew a lot about unemployment and poverty too. . . .

"Yes, God loves us, even in our poverty. God didn't create these conditions. I don't believe God wants our lives to be just a grinding struggle to survive.

". . . The support of our Church community gives me hope, that together, we can work for a better world . . . for peace in our barrio . . . and maybe even peace in the world." (Quoted from the Columban Fathers' video *Charo of the Barrio*)

In living conditions that seem hopeless, Charo chooses to act on the basis of her hope that God's Reign will come. Hope gives Charo the conviction that just as Jesus was raised from the dead, new life can come from even the most desperate of circumstances.

Above: Charo lives in a poor barrio of Lima, Peru, and works to build a more just society. She says, "To keep my hopes alive, I need to be with people who have faith and hope."

Love

Christian love is lived faith and hope. It is the crown of all the virtues and an intimate participation in God's life—and God *is* love (1 John 4:8,16). Without love, all other virtues are empty.

The power of God's love and the challenges it brings to human life can be experienced in many ways. Consider the response of Frank and Elizabeth Morris:

When their only son was struck and killed by a drunk driver, Frank and Elizabeth Morris of Kentucky were consumed with the idea of revenge. "We wanted him dead," Mrs. Morris admitted.

They soon realized, though, that their reluctance to forgive was eating away at them. They decided to visit the youth in jail. Then Mrs. Morris began helping him in his struggle against alcohol abuse. "The accident had already wiped out one very special life. I didn't want to see it waste this young man's life, too," she said.

Since the Morrises made the decision to speak words of forgiveness, the young man has quit alcohol, become an active church member, and lectures for Mothers Against Drunk Driving. ("Say It with Love," *Christopher News Notes*)

God's love challenged the Morrises to love the young man in a new and radical way. The virtue of love fueled their faith in God's power to bring about change, and it strengthened their hope that new life could emerge from their personal tragedy.

The virtue of love is at the heart of all other virtues. Without love, faith is simply theoretical ideas and hope is just self-centeredness. All virtues, to be fully and truly lived, must be infused with love.

In his First Letter to the Corinthians, Saint Paul gave us perhaps the most famous description of Christian love:

If I speak with human tongues and angelic as well, but do not have love, I am a noisy gong, a clanging cymbal. If I have the gift of prophecy and, with full knowledge, comprehend all mysteries, if I have faith great enough to move mountains, but have not love, I am nothing. If I give everything I have to feed the poor and hand over my body to be burned, but have not love, I gain nothing.

Love is patient; love is kind. Love is not jealous, it does not put on airs, it is not snobbish. Love is never rude, it is not self-seeking, it is not prone to anger; neither does it brood over injuries. Love does not rejoice in what is wrong but rejoices with the truth. There is no limit to love's forbearance, to its trust, its hope, its power to endure. . . .

There are in the end three things that last: faith, hope, and love, and the greatest of these is love. (1 Corinthians 13:1–7,13) **14**

The Moral Virtues

Although, faith, hope, and love are gifts from God, our readiness to accept them and live our life in accord with them requires some preparatory work on our part. The **moral virtues**, which we can acquire and nurture through our own efforts, enable us to do this. They are the building blocks of our character.

Later on in this course, we will see how Jesus lived the moral virtues and study ways that people today, especially young people, are challenged to live them. For now, we will stick to a quick overview of these virtues.

The Cardinal Virtues

Four moral virtues stand out because they are powers or abilities that all the other virtues hinge upon. Called **cardinal virtues** (from *cardo,* the

14
Suppose that Irma Acuna, Charo, and Frank and Elizabeth Morris had been closed to God's grace and its impact on these virtues. Describe in writing how different their lives might have been.

Other Moral Virtues of Jesus

Jesus' life shows us a host of other virtues. The following seem central to understanding what it means to be fully human:

- *Honesty.* The ability to seek and uphold the truth
- *Respect for persons.* The ability to treat each person as worthy and as loved by God
- *Compassion.* The ability to respond to the suffering of others
- *Respect for creation.* The ability to see all of the natural world as good, as a gift from God, and as deserving of respectful care
- *Reverence for human life.* The ability to hold human life as sacred and to treat it as a gift from God
- *Peacemaking.* The ability to try to resolve conflict in a creative, loving way **15**

The cooperative relationship between the theological and moral virtues gives us a good picture of what Christian moral life is all about. Living as fully human persons in our daily life is a creative partnership between each human person and God. For us to reflect God's love in the world as fully human persons, as Jesus did, means that we have the responsibility to accept God's gracious presence in our life.

Latin word for "hinge"), they are wise judgment, justice, courage, and wholeness. (Catholics have traditionally termed these virtues prudence, justice, fortitude, and temperance, respectively. In this book, however, more familiar terms are being used.) As you will see from the definitions, wise judgment is the basis of all the rest, without which no other virtues can be cultivated.

- *Wise judgment.* The ability to figure out what is right in a practical situation and to act on it
- *Justice.* The striving to ensure the well-being of others as well as ourselves
- *Courage.* The ability to do what is right (the good) in the face of harm or the threat of injury, whether psychological or physical
- *Wholeness.* The balancing of all the parts of the self to create a dynamic and harmonious order

For Review

- Define the theological virtues of faith, hope, and love.
- Name the four cardinal virtues and the other virtues of Jesus to be covered in this course.

■

Above: We can acquire and nurture the moral virtues, the building blocks of our character, through our own effort.

15
Of the ten moral virtues to be studied in this course, which one do you think is most needed in the world today? Explain your answer in a paragraph.

The Virtues

The theological virtues, gifts from God that take us to God, are the crown of the Christian life. The moral virtues are the building blocks of our character. Chief among them are the cardinal virtues.

Theological Virtues

- Faith
- Hope
- Love

Cardinal Moral Virtues

- Wise Judgment
- Justice
- Courage
- Wholeness

Other Moral Virtues

- Honesty
- Respect for Persons
- Compassion
- Respect for Creation
- Reverence for Human Life
- Peacemaking

Help!

Perhaps you have been reading this chapter with a growing sense of just how challenging Christian morality is. You have seen examples from Jesus' life and other persons' experiences that show what the Christian moral vision looks like. While admiring these noble deeds and attitudes, some readers may feel it is all very idealistic and beyond them. They may be feeling a bit overwhelmed: "You don't expect me to be like *that*, do you?"

Relax. Living our way into Jesus' vision of what it means to be human is just that: it takes a lifetime. To become a morally mature Christian is to become a person of substance, a person with a strong inner core. That does not happen easily. Nor does its accomplishment rest entirely on our shoulders. With the gift of grace, God has made a commitment to help us on our way.

People who set out on the journey to grow in Christian morality do not make the trip alone. Even the totally dedicated monks and hermits in the fifth century who went to the desert to follow Jesus could not hack it alone. This is the advice of a desert elder who knew this truth from experience: "'If you should see a young monk trying to climb up to heaven by himself, grab his foot and throw him down to the ground. What he's doing is not good for him'" (quoted in *Youth Update*).

In the spirit of that wise old monk, the next chapter considers the many helps that are available on the journey to becoming fully human.

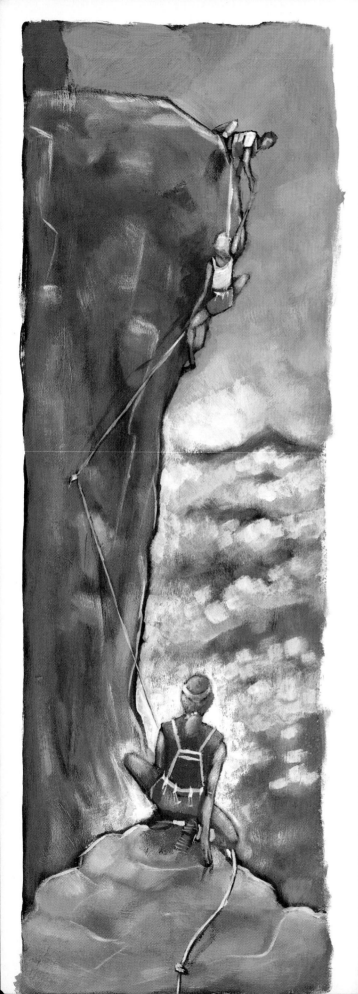

3

Helps
Along the Way:
A Journey
with Others

THE Christian vision and goal of morality, as discussed in chapter 2, is that we become the fully human persons that God created us to be. We are made in God's image, and Jesus' life shows us what God and humanity are all about—and that is *love*. Following Jesus' example, Christians down through the ages have lived up to their humanity by developing the virtues of Jesus in their own life. This process is a lifetime journey, and it cannot be undertaken alone.

This chapter shows why we do not make this journey on our own and describes the helps that are available to us throughout our life.

Beyond Independence

Much of adolescence is spent struggling to move from being dependent on our parents toward becoming more independent, able to do things for ourselves. Such movement is a necessary and valuable part of our growth toward maturity. What we soon realize, however, is that we cannot be independent if that means being separate from others, as illustrated in the following story: **1**

Cheryl tossed the hooded sweatshirt that she had borrowed from her mom into the suitcase. With a hard push on the cover, she managed to close and lock the bulging suitcase. She had to leave for the airport in thirty minutes. Butterflies the size of vultures careened through her stomach. Going to Alaska by herself to work in a fish cannery for the summer still seemed like a loony dream. But studying her flight schedule one more time convinced Cheryl that indeed she would soon be hundreds of miles north, away from home and on her own.

Two years ago when she had first heard her cousin Wendy talk about working in Alaska, Cheryl had paid only polite attention. At that time her main concerns had been getting out of high school and seeing Jeremy, her boyfriend, as much as she could. But Wendy's excitement, adventure, and haul of cash stuck in Cheryl's memory. By senior year, Cheryl realized that if she was going to pay her college expenses, she would need to make more money than her current job at Donut World could offer. Almost as important, Cheryl wanted to strike out on her own, to try something really different. Her boredom at the sameness of home and school, and even her friends, had reached an intolerable level. Cheryl knew she had to prove to herself that she could go it alone, without any of the people she usually depended on. So one night, on a whim, she called Wendy.

If Wendy's description of lecherous and lonely men, smelly bars, lack of female companions, long hours of hard work, and the stench of the canneries was intended to stifle Cheryl's interest, it failed. Cheryl forced Wendy to talk about the good pay and the beauty of Alaska.

"Well, can you talk to your brother-in-law?" Cheryl prodded.

Reluctantly, Wendy said she would try, but she couldn't promise that he'd help.

When Cheryl announced her summer plans, most of her friends laughed. But Pete, a silent sort of guy, came up excitedly and told her: "That's great. I wish I could join you. Go for it!" For the next several days, Pete and Cheryl talked of nothing but Alaska. They came up with a million reasons why it was a great idea, but in the end, Pete knew he had to stay home and work out. He didn't want to jeopardize his basketball scholarship. But their talks only fired Cheryl's enthusiasm.

1
Answer these questions in writing:
• In what ways are you trying to move toward more independence from your parents?
• What is the hardest thing about becoming more independent? the easiest thing?

Cheryl had begun her campaign to convince her parents to let her go. After two months of Cheryl's browbeating, pleading, and reassurances, her parents consented. Meanwhile, Wendy's brother-in-law Bud had agreed to take Cheryl on to do inventory in the cannery office. But "when I don't have work in the office, you'll have to work out in the plant, gutting and cleaning fish," he had added. Cheryl winced slightly at the specter of a sea of salmon entrails, but she stuck to her plans.

Bud's directions on how to get to the small town where she would be working seemed vague—a fact that Cheryl had conveniently kept from her folks. Bud had suggested that she catch a ride from the airport to the city, get a bus from the city to a town near the cannery, and probably call the cannery about a ride from there. Now, as she dressed, Cheryl wondered if she shouldn't have nailed down the arrangements. Bud's description of the living quarters made them sound adequate, but Wendy painted a picture of teeming vermin—and of bears knocking down the doors. Cheryl guessed that the truth lay somewhere in the middle.

Cheryl checked her purse to be sure that she had her money, plane ticket, and other essentials. The amount of cash she was taking seemed pitifully small, but she didn't want to borrow any more from her parents. They had agreed to give her money for airfare, especially after she had hinted that she wanted to drive to Alaska. Cheryl was determined that the money would only be a loan. After all, she wanted to do this by herself.

The drive to the airport passed quietly. Even her usually chatty father only mumbled a few vague warnings about not staying out too late and about "men." Cheryl's attempts at lighthearted banter about the sun being out twenty-three hours a day were met with silence.

As the plane roared down the runway, Cheryl shivered a bit. But soon she was calmly staring out the window at the city fading far below. She had done it; she was on her own.

The Myth of Rugged Individualism

Cheryl's desire to strike out on her own, to make it by herself, is familiar to many of us. It speaks of the rugged individualism that is so much a part of North American values: "I can go it alone. I don't need help. I'll struggle through on my own, and I'll be a better person for it." **2**

In her decision to make the trip to Alaska, Cheryl shows signs of growing *independence.* At this point in her life, this is a courageous step. But in the process of traveling to Alaska, Cheryl also experiences *interdependence,* even though she may not be aware of it at this point. At every step along her journey, she is supported by family, friends, and institutions (the airline, the cannery, the bus system, and so forth).

Even Cheryl's past is with her as she makes her journey. A past filled with thousands of relationships, interactions, and learnings has given Cheryl job experiences, a sense of adventure, the value she places on making money for college, even the know-how to count the inventory. As Cheryl's story illustrates, going it alone is not really possible. We can also ask, Is going it alone even desirable?

The Gift of Relatedness: Enriching Our Experiences

The story of Cheryl's physical journey to Alaska is useful for understanding the moral journey— our lifelong task of becoming the person we were created to be. Like Cheryl, many people hold a

---

2
In a paragraph, describe a character from literature, the movies, or television who espouses the attitude of rugged individualism.

rugged-individualist notion of their life's journey: they believe that becoming their own person means they must be independent of the influences or support of family, community, social institutions, and their past. They may assume that independent moral decision making means, "Nobody can tell another person what's right or wrong. Everyone has to decide within themselves what's right for them and do it. Other people can decide what's right and wrong for themselves, and I'll decide what's right for me."

This statement contains an element of truth—persons are each responsible for their own decisions, and they must make decisions based on what they know to be the good. But does each person really figure things out alone? Is there no shared wisdom to help us decide what is right? Is everyone a "moral universe" unto themselves? **3**

Just as Cheryl's physical journey to Alaska is not possible without the help of others, we do not travel the moral journey alone, either. All along the way, we are accompanied by what others have given us, both in our present and in our past—

including the family, religious, and cultural heritage we have been given. As Cheryl did, we may become more confident in our ability to figure things out, to strike out in courageous directions, and to rely on our inner resources. But we are kidding ourselves if we think that means we are going it alone. Besides that, when we try to exclude others from our journey, we cheat ourselves out of a great deal of what life has to offer.

We are by our nature, as beings created in God's image, relational. We are connected to others. Just as a baby cannot survive physically without other human beings, we cannot grow spiritually or morally without others. Our interdependence and relationships with others are a great gift, for they are significant vehicles for experiencing God's grace. **4**

Sources of Support

Support for our growth as moral persons can take many forms. Among the most significant are the following:

1. our relationship with God, the source of our life
2. our community
3. basic moral principles
4. civil laws
5. the teachings of Jesus and the Scriptures
6. the teachings of the church

For Review

- Why is it not really possible to "go it alone" in life?
- What does it mean to say that human beings are relational by nature?
- List the six significant sources of support for our moral growth.

■
Above: The notion of rugged individualism, which assumes that people should make the journey of life without help from others, is a familiar part of North American values.

3
Does the rugged-individualist approach to life make sense to you? In writing, explain why or why not.

4
Think back on two or three relationships that have been significant in your life, even if you and the other person did not get along. Describe these relationships, and then explain how they can be thought of as gifts from God.

Tuning In to God

Our primary source of support for the moral journey is our relationship with God. Everyone by nature has a relationship with God: we are all loved by God unconditionally, and likewise, we are all called to love God with our whole heart and mind—relationships are always a two-way street. This does not mean, though, that all people are aware of, or draw strength from, their relationship with God.

God's love for us is like radio waves. They are always out there, but we can miss them if we do not tune in the right station on the radio. Prayer is like tuning in, getting in touch with God, who knows us and loves us in our depths. In our journey to become the person we are meant to be, it seems essential for us to be in touch with the One who knows us at our core.

Praying Our Experiences

The most natural way for most of us to pray to God is to "pray our experiences." Persons who pray this way unfold before God their memories and feelings. They share with God who they are right now and how they are feeling—whether that be happy, excited, hurt, or angry. They let the details of their life tumble out before God. They turn these experiences over reflectively in their mind and heart, trusting that God's presence is somehow there in those everyday realities. Donna, age fifteen, says this about what praying her experiences has done for her:

"When I've had a lousy day and people have said mean things, it just helps to think God has a purpose for me, he knows what's going on in my life, and he's got a part in all that happens to me. That's what keeps me going when I feel like an absolute zero—

that God has a special purpose for me." (Quoted in *Campus Life*)

What can we expect from God when we pray—immediate answers to questions? a sudden turn-around in our personality or fortunes? Rather than expecting God to answer our questions or change us right away, we need to see prayer as a way of gradually living closer to the center of who we are, because that is where God can be found.

Rainer Maria Rilke, an early twentieth-century German poet, once wrote a now-famous letter to a young man who was having trouble figuring out his life. Rilke's words speak eloquently of what many believers know as prayer:

Be patient toward all that is unsolved in your heart and try to love *the questions themselves*. Do not now seek the answers, that cannot be given you because you would not be able to live them. And the point is, to live everything. *Live* the questions now. Perhaps you will then gradually, without noticing it, live along some distant day into the answer. . . . Take to yourself whatever comes with great trust, and if only it comes out of your own will, out of some need of your inmost being, take it upon yourself and hate nothing. (*Letters to a Young Poet,* pages 33–34) **5**

Grace: God-with-Us

Before we can tune in to God, though, we have to be aware that God is there within us and our experiences, ever present in our lives. God's loving presence with us is what Christians call grace.

A Parable of Grace

Here is an image of grace to consider, in the form of a parable based on a real incident:

Many years ago Ignace Jan Paderewski, the famous composer-pianist, was scheduled to perform at a great concert hall in the United States. Present in the audience that evening were a mother and her fidgety nine-year-old son. Weary of waiting, he squirmed constantly in his seat. His mother had hoped her boy would be encouraged to practice the piano if he could just hear the immortal Paderewski at the keyboard. So with great reluctance, her son had come with her.

As the mother turned to talk with friends, her son could stay seated no longer. He was impulsively drawn to the keys of the grand Steinway piano with its leather tufted stool on the huge stage flooded with blinding lights.

Without much notice from the sophisticated audience, the boy sat down at the stool, staring wide-eyed at the black and white keys. He placed his small, trembling fingers in the right location and began to play "Chopsticks." The roar of the crowd was hushed as hundreds of faces turned in his direction. Irritated and embarrassed, they began to shout: "Get that boy away from there! . . . Who'd bring a kid that young in here? . . . Where's his mother? . . . Somebody stop him!"

Backstage, the master pianist overheard the sounds out front and quickly put together in his mind what was happening. Hurriedly, he grabbed his coat and rushed toward the stage. Without a single word of announcement, he stooped over behind the boy, reached around both sides of him, and began to improvise a counter-melody to harmonize and enhance "Chopsticks." As the two of them played together, Paderewski kept whispering in the boy's ear repeatedly, "Keep playing, don't quit, son." (Adapted from an editorial by Truitt, "He Can Enter Our Stage of Life")

5
Write a prayer about some question that is still "unsolved in your heart," asking God's help in your experiences as you "live along some distant day into the answer."

Like the master pianist, God can surround us, improvising in our life to make a masterpiece, even out of our deficiencies. This is the wonder and gift of a grace-filled life. But we can be either open to grace or closed to it. The little boy could have slunk away in shame rather than playing along with the master's help. God's grace never takes away our freedom to choose. **6**

The Power of Grace

Accepting the gift of grace is what it means to have faith. An example of such grace-filled faith comes from South Africa. Archbishop Desmond Tutu, a black leader in that country, was once asked what role faith played in the struggle to end apartheid, a system of strict separation of the races. In response, he told this story:

"You meet so many wonderful people, people who have suffered and remained faithful. One such person is a man I met when I was praying with the people in Mogopa one night. [Mogopa was a black village that the white government was 'moving' as part of a forced population removal program during the 1980s.] Now this is someone whose house was going

to be demolished the next day. Clinics, churches, and shops had been demolished already. And the people were going to be moved at the point of a gun. And he got up, and he prayed, in the middle of the night, 'God, thank you for loving us.'

You couldn't have heard a more nonsensical prayer in the middle of that kind of situation. And yet, here was a man who didn't seem to know any theology but who could offer a prayer of thanksgiving." (Quoted in *Sojourners*)

The depth of this man's faith enabled him to see God's love, even in a time of great hardship. The struggle to end apartheid climaxed in 1994 when Nelson Mandela, a black leader who had been a political prisoner for more than twenty-five years, was elected president of South Africa. Such is the power of grace.

For Review

- How can people "pray their experiences"?
- What is grace?

■
Above: Archbishop Desmond Tutu, with young South Africans, carries a rough wooden cross in a religious service held in a Soweto township church at a meeting to explore ways to fight apartheid.

6
Apply this parable of grace to an everyday situation in which God's grace works in a person's life. Record the situation in writing; be sure to show how the parable applies to it.

Community: A Network of Relationships

Perhaps the most common means for us to experience God's gracious activity in our life is through our personal relationships and our communities.

Every person is born into a network of relationships, and from birth onward that network grows and evolves—expanding from parents and family to friends, to adults like teachers and coaches, to a faith community, to organizations and groups we belong to, and to heroes whom we admire and who influence us. This community is the most obvious, visible source of support for our journey to becoming fully human.

Parents and Family

Parents and family form the natural and first community for a person. Whether good or bad, values are experienced in the family; patterns for dealing with other relationships are learned there, too. From the positive side, a family can be a testing ground for dealing with life.

At this point in your life, you are generally trying to establish yourself as an individual, independent of your parents and family. But this does not mean that you cannot look to your family for support. In a conversation with students at a Catholic high school in California, a junior girl put it this way:

It's good to get your parents' opinions about moral things. When you're in a dilemma, you have to think on the spot, right now. If you've talked with your parents about their opinions ahead of time, it's a better help. At least you know what they think.

One boy, a sophomore, expresses the need for quality communication in families:

I think America is falling away from our value system. Drugs are tearing us apart. There's got to be a switch in families; we have to grow closer. We can't be together all the time, but at least we can have some meaningful time together. Maybe kids should bring home the stuff they're learning about in school, like pamphlets on issues—drugs, sex, AIDS—to bring up a discussion at home. **7**

Friends

Recall the story from chapter 1 about Frank and his buddies, who were stopped by the police after drinking and taking signs from the zoo. Frank's brain was not choosing his own behavior that night—his buddies and his needy emotions were.

Friends can be the source of powerful peer pressure, and that pressure can be constructive as well as destructive. But another kind of friendship often develops during the high school years—a kind that does not use pressure tactics at all. This is the kind of relationship in which two people can talk honestly with each other—about their feelings, problems, and dilemmas—knowing that the other person is going to listen and respond sincerely from his or her own wisdom and experience.

These *real* friends will not tell you only what you want to hear; they will challenge your opinions when they disagree, expose you to different ways of looking at a situation, and help you to not be phony about your motives. Real friends help you to be real. They are great sources of support on your journey. **8**

7
Have you discussed any moral issues with your parents? If so, explain in writing what you have learned about your parents' views on one of these issues. If you have difficulty discussing moral issues with them, write about what you and your parents might do or say to make it easier to talk openly.

8
Do you have a friend with whom you can talk honestly about your feelings and dilemmas, knowing that your friend will not just tell you what you want to hear? If so, write a letter to your friend, thanking her or him for this gift of honesty.

Other Adults

For many young people, adults besides their parents play a significant role in their development. A caring adult—whether a teacher, grandparent, counselor, or priest—can make a tremendous difference in the life of any young person, but especially in the life of someone whose parents were not able to give the love and structure that their young person needed. Consider this example:

On a national TV news show, a counselor at a community agency in Little Rock, Arkansas, was interviewed about his work in helping poor people to improve their lives and to break out of a generations-old cycle of poverty.

The counselor was convinced that in addition to programs of opportunity for poor people, there had to be caring adults who would give people caught in that cycle a different message about themselves— that they are good, that they can make it, that someone *believes* in them.

As the interview progressed, it became clear where this man's conviction came from. He himself had been caught in a cycle of poverty and abuse as a young boy. He had come from a desperately poor family. His mother had been repeatedly abused by men and had no strength to defend her son from them. One time, one of these men had put her son into the hot oven of a wood stove they used for cooking, as punishment for misbehaving. The mother had stood by helplessly. Finally, a neighbor had rescued the boy from the oven.

The man told the horrifying story as one who had survived a nightmare. Why, the interviewer asked, hadn't he grown up to become just another victim of the cycle of abuse, trapped in a life of hopelessness, crime, drugs, and destructive relationships? The man answered that his grandmother had intervened in his life, giving him a strong, clear message: "You are *worth* something. You can *be* something. I believe in you." The boy's grandmother had given him the hope he needed to break out of the cycle of abuse and poverty.

Caring adults are available for young people to rely on, whether the youth have come from bad home situations or not. You may be familiar with adults who are particularly good at giving support, encouragement, and guidance to young persons— at your school, in your parish, in your extended family, or in your community. Some of these adults may have played a part in turning someone's life around. **9**

In some situations, a young person needs the help of a professional. Nancy, a fifteen-year-old, describes what happened when her parents were going through a divorce:

■
Above: A caring adult can make a tremendous difference in the life of any young person.

9
List some adults you know who are good at giving support, encouragement, and guidance. Next to each adult's name, identify a characteristic that makes the person appealing to you.

"Looking back, I think it was Dr. Schwartzberg who pulled me through. Without his help I would probably have turned to drugs or liquor because they would have been my only means to escape from all the problems I had. . . . I think that when parents are getting divorced it's smart for the kids to go see someone, and I think they should understand that this doesn't mean they're crazy. It's stupid for anyone to say, 'I don't need a psychiatrist—they're for crazy people,' because that's not true. Counseling just helps you to understand yourself and your problems." (Quoted in *Campus Life*)

A Faith Community

The community within which persons share a religious belief typically has two dimensions. Parishes offer a faith community at the local level. But local churches are part of a larger faith community, such as the whole Catholic church, which spans many countries, cultures, and times. Both levels can be sources of support for the moral journey.

Your Local Parish or Congregation

A parish or other group that offers the potential for a faith community can be especially important. For young persons, this may be a parish youth group, a Christian organization at a high school, or a campus ministry program at a college. The important thing is to find other people who are struggling to deal with life out of a shared faith vision. Such groups don't "talk faith" all the time, or even most of the time, but individuals in them know that no matter what they do together or talk about, they are trying to live out of a common search for the meaning in their life.

Here is the comment of Rebecca, a member of a parish youth group:

"I had problems, problems with my parents and problems at school. What I found out was, so did everybody else. And most of us who checked these things out there at the parish rap sessions felt like God was in on the situation somehow, almost like it wasn't right to think of my life as *problems*." (Quoted in *Youth Update*)

Although a dynamic local faith community that supports people's growth in everyday life is not always easy to come by, it is potentially there in our parishes and Catholic schools. Sometimes it takes a bit of searching to find—or start up—what you need to sustain you, but it is worth the effort. **10**

The Communion of Saints

No local faith community could exist for long without support from and interaction with a wider community. This wider faith community is what we call the church, the community of all people who share a faith grounded in Jesus Christ. Sometimes the church is referred to as the **communion of saints**, the union of all good and faithful persons throughout history, both living and dead.

From the communion of saints we can draw upon the strength and companionship of those who have made or are making the journey to become their true selves and bring about the Reign of God in the world. People who are trying to live a good life are never alone; they are part of a great community that spans all time and space.

Consider the communion of saints in this way: Perhaps someone very important to you has died. Maybe that person—a grandparent or a parent or a friend—loved you specially, made you feel important, shared fun times with you. When people we love die and leave us, we miss them terribly and grieve their loss for a long time. But they are still

10
Interview a parish youth group leader or a high school campus minister to find out how the parish or school program supports young people in their struggles to deal with tough issues. Write up your findings.

The Great Cloud of Witnesses

Here are some words on the meaning of the communion of saints from Vincent Harding, an African American minister and long-time leader in the peace and justice movement:

> Not only is there this tremendous, magnificent, welcoming, loving host of folks who are prepared to welcome us into the light beyond this life, but also they are available to us now, on this side of death. Yes, the same cloud of witnesses is here now to help us live in the light; here to help us walk in the light; here to help us be enlightened in the fullest and deepest sense of that word, to help us walk in the truth.
>
> And if there's anything I want to share, it is my conviction of how important it is that we get past any sense of spookiness, strangeness, or fear about the reality of this great cloud of witnesses whose fulfillment cannot take place without our own [fulfillment]. I would call us to see and appreciate these folks who are like a great cheering squad for us. In the midst of everything that seems so difficult, that seems so powerful, that seems so overwhelming, they are saying to us: "We are with you," and "There is a way through; there is a way to stand; there is a way to move; there is a way to hope; there is a way to believe. Don't give up!"
>
> To know them, to know that they are present, is to know that regardless of how alone we feel sometimes, we are never alone. We are *never* alone: nowhere, no how, in nothing. Never. ("In the Company of the Faithful")

with us, present to us in our thoughts and memories, living on in us, and pulling for us. They have joined the "saints in heaven," and they still care about us, the "saints on earth."

These saints in heaven are good people who tried to draw close to God in their life. Some of them are famous people whom we can get to know through books, but most are not known to anyone today. Yet, all these millions of people are united with us in the communion of saints because they helped make our world a better place. Like our loved ones who have died, they send us their strength to help us on our journey. **11**

When Christians pray with the saints, they are not worshiping the saints. Rather, Christians are acknowledging that they are not alone but are surrounded by a great "cloud of witnesses" (Hebrews 12:1), who are a source of strength.

Heroes

You might not think of heroes as part of your community, especially remote figures like media celebrities, sports stars, activists, political leaders, or religious leaders. But they can be a significant part of your life because of the values and the lifestyle they communicate. They may touch your life as closely as a friend does, by offering a model of the kind of person you want to become or be like. Obviously, picking your heroes carefully is as important as picking your friends.

Who are your heroes? In addition to contemporary figures and celebrities, think of historical persons and persons who are not well known. What values and lifestyles do your heroes communicate to you? **12**

Organizations of Support

Many people find that support groups of individuals who have problems or concerns similar to their own can offer a great deal of support and guidance. A successful model for such support groups is Alcoholics Anonymous, started in the 1930s by two recovering alcoholics. It has spawned numerous offshoots, for instance, Alanon (for family members of alcoholics), Alateen (for teenage children of alcoholics), and Adult Children of Alcoholics.

Other support organizations exist—including groups for chemically dependent persons, children who have lost a parent through death, overeaters, parents who have lost a child, those addicted to gambling, families of mentally ill persons, children of divorced parents, divorced and separated adults, survivors of physical and sexual abuse, and abusers themselves. School counselors and pastors are usually familiar with the groups that exist in their community. **13**

People are often drawn to join a support group because they feel powerless. The empowering nature of these types of groups stems from the fact that human beings are truly relational. By coming together and sharing a common desire, many people are discovering the potential for growth and healing that such support groups can offer.

For Review

- Describe briefly how each of these community members can be a source of support for one's moral growth: parents and family, friends, other adults, a faith community, heroes, and organizations of support.

11
Name one of the saints in heaven whom you admire, well known or not. Write an imaginary dialog between you and that saint, in which you ask him or her for some advice or strength on some issue you are facing.

12
Make a list of people whom you think teens in your country most admire. Next to the name of each one, identify what values and lifestyle that person communicates. Then do the same with a list of people whom *you* most admire.

13
Do some research to find out the names of at least five support groups available to teenagers in your community or region. What is the focus of each group?

Sources of Help from Society

Besides the world of our immediate community, with its personal relationships, other sources of help are available to us from the wider human community, or society. One such source is the basic moral principles that have been expressed over the ages and that have validity as time-honored guides for living. Civil laws, or laws made by governments, are another primary means by which the society supports our growth as moral persons.

Basic Moral Principles: Lessons of the Ages

Basic moral principles represent the wisdom of human experience over the ages. These principles are not collected into any one book, nor are they agreed on by every human being. But, as discussed on page 15, some principles are so widely held that we can think of them as universals. Here are a few of these principles:

Do good; avoid evil. This most basic moral principle, the starting point for morality, was articulated by Aristotle, an ancient Greek philosopher, and is held by all the world's major religions. All other moral principles flow from this one.

Do unto others . . . As discussed in chapter 1, the world's major religions carry an expression similar to the Golden Rule familiar to Christians: "'Do to others whatever you would have them do to you.'" (Matthew 7:12)

The end does not justify the means. Classical philosophy and the major world religious traditions have upheld the principle that having a good end (goal or purpose) does *not* justify the use of evil means (method) to achieve that end.

For instance, after the pressure of final exams, suppose some teenagers want to celebrate the end of the school year by unwinding and having some fun. That is a good end, or purpose. But suppose that their method of celebrating is taking a fast, reckless drive through downtown. That would be a bad means to a good end. The good end of having fun does not justify the bad means of driving recklessly.

Here's another example: The end of passing a test, good as it may be, does not justify cheating as a means for achieving that end.

Sometimes, as in the previous examples, this principle of the end not justifying the means seems clear enough. But in other cases, it becomes more difficult to discern what is right, because conflicts arise between the principle and reality. When these conflicts occur, people call upon other principles, such as the classic philosophical principle of *proportionality*. This principle states that if the end to be achieved is clearly so good that it outweighs the harm done by the bad means, then the means *could* be justified. This has been the usual way in which many Christians have justified war, saying that the good to be done (for instance, getting rid of Hitler in World War II) outweighs the harm of the means (the suffering of war), and no other means are available.

The principle of proportionality, of course, cannot always be applied in clear-cut ways. Difficult judgment calls will always be required in matters of morality. For instance, in considering the morality of war, many other Christians believe that war can never be justified, especially the kind of war of massive destruction that contemporary weapons make possible.

Follow what nature intends. Known in philosophy as natural law, this principle is not actually a law written down someplace but, rather, an approach to making decisions that respects the nature of things, especially human nature. Briefly, natural law tells us this: Learn a lesson from nature. Follow what is natural for human beings and the rest of creation. Do not violate the nature of things. For instance, it is natural for parents to care for their children; this is nature's way of continuing life.

Consider how natural law could apply to humans' tampering with the earth's environment. For example, it is natural for the earth to have a protective ozone layer around it to shield animals and plants from the destructive effects of ultraviolet light. Human beings' damaging of the ozone layer through pollution could be considered a violation of natural law. **14**

Civil Laws: Moral in a Just Society

Civil laws, that is, laws made by governments, can be sources of help for us in our moral development, but only in a limited, minimal way. Laws ensure public order, provide for the common good, and guarantee access to basic rights. At the least, citizens should obey such laws.

It is possible, however, for an individual to go through life without ever breaking a civil law but still be morally stunted. Obeying all civil laws does not necessarily mean we are behaving in a morally mature way. But breaking civil laws that are just is definitely immoral. In a fundamentally just society, we can assume that the laws are just, even the ones that inconvenience us, such as parking regulations or age limits for driving. We do not need to debate the fairness of every regulation before deciding to obey it.

14
List three other examples of what could be considered violations of natural law.

However, in some societies, especially fundamentally unjust ones, many of the laws are unjust. In these cases, the church says that we are not only allowed to break the law but we may even be obligated to do so. Such acts, performed nonviolently and with an acceptance of the consequences of jail, fines, or sometimes even death, are called civil disobedience. Historically, acts of civil disobedience have been performed by conscientious Christians as well as by members of other faiths and persons who claim no particular faith. Civil disobedience does not guarantee that unjust laws will change at once, but it does allow the voice of conscience to be heard. Here are some examples of unjust laws that have been broken by conscientious people around the world:

- slavery laws in the United States up until the Emancipation Proclamation of 1863
- legal discrimination, to the point of genocide, against Jews and other minorities in Hitler's Germany
- laws against free speech in a dictatorship **15**

For Review

- List four moral principles that are considered universals.
- What is a Christian approach to deciding whether to obey or disobey civil laws?

■
Above: In an instance of civil disobedience in 1989, a Romanian tank driver takes his stand with the people who are demanding democracy.

15
In a periodical from the last five or ten years, find an account of an act of civil disobedience. Write about what prompted the civil disobedience, the rationale of the dissenters, and whether you agree or disagree with their action.

Christian Teachings

The Teachings of Jesus and the Scriptures

As discussed in chapter 2, for Christians, Jesus is the model of living a fully human existence. The great commandment of love—that we love God above all else and our neighbor as ourselves—sums up the ethical teachings of both Judaism and Christianity.

But the Scriptures also spell out the meaning of an ethical life in more specific ways.

The Ten Commandments

Certainly the Ten Commandments are basic—so basic that they can be considered the moral minimum that we must do or avoid doing (see page 40). Doing the moral minimum might keep us from gross immorality, but it is not enough to guarantee we will become moral adults. We might compare it to studying just enough to get a passing grade but not enough to get an education. **16**

As one proverb puts it, the law is found at the foot of the mountain, but uphill from the pit. When people break a law, such as one of the commandments, they leave the mountain and are headed for the pit. But those who hear the call to a moral life choose not to wander near the pit, seeing how close they can come to it without falling in. Rather, they see themselves as being called to the top of the mountain, and they strive to reach it.

The Sermon on the Mount

The **Sermon on the Mount** in Matthew's Gospel (chapters 5–7) is a collection of many of Jesus' teachings about how to live and relate to other people. First, Jesus proclaims the **Beatitudes.** These are descriptions of people who are living the Reign of God in their own life—the poor, the sorrowing, the hungry, the meek, the persecuted. Jesus calls them blessed, or happy, because they know how needy they are and thus have room in their hearts for God. **17**

After the Beatitudes, Jesus gives his disciples some startling guidelines for how to live out the law of love. Here they are summarized briefly:

- Love your enemies and be good to those who hate you. Pray for people who hurt you.
- Do not condemn what is in other people's hearts. Only God can judge. Pay more attention to working on your own weaknesses than on the weaknesses of others.
- Be as concerned about your intentions—what is in your heart—as you are about your actions.
- Do not spend your whole life making yourself secure and comfortable; dedicate yourself to the things of the Spirit, and God will take care of you.

16
Rewrite the Ten Commandments so that they express positive ideals. For example, "you shall not kill" could be expressed as "protect human life."

17
In the Beatitudes, Jesus turns people's expectations upside down. In a paragraph, give an example from your own or another person's life of how happiness came in a surprising way, a way that does not fit the popular notions.

The Beatitudes

"Blessed are the poor in spirit,
  for theirs is the kingdom of heaven.
Blessed are they who mourn,
  for they will be comforted.
Blessed are the meek,
  for they will inherit the land.
Blessed are they who hunger and thirst for
    righteousness,
  for they will be satisfied.
Blessed are the merciful,
  for they will be shown mercy.
Blessed are the clean of heart,
  for they will see God.
Blessed are the peacemakers,
  for they will be called children of God.
Blessed are they who are persecuted for
    the sake of righteousness,
  for theirs is the kingdom of heaven."

(Matthew 5:3–10)

Christians and non-Christians alike have been inspired for centuries by Jesus' Sermon on the Mount. One of them was Mohandas K. Gandhi of India, the Hindu statesman who led the movement of nonviolent resistance to British colonial rule, which ended in 1948. During the 1950s and 1960s in the United States, the Baptist minister Martin Luther King Jr., led a similar nonviolent campaign to end racial segregation and discrimination. King, too, found his inspiration in the Sermon on the Mount and in the nonviolent example of Gandhi.

During the 1980s and 1990s, Gospel-inspired peace organizations such as Witness for Peace, Pax Christi USA, and the Fellowship of Reconciliation maintained an international, nonviolent presence in such war-torn nations as Nicaragua, El Salvador, the Philippines, and Haiti. Eastern European Christians were leaders in the movement to transform their nations from dictatorships to democracies—again, many were inspired by the nonviolence of Jesus, Gandhi, and King. Religion and religious ideas played a critical role in the upheaval that led to the overturning of unjust regimes in, for example, Poland and Argentina. All of these examples involved campaigns of civil disobedience by citizens of those countries.

Other Teachings of Jesus

Jesus' moral teachings can be found not only in the Sermon on the Mount but throughout the

Gospels. By the example of his life and through parables, Jesus taught his followers to look at the world in a fresh, new way, to see the mysterious reality of God's presence in everyday life.

Most of Jesus' parables are about relationships: God's with human beings, human beings' with God, and human beings' with one another. You are probably quite familiar with the parable of the prodigal son (Luke 15:11–32), about forgiveness; and the parable of the good Samaritan (Luke 10:29–37), about compassion for persons who are considered different from us, even enemies. **18**

The Teachings of the Church

In searching for help and insight for their moral development, it makes sense for Christians to turn not only to Jesus' teachings but also to the community that has tried to apply and live out those teachings for centuries, in good times and in bad. To consider the importance of church teaching for our development as full persons, it is helpful to put that teaching into the context of the church's long history.

Christianity has "been around the block" a few times. Over its nearly two-thousand-year history, the Christian church has experienced great trials and renewals, and, as often comes with age, it has accumulated a wealth of wisdom that can be drawn upon in a person's growth.

A Community That Has Struggled and Searched

After Jesus died and was raised from the dead, a fledgling community of believers was born, the Christian church that would carry on Jesus' mission and message. Over the centuries, Christianity grew, endured persecutions, struggled with painful

18
Rewrite as a contemporary story the parable of the prodigal son or the parable of the good Samaritan.

■
Above: Catholic church teaching can be viewed as the wisdom of a community of believers who have been trying to live out Jesus' teaching for twenty centuries.

From the Roman Catholic Church's Teaching Voice

A U.S. Cardinal on a Consistent Ethic of Life
The spectrum of life from womb to tomb creates the need for a consistent ethic of life. For the spectrum of life cuts across the issues of genetics, abortion, capital punishment, modern warfare, and the care of the terminally ill. . . .

Those who defend the right to life of the weakest among us must be equally visible in support of the quality of life of the powerless among us: the old and the young, the hungry and the homeless, the undocumented immigrant and the unemployed worker. (Cardinal Joseph Bernardin of Chicago, "Call for a Consistent Ethic of Life")

The U.S. Bishops Speak Out on Immigration
In solidarity with our brother bishops in California, we . . . want to express our concern over the passage of California's Proposition 187—denying most health care, social service and educational benefits to undocumented persons. . . . We regret the passage of Proposition 187. . . . Health care and education are among the basic rights to which all people have a moral claim.

. . . In seeking to cure social and economic ills, this proposition strikes at the most vulnerable among us—children, the sick and the needy—without addressing the larger social and political causes for the problems. . . . In an attempt to deal with today's economic downturn and to force people to flee from the United States, this law seeks to enlist public servants—teachers, medical professionals and others who enter their professions desiring to serve society—to police the populations they serve.

"We are one human family, whatever our national, racial, ethnic, economic and ideological differences. We are our brothers' and sisters' keepers." ("National Conference of Catholic Bishops President's Statement on Immigration Debate")

A U.S. Bishop on Sex and Teenagers
Abstinence should be thought of not just as a "no" to sexual activity, but also as a "yes" to one's future and to one's future spouse. It is a "yes" to one's own inner potential, to one's ability to love and to express love. It is a "yes" to trust, faithfulness, and friendship. (Archbishop John R. Roach of Minneapolis-Saint Paul, *Grateful for the Gift*)

Pope John Paul II Speaks at World Youth Day 1993
The Good Shepherd . . . sees everything that threatens life. . . . He sees so many young people throwing away their lives in a flight into irresponsibility and falsehood. Drug and alcohol abuse, pornography and sexual disorder, violence: These are grave social problems which call for a serious response from the whole of society. . . . But they are also personal tragedies, and they need to be met with concrete interpersonal acts of love and solidarity in a great rebirth of the sense of personal answerability before God, before others and before our own conscience. We are our brothers' keepers!

splits in its membership, and wrestled over the implications of Jesus' message for the people of each new era. The Christian church upheld Jesus' vision more nobly at some times than at others.

Through all the growth, upheaval, and change, Christians believe that the Spirit of God has been and is at work in the church, bringing about a renewal of Jesus' vision in the hearts of its members and in its teachings in each new age.

The Christian church is not perfect and has never claimed to be so. It is an institution in process—a pilgrim church on a journey to becoming the full expression of Jesus in the world. Its journey is not unlike our individual journey to becoming fully human. The church's journey thus far is a powerful experience for us to learn from, especially because that experience is guided ultimately by God's Spirit.

A Wide-angle View

In spite of its imperfections, the Christian church is a community whose members, with all their limits and weaknesses, have struggled and searched together for two thousand years to figure out and live out the vision of Jesus. This gives the church a unique, wide-angle perspective on the human experience. Thus when the **magisterium**, or teaching voice of the Catholic church—as expressed by the pope and the bishops—speaks, we have good reason to listen well to what it has to say.

The Catholic church has not arrived at its present insights or teachings lightly but only after years, even centuries, of living with and reflecting on its experiences in light of the Gospel. The wisdom of age has taught the Catholic church, an institution with over 800 million members worldwide, to proceed cautiously in the development of its teachings.

The value of Catholicism's cautious, wide-angle view is that it guards against making decisions without looking at all the implications. In our moral decision making, we often look at our dilemmas from within a quite narrow view; we tend to see only our immediate concerns and desires and to screen out the bigger picture. A good friend is not one who just tells us what we want to hear, reinforcing our narrow view of things. Rather, a good friend sometimes tells us what we do *not* want to hear, in order to help us see beyond our own nose. Think of the Catholic church as a good friend who at times tells us things we do not want to hear, but tells us out of love, experience, and wisdom. Smart people listen to such friends; they do not dismiss their insights as old-fashioned. **19**

Creating human beings as relational (connected to others) is God's way of enabling us to experience grace. In addition to faith and our relationship with God through prayer and worship, God's grace can be experienced in every area of daily life. Whether it is in a relationship with a family member or through laws governing how we conduct ourselves in society, God can be found working in our life to help us become fully human.

For Review

- List the Beatitudes.
- What are four other moral guidelines for living the law of love from Jesus' Sermon on the Mount?
- What is the value of the church's wide-angle view for moral decision making?

Facing page: Pope John Paul II meets with young people in Los Angeles during his 1987 visit to the United States.

19
Respond in writing to this statement:
- The church is a good friend who, out of love, experience, and wisdom, at times tells us things we do not want to hear.

Sin:
A Violation of Relationships

Relationships through which we experience God's grace in our life help and support us on our moral journey. But **sin** is ultimately a violation of relationships. When we lie to our parents, we violate our relationship with them because they can no longer trust us; when we refuse to turn to God in prayer, we are rejecting God's transforming gift of grace. At another level, our efforts to prove we are better than others often stem from our own insecurities about ourselves, our own inability to love ourselves. Sin cuts us off from ourselves, others, and God. **20**

The reality of sin in the world often acts as a giant pothole in our road toward moral maturity. Rather than making our journey to full humanness by following a straight line toward goodness, we end up mostly zigzagging our way through life in spite of our intentions to do otherwise. Even the great Apostle Paul admitted this about his own tendency to get off the track: "What I do, I do not understand. For I do not do what I want, but I do what I hate. . . . For I do not do the good I want, but I do the evil I do not want" (Romans 7:15,19).

Original Sin and Actual Sin

Christian belief holds that we are created good and that we have a natural thirst within us for goodness. But according to the story of the Fall, Adam and Eve rejected that goodness. Their **original sin** left a legacy of sin in the world, a legacy of broken relationships. Sin is "inherited" as a part of the human condition: we experience ourselves as estranged from others and from who we really are

through feelings of powerlessness, brokenness, and insecurity, and through suffering and pain. When we give in to the evil and the violation of relationships we find around us in the world, we make that evil our own. This is known as **actual sin**—what we ourselves do to keep sin going in the world. Actual sin, however, can be done either by **commission** (doing an act of wrong, such as stealing) or by **omission** (neglecting to do something required, such as failing to speak up when someone else is wrongly accused of something).

Sin Breeds Sin

Sin tends to engender further sin, resulting in more and more damage to relationships. Of equal significance is the fact that both individuals and groups participate in actual sin: sin occurs at the social level, involving groups of persons or whole societies, as well as at the personal level.

Personal Sin

When individuals knowingly, willingly do something that hurts their relationship with God, self, neighbor, or nature, this is known as **personal sin.**

For example, consider the spot Mick got himself in after telling a lie to his parents:

When my parents asked me how that pint bottle got in my coat pocket, I told them that Jes must have snuck it in there the other night when I gave him a ride home. I said, "I saw him drinking from it earlier that night—that's why I offered to take him home."

Wouldn't you know it, my parents wanted to call Jes's folks because "they should be aware that their son might have a drinking problem." The next thing I knew, I was rattling off a story about how I really didn't think that was a good idea because if Jes's par-

---

20
List ten actions that would be considered sinful if they were done knowingly and freely. For each action, indicate how it violates a relationship with oneself, others, or God.

ents found out he was drinking at all, they wouldn't let him go out for basketball. I told them they're real strict with Jes, they jump on him for the littlest thing, and he hardly ever drinks—this was, like, the first time this year. But my folks said they had to do the "right" thing and call.

Well, finally I had to come clean: "Jes had nothing to do with the bottle. Jacquo and I were passing it at the movie Friday night. Jes didn't even know we had it." Jes would have been in deep trouble if my parents had called his.

Lies are notorious for their tendency to pave the way for more lies and to multiply damage in relationships. Lies have a way of cornering us, making it very hard to get ourselves out of them and "come clean" as Mick did. Personal sins of all kinds are much like lies in that they tend to trap us and make it difficult for us to get free.

Social Sin

When a whole group or society participates in a process or a system that harms human relationships, this is known as **social sin.** Everyone in the group or society shares, in some degree, the responsibility for the damage caused.

Discrimination on the basis of gender, or sexism, is a good example of how sin crosses over from the personal level to the social level. At the root of sexism are the beliefs that women are not as competent as men, that women's concerns are not as important as men's, and that women's talents are of less value than men's.

When women, or any group of people, are given the message from childhood on that they do not have much to offer or that what they do offer is second-rate, they tend not to offer much. The negative message becomes a self-fulfilling prophecy. As the famous ex-slave and abolitionist Frederick Douglass expressed it, "'If nothing is expected of a people, that expectation will be fulfilled completely'" (quoted in *Overview*).

Because of such a self-fulfilling prophecy, gifts can get buried and potential stifled; this negative reinforcement often blocks or seriously damages persons' self-esteem and therefore their ability to reach their potential as fully human persons. The "isms" mentioned in chapter 1—racism, sexism, ageism, and so on—all operate in this destructive way to block the potential of whole groups. A person who unthinkingly goes along with one of these "isms" participates in social sin. Much of the time, social sin is done through omission—looking the other way, allowing an unjust societal practice to continue without protest. **21**

Harm to Oneself

Sin violates relationships not only with others but also with oneself. In the following instance, Megan, age sixteen, becomes aware of the damage she has done to herself as well as her sister:

It had been another one of those horrible screaming matches with her sister, Evie. Over what? The fact that Evie had borrowed her blouse. Megan could hardly believe the argument could have gone so far over a stupid blouse.

Yes, she had been angry and her sister had been defensive. But then what happened to spin them both out of orbit? A lot of hurtful, ugly things had been said. When Evie had called her stingy and selfish, Megan had pulled out all the stops. She didn't hold back on the accusations that Evie was irresponsible, lazy, insecure, and furthermore, unattractive to boys. In this fit of hurling insults, Megan unloaded every resentment she had ever felt toward Evie. Then came the biggest cut: "I heard Alan say he knew you wanted to go to the homecoming dance with him, but he wouldn't be caught dead on a date with you."

When the screaming and the tears were over and both girls were back in their rooms, Megan felt so exhausted she did not know how she would be able to do her homework. But worse than the exhaustion, she felt rotten about what had happened. She felt terrible for Evie. But she also felt bad for herself. Megan realized she had sunk to a new low. She did not even want to look at herself in the mirror. Throwing herself on her bed and sobbing, Megan felt worse as a person than she had felt in a long time.

Megan is keenly aware of how she has hurt her sister and herself. Not everyone realizes how they hurt themselves as well as others by sinning. Often we try to deny that what we have or have not done is a sin, thus preventing ourselves from ever facing up to the damage we have done to ourselves and to others. Megan's painful remorse is the first step toward healing her relationship with God, herself, and her sister.

Mortal Sin and Venial Sin

According to Catholic belief, persons can choose to cut themselves off so severely from God, self, and others that their whole life direction is toward sin. This is a condition traditionally called **mortal** ("deadly") **sin**. This type of sin is appropriately named, for a person in a state of mortal sin has deadened himself or herself to goodness and life.

Usually when people sin, however, they are not turning their whole life direction away from God and goodness. Rather, they are in a condition of **venial sin**, which means they are choosing to hurt their relationship with God, self, and others but not to cut it off completely. This is a sad state to be in, but one that we have all frequently experienced. **22**

For Review

- What is sin?
- Define original sin and actual sin.
- How does personal sin differ from social sin?
- What is mortal sin? venial sin?

21
In a paragraph, give an example of social sin that exists in this country. Explain how this sin happens through both omission and commission.

22
In writing, tell whether you agree or disagree with this statement and why:
- It is possible to make a list of wrong actions and label each one as either a mortal sin or a venial sin.

Grace as God's Mercy, Forgiveness, and Empowerment

More Powerful Than Sin

Because we are relational beings, the path away from sin to healing cannot be traveled alone. In the midst of our brokenness, God is still with us. And without God, we are powerless against sin.

From the Christian perspective, human life and history are not determined by sin. Christians believe that in Jesus' life, death, and Resurrection, God has broken through the darkness and evil of sin to triumph over it. God's love, mercy, and forgiveness for us are far more powerful than all the sin in the world. The reality of **grace**, God's loving presence within us, acts to free and empower us for good. The grace of God's mercy and forgiveness is a gift, not something we earn. Further, grace not only frees us from the power of sin in our life, it also takes us way beyond what we could do on our own.

Consider the story of the man who wrote the much-loved Christian hymn "Amazing Grace":

In his youth, John Newton (1725–1807) was an atheist. He led a decadent, sinful life while a sailor in the British Navy, briefly became a slave in Africa, and later profited from the slave trade as the captain of a slave ship. At one point, when Newton almost died during a raging storm at sea, he had a profound experience of faith in God. Later he became a Christian, one of England's most beloved preachers and hymn writers, and a leader in the struggle to abolish slavery. He felt profound remorse that he had ever participated in the inhumane slave trade. John Newton knew the amazing power of God's forgiving grace.

Letting God's grace work in us is the way to real freedom and empowerment. With God, all things are possible. **23**

23
Persons can experience God's grace without being aware of it. Write about a time in the last week or month when you were open to an experience that you can now identify as God's grace.

"Amazing Grace"

You may be familiar with the much-loved
Christian hymn "Amazing Grace." Here are
the words of the hymn:

Amazing grace, how sweet the sound
that saved a wretch like me.
I once was lost, but now I'm found;
was blind, but now I see.

'Twas grace that taught my heart to fear,
and grace my fear relieved.
How precious did that grace appear
the hour I first believed.

Thru many dangers, toils and snares
we have already come.
'Twas grace that brought us safe this far,
and grace will bring us home.

How sweet the name of Jesus sounds
to a true believer's ear.
It soothes his sorrows and heals his wounds,
and drives away his tears.

Reconciliation: Healing What Is Wounded

Opening ourselves up to God's grace and love brings about healing in our relationships that have been wounded as a result of sin. This healing, called **reconciliation**, brings us back in touch with God, nature, one another, and ourselves.

Person-to-Person

Reconciling with God might sound like a fairly easy thing to do. We just have to say, "I'm sorry, God," right? But reconciliation is not that simple. It involves facing ourselves honestly, not kidding ourselves about what we have done and the hurt we have caused, and then taking the necessary steps to bring our wounded or damaged relationships back together. We cannot be reconciled with God without being reconciled within ourselves and with each other.

The following story illustrates the person-to-person reconciliation that all of us are called to:

Rudy pulled his English book out of his locker and hurried to class. He didn't notice the note that fell out of the book, but his friend Dennis did.

Picking up the crumpled sheet, Dennis started after Rudy, but when he noticed that he had only two minutes to get to class on the third floor, he crammed the note into his jeans pocket and dashed up the stairs.

As the history teacher droned on, Dennis remembered the note. To relieve his boredom, he pulled it out, unfolded it, and began to read:

Rudy, stop calling me. Your too serious; I got bored on our dates. You should loosin up. You spend so much time with computers, people think your a nurd.
Amy

Dennis smiled, wishing class would end so that he could show the note to Vito and Ramon. They'll love this, he thought. She can't even spell. What a loser.

When Rudy got to his locker the next day, a piece of bright yellow paper hung from it. "People think your a nurd" was written in large letters across it. Dennis and Vito watched as Rudy furiously snatched it off the locker, balled it up, and threw it on the floor.

"He's got it bad," Vito laughed.

Thinking that they could get Rudy to finally see how weird Amy was, Dennis, Vito, and Ramon kept up their campaign, somehow expecting that Rudy would eventually start laughing at it all. Over the next couple of days, Rudy found phrases from the letter stuffed in his desk, his books, and even in his P.E. locker. Anger, humiliation, and embarrassment twisted inside him. He had really cared for Amy. The hurt was compounded by the thought that someone had her note. He wondered if the whole school knew that she had called him a nerd and a boring date.

On the fourth morning of his humiliation, as Rudy walked toward his locker, he saw Dennis stuff a piece of paper in one of the slots of his locker. It was the same yellow paper as before. Realizing that Dennis, whom he had considered his best friend, had been the one torturing him, Rudy dropped his books, ran down the corridor, and jumped on him. All the anger and humiliation surged up as he hit Dennis above his left eye. Rudy's fist came back bloody. As he looked at his fist, hands grabbed him from behind.

While nursing his swollen eye the next day, Dennis had a lot of time to think about the way he had been treating Rudy. He couldn't blame Rudy for being so mad. He had to figure out a way to repair the damage to his friendship with Rudy—they had been best friends since seventh grade. He hoped that Rudy would accept his apology.

That night Dennis went over to Rudy's house. His heart pounded like a jackhammer as the door opened. Before Rudy could close the door on him, Dennis stepped into the house and started, "Rudy, I'm really sorry. I don't know why I wasn't thinkin' right. I gotta clear this up with you. . . ." **24**

The Sacraments as Healing Signs of God-with-Us

Two of the Catholic church's seven sacraments —Reconciliation and the Eucharist—offer Catholics ongoing opportunities to celebrate the healing power and forgiveness of God in their life.

The Sacrament of Reconciliation. In the Catholic tradition, Reconciliation is the sacrament by which we "come back home" to God, ourselves, and others in the community.

When we are in a sinful state, we are denying others of the best possible self we can be. We owe it to others to be that best self, and when we are not, the community is worse off as a result. Thus, sin has a communal dimension. We need to be reconciled not only with God but with the community we have hurt. **25**

The healing love and forgiveness of God—God's grace—is discovered in the sacrament and celebrated when persons move through this process:

- face themselves honestly, recognizing their own hurts and weaknesses, and their capacity to hurt
- share that recognition in confession with a priest, who represents the church community
- receive the priest's words of advice and absolution as he welcomes them home into God's acceptance and forgiveness in the name of Jesus
- resolve to let God's love and mercy work in them to free them from sin

Acceptance and forgiveness free us within to become who we are meant to be. This is the empowerment that comes from reconciliation.

The Eucharist. For Catholics, the celebration of the Eucharist is both the source and the fruit of the faith-life of the community that is the church. In the Eucharist, the members of the community are brought into oneness with God through being nourished by the living Jesus under the forms of bread and wine. The Eucharist is about people growing closer to God, but at the same time, it is about people growing closer to one another.

In Reconciliation, Catholics experience themselves as reconnected—to themselves, to others, and to God. In the Eucharist, Catholics can pour out their thanksgiving to God for the forgiving, healing, and empowering gift of grace.

For Review

- What do Christians believe about the power of God's grace versus the power of sin?
- How do the sacraments of Reconciliation and the Eucharist offer the chance to celebrate God's healing love and forgiveness?

24
What things do people typically say to themselves that prevent them from being reconciled with another person? List several examples.

25
Give an example in writing of how a community can be worse off when one of its members is in a sinful state.

A Power Greater Than Sin

We can depend on this fact: we do not make the journey of life alone. God ensured this by our very nature, which is relational. When we are able to see interdependence as a gift, it can be a great source of strength for our moral journey. We are then able to reach out to the many helps along the way—to our community, to basic principles and religious teachings, and to our relationship with God. **26**

But when we stumble, we can be assured that God's power is far greater than the power of our own sin and weakness or the power of all the sin in the world. With God's grace, we can be confident that all things are possible.

■
Above: In the Eucharist, members of the community are brought into oneness with God and one another.

26
Write a response to a person who says, "Morality is a private thing between God and me."

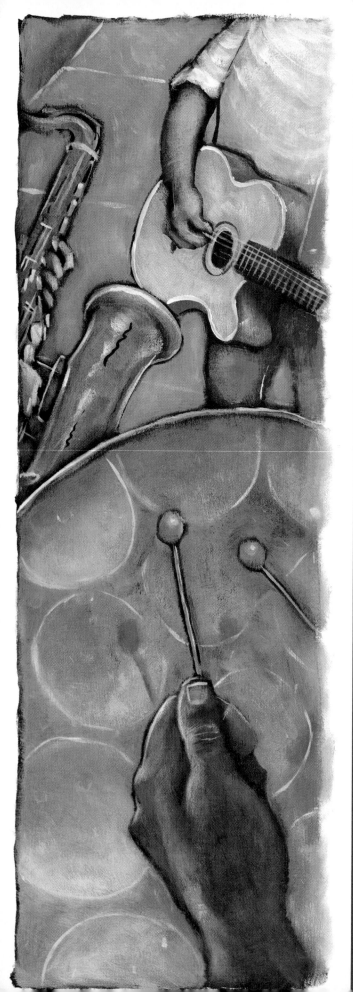

4

Moral
Decision
Making:
Listening
to Reality

BECOMING the person you are meant to be is a lifelong project, involving thousands of decisions. Some decisions you will make in a split second; others, after weighing the pros and cons; and still others, as the outcome of perhaps years of struggling to decide.

This chapter outlines a practical process for moral decision making consistent with the Christian vision of morality and with the helps for the journey described in chapter 3. Before getting into the specifics of the process, consider the following incident about the decision-making approach of a judge from the Old West:

The story has it that when New Mexico became part of the United States and the first court session opened in the new state, the presiding judge was a hardened old former cowboy and Indian fighter.

He took his place on the bench and the case opened. A man was charged with horse stealing. The case for the prosecution was made; the plaintiff and his witnesses were duly heard.

Whereupon the attorney for the defendant stood up and said, "And now, Your Honor, I should like to present my client's side of the case."

Said the judge, "Sit down. That won't be necessary. It would only confuse the jury!" (De Mello, *Taking Flight*, pages 185–186)

This judge made his moral decisions strictly from his biases. He listened to only one side of the case before him—the side he agreed with! His stance was, "Don't confuse me with the facts." **1**

Good decisions require an open attitude. The approach to moral decision making presented in this chapter helps to open the windows of the heart and mind to all of the reality that needs to be considered.

A Process for Moral Decision Making

Let's begin by looking at the process of moral decision making in action in the life of one young couple. The following is based on an interview with the couple that took place when both members of the couple were twenty-three years old.

One Couple's Decision

Marie and Vince were interviewed as part of a study of the attitudes of young adults about sexuality. They were both seventeen when they started dating. They dated for over five years before they got married. The interview focused on their decision of whether to have sexual intercourse before they were permanently committed to each other in marriage. During the interview, it became clear that Vince and Marie placed a great deal of importance on open and honest communication and on working out issues together.

For the interview, Vince and Marie were asked to discuss their relationship, dating, and sexuality—in particular, their decision about whether to have sex while dating. In making the particularly important decision concerning premarital sex, they had considered several of the elements of the decision-making process recommended in this chapter—without being consciously aware of, or able to explicitly spell out, such a process.

Marie: We started dating at the beginning of senior year in high school. We got off to a rocky start, partly because I just wanted to have a boyfriend and hadn't really had one until Vince. Anyway, by January, I had fallen for this guy here real hard.

1
In writing, give an example of a situation in which a person has an attitude similar to the judge's attitude in this story.

What was awful was that I wanted to go to college in a different state. Vince couldn't.

Vince: We both knew what we wanted. That was a big factor in shaping our relationship, having goals. College was a biggie.

Marie: I liked the fact that he didn't *demand* that I stay back in Illinois with him. I mean, it was unspoken that I would do what I had to do, and he was okay with that. But then it sunk in that we'd be hundreds of miles away from each other for the next four years. For a while we talked about going to the same school, but then we talked about how we could deal with long distance if we had to.

Vince: I hated it, but our individual goals were just too important to each of us. I knew I wanted engineering but couldn't afford to go to college out of state. It wouldn't have been fair for me to get what I wanted and to demand she stick around.

Marie: We talked and talked about all this. If we weren't individually happy, we'd be a lousy couple, and I'd start to resent him. But then we didn't want to be me-centered either.

Vince: As far as the sexuality thing goes, we talked a lot about that, too. Definitely if we couldn't be around for each other, having sex would be a problem. I wanted us to get to know each other first, you know, like attitudes, friends, family, and all sorts of things. Otherwise, it would be like sex with a stranger, impersonal.

Marie: Really, we had to get to know each other. I'm happy because that way our relationship unfolded slowly.

Vince: Sex touches all levels of life. We talked about our feelings a lot. I mean, it's all intertwined, right?—ideas, goals, and feelings. We both really agreed on how important it was to talk through our thoughts and feelings.

Marie: Another thing is we wanted to feel safe with each other. That only comes when two people know each other real well.

Vince: Family was a big thing, too. Part of knowing each other was knowing each other's family. It's like climbing a ladder. Each step of getting to know each other made us see different things. It started with physical attraction, but there was a lot more involved.

Marie: Another thing about families—my family, and yours, too *[Vince nods]*, taught me commitment. I just do not quit. I'll stick to things even sometimes when I should give up. I learned never to give up on a relationship I'm committed to. We've been fed all this Prince Charming stuff, the perfect man. Garbage. Nobody's perfect, so I want to hang in there and work things out.

My family was chaotic in a lot of ways, and in high school my self-esteem often took a beating, but they did push me to be honest. One reason I couldn't have sex before we were committed was because—this might sound silly—if I couldn't tell my mom, I couldn't do it. We were just always honest with each other. I couldn't break the trust with her. **2**

Vince: I wasn't under that kind of pressure, but my folks never once told me to shut up. So I could talk about anything. And both our families make a point of saying "I love you." Sex isn't the only way of expressing love. Maybe if people knew they were loved they wouldn't need sex so bad.

Marie: There was pressure from other kids to have sex. They'd tell us we were the perfect couple. It freaked them out that we didn't have sex. I just wanted a date for homecoming when we started!

Vince: At college, everybody talked about sex. I just didn't say anything. Let them think what they want. It's none of their business.

2
Interview another person about how she or he made an important decision, and then write up the interview.

Marie: As a woman, I was afraid of letting anyone think I was having sex.

Vince: Males brag about it a lot. When we first went out, sex was a big question. I mean, a lot of couples have sex to hold their relationship together when they don't have much else in common. It's stupid, but without other things to do together, sex becomes the only thing.

Marie: I would have felt bad about myself if I'd had sex. Pregnancy is a big thing, too. Men don't worry as much about that, even though they should. I knew both Vince and I would suffer the consequences. Sex had too many implications for each of us and our futures.

Vince: Sex can't be the focus of a relationship. A person can't live for it.

Marie: Besides, I wanted sex to be fun, a happy thing. If I had to worry all the time, how could I be happy with it?

Another thing that helped was that our church had youth group sessions on sexuality led by a married couple. That helped a lot. We got to ask all the questions we were afraid to ask—anonymously. And then a retreat was good, too. We spent a lot of time talking about setting boundaries. You really do have to be clear about your boundaries.

Vince: Sexuality is more than sex. There's all kinds of ways of being intimate besides physically.

Marie: Kids have sex because it's symbolic of being adult and because of pressure. Bogus TV ads and music make it seem so glamorous.

Vince: TV especially—there's too much hype.

Marie: I wanted to be normal and not feel pushed into anything; there was too much pressure from society to have sex. Sex takes lots of thought. It's too important to be laughed off or taken lightly. So we decided to wait.

■

Above, left and right: Decisions about sexual expression in a relationship require honest communication.

LISTEN to Reality

Remember the judge who decided the horse stealing case after hearing only one side? He lacked an attitude of listening. Marie and Vince, on the other hand, showed openness in how they dealt with the decision about their sexuality.

Our action-oriented culture tends not to value listening because the idea has overtones of being passive and of not having any choices, as in, "Sit and listen to what I tell you!" In moral decision making, however, a very different image of listening emerges. This dynamic process requires an active sense of listening.

To listen actively is to be open to the world around us. When we listen, our mind must be engaged, working on what we hear and sorting it out. Only then can we evaluate what we hear and know in our heart how we must act. **3**

Active listening also requires the element of humility. To listen humbly is to be open to the opinions, insights, and observations of others. An attitude of humility promotes active listening by preventing us from presuming that we have all the answers and do not need to listen closely to others.

The elements of good moral decision making can be thought of as ways of listening to reality. Appropriately, the first letter of each of the elements spells out LISTEN:

L **Look for the facts.** Figure out what the real situation is.

I **Imagine possibilities.** Consider consequences, creative approaches, options.

S **Seek insight beyond your own.** Look for help from family, religion, wise persons, and moral principles.

T **Turn inward.** Examine your own feelings, insights from experience, motives, and values.

E **Expect God's help.** Believe that God is present in your life, especially in your honest attempts to seek the truth.

N **Name your decision.** Even if it is simply to say you are postponing a decision, say so. Don't just let yourself and events drift.

What is the "reality" that we must listen to? It includes these facets:

- all of the circumstances and details of a situation, both internal and external
- the plain facts
- the potential options and consequences
- the insights available from persons near to us and from wise teachings
- our own inner reality of feelings, motives, and values
- the presence of God's help in the situation

An effective decision-making process is a way of listening to, and therefore thinking more clearly about, as much of reality as we can so that we can choose the best course of action.

Picture the LISTEN process as a pie cut into six pieces, like the diagram on the next page. Consider each of the pieces of the pie as they were evidenced in Marie and Vince's interview.

Look for the Facts

In the first piece of the LISTEN pie, look for the facts, the aim is to identify what is going on, or what is involved in the situation. Like a newspaper reporter, the person needs to figure out the who, what, when and where, why, and how of the matter. Any of these details might influence how the situation could best be resolved.

In Vince and Marie's decision about premarital sex, they showed an awareness of these factors:

- *Who.* Vince and Marie were aware of each other as individuals with their own valid goals and

---

3
Contrast a time when you listened to someone in an *active* sense with a time when you listened in a *passive* sense. Make a list of several adjectives that describe you *(a)* as you listened actively and *(b)* as you listened passively. Which kind of listener would you rather be?

L — **L**ook for the facts.

I — **I**magine possibilities.

N — **N**ame your decision.

S — **S**eek insight beyond your own.

E — **E**xpect God's help.

T — **T**urn inward.

dreams, and as cared for by the other. They also knew where their families stood on the issue of premarital sex.

- *What.* They knew their decision was about whether to have sex—with all the physical, emotional, and psychological intensity that sexual intercourse entails.
- *When and where.* Vince and Marie recognized that they were not at a stage of permanent commitment, that they both still had a lot of growing to do, and that they needed to know each other much more deeply before they would be ready for a commitment. They were also facing a geographical separation that would complicate their relationship.
- *Why.* Vince and Marie were aware of various reasons that many young persons have sex be-fore marriage: to keep the relationship together, to feel adult and glamorous, to do what other people expect, to feel loved when they do not already feel lovable, and to express genuine love.
- *How.* Marie was convinced that sex should happen in an atmosphere that is worry-free, fun, psychologically safe, and committed. Vince discussed how sex touches every level of life and should come from a sharing of those many levels over a long period of time. They both recognized that they could be sexual and intimate as a couple in other ways than by having sex. **4**

Imagine Possibilities

The second piece of the pie, imagine possibilities, is a way of anticipating consequences—long-term as well as short-term. A high school senior

---

■
Above: Picture the LISTEN process as a pie cut into six pieces.

4
Focus on a difficult moral decision that you have had or will have to make. Identify in writing the *who, what, when and where, why,* and *how* of the matter.

remarks on this: "It's hard for most kids to think about the long-term effects of what they're doing. They look at the short-term effects—like whether they'll get caught—but thinking about what's way down the road takes some maturity." **5**

In Vince and Marie's case, they had thought about the long-term effects that sex might have for them. For one, they foresaw a too-rapid development of intimacy that might quickly evaporate because it was not based on real knowledge of each other. In the long term, they wanted their sexual relationship to be solidly founded on close personal knowledge of each other. Marie anticipated the breaking of trust with her mother—and, of course, pregnancy. They figured that for persons who are not committed to each other, sex could be an artificial way to keep a relationship together when it does not have much else going for it.

Another way that we can imagine possibilities when trying to make a decision is to be creative in coming up with options or solutions to our dilemma. For instance, Marie and Vince found other ways to express intimacy. They discovered that their options were not simply to have sex or not but that they could find ways to communicate closeness at many levels. If they had confined their options to sex versus no sex and not seen other possibilities for closeness, they would have missed out on the chance to build a rich, deep relationship. **6**

Seek Insight Beyond Your Own

The third piece of the pie, seek insight beyond your own, calls upon the helps for the journey detailed in chapter 3: community—including family, friends, organizations and professionals that offer support, the example of heroes, and a local faith community; laws; moral principles; and the teachings of Jesus and the church. As discussed in that chapter, it is unwise to seek the insights of certain people or organizations just because you know they will tell you what you want to hear. Mere confirmation of your own opinions ends up cheating you of the help that you could receive from people who genuinely care about you and would not hesitate to disagree with you if disagreement were needed. **7**

Marie and Vince found that they had to weigh the advice of their friends carefully. Their friends turned out to be more sources of pressure than of insight. Although Marie apparently did not talk directly with her mother about the decision of

---

■
Above: Thinking about what is way down the road—the long-term effects of a decision—takes maturity.

5
Consider a moral choice that you typically have to make, involving at least two options. For each option, list the possible short-term and long-term consequences that you can imagine.

6
Think of a situation in which you supposedly must choose between two options. Stretch your mind to create a list of alternative solutions to the dilemma.

whether to have sex with Vince, she knew where her mother stood, and it was a strong position against premarital sex.

Vince and Marie's church youth group gave them an opportunity to learn about sexuality from persons who shared their same faith perspective. In the interview, Marie did not detail what was covered in the youth group's sessions with the married couple, but we can imagine that Christian insights on sexuality were conveyed to the young persons, including the church's position that sex is for marriage only.

Turn Inward

In the fourth piece of the pie of decision making, turn inward, we listen to our values and desires, our motives, and our feelings—our gut-level sense of things. This *inner reality*—the inner world of the person making the decision—is as important as the outer reality and needs to be listened to just as closely.

Vince and Marie spent a lot of time and energy on turning inward, listening to their heartfelt desires. They were physically attracted to each other, but they wanted sex to be an expression of a deep, lifetime relationship based on knowing each other well. Marie knew she didn't want to be dishonest about sex, keeping it a secret from her family. She wanted to feel relaxed about sex, not pressured. Vince knew he wanted intimacy to mean closeness at many levels, not just the genital level.

We need to take seriously our personal values, needs, insights, and feelings. Sometimes a heartfelt decision that seems unable to be explained logically is the best one we could make. But we cannot rely solely on our heart when we make decisions; feelings must be balanced by the other elements of the decision-making process.

A challenging piece of advice comes from the Greek historian Plutarch: "Know thyself." Knowing yourself includes an awareness of your motives for doing or not doing something, your true reasons.

Marie and Vince had looked seriously into their own motives, questioning why they might have wanted to have sex before they were committed permanently to each other. They considered the pressures they were under from friends and society. Vince must have wondered if the desire to brag about his sexual achievements to other college men was a factor for him. Marie knew that the chaos she had known in her own family and the beating her self-esteem had taken were potential weak spots for her that might have motivated her to have sex to prove she was okay. This couple spent a good deal of energy examining their motives.

If we are able to search within ourselves and uncover the layers of our possible motives about a given action, we are wise persons. We usually find that we have several motives going at once, some admirable and others not so admirable. We cannot expect that our motives will always be totally pure. But when we listen very carefully to our inner reality, we can see all our motives more clearly and then decide which ones we want to base our decisions on. **8**

Expect God's Help

The fifth piece of the pie, expect God's help, means that we recognize God is with us in our struggle with any and all decisions, and we can draw strength from God. Through prayer we can ask God to listen to us, as well as to help us listen to reality with an attitude of openness to truth. **9**

7
Write a dialog about a person seeking advice about a moral issue from a friend in order to hear only what he or she *wants* to hear.

8
Reflect on a moral choice you have made in the last week. For each option you could have chosen, look inward and identify in writing as many motives as you can think of for choosing that option.

9
Write a brief prayer that a person could say in the midst of making a difficult moral decision.

Although prayer was not specifically discussed in the interview, Marie mentioned having gone on a retreat that enabled her to reflect on issues of her own sexuality and the need to set boundaries. We can assume that the retreat involved prayer—reaching out to God for support—and that Marie was aware of God's presence with her in her efforts to decide how to be a sexual person with integrity.

Name Your Decision

The sixth piece of the pie, name your decision, calls for some resolution of the dilemma and a consciousness of where the matter now stands. Drifting—letting things just float off without an awareness of any decision at all—invites passivity and a lack of direction and focus in a person's life. And not deciding is itself a decision, although not a helpful one most times. In naming our decision, we take responsibility for how we are to act given all that we have "heard." Drifting, or avoiding decisions and responsibility, undermines the freedom and power we have to shape our life. As someone once put it, "If you don't know where you're going, you might end up somewhere else."

Of course, many situations cannot be resolved quickly one way or the other. In such cases, even postponing the decision and recognizing it as a postponement ("I will give this a month, then I'll try to make a choice again") is a way of naming a decision. Postponing a major decision can be a wise choice, especially in situations where more information is needed to make the decision. But holding out indefinitely is not good either. Vince and Marie could have put off indefinitely their decision about whether to have sex, in which case they might have wandered into having sex without resolving their feelings about it. Instead, they came to a resolution together: They would wait to have sex. **10**

A Process with Many Dimensions

You may be wondering if the ideal way to make decisions is to go through the six pieces of the pie as steps, in some sort of logical sequence or order. Reflecting on your own experience will probably remind you that decision making is rarely, if ever, that neat and orderly. In reality, all the various elements that go into making moral decisions are interconnected. And many parts of the LISTEN process take place at the same time, with varying levels of awareness on your part.

Thus we can look at moral decision making overall as a process of paying attention to a set of distinct elements of reality—the LISTEN elements. When it comes to actually making decisions, however, the process becomes more complicated than that, because real life itself is complex and includes many dimensions. Circumstances, motives, advice from others, religious teachings, values, gut-level feelings, and anticipation of consequences all overlap and influence one another.

Intuitive Decisions

In many decisions, we have only a fleeting awareness of sorting through the factors. Our decision may seem to be arrived at automatically or intuitively, but it may still be a well-made, wise choice. For instance, a person may decide in an instant to go with friends to a movie on a Friday night rather than to a party where there will be heavy drinking and drug use. Often, decision making is simply a matter of relying upon the wisdom gained from past experiences.

10
In a paragraph, describe a case in which it is wise to postpone making a decision for a definite time period.

Like a Blueberry Pie

Given the image of a pie, some people might think of the LISTEN process as a nice, firm cheesecake cut into pieces that come out neat and separate when lifted from the pan.

But as this chapter points out, moral decision making is about listening to the full reality of life, and life is never so neat and orderly. Instead, the LISTEN process of moral decision making is like a runny, messy blueberry pie. From the top, it looks fairly neat, cut into six separate pieces. But when you try to lift any one of the pieces out, you see that they all run together.

After Careful Reflection

Other decisions require a much more conscious, up-front awareness of what is needed to make a good choice. More deliberate, careful reflection is called for when many factors are unknown or unclear, when issues have to be sorted out to determine what is relevant, when many motives are at work, when values or needs are in conflict, when the consequences may have a major, long-term effect, and so forth. In a case like Vince and Marie's decision of whether to have sex when they were not permanently committed, the couple's process of sorting through the elements of reality took a long time, perhaps months. By then, they were able to come to a definite decision they both felt good about. **11**

Not a Perfect Process

Of course, it is possible to sincerely go through the LISTEN process and come up with a decision that is not good, that does not promote full humanness. Because we human beings are imperfect and limited, we can never guarantee that our own deliberations will turn up conclusions that are objective and morally right. A decision to do an action could be objectively wrong but subjectively right. That is, in God's eyes the decision and action could be wrong (objectively, in reality, wrong)—not good for the person or the situation. But due to the limited grasp that any human being can have of the whole picture, the decision and action might seem right in the eyes of the person (subjectively right).

However, following the LISTEN process sincerely gives us a better chance to discover what is objectively right than if we made our decisions willy-nilly or simply from our biases and inclinations. We may be limited in our grasp of reality, but the LISTEN process expands our vision to help us see with clearer eyes.

For Review

- List the elements of the LISTEN process.
- What kinds of facts does a person need to find out before making a moral decision?
- How does creativity play a part in making moral decisions?
- Where should people seek insight when making moral choices?
- Why is it important to examine our motives?
- How does God help us in moral decision making?
- How does drifting in moral decision making work against us?

■
Above: Because we are limited human beings, we cannot guarantee that our own deliberations will always turn up conclusions that are objective and morally right.

11
If you did activity 2, go back to your write-up of the interview and identify which elements of the LISTEN process the person you interviewed used in making her or his decision.

A Matter of Conscience

Marie and Vince, in deciding whether to have sex, showed evidence of following their consciences. **Conscience** is the inner sense of right and wrong that enables individuals to discern moral choices freely. In Vince and Marie's case, they knew that in order to feel good about themselves as persons, they had to be comfortable with their decision concerning premarital sex. For them, having sex outside of a permanently committed relationship would have violated their sense of what was right and good about sex and sexuality.

On Following Your Conscience

This question often arises in discussions of morality: Should I always follow my conscience? The Catholic church's answer to this question is clear: **Yes, you should always follow your conscience, but you must also make a sincere effort to** *form* **your conscience rightly and honestly.**

The hazard of saying "follow your conscience" is that people may assume that they can claim they are acting in good conscience when, in reality, they have not formed their conscience at all. Saying "I'm just obeying my conscience" can be a way that people rationalize doing what they wanted to do in the first place. The injunction to follow a well-formed conscience carries with it the responsibility of individuals to actively develop their conscience.

Although an inner sense of right and wrong is part of our nature as human beings, our conscience is formed or shaped by many sources over a lifetime. Some of these sources are internal, others are external.

For example, the family environment that we grow up in is likely to be a primary source for our understanding of right and wrong. Parents who have a habit of communicating directly with each other about important issues are passing on to their children a sense of honesty. A family in which an alcoholic parent lies to hide his or her problem may implicitly teach the children that lying is usually better than honesty.

External sources, however, do not totally determine our sense of right or wrong. A person raised in a family in which lying is a common practice may recognize the harm caused by lies and so, knowing from within that lying is usually wrong, may resolve not to lie.

A well-formed conscience is developed by listening to the full reality of life, including your own insights and experiences along with those of others. Employing the LISTEN process of decision making repeatedly is one way to gradually develop a well-formed conscience.

A Healthy Conscience at Work

Like a Good Friend

Conscience plays a critical role in moral decision making; without it we would be like strangers traveling in a foreign country with no map or language skills to help us read the road signs. In fact, conscience ties together or integrates the pieces of the decision-making pie. At the very least, our conscience is a starting place for making moral decisions. Ultimately, however, our conscience guides the direction of our whole life; thus, it is important to form our conscience as well as possible.

A well-formed and well-listened-to conscience is a good friend when it comes to making moral decisions. Like a true friend, your conscience will tell you what you need to hear rather than what you want to hear. Heeding your conscience usually leads to a sense of peace with yourself, a sense of integrity, of being true to yourself. Deep inside, you can feel good about your decision. **12**

Healthy Guilt?

Our society often gives us misleading messages about guilt: "A guilty conscience is not healthy. It's a sign of psychological problems." When guilt is warranted, or deserved, it can actually be a sign of mental and moral health, a vital sign that our conscience is alive and well. Warranted guilt occurs when two conditions are met: (1) we know an act is wrong and (2) we do it anyway. Warranted guilt functions to alert us when we have waded into waters that are morally dangerous.

Sometimes people do not deserve the full measure of blame because they did not know an action was wrong. Perhaps they were too young to understand or were ignorant of what they were doing. People can also suffer undeserved guilt if they believe that an act is wrong, when in fact it is not wrong. Let's look at this last problem more closely.

When Conscience Gets Off Track

Obviously, no one's conscience is as completely formed as it could be, often through no fault of the person. Neglect or indifference to right and wrong can also result in an ill-formed conscience. When a person's conscience is skewed, her or his experience of guilt usually is, too.

Some distortions of conscience include the following:
1. a wrongly formed conscience
2. a lax conscience
3. a legalistic conscience

Wrong Information and Bad Advice

Through no fault of their own, people are sometimes given information or assumptions about right and wrong that are mistaken. These people have a **wrongly formed conscience.**

For example, something judged right at one time in history, such as slavery, may be recognized as grossly immoral at a later time. You may recall Mark Twain's novel *The Adventures of Huckleberry Finn,* in which Huck helps the slave Jim escape from his owner, Miss Watson. Together, Huck and Jim have many adventures on their journey down the Mississippi River on a raft.

Huck, however, is convinced that he is doing something "low-down" by helping Jim escape; after all, helping someone's property to get away is like stealing! He wrestles with his conscience over whether to reform himself and do the "right" thing by sending Miss Watson a note telling her of Jim's whereabouts. For Huck, this decision has eternal consequences—he believes his choice may determine whether he goes to heaven or hell after death. At last Huck writes the note and finally feels "washed clean of sin." But then his heart starts to speak to him, reminding him of his now-close friendship with Jim and all their risky adventures on the river. He looks at the note to Miss Watson:

I took it up, and held it in my hand. I was a-trembling, because I'd got to decide, forever, betwixt two things, and I knowed it. I studied a minute, sort of holding my breath, and then says to myself:

"All right, then, I'll *go* to hell"—and tore it up.

It was awful thoughts and awful words, but they was said. And I let them stay said; and never thought no more about reforming. I shoved the whole thing out of my head, and said I would take up wickedness again, which was in my line, being brung up to it, and the other warn't. And for a starter I would go to

---

12
Reflect in writing on a time you chose to pay attention to your conscience versus a time you chose not to. Describe your feelings in each case.

work and steal Jim out of slavery again; and if I could think up anything worse, I would do that, too; because as long as I was in, and in for good, I might as well go the whole hog. (*Adventures of Huckleberry Finn,* pages 284–285)

Mark Twain, in commenting on his beloved character Huck ten years after the novel was written, said, "'In a crucial moral emergency a sound heart is a safer guide than an ill-trained conscience'" (quoted in Blair, *Mark Twain and Huck Finn,* page 143). Huck's belief that it was right to turn Jim over to his slave master, a commonly held "moral truth" of that time, in Twain's words, "'shows that that strange thing, the conscience . . . can be trained to approve any wild thing you *want* it to approve if you begin its education early and stick to it'" (page 144).

If something immoral was thought by many people, even devoutly religious persons, to be right at one time in history, that does not mean it used to be right and now it is wrong. It means that people's consciences were objectively in error—wrongly formed—in the past. **13**

Unwarranted guilt. Out of his wrongly formed conscience, Huck feels guilty about helping Jim run away from slavery. And, according to the civil law and the moral understanding of the time (the early 1800s), Huck was guilty of both a crime and a sin. But Huck suffers from unwarranted guilt because he was doing what was morally right—helping another human being escape the inherently evil system of slavery. Huck has no real or justifiable reason to feel guilty or regret his actions because what he did was not wrong. Of course, the fact that Huck's guilt was undeserved does not lessen it, and his decision is all the more heroic because of the inner pain it brings him.

Indifference to Right and Wrong

Someone in Huck's shoes, assuming he is wearing them, can end up with a confused sense of right and wrong. Part of Huck knows that he is doing the right thing, but he is just as sure that he is headed to hell. We might say his conscience is overtaxed.

In the reverse case, when persons habitually sin in a certain way, their conscience gradually gets distorted. Actions that once seemed wrong begin to seem less wrong, or not wrong at all. This insensitivity to right and wrong is often called a **lax conscience.** For example, consider the following example:

Leo has gotten a job as a waiter at a family restaurant where the manager is often not around. Leo is supposed to pay 50 percent of the price for any food or

---

■
Above: Because of a wrongly formed conscience, Huck is convinced that he is doing something "low-down" by helping Jim escape from slavery.

13
Research and write about an immoral practice other than slavery that was once considered morally right by most people.

Jesus and the Law

In his day, Jesus challenged the legalistic mentality of the Pharisees, who insisted on the strictest interpretation of the Jewish Law. When they criticized Jesus for curing a man's withered hand on the Sabbath, which was supposed to be a day of complete rest, Jesus answered:

"Which one of you who has a sheep that falls into a pit on the sabbath will not take hold of it and lift it out? How much more valuable a person is than a sheep. So it is lawful to do good on the sabbath." (Matthew 12:11–12)

When Jesus' disciples were hungry and so pulled off heads of grain as they walked through a field of wheat on the Sabbath, they were attacked by the Pharisees for breaking the Law. Jesus responded, "'The sabbath was made for man, not man for the sabbath'" (Mark 2:27). Jesus believed in following the spirit of the Law, which often also meant following the letter of the Law— but not always.

beverages he eats or drinks while on the job. After about a week, Leo sees that most of the other employees just take a glass of Coke whenever they want without paying, so he follows suit.

In another week, Leo realizes that he can easily eat a burger without paying for it. Soon he is accustomed to sitting down to a whole dinner, complete with a hot fudge sundae, on the house. The next step is that when his friends come in every evening, he offers them a free burger—"on me."

Leo's habits have gradually created a lax conscience, one that judges that what is wrong is not so wrong after all.

Too little guilt. In the case of a lax conscience, persons become less and less sensitive to right and wrong, and they can experience too little guilt. They feel immune to guilt because they have become so accustomed to sin. A bad act becomes "okay" in their mind, and thus they lose the awareness of sin that is the sign of a healthy conscience. But having a lax conscience does not excuse persons and make them less accountable for their actions. They are still objectively guilty and culpable even though they may not feel guilty or remorseful. **14**

A Stickler for Rules

When persons are so caught up in obeying rules perfectly that they cannot see the real needs of a situation, they have a **legalistic conscience.** They have trouble recognizing the more important aspects of reality; they "cannot see the forest for the trees." For example:

Molly, age sixteen, knows that her high school's policy requires that students who need to leave campus during school hours must have permission from the principal's office. She has an appointment at the eye doctor's at 2:00 p.m. to see about replacing her broken glasses, and she has brought a note from home to excuse her from school early.

14
Corruption in business or government usually involves laxness of conscience. Focus on one instance of such corruption from a past scandal covered in the news. Write about how lax consciences may have played a role in the corrupt practices.

However, when she goes to check in at the principal's office at 1:35, unexpectedly the office door is locked. Molly does not know what to do. She feels she cannot possibly leave the campus without permission from the office. She waits by the office door until 1:55, then, giving up, she goes back to class and misses the appointment with the eye doctor.

People bound by a legalistic conscience find a great deal of security in adhering to rules. They are afraid of making mistakes, of being caught and found blameworthy, even when common sense dictates that a rule ought to be broken. Sometimes, as in Molly's case, fearfulness keeps people from thinking of creative alternatives. Molly could have looked for someone to give her permission or tried to get permission from her homeroom teacher. If time was short, she could have just left the campus, knowing that she had a note from home and that getting to the appointment was crucial to her eyesight.

At the extreme, persons with a legalistic conscience constantly scrutinize their every action for signs of wrongdoing, which can be paralyzing. Such persons need the guidance of a responsible, wise friend or pastor who can help them put their sense of right and wrong into perspective.

Excessive guilt. Persons with a legalistic conscience are prone to being overly sensitive about their blameworthiness. The guilt they feel exceeds, or is out of proportion to, the severity of their wrongdoing. Suppose Molly had left campus without permission to go to her appointment. Given her strong legalistic conscience, Molly's sense of guilt could easily have overwhelmed her. She might not have been able to get to sleep that night because she felt so bad about not getting permission to leave. By morning she may have built up so much anxiety that she has a stomachache and cannot go to school. Excessive guilt can get in the way of making a clear judgment about the moral significance of an action. **15**

Guilt Versus Shame

Guilt signals to us that we are uncomfortable with our own behavior. Even though guilt can be misunderstood or distorted, it can also be a healthy and constructive part of our growth as fully human persons. Shame, on the other hand, is always destructive. The message of shame is that as a person we are not good. To be shamed by someone is to be told, in effect, "You are worthless as a person." Individuals should not feel or be made to feel shame about themselves.

The Christian tradition affirms that God forgives our wrongdoing; we are cleansed of our guilt when we admit to it and accept God's forgiveness. But Christian tradition also strongly affirms that God loves us and accepts us unconditionally. As creatures made in God's image, we are fundamentally good; shame denies this basic goodness.

For Review

- What is conscience?
- What is the Catholic church's position on whether to always follow one's conscience?
- How does a well-formed conscience act like a friend to us?
- Briefly describe the three distortions of conscience.
- How does guilt differ from shame?

15
Give three examples of cases in which a rule or a law could be broken in good conscience.

Listen to Your Conscience

The phrase *listen to your conscience* might conjure up images of attentively waiting for a voice to speak from within and then heeding that voice's command. By now, it is probably clear that this is a limited, even mistaken, image of conscience—and of moral decision making.

Listen to your conscience means a great deal more than heeding the commands of an inner voice. It means "listen to the whole reality of a situation." That whole reality includes your inner world of feelings, values, insights, and motives. But it also includes objective circumstances; the possible consequences; the wisdom of others who have much to teach, such as Jesus, the church, and parents; and the help of God, who journeys with you in all your decisions.

Something Inside

As we learn how to listen to the full reality of situations that require a moral decision, a well-formed conscience begins to take shape within, ready to be a friend to us when we need it. Consider the significance of listening to one's conscience in the following situation:

The store was crowded with the usual Saturday afternoon bustle. Gary had been looking at stereo albums. His friend Ron came over from the sporting goods department where he had been checking out fishing equipment. "Come with me to the fishing stuff. I saw some neat lures." Gary put down the album and followed. The lures were unusual—wild reds and glittering greens with shredded rubbery tails. Gary could imagine a largemouth bass slamming into them.

Ron glanced over his shoulder. "Check out the security," he mumbled.

"You've got to be crazy," Gary whispered back. "This place is crawling with undercover cops."

"Come on! Is the coast clear? It's only a couple of fishing lures. Who'll know the difference? What are you, a chicken?" Gary's heart pounded. He wanted to say yes. "I don't want to be part of this," he found himself muttering.

"Fine friend you are. A buddy needs help and you back out."

Gary *was* Ron's friend. Maybe he should go along. After all, *he* wasn't taking anything. After all, he was just a lookout. But something inside him couldn't do it. "You're alone in this one, buddy," Gary told Ron and walked away. (Rapien, "Want to Be Friends?") **16**

It Comes Down to You

In the final analysis, you, and no one else, are responsible and accountable for your decisions. You cannot blindly follow the teachings of anyone, even the church. You must be sincerely convinced that your actions conform to the will of God (that is, they are oriented to the good).

There are no easy, automatic rules to follow that will ensure you are doing God's will. The LISTEN process is a good place to start, however. To become a person of integrity, you have to listen to the fullness of reality and come to your own decisions.

For Review

- What does the phrase *listen to your conscience* mean?

16
Often we must make a moral decision quickly, as Gary did, relying on "something inside"—our conscience. Write a paragraph about the kind of conscience you relied on in making a moral decision that required a quick response.

Looking Back—and Ahead

In Review

The first part of this course, chapters 1–4, has offered a framework for looking at morality from a Catholic Christian perspective. Here are some key points from those chapters:

1. Morality is about choosing the kind of person you are now and are becoming.
2. Human beings are created in God's image and are loved unconditionally by God. Jesus embodied God's love in his humanity, showing us how we can be fully human, reflections of God's love.
3. Human beings are relational by nature. We require the help of God, the community, the society, and the teachings of Jesus and the church in our journey to becoming fully human.
4. To make a moral decision, we need to listen to the whole reality of a situation. The LISTEN process is a tool for making good moral decisions from a well-formed conscience. **17**

What's Ahead

The next ten chapters look at how good decision making and the building of a virtuous character can happen in everyday life. Each chapter will focus on a different virtue of Jesus.

■

Above, left and right: We experience our conscience as "something inside" us that we can rely on like a good friend.

17
Which one of the four key points from chapters 1 to 4 has been most significant for you to consider? Explain your answer in writing.

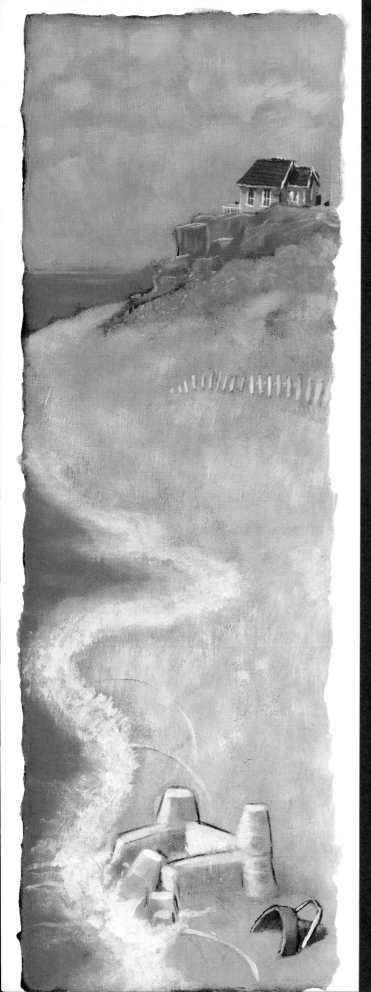

5

Wise Judgment:
Good-
Conscience-
in-Action

The Moral Virtues: Habits of Love

Jesus showed us how to love in our everyday encounters with others, and his brand of love—the binding force of all creation—is lived out through the moral virtues.

Recall from chapter 2 that with God's help, we must work at building the moral virtues within us. (The theological virtues of faith, hope, and love, on the other hand, come from God as gifts.) Each of the ten chapters of the second part of this course takes a close-up look at one of the **moral virtues**, those good habits that reveal our inner readiness to do good, the habits of a life of love.

The Cardinal Virtues: Hinges of the Good Life

Of the moral virtues, four stand out as foundational to all the rest. In the Christian tradition, these four are called the cardinal virtues (from *cardo,* the Latin word for "hinge"). These four virtues are the hinges upon which all the other moral virtues swing: **1**

- wise judgment
- justice
- courage
- wholeness

A House Built on Rock

Persons who make wise judgment a part of their character cannot be easily diverted from the good by a closed mind or by self-deception. Wise judgment is good-conscience-in-action.

Speaking about a person who puts a well-formed conscience into action, Jesus said:

"Everyone who listens to these words of mine and acts on them will be like a wise man who built his house on rock. The rain fell, the floods came, and the winds blew and buffeted the house. But it did not collapse; it had been set solidly on rock. And everyone who listens to these words of mine but does not act on them will be like a fool who built his house on sand. The rain fell, the floods came, and the winds blew and buffeted the house. And it collapsed and was completely ruined."

When Jesus finished these words, the crowds were astonished at his teaching. (Matthew 7:24–28)

The virtue of wise judgment is like a house built on rock—sure, steady, solid, not easily blown over. With its firm grounding, this virtue provides the secure, lifelong foundation upon which all the other virtues can flourish.

For Review

- How is Jesus' love lived out in daily life?
- Why are the cardinal virtues so important?
- Why is a house built on rock a good image of the virtue of wise judgment?

1
Describe in writing what would happen to a door if the hinges were loose or improperly installed. Explain how the hinges of a door are like the cardinal virtues.

The Character Cycle

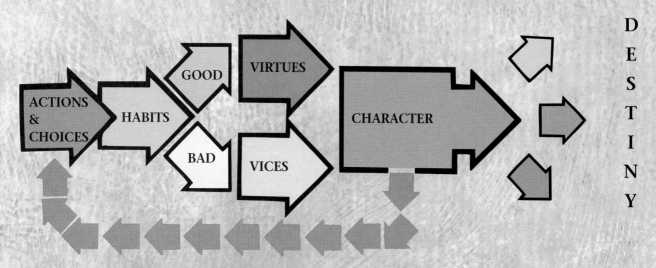

As discussed in earlier chapters, virtues become a part of our character when we practice them regularly. Building a virtuous character cannot happen overnight; it involves practice and experience. It is like performing feats of magic, a process that the master magician Doug Henning once described in an interview.

First, Doug said, he practices a difficult trick until it is a habit. Then he continues to practice the trick until it becomes extremely easy for him to do. Even then he practices it some more, until finally the trick is so simple for him that it *seems* magical to other people watching it.

Obviously, Doug Henning's magic does not just "happen." Likewise, the more we practice the virtues discussed in the remainder of this book, the more likely they will become part of who we are.

Our character is that unique mix of qualities, virtues, vices, talents, and weaknesses that makes us who we are as persons. And once our character starts to take shape, it affects our actions and moral choices. (See above diagram.)

Thus, our character may become a loving, deeply human one—or it may not. It depends on our daily moral choices. As we grow beyond childhood, our character begins to shape those daily choices more and more.

Chapter 1 posed the question, What kind of person do you want to become? Figuring out the answer to that question is the most important decision of your life. Your destiny depends on it.

- Think of a once-difficult action or behavior that you now do with relative ease, as if magically. Write about your efforts and how they led to your mastery of that action or behavior.

Good-Conscience-in-Action

Of the cardinal virtues, **wise judgment** (traditionally called prudence) comes first in importance because it includes both the ability to make decisions according to a well-formed conscience and the willingness to carry out these decisions.

Think back to the discussion of the LISTEN process of moral decision making in chapter 4. When we use the LISTEN process, we are actually listening to the whole reality of a situation. We are forming our conscience, equipping it to make a good choice. Wise judgment takes us to the next step. It is good-conscience-in-action.

Jesus and the Accused Woman

Read the following passage from John's Gospel, which illustrates Jesus' wise judgment and shows some of the characteristics of this virtue:

But early in the morning [Jesus] arrived again in the temple area, and all the people started coming to him, and he sat down and taught them. Then the scribes and the Pharisees brought a woman who had been caught in adultery and made her stand in the middle. They said to him, "Teacher, this woman was caught in the very act of committing adultery. Now in the law, Moses commanded us to stone such women. So what do you say?" They said this to test him, so that they could have some charge to bring against him. Jesus bent down and began to write on the ground with his finger. But when they continued asking him, he straightened up and said to them, "Let the one among you who is without sin be the first to throw a stone at her." Again he bent down and wrote on the ground. And in response, they went away one by one, beginning with the elders. So he was left alone with the woman before him. Then Jesus straightened up and said to her, "Woman, where are they? Has no one condemned you?" She replied, "No one, sir." Then Jesus said, "Neither do I condemn you. Go, [and] from now on do not sin any more." (John 8:2–11)

In this incident, three characteristics of Jesus' wise judgment stand out:

1. Seeing reality clearly. Jesus knows what is going on. He grasps the whole reality of the situation: a woman is about to be stoned to death for adultery, as prescribed by law. He knows that in his culture an adulterous woman suffers extreme punishment. But a man who commits the same act can walk away free (as long as the woman he was with is not married). Jesus also understands this:

a. that the punishment is too severe

b. that the woman is being treated unjustly because she is a woman

c. that the scribes and the Pharisees are trying to trap him into saying something contrary to the Law of Moses

Jesus has his eyes wide open, an essential feature of wise judgment.

2. Figuring out the good—what is most needed in the situation—and the best way to achieve it. Jesus knows immediately that the punishment the woman is about to suffer is out of proportion to her crime. How can he save her from death and from her sin, and still confront the Pharisees and scribes with their own hypocrisy?

The story says Jesus wrote on the ground with his finger. We do not know whether he actually wrote something meaningful. Maybe Jesus was just taking a few moments to figure out the response most likely to achieve all the desired objectives.

A Story of Wise Judgment

"Once there was a wise old woman . . . who lived in a small village. The children of the village were puzzled by her—her wisdom, her gentleness, her strength, and her magic. One day several of the children decided to fool the old woman. They believed that no one could be as wise as everyone said she was, and they were determined to prove it. So the children found a baby bird and one of the little boys cupped it in his hands and said to his playmates, 'We'll ask her whether the bird I have in my hands is dead or alive. If she says it's dead, I'll open my hands and let it fly away. If she says it's alive, I'll crush it in my hands and she'll see that it's dead.' And the children went to [her] and presented her with this puzzle. 'Old woman,' the little boy asked, 'This bird in my hands—is it dead or alive?' The old woman became very still, studied the boy's hands, and then looked carefully into his eyes. 'It's in your hands,' she said." (Quoted in Heyward, *Touching Our Strength,* page 73) **2**

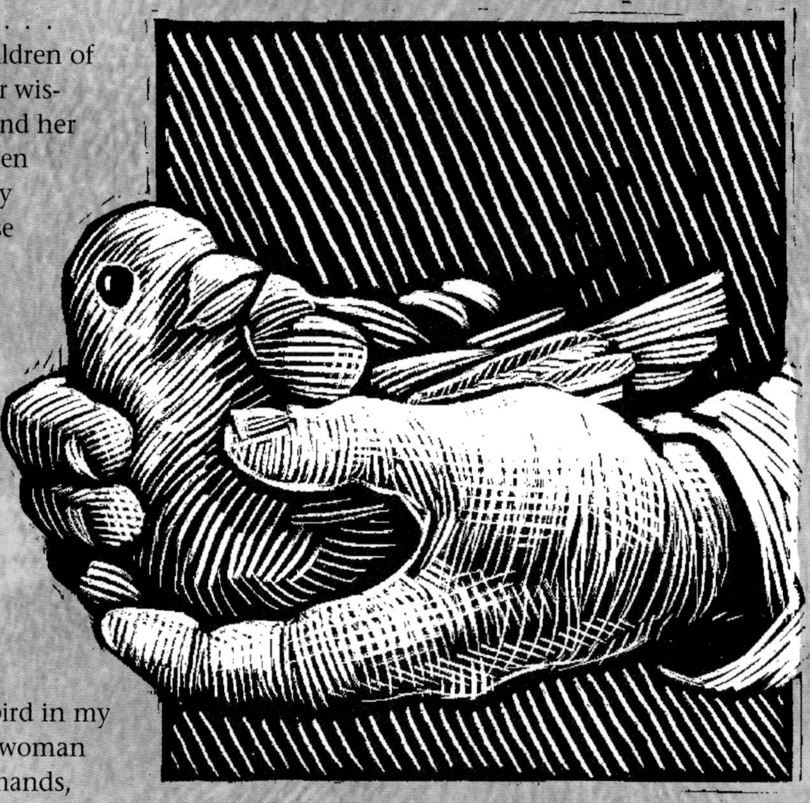

2

Explain how the woman in this story shows evidence of these dimensions of wise judgment:
1. seeing reality clearly
2. figuring out the good—what is most needed—and the morally best means to get to that end
3. knowing her own feelings and motives

After reflecting, Jesus responds, "'Let the one among you who is without sin be the first to throw a stone at her'" (John 8:7). Jesus' words must have haunted his listeners for a long time. It was the right answer in every way—the most appropriate, best means available to achieve the good. **3**

3. Knowing his own feelings and motives. We can assume that Jesus does not want to get himself into dangerous trouble with the influential scribes and Pharisees. They are already hostile to Jesus because of his claim that God has sent him. To confront them with their own hypocrisy must be a frightening prospect for Jesus.

Perhaps Jesus used the time spent writing on the ground to also turn over in his mind his motives and emotions. He may have been trying to ensure that his own fears—and maybe even a desire to get the best of the scribes and the Pharisees—did not hinder him from responding in a loving, truthful, and effective way.

Jesus was able to see through the phoniness and deception that often characterized the people with whom he associated. He could cut right through all that to discover what would accomplish the good and to act accordingly.

A Different Kind of Wisdom

Taking the Necessary Risks

If wise judgment meant simply being practical and choosing the safest route, some people might argue that Jesus was not a very wise or prudent person. But making wise judgments and acting upon them is not about avoiding all risks. Being wise and prudent involves sorting out the difference between those risks that are needed to accomplish a good end and those that are not needed. Then, when the necessary risks are figured out, the wise person is willing to take the risks required to accomplish the good.

In the incident with the woman about to be stoned, Jesus had no totally "safe" way to answer the challenge of the scribes and Pharisees. In the midst of those tricky circumstances, Jesus saw what he needed to do and followed through with it. Jesus took the necessary risks for the sake of the good in many other situations as well. For instance, read these Gospel passages:

1. the story of the penitent woman (Luke 7:36–50), told on pages 27 and 28 of this text
2. the healing of the man with a withered hand (Matthew 12:9–14)
3. the cleansing of the Temple (Mark 11:15–19)
4. the story of the tribute money (temple tax) (Matthew 17:24–27)

Unconventional Wisdom

During his ministry, as well as throughout the centuries following his death, the wise judgment of Jesus has often confounded his followers. Many of the things Jesus said or did seem guaranteed to get him in trouble. Ordinary, or conventional, wisdom would judge that Jesus acted foolishly. Cautious people might argue: "Why did Jesus do so many things to make the scribes and Pharisees angry with him? Wouldn't he have been better off if he had been nice to them and tried to win their support and cooperation, like any good and wise politician would? Maybe then he wouldn't have gotten himself killed. What makes Jesus so wise?"

Cardinal John Henry Newman, a famous nineteenth-century Catholic writer, clues us in to the unconventional wisdom of Jesus: "'Wisdom is the clear, calm, accurate vision and comprehension of the whole course, the whole work of God'" (*The Book of Catholic Quotations*, page 918). The

3
List alternative responses to the one Jesus chose in this story. In writing, evaluate the wisdom or lack of wisdom in each response.

challenge of being a follower of Jesus is to do what is good and loving—what is in line with the whole work of God—even though it might seem foolish by customary standards. **4**

Now that the major dimensions of wise judgment have been identified, let's look at them in some contemporary cases and see how the parts of the LISTEN process apply.

For Review

- What is wise judgment?
- Name three characteristics of wise judgment.
- How does wise judgment differ from simply being practical and choosing the safest route?

Seeing Reality Clearly

The Offensive Oil

In the story of the woman about to be stoned, seeing reality clearly meant that Jesus assessed what was really going on in the situation. Wise judgment also calls for considering all the information important to making a good decision.

Consider the choice made by Russ after he changed the oil in his car:

Russ had worked hard to put together enough money to keep up his car. Despite its seven years, the body sported a clean finish and no dents. The engine purred. Even so, with the cost of the insurance and the monthly loan payments, Russ tried to economize where he could.

He had just finished changing the oil, his first time doing so. A local parts store had run a special on 10W–30 HD oil. He had purchased a good filter on special, plus a filter wrench and a pan to drain the used oil into.

Looking down at the black mess in the catch-pan, Russ mumbled, "Oh man, what am I gonna do with it?"

Russ considered dumping it in the garbage but realized that the galvanized trash can leaked. Besides, the garbage collectors would be angry. His dad would not like it if he just left it in the garage. Then he spied the storm-sewer drain at the end of the driveway. Figuring this was okay, Russ carefully carried the sloshing pan of oil to the sewer and slowly poured it down. Then he wiped out his new oil pan and tidied up the garage. Russ felt good about his accomplishment and about being neat, so he got into his car and headed to Dairy Queen to celebrate.

■
Above: In this detail from "Christ in the House of Simeon the Pharisee," a sixteenth-century painting by Paolo Veronese, Jesus shocks the Pharisee Simon by accepting the love of a sinful woman.

4
Write up an example of a person's action that would be judged foolish according to the conventional wisdom of society but wise according to the unconventional wisdom of Jesus.

- What do you think of Russ's decision to pour the oil down the storm-sewer drain? (Keep in mind that the purpose of a storm sewer is to carry away rainwater, not sewage, and this storm sewer empties directly into a nearby lake.)
- What parts of the LISTEN process should Russ have considered?
- In what other ways could Russ have disposed of the used oil?
- Why is pollution a moral issue? How do apparently small actions pile up to make big problems?
- Are good intentions enough to make a decision good? Explain your answer in terms of Russ's dilemma.

A Public Responsibility Too

The moral duty to see reality clearly and practice wise judgment is not limited to individuals acting in private situations. Making good, wise decisions at the public level is important as well.

One example of wide-scale imprudence is the savings and loan industry scandal in the United States, a crisis that emerged during the late 1980s. It has been called the worst financial scandal in the nation's history. The facts show that the money problems of thousands of savings and loan institutions were rooted in the failure of both the savings and loan companies and the United States government to see reality clearly. The institutions made bad loans, and the federal government agreed to bail them out. These mistakes have cost more than 500 billion dollars, and will influence the U.S. economy for decades.

Failure to use wise judgment can also be seen in national planning for energy alternatives. Since the early 1970s, we have known that the sources of energy that power industrialized economies are running out. Fossil fuels such as oil and coal took millions of years to form but have been consumed in a little over a hundred years, mostly in recent decades. The use of these fuels has been a major factor in the global environmental crisis. Emissions from automobiles and other fossil fuel-powered machinery have led to the problem of global warming and other climatic changes.

The development of nuclear power has offset some reliance on fossil fuels, but at a great cost. Radiation leakage from nuclear power plants can contaminate cities and towns for miles around and can even threaten the quality of life in other parts of the globe. In addition, when nuclear fuels have

become too irradiated to be put to further use, they must be discarded. But more than fifty years after the first nuclear explosions, no satisfactory method has been devised to dispose of these wastes, which remain a hazard to humans and the environment for thousands of years.

Yet instead of shifting government and corporate money into developing renewable, nonpolluting energy sources (such as wind and solar power), North Americans have closed their eyes to the reality by using more fossil fuels than ever in the last two decades and continuing to build a greater dependence on nuclear power.

Unwise decisions, like lies, often have a way of multiplying, making a bad situation even worse. In both the savings and loan and energy crises, government, corporations, and voting and consuming citizens in most cases have failed to see clearly. They have not looked ahead at the possible consequences of their decisions. Hindsight, looking back on something, does not help much after the damage has been done. The virtue of wise judgment challenges us to evaluate the possible consequences of our choices before taking action. **5**

For Review

- Briefly describe two examples of failing to see reality clearly at the public level.

■

Above, left and right: The failure to develop solar and wind-generated sources of energy is an example of a public lack of clear vision.

5

Focus on another public policy issue that requires wise judgment. In writing, express your opinion about the wisdom or lack of wisdom of government and corporate decisions on the issue.

Sizing Up the Good and the Best Way to It

Crisis on the River

Here is a story involving quick decisions about what is most needed—the good—and how to achieve it:

The Black River was perfect for a leisurely canoe trip. The sandy bottom glistened through the clear, easy-flowing water. Even the rapids were gentle. The frequent sandbars provided great places for picnics and sunbathing or beaches from which to swim.

B.J., Mia, Al, and Kathy had been canoeing for a couple of hours. Calling back to the other canoe, B.J. declared break time for lunch, and they nosed their canoes into a sandbar overhung by a huge willow tree.

After eating their picnic, B.J., Al, and Kathy dozed in the cool shade of the willow's branches.

Mia got bored watching the other three snooze. Pulling off her sneakers, she waded into the shallow water. Her feet sank comfortably into the soft sand. But when she took another step, a sharp pain ripped through her foot. She jumped back quickly and screamed. Blood poured from a semicircular cut in her foot. Mia yelled again, beginning to feel nauseated from the sight of the blood.

B.J., Kathy, and Al carried Mia to the sandbar. Al poured water from the canteen over the gash in Mia's foot. A jagged, deep, five-inch cut sliced through her instep. Kathy covered the wound with a fairly clean bandanna that rapidly turned wet and bloody.

"Al, gimme your T-shirt." Kathy ripped it into strips and wrapped it tightly around Mia's foot.

"We've gotta get her to a doctor, quick."

"We passed a farmhouse about a quarter mile back. Maybe somebody's there." B.J.'s anxious voice reflected the concern they all felt.

Without missing a beat, B.J. cleared the extra gear out of the larger of the two canoes. "We'd better all get into the green canoe since we're going to be paddling upstream. We can get the rest of this stuff later."

"You need to elevate your leg, Mia. Keep it up on this crossbar," Kathy instructed as B.J. and Al helped Mia into the middle of the canoe. Mia grimaced and struggled to stay alert.

• • •

Kathy came back around the corner of the farmhouse just as B.J. and Al arrived at the front door, carrying Mia. "Nobody's home, but there's a pickup with the keys in it."

"Maybe we can fix her foot and then call for a doctor to come out here." Al realized immediately how dumb that sounded.

"Can't wait that long, Bozo," Kathy snapped. "Besides, I already stuck a note in the door with our names and where we're taking the truck."

"Let's get Mia in and go," B.J. ordered. "There's a small hospital in the next town downriver."

"We can't steal somebody's truck," Mia tried to object, as B.J. and Al lifted her off the ground.

Kathy looked at Mia, not believing what she had heard. "Be quiet, Mia. You're delirious."

As soon as she sat down in front, Mia slumped over onto Kathy's lap, her face bone white. In moments B.J. had the pickup flying down the gravel road. **6**

- How did Mia's friends use the second piece of the LISTEN process, imagine possibilities?
- What was most urgently needed in the situation? What other needs did they take, or should they have taken, into account?

Why Worry About the Means?

"The end does not justify the means" is a basic moral principle that is central to practicing wise judgment. Many people make the mistake of focusing only on the end, or goal. They give the end top priority over everything, including the means, or methods, they use. They wonder: Why worry about the means? It's what I accomplish that's really important!

A classic example of a debate over means and ends is the question of whether peace can be achieved through violence, such as war. Indian leader Mohandas K. Gandhi (1869–1948) based his support for nonviolent resistance, rather than armed revolution, on the principle that the end does not justify the means: "The means may be likened to a seed, the end to a tree; and there is just the same inviolable connection between the means and the end as there is between the seed and the tree" (Gandhi, *Indian Home Rule*). In other words, violence tends to foster more violence; lies tend to beget more lies; and so on. Likewise, trust tends to encourage deeper trust; honesty tends to promote further honesty, and so forth. The means *does* matter.

6
Describe in writing an urgent situation that required a wise decision of you. What did you decide and how did the situation turn out? Would you make the same choice again? Why or why not?

■
Above: Mohandas K. Gandhi of India led a campaign of nonviolent resistance that eventually brought an end to oppressive British rule.

- What did you think of Mia's friends' decision to borrow the farmhouse truck without permission? Was it the best means to the good? What would you have done?

Other Circumstances

Circumstances often influence what we should or should not do in a moral situation. Consider how these "what ifs" might have made a difference in the story of Mia and her friends:

- What if the only available vehicle had been a new, expensive car?
- What if the keys had not been in the truck? Would it have been okay for them to break into the house? If they had broken into the house, what should they have done?
- What if a similar incident took place in a more populated area?

The Wrong Means?

Recall the principle discussed in chapter 3: The end does not justify the means. It may seem that Mia's friends violated this principle by their choice of means—taking the truck to get Mia to the hospital. After all, they did take something that did not belong to them and justified it by presuming that getting Mia to a doctor was more important.

Although the crime of stealing typically involves "taking" something belonging to someone else, at its heart is the *attitude* of not caring about or respecting other people's property. Based on this criterion, Mia's friends certainly cannot be accused of stealing, especially since they left a note for the truck's owners letting them know what had happened.

The virtue of wise judgment often involves the ability to evaluate the means we are using to accomplish a good end, such as in this case. **7**

Sticky Situations

Figuring out what is most needed in a situation and the best way to it is often the toughest task of moral decision making. Many situations are not as clear-cut as in the story about Mia and her friends. Sticky situations make it clear that practicing wise judgment is not always easy.

Caught Between Two Goods

Sometimes we feel caught between two or more goods, and each one seems just as important as the other. But going for one of these goods appears to rule out going for the other one. And it seems impossible to figure out which one is more important.

In some cases, young people find themselves in particularly tough, even life-and-death, circumstances. Take, for example, the experience of some inner-city high school students. The following is based on a number of such incidents experienced by teens:

Recently, three shooting incidents have occurred near Tony's high school. The drug problem in the school has escalated in the past few months. The shootings are just the latest in a growing list of assaults upon students by people desperate for the cash to support their drug habit. It's not uncommon for kids to get beat up while going to and from school, especially for their high-priced sneakers or jewelry. Even carrying their books makes them a possible target.

Tony and his friend Zeke have worked out a strategy for getting to and from school as inconspicuously as possible. They try to take a different route every day, to vary the time they leave home or school, and to not wear any nice clothes, gold chains, or even watches. Also, they do as much of their homework at school as they can so they don't have to carry any

---

7
Write down a good end, or goal, that you want to reach. List at least five means to that end. Next to each means, evaluate its moral goodness. Finally, choose which means would be morally acceptable ways to reach the end.

books back and forth. Even with these precautions, though, they know that just trying to get to school at all puts them at risk. They never know when they might be cornered or trapped like the five students who were injured in the earlier assaults.

Tony and Zeke are caught between two goods, both of which seem overwhelmingly important:
- the need to get an education so they can prepare for their future
- the need to simply stay alive

In situations like these, even using wise judgment cannot always point us toward an ideal solution. However, it can help us work things out so that both goods can be met to the greatest extent possible given the circumstances we have to deal with. **8**

An Obstacle Course to the Good

In other cases, we can sort out what is most needed, but the path to the good is blocked by enormous obstacles—such as fear of losing a job or being ridiculed. These pressures seem to work against going for the good.

Obstacles and pressures, tough as they can make things, never let us totally off the hook in moral situations. They call for the virtue of courage, which will be covered in chapter 7. Even when we are faced with obstacles that are beyond our power to overcome, we have a responsibility to make the best decision we can. Regular practice of the virtue of wise judgment in less-complicated matters prepares us for dealing with such sticky situations.

For Review
- Why is it important to evaluate the means available to achieve a good end?

Spotting Inner Blocks

The Activities Sign-up

Motives, or the "whys" behind an action or decision, can play a crucial role in determining the decision's moral goodness. (Recall the issue of taking the truck in the canoe trip story.) Wise judgment helps us to sort through possible motives and see which ones are really at work in us. It also helps us to decide which of our motives are positive and which are negative.

Listen in on a conversation between Lena and Stacey during the first week of their senior year:

Glancing down the list of activities offered by the school, Lena rattled off her preferences to her friend

---

8
Give an example from your own experience of being caught between two important goods that seemed to exclude each other. Tell in writing how you tried to resolve the dilemma.

■
Above: Even deciding what activities we want to be involved in requires an understanding of our own motives.

Stacey: "I'm joining the yearbook staff. No way do I want our yearbook to look as dippy as last year's. It was so-o-o boring! Besides, if I want to get into the journalism program at the university, I'd better get some experience. First place in the state speech tournament would look good on my application, too. No coming in second to Belinda Meyer this year!

"Pep band's a definite repeat," Lena continued, "especially since they got rid of ol' what's-her-name as director."

"Do you think I should run for student council? Randy Toma's going to. He makes me ill, the way he's so into *leadership*."

Stacey could hardly believe this was the same friend she had talked with the week before on the very same subject. In exasperation, she said, "I thought you wanted to cut back this year! All you did last year was complain about being too busy to get your homework done. Remember all the times I bailed you out? And I thought you said pep band was a waste?"

Defensively, Lena replied, "Yeah, but remember what the guy from the U. said on College Night last spring—the more activities I'm involved in this year, the better my chances of getting in."

"I'm sticking with things I really enjoy," countered Stacey. "The U. will have to take me for who I am."

"Hey, all I'm trying to do is have a great year!" Lena shrugged as the bell rang for first period. **9**

- Does choosing extracurricular activities call for moral reflection?
- Sort out Lena's motives. Which do you see as admirable and which as less admirable? Why?
- Which parts of the LISTEN process deal with examining motives in moral decision making?
- Suppose that Lena never does reflect on her motives for joining activities. What can you predict might happen to her later on, in college or after college?

Fooling Ourselves with Rationalizations

Often we have a mixture of motives for what we want to do. Some of them are good, legitimate reasons. But when our reasons are not so admirable and we do not want to admit them even to ourselves, we may come up with rationalizations, or false motives. These are attempts to trick ourselves and others into believing that we are doing something for good reasons when we really are not. In other words, it is a form of lying, especially to oneself. (Note that rationalizing is different from the human ability to reason things out, to be rational and logical.) As we take on the habit of wise judgment, we move away from rationalizing and begin to acknowledge what *truly* motivates us, even when we are not so proud of our motives. **10**

Here are some examples of rationalizations:

1. "Our company can hire only part-time employees so that we can be flexible with our scheduling. Besides, these people don't really want full-time work."

2. "I'm too tense to study for the big test I have tomorrow. I need to relax first, so I will go over to my girlfriend's to watch a movie."

3. "I'd really love to spend more time with my kids, but there's so many other things pulling at me. Besides, I don't think they even notice that I'm away in the evenings."

4. "My husband's under a lot of pressure these days. When things are going better, he hardly ever hits me. Besides, what would he do if I left him? I know he'd just fall apart."

- What are some likely true motives behind each of these rationalizations?
- For each of these situations, imagine some consequences that could result.

9
Focus on a choice you made in the last week and list the admirable and less admirable motives involved in that choice.

10
In writing, offer three examples of rationalizations that you have heard. For each one, identify the true motives you think may lie behind the rationalization.

A Matter of Life and Death: It's Your Decision

Based on a real incident, the following story offers four possible conclusions. The situation calls for the highest degree of wise judgment, because it involves life and death. Read the story and choose the conclusion that you think demonstrates wise judgment. Be prepared to explain your choice.

Melanie tried to sleep, but she kept thinking about Kelly. For days, Kelly had moped around school. She had lost weight and let her appearance go. For the last few days, Kelly had worn the same jeans. Her blouses were wrinkled, and her hair was matted and dirty. People whispered their worry, but when they asked her how she was doing, Kelly snapped at them.

Tonight Melanie's worries came to a head. Right after school that day, Kelly had given her a picture of the two of them from a party last year, a novel that meant a lot to Kelly, and some other little prized objects. Kelly had simply stated, "I want you to have these. I don't need them anymore."

After more tossing and turning, Melanie flicked on the light by her bed, threw back the covers, and sat up, staring at the phone. Even though the clock read 11:45, Melanie decided that she had to call Kelly.

The phone rang five, then six times. Melanie wondered if her call was too late. Finally, she heard Kelly's voice, low and sad. "Hello. Who is it?"

"Kell, it's me, Melanie. I just had to call. You've been so sad lately. I got scared when you gave me your stuff this afternoon."

Kelly tried to speak but choked up. "I'm so scared. . . . I don't want to do it. . . . I can't take it anymore."

Melanie froze, realizing that Kelly was at the end of her rope. "What do you mean? What are you going to do?"

"You wouldn't tell anyone?"

From the suspicion in Kelly's voice, Melanie knew that if she wavered on this, the conversation would be over. "No, I won't tell anyone."

"Promise?"

"Promise." Melanie's anxiety increased. If she heard what she thought was coming next, she didn't know if she could promise.

"I've got all these pills. Remember when my back got hurt? I saved all the painkillers." Her voice faded into mumbling.

"Kell, are you okay?"

"Tell my mom and dad it's not their fault."

"Are your folks there? Can you talk to them?"

"They're gone to a Christmas party. Why? You won't try to tell them, will you?" Fear etched Kelly's voice.

"Oh, God, Kell. What are you going to do?"

"You sure you won't tell anybody?" Silence. "You won't try to stop me?"

"I promised." Melanie hated this, not sure now that she would keep her promise.

"I'm going to go now. Remember, you promised. I just feel too awful." Melanie heard the phone click.

Tears streamed down Melanie's face. Panic nearly gripped her. She had to do something quickly.

■

Above: "Stress," an oil painting by student Shawn M. Beirne of Holy Cross High School in Louisville, Kentucky, reminds us that young people often face situations where the ability to use wise judgment is necessary.

Conclusion 1

Throwing on her clothes, Melanie grabbed her purse and ran to her mom's car. The drive to Kelly's house would only take ten minutes. If she could just talk to Kelly, maybe things would be okay.

Conclusion 2

Melanie knew that she could not handle this. Realizing that time was important, she dialed 911 and explained the situation. The operator said he would dispatch a squad car.

Conclusion 3

Melanie knew that she could not handle this alone. Realizing that time was important, she dialed 911 and explained the situation. The operator said he would dispatch a squad car. Throwing on her clothes, Melanie grabbed her purse and ran to her mom's car. The drive to Kelly's house would only take ten minutes. Maybe the police would already be there.

Conclusion 4

Melanie knew that she could not handle this alone. The only other person that Kelly might trust was their friend Missy. Together maybe they could convince Kelly that everything was going to be all right. She called Missy, got her out of bed, and explained the situation. Then she ran to her mom's car and headed out to pick up Missy.

- What reality must Melanie see clearly if she is to make a good decision?
- What is most needed in the situation and what is the best means to that good? Does a conflict of competing goods exist, and if so, which is more important?
- Which of her emotions or motives must Melanie consider if she is to make a good decision?

- What part or parts of the LISTEN process of decision making do you think would be most critical for Melanie to consider in this situation? How might those considerations affect her decision at the end of the story? **11**

For Review

- What is a rationalization? How do rationalizations get in the way of good moral decision making?

Tending Life's Garden

The poet Samuel Taylor Coleridge was visited by an admirer one day. During the course of the conversation the subject somehow got around to children. "I believe," said the visitor, "that children should be given a free rein to think and act, and thus learn at an early age to make their own decisions. This is the only way they can grow into their full potential." Coleridge interrupted the man at this point. "I would like you to see my flower garden," said the poet, and he led the man outside. The visitor took one look and then exclaimed loudly, "Why, that is nothing but a yard full of weeds!" "It used to be filled with roses," said Coleridge, "but this year I thought I would let the garden grow as it willed without my tending to it. This is the result." (Wharton, *Stories and Parables*, page 35)

Our lives are like the poet's garden—thoughtful care and attention are required if we are to flourish. The quality of that care has its foundation in our ability to practice wise judgment, the virtue upon which all the other virtues are built.

11
Which conclusion to this story do you think reflects wise judgment? Explain your choice in writing.

6

Justice:
Love's Minimum

JESUS used an engaging method to teach the people of his day: he told stories, or parables, which contained an element of surprise to shake people out of their customary thinking patterns. Jesus longed to give people a new view of reality—God's view, which was often not what people assumed it to be. Thus, his stories were full of surprises.

Living Justly

Picture a cluster of people around Jesus, many anxious to be assured that they are among the "righteous." Jesus affirms that to be saved you must love God wholeheartedly and love your neighbor as yourself. Then, in response to one listener's follow-up question, "Who is my neighbor?" Jesus tells this story:

The Good Samaritan

"A man was going down from Jerusalem to Jericho, and fell into the hands of robbers, who stripped him, beat him, and went away, leaving him half dead. Now by chance a priest was going down that road; and when he saw him, he passed by on the other side. So likewise a Levite, when he came to the place and saw him, passed by on the other side. But a Samaritan while traveling came near him; and when he saw him, he was moved with pity. He went to him and bandaged his wounds, having poured oil and wine on them. Then he put him on his own animal, brought him to an inn, and took care of him. The next day he took out two denarii, gave them to the innkeeper, and said, 'Take care of him; and when I come back, I will repay you whatever more you spend.'" (Luke 10:30–35, NRSV)

For Jesus' Jewish audience, this story had an unexpected twist: the man who behaved like a real neighbor, that is, the Samaritan, was a member of a group of "distant cousins" to the Jews, whom the Jews looked down on and tried to avoid. This despised foreigner, not the Jewish priest or the Levite, was neighborly enough to recognize *and* care for another person's needs, even though the injured man was not one of his own people.

Often the parable of the good Samaritan is cited as a story of compassion and love, and it certainly is that. However, it is also a lesson in the virtue of justice. **Justice** is the striving to ensure the well-being of others, as well as ourselves. Let's look further at this parable as a lesson in justice.

The Actions of the Samaritan

Just persons strive to promote the conditions that enable others and themselves to have a basic level of well-being. Obviously, the injured man in the parable was in danger of death and deserved to be helped. Justice prompted the Samaritan to respond, to at least get the man out of the road and to a safe place where he could be cared for. Beyond that, the Samaritan, out of compassion, took care of the injured man himself and left money for his continued care with the innkeeper. By his actions, the Samaritan also enhanced his own just and compassionate character. **1**

The Actions of the Avoiders

The priest and the Levite show us clearly what it means to be unjust, or how to cause injustice. (Injustice is both the lack of concern for, and the violation of the well-being of, others or oneself.) The priest and the Levite endangered the injured traveler's well-being by avoiding him. In addition, their avoidance made them harder, colder persons.

1
Write a paragraph about someone who has been like the good Samaritan for you.

Most injustice, in fact, happens in a similar way—through sins of omission more so than commission. It becomes easy for people who are relatively well-off to simply turn away from those who lack the basics for well-being.

Love and Justice

The parable of the good Samaritan is thus a story about justice as well as about love and compassion. The great commandment of love cannot be fulfilled apart from justice. We cannot love and practice injustice at the same time.

Pope Paul VI called justice **"love's minimum requirement."** In other words, loving actions are first of all just actions. The U.S. bishops also noted the link between justice and love in their 1986 pastoral letter *Economic Justice for All:* "Nor is justice opposed to love; rather, it is both a manifestation of love and a condition for love to grow" (no. 39).

At times the connection between love and justice is forgotten. For instance, a couple who are going together may call their relationship "love." But if one is trying to use the other for her or his own purposes, this is unjust. The relationship must first be just if it is to be loving. **2**

For Review

- Define the virtue of justice.
- How are love and justice connected?

■
Above: The parable of the good Samaritan, depicted in this painting by a Nicaraguan peasant, speaks of justice as well as compassion.

2
Create an imaginary dialog between two persons who are supposedly in love but whose relationship is actually unjust.

The Hebrew Prophets Call for Justice

The call for justice runs deep within the Hebrew
Scriptures:

> Woe to him who builds his house by
>   unrighteousness,
>   and his upper rooms by injustice;
> who makes his neighbors work for nothing,
>   and does not give them their wages;
> who says, "I will build myself a spacious house
>   with large upper rooms,"
> and who cuts out windows for it,
>   paneling it with cedar,
>   and painting it with vermilion.
> Are you a king
>   because you compete in cedar?
> Did not your father eat and drink
>   and do justice and righteousness?
> Then it was well with him.
>
> (Jeremiah 22:13–15, NRSV)

> Therefore thus says the LORD, the
>   God of hosts, the LORD:
>
> . . . .
>
> I hate, I despise your festivals,
>   and I take no delight in your solemn
>   assemblies.
> Even though you offer me your burnt offerings
>   and grain offerings,
>   I will not accept them;
> and the offerings of well-being of your fatted
>   animals
>   I will not look upon.
> Take away from me the noise of your songs;
>   I will not listen to the melody of your harps.
> But let justice roll down like waters,
>   and righteousness like an everflowing stream.
>
> (Amos 5:16,21–24, NRSV)

> Is not this the fast that I choose:
>   to loose the bonds of injustice,
>   to undo the thongs of the yoke,
> to let the oppressed go free,
>   and to break every yoke?
> Is it not to share your bread with the hungry,
>   and bring the homeless poor into your house;
> when you see the naked, to cover them,
> and not to hide yourself from your own kin?
>
> (Isaiah 58:6–7, NRSV)

■
Above: "Is not this the fast that
I choose: . . . Share your bread
with the hungry, and bring the
homeless poor into your house?"
(Isaiah 58:6–7, NRSV).

The Grounds for Justice

Understanding the roots of the notion of justice can help clarify why justice is so important to the Christian vision of morality.

Valuable in God's Eyes

We want to be loved for *who we are,* not for *what we do.* We want others to recognize our inherent value. The desire to be loved in this way touches upon a biblical insight that is at the heart of moral behavior:

- **All of God's creation is good and therefore has worth.**

The demands of justice spring primarily from this insight.

Value restricted to usefulness leads to all sorts of abusive situations and injustices. The illegal killing of elephants in Africa for the sole purpose of obtaining their tusks for ivory is one consequence of this narrow idea of value. Similarly, aborting unborn children who have Down's syndrome is often defended with the claim that such children are a burden to families and to society—that they are not useful contributors.

Christian belief, however, affirms that human persons, and indeed *all* living things, are valuable in God's eyes by the very fact that they are creatures of God. Their worth comes from within, not from someone else who judges them to be employable or enjoyable. The task of justice is to make sure this dignity is not violated.

A Matter of Rights and Obligations

The concept of rights flows from this inherent, God-given dignity. **Rights** are those things that we must have if we are to actually *be* what God created us to be. Rights are what is needed for basic well-being, and this applies to all of creation, not just human beings. Thus, justice is a matter of fulfilling the rights of both human and nonhuman creation.

Basic Rights and Well-being: A Case in Point

The situation of Laura can give us some idea of what it is like to be deprived not only of a home but of the right to a good education. At the time she was interviewed, Laura was staying with her four children in one room of a dilapidated, frightening welfare hotel for homeless people in Manhattan. Writer and social justice advocate Jonathan Kozol describes his encounter with her:

The woman . . . is so fragile that I find it hard to start a conversation. Before I do, she asks if I will read to her a letter from the hospital. Her oldest son has been ill for several weeks. He was tested in November for lead poisoning. The letter tells her that the child has a dangerous lead level. She's told to bring him back for treatment. She received the letter some weeks ago. It's been buried in a pile of other documents she cannot understand. . . .

"I cannot read," she says. "I buy the *New York Post* to read the pictures. In the grocery store I know what to buy because I see the pictures. . . .

"If there are no pictures I don't buy it. I want to buy pancakes, I ask the lady: 'Where's the pancakes?' So they tell me. . . .

"I know my name and I can write my name, my children's names. To read I cannot do it. Medicines: I don't know the instructions. . . .

"I can read baby books—like that, a little bit. If I could read I would read newspapers. I would like to know what's going on. My son, he tells me I am

The Catholic Church and Human Rights

In their 1986 pastoral letter *Economic Justice for All,* the U.S. bishops summarize the teaching of the Catholic church on human rights, as outlined in Pope John XXIII's 1963 encyclical *Peace on Earth.* The bishops also point out that the church's teaching strongly supports the U.N. Universal Declaration on Human Rights.

These rights include the civil and political rights to freedom of speech, worship and assembly. A number of human rights also concern human welfare and are of a specifically economic nature. First among these are the rights to life, food, clothing, shelter, rest, medical care and basic education. These are indispensable to the protection of human dignity. In order to ensure these necessities, all persons have a right to earn a living, which for most people in our economy is through remunerative employ-

ment. All persons also have a right to security in the event of sickness, unemployment, and old age. Participation in the life of the community calls for the protection of this same right to employment, as well as the right to healthful working conditions, to wages and other benefits sufficient to provide individuals and their families with a standard of living in keeping with human dignity, and to the possibility of property ownership. These fundamental personal rights . . . state the minimum conditions for social institutions that respect human dignity, social solidarity and justice. They are all essential to human dignity and to the integral development of both individuals and society, and are thus moral issues. Any denial of these rights harms persons and wounds the human community. (No. 80)

■
Above: Fundamental human rights are denied to those who live in dire poverty, such as the people living in this Venezuelan slum.

stupid. 'You can't read.' You know, because he wants to read. He don't understand. . . . People laugh. You feel embarrassed. On the street. Or in the store." She cries. "There's nothing here. . . .

. . . "I sign papers. Somebody could come and take my children. . . . 'Sign this. Sign that.' I don't know what it says. Adoption papers I don't know. This here paper that I got I couldn't understand." (*Rachel and Her Children,* pages 102, 104–106)

Education is a human right. Lacking education, Laura is prevented from caring adequately for the well-being of her family.

The Rights of Persons
Basic human rights can be divided into two main categories:

Survival rights. Certain basic needs must be met if a person is to survive and live a bearable existence. Minimum survival needs include food and water, shelter, a means of livelihood, nurturing of the young, physical safety, and health care.

"Thrival" rights. However, as Laura's experience shows us, meeting mere survival needs is not adequate for reaching one's full potential as a person. In addition to survival, justice is concerned with what can be called "thrival." To thrive is to grow, to become enriched, to be full of life. Education and literacy are among the requirements for human "thrival"—along with respect, privacy, freedom of speech, freedom of conscience, religious liberty, and participation in decisions that affect us. (Chapter 10 focuses on the "thrival" right of respect for persons.) **3**

The Rights of Nonhuman Creation
Issues of justice are not limited to relationships between human beings. The essential goodness and value of all creation means that nonhuman creation has rights as well. Thus, human actions toward the rest of creation are a matter of justice. Concern for justice with creation, or ecological justice, is relatively recent for most Christians. It involves new ways of viewing ourselves and the world in which we live.

Obligations in Relationships
The fact that all members of God's creation have rights implies an obligation on the part of human beings to respect those rights. A person or a thing has a right to what is needed to fulfill its very nature—to have what belongs to it, so to speak. In the case of persons, each of us has an obligation to respect not only our neighbors' rights but our own rights as well.

When relationships include respect for rights, they function as God intended: they make life a rich, fulfilling experience. Justice is the guardian of rights, because honoring rights is essential for dignity and integrity.

Dimensions of Justice

Relationships take place at several levels, and so justice has several dimensions. The first three dimensions refer to relationships among human beings; the last dimension, to relationships between humans and the rest of creation.
- **Individual justice** is concerned with obligations between individuals, one-to-one relationships.
- **Social justice** is about obligations that individuals and subgroups within society have toward their community or the society as a whole.
- **Distributive justice** deals with the obligations that the society has toward all its members, and the role of governments, corporations, commu-

---

3
Write a brief essay explaining which of the "thrival" rights is most important to you and why.

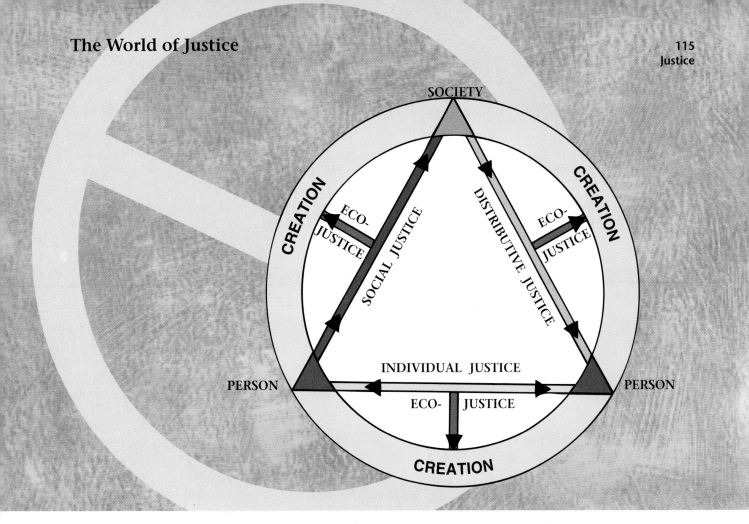

nities, and individuals in the just distribution of society's resources.
- **Ecological justice** is concerned with the obligations that human beings have to all the rest of creation.

Each dimension of justice expands the notion of justice to a bigger world, so that all human relationships—from the one-to-one to the global—can be seen as realms for the virtue of justice. The first three dimensions of justice will be covered in this chapter. Chapter 12 will cover ecological justice.

As you read through the following stories and cases that show the first three dimensions of justice at work, keep in mind this point: Although the different dimensions of justice can be distinguished from one another, all forms of justice are intertwined, as the above diagram shows. Individual justice, social justice, distributive justice, and ecological justice are fused together by a common purpose—fulfilling the great commandment of love.

For Review

- From what biblical insight do the demands of justice primarily spring?
- What are rights?
- What needs come under the category of survival rights? "thrival" rights?
- Describe the four dimensions of justice.

■
Above: Justice has several dimensions: individual, social, distributive, and ecological.

Individual Justice: One-to-One Fairness

The simplest form of justice is one-to-one. In general, individual justice focuses on the obligation that one person has to another because of a relationship they have—by contract, deal, family ties, friendship—such as this brief relationship of customer and clerk:

The scene is Ben & Jerry's ice cream and frozen yogurt parlor on Eighth Avenue and 43d Street in Manhattan. A young man reaches over the counter in excited delight for his choice du jour: a sugar cone containing a generous scoop ($2.65) of cappuccino frozen yogurt. He heads for the street. Seconds later he is back, brandishing his now empty cone sadly.

"My cappuccino frozen yogurt fell out of the cone as soon as I got outside," he says, a little-boy look on his face.

The clerk shrugs. "What do you want me to do?" he asks. "You wanted yogurt in a cone; I gave you yogurt in a cone."

"But you didn't push it down deep enough," the sad man says.

"No one ever told me that before," the clerk insists.

"Refill his cone," another customer says. The clerk remains unmoved. A chorus of grumbles.

"Ben and Jerry would want you to!" a woman joins in. That does it. The clerk looks at her, moves his gaze to a mural of contented-looking cows, then back to the man with the empty cone. With a sigh and a smile he presents him with a new tightly packed cone.

"From Ben and Jerry," he says. (The New York Times) **4**

Fulfilling a debt or obligation is a way of honoring the rights of the person to whom the debt or obligation is owed. So is respecting other people's personal property. Such actions establish good relations between individuals. The frozen yogurt clerk assumed he had fulfilled his obligation to his customer. Confronted in a non-abusive manner by the customer (and by "public opinion"), he found that he was mistaken and corrected the problem with an act of one-to-one fairness.

Following through on obligations and dealing with others respectfully have a lot to do with a sense of what is fair, what we owe to others for their basic well-being. Justice at the individual level can be thought of as one-to-one fairness.

In the United States, where individual rights have always been so important, this form of justice has traditionally held a high position in people's awareness. Nevertheless, we all know that violations of fairness still abound. The next two stories offer examples of situations calling for individual justice.

A Deal's a Deal

When two people have come to an agreement on what they expect from each other, they have a "deal." Each person is obligated to keep his or her part of the bargain. Here is a situation in which a deal becomes messy: **5**

In February, Art got into a financial jam and borrowed seventy-five dollars from his friend Jake to cover his expenses for a ski weekend they went on together. Jake said Art could pay back the debt whenever he got the money, and Art figured that it wouldn't be too long because he was going to start a part-time job on weekends in March.

It is now May 1, though, and Art has not saved enough to pay back Jake because of some "unexpected" expenses that came up—his class ring, a concert

---

4
Have you ever thought that you were being treated unfairly, only to find out later that the opposite was true? Describe the incident in writing.

5
List three deals you have been involved in, telling what each side promised in each case. Next to each deal, indicate whether the persons kept their side of the bargain. And if they did not, why not? Then finish this sentence:

• From my experience with making deals, I have learned . . .

Affirmation: An Overlooked Need

Often overlooked in our critical society is the need for affirmation from others. This need falls within the broader category of respect. Human beings need affirmation, including thanks and praise, as much as a dry, parched earth needs rain. Although we can survive physically without affirmation, our spirit cannot flourish without it. We have all probably known persons whose spirits seemed dry and lifeless because they were thirsting for some recognition of their worth.

Here are a few examples of simple affirmations we can give to one another:

- It's fun to be with you. You always have such a neat way of looking at things.
- I always look forward to this class.
- I know you can figure it out. You've got good judgment.
- What you said really got me thinking. I'm glad you said it.
- Whenever you listen to me when I'm in one of my terrible moods, I feel better.
- The decorations for the homecoming dance look fantastic!
- You were well prepared for that talk. I was impressed.

he "couldn't pass up," and a birthday present for his girlfriend. Jake realizes that he won't be able to go to the prom unless Art comes up with the seventy-five dollars he owes him. Jake presses Art for the money, but Art complains, "Hey, I haven't got it. What do you want me to do, steal it? I can't go to the prom either, so get off my back."

- What could have helped Art and Jake to deal wisely with the debt before it came to this unjust situation?
- Now that they are in this predicament, what might be a fair solution?
- What problems may develop in Art and Jake's relationship if this situation is not resolved fairly?

Abuse in Families: A Grave Injustice

More than any other institution in society, the family has to be a place where a person's basic survival and "thrival" needs are met—such as the need for food, shelter, safety, and so on. In particular, parents owe their children a secure, loving environment in which they can be children and gradually take on responsibilities as they mature. Likewise, children owe their parents respect and cooperation. However, in too many families these expectations are breaking down, and grave injustices are being done.

Consider Eva's account of coming home from school on a typical afternoon:

As soon as I walk in the door, I see that my mother's drunk. Nothing new there. Like usual, I try to just get by her and go to my room to get ready for work, but sometimes it's not easy 'cause she's yellin' and yellin' at me, and I don't even know why. I've quit listening. All I know is, I gotta go to work, come home later, and get supper for me and my little brother. Mom will be out drinkin'. And I've got all these projects due for school the next day. Then I feel like I'm gonna explode. Sometimes I do—I scream at my mother, I call her names. Or I take it out on my brother and hit him—hard—when he won't do what I say.

- What basic needs of Eva and her brother are not being met?
- Can you imagine why Eva's mother might behave as she does? Do you think that she is responsible and culpable for her behavior? Why?
- Reflect on this statement in light of Eva's family situation: Violence and injustice breed more violence and injustice.
- Try to apply the LISTEN process of decision making to Eva's situation.

For Review
- How does keeping a deal convey a sense of justice?
- What do parents and children owe each other?

Above: A family should be a place where a person's basic survival and "thrival" needs are met.

Social Justice: Contributing to the Well-being of All

Social justice is concerned with what belongs to all people in common, to the community or society as a whole. As emphasized many times throughout this book, individuals need communities. These communities, too, have needs that must be met if they are to provide a healthy environment in which *all* the members can thrive. Social justice challenges individuals to do what they can to make sure these collective needs are met.

Being a just person in society means doing what you can to make your community, nation, and planet a better place to live. To quote Peter Maurin, cofounder of the Catholic Worker Movement, our purpose should be to build "'a society where it is easier for people to be good'" (quoted in *The Catholic Worker*).

The Common Good: The Ideal to Strive For

Social justice focuses on what is often called the **common good**—that is, the condition of the social whole that enables all its members to flourish. The common good stands as an ideal toward which every society must strive valiantly if it intends to be just.

What or how each person should contribute to the common good is not totally clear-cut. At the most basic level, citizens are legally required to contribute to the common good by paying taxes, serving on juries, and so on. And it is obviously wrong for people to steal public funds or damage resources that are meant to be used by the wider community.

Beyond these basic levels, though, there is no complete, things-to-do list that persons can follow and be assured that they are doing their full part. What each person must give to the community varies with the needs of the community and the personal circumstances of each member. One rule of thumb to follow for doing social justice is this advice from Jesus: "'Much will be required of the person entrusted with much, and still more will be demanded of the person entrusted with more'" (Luke 12:48).

At times, individuals and groups within society have to make sacrifices for the sake of the whole community. For instance, property owners can be required by law to sell part of their land to the city or some higher level of government so that a public road can be built or widened. Ultimately, however, the goal of the common good is to make sure that everyone's basic rights and needs are met. Contributing to the common good fosters the well-being of all individuals.

Creating a Society in Which It Is Easier to Be Good

Let's look at some concrete ways individuals contribute to the good of their community or the entire society.

Leaving No One Out

Creating a society in which everyone's needs are met and everyone's rights are respected is very different from aiming for merely satisfying the majority's needs. Social justice recognizes that when one person's rights are disregarded, everyone's rights are endangered. Sometimes the majority of individuals must let go of some of their desires in order to make sure that everyone's basic rights are

Day-to-Day Opportunities to Serve the Common Good

Here are some everyday, familiar examples of contributing to the common good:

- pitching in to help with household chores
- helping raise money for a class trip
- putting in a decent day's work at your job
- taking proper care of school textbooks that will be passed on to other students

Consider how, in each of the above examples, working for the common good ultimately benefits the individual.

being respected. The task of the just person is to figure out what is fair for everyone and to create situations in which everyone comes out a winner. Even everyday situations present opportunities to practice social justice, as these two students discovered:

Nick: At one of our class meetings last spring, we had to pick a place to go for our class trip. We thought it'd be no big deal. Were we ever wrong!

Coci: See, most of us were all psyched to go white-water rafting on this river at the state park. I guess it's supposed to be a lot of fun. There's even an outfitter who provides the rafts and guides for each boat. At the time, it seemed like the only suggestion that sounded really fun.

Nick: We were about to take a vote when Hilary stood up in the back of the room and pointed out that white-water rafting was probably not very safe for Tess and Ray. They are two kids in our class who use wheelchairs to get around.

Coci: Hilary didn't think it would be fair for all of us to go have fun while Tess and Ray stayed back at school or whatever. Everyone groaned. Most of us really had our heart set on rafting.

Nick: Then we all felt like scum because Tess and Ray were sitting back there with Hilary. It didn't really take that long to come up with a bunch of ideas for trips that Tess and Ray could go on, too.

Coci: Yeah. We ended up touring a movie studio, and it was great. Everybody seemed to have a really good time.

- What other kinds of situations might call for sacrifice on the part of the majority so that the rights of everyone are honored?

Above: Participating in fund-raising events is one way we can contribute to the common good.

- What would be some harmful consequences of aiming for a simple majority rule instead of the common good?

Service in the Community

Individuals can also do their part to create "a society where it is easier for people to be good" by becoming involved in community service activities and programs. In recent years, record numbers of young people have been helping in their communities. Here are some examples described in the magazine *Youthworker Update:*

- Young people ages seventeen to twenty-one from Boston-area schools are gathering food for the needy and fixing run-down playgrounds in the Boston City Year Program.
- Students on 350 campuses are helping out with social concerns like literacy programs and feeding the homeless under the Minnesota-based Campus Outreach Opportunity League; Operation Civic Serve is doing the same thing on 50 campuses in California.
- Public schools in Atlanta require high school seniors to put in seventy-five hours of community service before they graduate. **6**

Many students who volunteer their time and energy to community service testify to its positive effect on them. In other words, they were helped as much as those they intended to help, often in ways they did not expect. One college student looked back on the summer between her junior and senior years of high school, when she volunteered to work with poor people in Appalachia:

It had such an effect on me. Before that, I really was focused on high school as the only world I lived in. That's just the way you are when you're young—you think that high school is *it*, it's all that exists. Then when I spent the summer in Appalachia, my world started to grow, and I realized I was involved in a much bigger world than I thought—and that what I do in my life affects other people. It really changed me.

6
Find out what service opportunities exist for teenagers in your community, and then write a brief description of three of them.

■
Above: Young people volunteer their time and skill in neighborhood fix-up projects.

Social injustice saws at the limb upon which we all sit.

Doing Harm to the Common Good

Victimized by Public Vandalism

When people actively do harm to the common good, they are guilty of social injustice. This injustice can take place on a very broad scale, such as in the "merger mania" in which huge conglomerates gobble up smaller companies, frequently resulting in factory closings, job losses, and poor quality of products or service to consumers. Actions of this scale have an enormous impact on individual lives.

But harm to the common good can also happen at familiar, everyday levels. Consider Pete's plight and his feelings of being violated:

Pete splashed cold water on his sleepy eyes. This was one Saturday morning he couldn't sleep in till ten. He had to go over to the library as soon as it opened and start on a fifteen-page research project for his American literature class. It was due first thing Monday morning. Pulling a C on this assignment was critical; his grade depended on it. And so did his college career—passing this class would get him off academic probation. Pete shuddered at the thought of the scene his parents would make if he got kicked out of college after his first semester.

Though Pete was more on top of things than usual with this assignment, he now wished he had started a week earlier. But he'd been having trouble choosing from the list of recommended authors. By the time he went to get some suggestions from his professor five days ago, there was only one choice left.

"Looks like you get to research this author by default, Pete," his professor said with a slight smirk.

Pete anxiously wound his way through the endless stacks in the basement of the school's library, searching for the books he needed for his paper; this was not familiar territory. He needed two books in particular, the ones his professor had recommended. After about fifteen minutes of searching, he found them. Sighing with relief, Pete snatched them off the shelf and dashed up to the checkout desk.

With his can of Mountain Dew and package of Double Stuf Oreo cookies in front of him, Pete sat down at his desk, ready to take notes. As Pete opened the first book and then the second one, a wave of panic hit him. Now he knew why none of the other students had chosen this author. Some jerk had cut out huge geometric shapes in the middle of *each* page of *both* books except for the first twenty pages and the last ten!

"Now what am I gonna do?" Pete moaned as he buried his face in the maimed books.

- Do you think vandalism of public property is a social injustice?
- Pete is somewhat to blame for his predicament. Does this lessen the harm done to him?
- Why do people vandalize public property, or, for that matter, private property?

The Get-All-You-Can Mentality

As discussed earlier, individuals or groups may have to sacrifice some of what they want, or feel they deserve, so that everyone can share in the benefits and available resources meant for all. Ultimately, unwillingness to contribute to the common good ends up working against everyone's well-being. The get-all-you-can competitive mentality, illustrated in the following example, is one form this attitude can take:

The fishing industry used to flourish in a North American coastal region that is now very poor. A number of factors have contributed to the devastation of the region's economy:
1. The fishers have consistently exceeded the quotas for numbers of fish they can legally catch.
2. Fishery plants on shore have been increasing in number, competing for fish to process for export, and this has pushed up the prices of fish and brought about more illegal overfishing to fill the demand.
3. The problem is complicated by the fact that foreign fishing vessels have been illegally overfishing as well, outside the country's two-hundred-mile limit.

The consequent fish shortage has meant that plants have closed, putting thousands of workers out of jobs. The whole region is hurting.

- In the situation just described, what is the common good that the participants in the fishing industry need to strive for?
- How does the private behavior of the participants work against the common good?
- If you were a fisher in that situation, when everyone else in the area was overfishing, what pressures would you feel to also catch more than your quota of fish? What alternatives would you have?
- Reflect on this statement from a Catholic theologian in light of the above situation: "Social injustice saws at the limb upon which we all sit" (Maguire, *The Moral Revolution,* page 26). How does this statement also apply to other situations in society?

A Way of Life

Social justice, or contributing to the common good, is not simply a luxury for Christians, something nice to be done with extra time and energy after taking care of one's own individual needs. But neither is it a matter of running around frantically trying to take care of everyone's needs. The needs of the common good are vast and endless. It is not up to any one person to cover all the bases—she or he would burn out very quickly. Instead, each member of the community has the obligation to contribute what she or he can. In the words of one individual committed to social justice, "Individual efforts toward justice become currents that break down barriers when they are joined and directed at a common goal" (Vuyst, "Self-help for the Homeless").

For Christians, social justice is a way of life, a way of looking at reality and responding to it with a sensitivity to the well-being of all and not just oneself. The "all" includes people living now but also people who will come after us, who must live with the consequences of decisions we make today. A wise saying from the Six Nations Iroquois Confederacy sums up this responsibility: "In our every deliberation, we must consider the impact of our decisions on the next seven generations." **7**

For Review

- Define the common good. How does it differ from simply the good of the majority?
- In what way does social justice involve sacrifice?

■
Above: A society must be structured fairly so that everyone can participate. Here a group of people with disabilities protests for better physical access to buildings in downtown San Francisco.

7
Choose a public-policy decision that is being debated in your community, state, or nation today. Write about how that decision could affect people one hundred years from now.

Distributive Justice: Making the System Fair for Everyone

Just as individuals owe a duty to society, the reverse is also true: Society as a whole has the obligation to look out for the good of its members. Governments and private businesses have to be organized in such a way that burdens and benefits are shared and distributed fairly to individuals in society.

So distributive justice also has its eye on the common good. Remember, the common good is a complex of conditions needed so that *every person*, not just an elite group or even a majority, can achieve a life of dignity, a life filled with respect and hope. To the extent that a system is organized for the common good, distributive justice exists. (And, as you will see in the examples to follow, social justice and distributive justice often overlap.)

At the Global Level

At the global level, governments and corporations of the world's nations create economies that control the distribution of the world's resources, including food and fuels. At present, thedistribution of these resources is terribly unjust: industrialized nations consume far more of the world's goods than less-developed nations.

A Lesson from Jesus

In the following parable, Jesus contrasts the luxurious lifestyle of a rich man and the desperate plight of a beggar, Lazarus, at the rich man's gate. The story describes a one-to-one relationship, but it is also a potent symbol of the distributive injustice that exists today at the global level:

"There was a rich man who was dressed in purple and fine linen and who feasted sumptuously every day. And at his gate lay a poor man named Lazarus, covered with sores, who longed to satisfy his hunger with what fell from the rich man's table; even the dogs would come and lick his sores. The poor man died and was carried away by the angels to be with Abraham. The rich man also died and was buried. In Hades, where he was being tormented, he looked up and saw Abraham far away with Lazarus by his side. He called out, 'Father Abraham, have mercy on me, and send Lazarus to dip the tip of his finger in water and cool my tongue; for I am in agony in these flames.' But Abraham said, 'Child, remember that during your lifetime you received your good things, and Lazarus in like manner evil things; but now he is comforted here, and you are in agony. Besides all this, between you and us a great chasm has been fixed, so that those who might want to pass from here to you cannot do so, and no one can cross from there to us.'" (Luke 16:19–26, NRSV)

Vast Inequities: Lazarus and the Rich Man Today

In current economic systems, there is no guarantee that economic growth will benefit all members of society. In fact, vast inequities exist within industrialized countries despite constant economic growth. The gap between rich and poor is widening even in countries where citizens are, on the average, living comfortably. In the United States, for example, a growing "underclass" is caught in a cycle of poverty from which escape seems nearly

impossible. In an article on the movement of young people into volunteer service projects, a reporter made this remark: "'Over the past few years many of the children of affluence have begun to wonder, why, in a nation that is doing so well, do so many feel so bad?'" (quoted in *Youthworker Update*). **8**

But the gap between rich people and poor people is even more pronounced when we contrast the material conditions of life for average citizens in industrialized countries with those in nonindustrialized, or developing, countries. In his 1993 World Day of Peace message, Pope John Paul II pointed out that this economic gap not only violates human dignity but also threatens the well-being of the world community:

Many individuals and indeed whole peoples are living today in conditions of extreme poverty. The gap between rich and poor has become more marked, even in the most economically developed nations. This is a problem which the conscience of humanity cannot ignore, since the conditions in which a great number of people are living are an insult to their innate dignity and as a result are a threat to the authentic and harmonious progress of the world community.

The church's position on this situation is clear, and, in the pope's words, "it is a faithful echo of the voice of Christ: Earthly goods are meant for the whole human family and cannot be reserved for the exclusive benefit of a few." Society has an urgent responsibility to create economic mechanisms that will "ensure a more just and equitable distribution of goods."

The story of Lazarus and the rich man continues to have meaning for the contemporary world, and Pope John Paul II can help us see the connection:

We cannot stand idly by, enjoying our own riches and freedom if, in any place, the Lazarus of the twentieth century stands at our doors. In the light of the parable of Christ, riches and freedom mean a special responsibility. Riches and freedom create a special obligation. (*Justice in the Marketplace*, page 352)

- Christian faith holds that if any "members of the body" are hurting, the whole body hurts. Relate this belief to the economic gap that exists between industrialized and developing nations, and within industrialized nations themselves.
- In your own words, describe the "Lazarus of the twentieth century." Describe the rich man as well.

■
Above: Pope John Paul II says, "We cannot stand idly by, enjoying our own riches and freedom if, in any place, the Lazarus of the twentieth century stands at our doors." The gap between rich and poor is evident in the chronic inability of hundreds of millions of people to meet their minimum needs, while others feast lavishly.

8
Bring in a newspaper or magazine article that points out the gap between rich and poor people in your own community or country. Write a brief summary of the article.

- How might international structures be created and strengthened to ensure global distributive justice?
- What role can individuals play in affecting distributive justice at the global level?

Who's Responsible?

Who is responsible for the vast inequalities that exist in the world, for the persistent hunger that gnaws at so many of the world's people? As discussed earlier, most injustice is caused by omission—people simply looking the other way. The responsibility for injustice caused by omission is harder to pin down, of course, than injustice caused by a specific culprit who is caught red-handed. If Lazarus starved to death, was the rich man responsible? We could more easily determine responsibility for Lazarus's death if, say, a thief had come by, stolen what little bread Lazarus had, and kicked him to death. Instead, the responsibility is diffused, shared to a lesser but real degree by all the advantaged, well-fed people who looked the other way in the face of Lazarus's need. When good people do nothing, injustice flourishes. **9**

At the National Level

Within nations, governments and businesses are supposed to provide the structures to ensure that the goods in that nation are distributed among the people. For instance, in the United States, Social Security and minimum-wage laws are geared toward enabling people to have a basic income. Private health insurance, Medicare, and Medicaid (these last two are government programs) ensure a basic level of medical care. Even with these structures, however, many people are not receiving adequate income or health care.

Who's Responsible, Anyway?

Some people claim that they just want to lead a private life, minding their own business and not getting involved in controversial issues beyond their own family. They claim that they are neutral on the issues. Archbishop Desmond Tutu of South Africa, a long-time resister of his government's apartheid policy, had this answer for persons who do not want to get involved:

> If you are neutral in situations of injustice, you have chosen the side of the oppressor. If an elephant has his foot on the tail of a mouse and you say that you are neutral, the mouse will not appreciate your neutrality. (Quoted in *Social Concerns Bulletin*)

9
List some types of omissions by privileged people that can cause injustice to flourish for poor people.

Because education is a fundamental right to which everyone is entitled and because the government is involved in public education, we will focus on this issue as an example of distributive justice at the national level.

Quality Education: Owed to All

The public education system is one of society's ways to enable its members to survive and thrive—to live a full, meaningful life. A good education is crucial. It helps people prepare to be "producers" in society. It passes on the cultural life of society through the arts and sciences. It exposes people to the language, math, and thinking skills needed for creative, enjoyable, and responsible participation in life.

We hear that education is the key to an individual's future and that a nation that neglects education is putting itself in jeopardy. Yet the quality of public education in the United States is extremely uneven and, according to many studies, getting worse overall. Young people who receive a poor education live at a serious disadvantage all their life. Poorly educated persons have greater difficulty providing themselves with the basic necessities of life, such as food, shelter, and clothing.

"We All Lose When the Schools Lose"

In recent years, many U.S. citizens have been alarmed by the failure of the public education system to adequately prepare young people for life in society. Many businesses are concerned about the difficulty they have in finding skilled and even semiskilled workers—those who have basic reading and math abilities.

- In what ways does a poorly educated workforce jeopardize the common good in a society?

- Not all public schools are doing poorly, especially those in suburban areas. Why is this the case?
- What do teachers, parents, students, school board members, taxpayers, and the business community owe to public education?
- Do U.S. citizens whose children attend private schools have an obligation to support public education?

Above: We can try to change the business or agency we work for so that it is held accountable to the common good.

At the Individual Level

As is obvious from the discussion on education, individual citizens and consumers also share the responsibility to affect distributive justice. Governmental efforts to provide every person with an adequate education would not get very far without the contributions of individuals such as teachers and taxpayers at local levels of society.

The role of individuals in affecting distributive justice can vary a great deal. Here are a few of the many avenues for individuals to affect distributive justice:

Through Work

The most common way for individuals to contribute to making society's systems fair is through their work. We can try to change the business or agency we work for so that it is held accountable to the common good. Providing safe, well-made products at reasonable prices; designing management systems that promote fairness; following health and safety regulations; and so on—all these depend upon efforts and choices of individuals who work for the government or for corporations.

Through the Political Process

Distributive justice is also furthered when individuals become involved in the political process. Involvement can take these forms:
- becoming informed about issues and candidates
- working for an issue or a candidate
- voting in national, state, and local elections
- running for political office and serving as an elected official
- speaking up and putting pressure on agencies that may be neglecting their duties to the common good

Through Volunteer Organizations

Volunteering helps establish distributive justice as much as it does social justice. However, volunteer organizations and service projects must not be viewed as substitutes for governments' and corporations' responsibilities to further the common good. Rather, by volunteering their time and other resources, individuals can enhance the efforts of government and business to ensure that everyone's basic needs are provided for.

The virtue of justice has a place in all the levels of human relationships. As the following saying reiterates, each dimension of human justice—individual, social, and distributive—overlaps with the others, and with ecological justice as well:

Give people a fish, and they'll eat for a day.
Teach people to fish, and they'll eat for a lifetime.
Clean up the river, and you'll make sure
there are fish. **10**

For Review

- What does it mean to say that distributive justice exists in a society?
- Describe how the story of Lazarus and the rich man is a parable of global distributive injustice today.
- How does omission play a role in the creation and maintenance of distributive injustice?
- Describe three avenues by which individuals can affect distributive justice.

10
Rewrite the above saying to apply it to a situation of need that you are aware of globally, nationally, or locally.

Amnesty International: To Free All Prisoners of Conscience

Imagine disagreeing with your nation's leaders. Imagine, too, being picked up and thrown in jail because of that disagreement. In the United States we take for granted that such things just don't happen. They do go on in many countries, however, and that fact led to the creation of Amnesty International in 1961.

Amnesty International works on behalf of prisoners of conscience—people who have been jailed, anywhere in the world, because of their beliefs, ethnic origin, sex, or language, and who have not used or advocated violence. Amnesty has more than a million members in over 150 countries. The organization is independent—it is not attached to any government, political party, ideology, economic system, or religion. From that independent stance, Amnesty defines its goals:

- to free all prisoners of conscience
- to ensure fair and prompt trials for all political prisoners
- to abolish the death penalty, torture, and cruel treatment of prisoners
- to end political killings and "disappearances"

What Amnesty Does

Writing letters is at the heart of Amnesty's action. Members write letters on behalf of specific prisoners. Amnesty International provides the necessary information: the facts of the case, the names and addresses of the government officials to whom the letters should be sent, and suggestions about what to say in the letter.

What Can Students Do?

Amnesty International has more than eight thousand volunteer groups in over seventy countries. Among them are two thousand groups in high schools and colleges throughout the United States. These groups give students the opportunity to stand up for human rights and take action. Student groups sponsor letter-writing campaigns, fund-raisers, concerts, lectures, and other activities designed to call attention to human rights abuses around the world.

Success Stories

Amnesty International can boast of a great number of successes. Forty-three thousand cases have been taken up by Amnesty, and forty thousand have been closed. A typical success story was related by a Detroit-area Amnesty member. Her local group had taken on the case of Syrian citizen Abd al-Qahhar Saray. Saray had been imprisoned for more than twelve years, beginning in 1982, "without being charged, without a trial, and without being convicted of a crime. For all intents and purposes, his only crime was belonging to a group his government opposed" (Rhein, "A Liberating Flood Of Letters").

In December 1994, the Detroit Amnesty group received the good news. Saray—the married father of two, whose family had spent twelve years not knowing whether he was living or dead—was free. Amnesty's efforts had succeeded again, and the cause of human rights had taken a step forward.

For information about starting an Amnesty group, contact Amnesty International USA, National Student/Youth Program, 1118 22nd Street NW, Washington, DC 20037; phone 202-775-5161.

On Not Being Overwhelmed by Injustice

Our responsibilities to social and distributive justice are not as clear-cut as they are to individual justice. So some people react by assuming they have no obligations at the level of the common good—"I don't want to get involved." Others respond with excessive guilt and a burdened sense that the world's weight is on their shoulders— "I can never do enough." Still others would like to get involved in making the world a better place but think they cannot make a difference, so why try? Another group believes that if God is all-loving and all-powerful (as they have always been taught), God would not allow the terrible suffering and injustice in the world to continue; thus, they despair of God's existence and of the possibility that good can triumph over evil.

In answer to these various stances, a response consistent with Christian faith would be this:

- We all have a responsibility to the common good, and we need to discern how to best contribute according to our gifts and our life circumstances.
- We are not expected to carry the burden of the world's suffering on our shoulders or to feel guilty about all the injustice in the world.
- No one can change unjust systems alone, but millions of people, each contributing in their own way, can bring about a tidal wave of change with the help of God's Spirit.
- God has given human beings freedom and will not take it away from us. Thus, unjust situations are brought about by human freedom, not by God. And good can triumph over evil when persons respond freely to God's grace.

God is relying on us, with God's help, to bring about the reign of justice, love, and peace. **11**

Yet even with God's help, standing up to massive injustice and creating a just world may seem like impossible tasks. How can Christians who commit themselves to seeking justice keep their perspective and not become overwhelmed by the enormity of the suffering and need they see in the world? Here are some recommendations:

Use Your Power

Recognize that although you cannot immediately get rid of injustice in the world, you *can* do something. Write a letter to a government representative. Refuse to buy a boycotted product. Participate in a run-for-hunger event. Keep in mind that you may be limited in the time, energy, or money you can give to justice causes, but you are not powerless. Everyone can do something.

See Members of the Body

See yourself as part of the Body of Christ—one member whose contribution is unique:

"For as in one body we have many parts, and all the parts do not have the same function, so too we, though many, are one body in Christ and individually parts of one another. Since we have gifts that differ according to the grace given to us, let us exercise them." (Romans 12:4–6)

Belonging to the Body of Christ means, "I don't have to do it all. I will do what I can, knowing that I am part of something much greater than my own efforts."

Another helpful image is that of a symphony orchestra. Each instrument, if played well, contributes a beautiful sound. The sounds of the instruments differ, but together they produce the

---

11
Create an imaginary dialog between a person who has given up on the possibility of a just world and a person whose Christian faith motivates him or her to work for justice.

Members of Christ's Body: The Campaign for Human Development

The Campaign for Human Development (CHD) demonstrates one way that the members of Christ's Body can contribute to a more just society.

CHD was begun in 1969 by the United States Catholic Conference to raise funds to enable poor and low-income people to organize into self-help groups that attack the root causes of poverty. Through an annual collection in U.S. Catholic parishes, the campaign raises millions of dollars, most of which are distributed as grants to local self-help projects. CHD also educates Catholics about the church's stance of commitment to poor people.

In 1993, CHD gave grants totaling $6.6 million to 203 self-help projects—an average grant of $32,670. Here is a sampling of projects funded:

Churches Acting Together for Change and Hope (CATCH), Cleveland, Ohio. CATCH brings together members of inner-city congregations to develop plans of action to improve the quality of their communities on both immediate and long-term levels. Working with police, CATCH has created "safe zones" around churches. In one case, fifteen houses in

which drugs were being dealt were closed down—in one day. This success led to the challenge of renovating those houses and making them available to families. CATCH has also advocated legislation to decentralize the public school system, and is working with other organizations to restore an old baseball park and the neighborhood that surrounds it.

Land Stewardship Project, Stillwater, Minnesota. The Land Stewardship Project aims to strengthen moderate-sized family farms. Part of their work is to call public attention to the practices of financial institutions whose policies endanger the family farm.

Milwaukee 9 to 5, Wage Replacement for Family Leave, Milwaukee, Wisconsin. The Family and Medical Leave Act (FMLA) provides employees of companies with fifty or more employees with *unpaid* leave time for the birth or adoption of a child and the serious illness of a family member. The 9 to 5 project responds to the U.S. bishops' call for "personnel policies that more fully reflect our commitment to family life" (*Putting Children and Families First,* page 19). The project seeks to

take the FMLA a step further by advocating a law that provides public funds to replace two-thirds of the wages lost during the period of family leave.

Sin Fronteras Organizing Project, Border Agricultural Workers, El Paso, Texas. Sin Fronteras, initiated by farmworkers and activists, fights the injustices faced by farmworkers in western Texas and southern New Mexico. The project has two main goals: *(a)* to satisfy the immediate needs of agricultural workers and their families; and *(b)* to organize the workers in committees that will bring changes to the agricultural system and to the public and private institutions that now condone exploitation and poverty. Sin Fronteras directs El Centro de los Trabajadores Agrícolas Fronterizos in El Paso, a facility that houses the project's administrative offices and provides living space, a clinic, and other necessities for five hundred migrant workers during the harvest season.

The generosity of Catholics in the annual CHD collection enables thousands of poor people to improve their lives.

magnificent symphony. Each of us is just one instrument in a grand orchestra.

Remember It Is God's Work

Remind yourself that the work of justice is God's work, not just your own. God sustains those who seek justice. What God asks of us is not that we be *successful* in our efforts, but that we be *faithful*. The end product, in a way, is in God's hands.

Be a Joyful Community

Link up with other people who are trying to live justly, especially persons with whom you share faith. Have fun together; care for one another; pitch in on group projects; pray together. Doing the work of justice requires a support community.

Take the Long View

The struggle for justice also requires a long-range perspective on things. People of the nineteenth and early twentieth century who worked for an end to slavery, for free public education, for an end to child labor, and for the right of women to vote would be amazed today to see that their dreams have become reality. In the same way, people today who work to see injustice turned upside down play a part in the growing reign of justice. **12**

For Review

- Briefly summarize the recommendations for Christians to guard against becoming overwhelmed by the injustice they seek to change.

Living Out These Dreams

Vincent Harding, a minister and a long-time advocate for peace and justice, puts the virtue of justice into the wider context of living in faith and hope:

Living in faith is knowing that even though our little work, our little seed, our little brick, our little block may not make the whole thing, the whole thing exists in the mind of God, and that whether or not we are there to see the whole thing is not the most important matter. The most important thing is whether we have entered into the process. Like Martin [Luther] King talking to the old woman in Montgomery, Alabama, during the long bus boycott [of segregated buses in 1956], asking, "Mama, why are you walking like this, walking miles and miles to work? I mean, you're not even going to benefit much from this new situation yourself." And she said, "Dr. King, I'm not doing this for myself. I'm doing this for my grandchildren." That's why she could also say to him then, "Yes, Dr. King, my feets is tired, but my soul is rested."

That's how your soul gets rested . . . when you stop thinking, working only for yourself, and start dreaming, as the Native Americans do, for seven generations beyond us. Your soul gets rested when you realize that your life is not meant to be captured just in your own skin, but that your life reaches out to the life of the universe itself. And the life of the universe reaches into us and demands of us that we be more than we think we can be, demands that we live out these dreams. ("In the Company of the Faithful")

12
Which of the five recommendations seems most helpful to you? Write a paragraph on how it could help you.

7

Courage:
Facing Our Fears
for the Sake
of the Good

As discussed in chapter 5, wise judgment enables us to figure out the good in a given situation and choose to act for that good. This virtue was called good-conscience-in-action. Justice, which was covered in chapter 6, orients us to give to others (individuals, society, and the rest of creation) what is rightfully theirs, what they need for a basic level of well-being.

So wise judgment and justice focus on doing what is right. Anyone who has ever tried to do the right thing, however, can say this: It is one thing to *know* what is right and to be *inclined* to do what is right, but it is quite another thing to actually *do* what is right. Why? Because obstacles get in the way. One of these obstacles is the fear that we will somehow be harmed. Our own dread of being hurt can divert us from the good.

The Stuff of Heroes

Courage, the third cardinal virtue, enables us to tackle the fear and dread that stand in the way of our doing the good. Courage is the stuff of which heroes are made.

You probably have heroes in mind from history or current events, people who have risked their own security and even their life for the sake of something great and worthy. Abraham Lincoln, Martin Luther King Jr., Harriet Tubman (a black woman who worked on the Underground Railroad to free slaves), and Lech Walesa of Poland's Solidarity movement are a few examples of real-life heroes.

Epic literature is another source of heroic figures; *The Odyssey, Beowulf,* and *King Arthur and the Knights of the Round Table* provide examples of classic heroes. The heroes in these epics fit the typical portrayal of courageous persons—independent, strong, and fearless. But their brand of courage—surrounded by daring and adventure—does not match up well with the Christian concept of courage. In order to see what the Christian virtue of courage looks like, let's consider a more recently written epic, the three-volume Lord of the Rings, by J. R. R. Tolkien.

A Heroic Epic: The Lord of the Rings

In his trilogy, Tolkien transports us to a fantasy world called Middle-earth, inhabited by assorted strange beings—among them, tree-like walking creatures, wizards, trolls, and hobbits. Hobbits are three feet tall, furry-footed, content little people who love fun and parties, gardening, and staying at home in their cozy, quiet dwellings.

One of these gentle hobbits, Frodo Baggins, is appointed by his community to carry a powerful, evil-enchanted ring back to the place where the ring originated, in the horrible land of Mordor, ruled by the enemy Sauron. There the ring can be destroyed in the volcanic fire in which it was forged, so that Sauron can never use it to enslave Middle-earth.

Frodo is afraid of the powerful ring; thus, he is not crazy about accepting his task. But he is chosen to be the ring-bearer precisely because of his cautiousness. Other, stronger persons have been destroyed by the ring's evil power because they thought they could exploit it. In his fear, Frodo respects the power of the ring and avoids using it. So, with a few companions, he embarks on a long, perilous journey to Mordor.

Along the way, Frodo's "fellowship of the ring" meets with terrifying events and monsters. As Frodo

Above: Frodo, hero of the Lord of the Rings trilogy, is not by nature a daring, fearless, strong fellow. But Frodo shows us a model of the Christian notion of courage.

struggles to keep the ring out of the hands of Sauron, he is pursued by hideous riders, attacked by terrible goblins, stung by a huge spider, imprisoned in a tower, and beaten and wounded. When he does use the ring to get out of a tight spot, Frodo feels drawn to its evil, and he must destroy the ring before its corruptive power overwhelms him.

When Frodo arrives at the base of the volcano into which the ring must be cast, he is exhausted and starved. He has also become possessed by the ring's dark power. Sam Gamgee, Frodo's faithful servant, has to carry Frodo on his back up to the mouth of the volcano, where, in a final surprising event, the mission is accomplished.

Lessons from Frodo: What Courage Is Not

Looking at Frodo as a model of courage, we can understand this virtue more clearly. Earlier it was said that courage enables us to tackle the fear and dread that stand in the way of our doing the good. But what is *not* meant by courage?

Risk taking for its own sake. The willingness to take risks is not automatically a sign of courage. (A person who drives recklessly simply for the thrill of it is not courageous but foolhardy.) Frodo would rather avoid the perils of the journey; he longs for the comforts of his home and garden.

Proving oneself. Courage is also not about proving oneself to others. Persons of courage are less concerned about their own reputation than about the good they are trying to promote. Frodo is not out to prove his worth to the other folks of Middle-earth; hobbits naturally avoid glory. At the same time, Frodo has no wish to fail all those who count on him to destroy the ring.

Being fearless. Macho heroes of action movies, such as James Bond and Rambo, act fearlessly in the face of grave danger, without so much as a wrinkle of anxiety. A lack of fear has been confused with courage. This is a false notion because being courageous does not mean having no fear. Cowardice, the true opposite of courage, is the inability to face our fears and deal with them directly and honestly. Even though Frodo shakes with fright, he is no coward; he does not let his fear stop him from doing what he must do. **1**

Going it alone. Acts of courage are seldom, if ever, single-handed accomplishments. Even the Lone Ranger wasn't alone! Doing good in the face of fear requires a supportive environment. Knowing that we can turn to other people—even if only in thought—can help us regenerate our energy and carry on with our task. In Frodo's case, it was not he alone who destroyed the ring and defeated Sauron. This monumental task was possible because of the network of support created by the fellowship of the ring. Above all, it was the love and friendship between Frodo and Sam that overcame the final hurdle of the journey.

Saving the day in one bold stroke. Another misunderstanding of courage is the belief that courage happens only in a dramatic, highly noticeable activity. It can be spectacular to see courage in action. However, this virtue often operates more quietly, without fanfare and attention. Courage typically involves hanging in there during tough times rather than saving the day with bold moves. Even the mission of Frodo and his companions, dramatic as it was, entailed many months of taking things one day at a time.

The courage of hanging in there requires endurance and patience. These qualities do not involve a passive resignation to circumstances. Instead, endurance and patience require a vigorous holding fast to the good over time. They are active qualities, not passive. Furthermore, endurance and patience strengthen us to face and plow through the day-in and day-out barrage of obstacles that would cause a lesser person to give up. **2**

What Courage *Is*

Genuine **courage** is the ability to do the good in the face of harm or the threat of injury, whether physical or psychological. What conditions, then, make an act courageous? There are three:
- **choosing to act for the good**
- **being threatened by harm**
- **loosening the grip of fear**

For Review
- What lessons about courage can we learn from Frodo?
- Define courage. What makes an act courageous?

1
In writing, describe a hero from literature, movies, or television who exemplifies what is *not* meant by the Christian virtue of courage.

2
Give an example from your own life or the life of someone you know of the opportunity to practice the courage of hanging in there.

Choosing the Good

The key feature of all moral behavior is choosing the good. Courage entails, above all, going for the good. It means being so devoted to the good that a person does not get sidetracked from it by fears of personal harm or suffering.

A story is told of a traveler who made a religious pilgrimage:

An old pilgrim was making his way to the Himalayan Mountains in the bitter cold of winter when it began to rain.

An innkeeper said to him, "How will you ever get there in this kind of weather, my good man?"

The old man answered cheerfully, "My heart got there first, so it's easy for the rest of me to follow." (De Mello, *Taking Flight,* page 159)

The pilgrim's heart was so attached to his sacred destination that the frightening, dangerous journey was, in a sense, easy for him. He "fell in love" with the good, and the vision of that good sustained him through fearsome conditions.

Civil rights activists in the United States have another way of talking about focusing on the good. They remind each other to "keep your eyes on the prize." Both phrases summon us to follow in Jesus' footsteps, to imitate his single-minded focus on the good. **3**

The following comments by Eric, a nineteen-year-old, illustrate courage, going for the good in spite of fears:

Deciding to go to college on my own was scary, but I've got to make the best of my life. I have enough use of my arms to move my wheelchair on relatively flat places. Anyway, the university arranged for a guy to help me get out of bed and get dressed in the morning, and to help me get ready for bed at night. That's the tough part.

But, you know, ever since the car accident, I've really had to adjust my priorities. I wanted to go into mechanical engineering, but now I want to do computer graphic design. Maybe I can even teach it someday, show kids that you can do a lot of things, even if you've got a disability.

Sure, I'm plenty afraid. Being a college freshman is an adjustment, let alone being a quadriplegic. Moving five hundred miles from home took getting used to, but what are my options? Sitting at home, going nowhere? No way!

- What is the overriding good that keeps Eric motivated, in spite of obstacles?
- Put yourself in Eric's place. Imagine you have been paralyzed in a car accident in your sophomore year of high school. What fears would you have about moving away from home to college?
- Consider how Eric may have used elements of the LISTEN process of decision making without being consciously aware of that process.

Going for the good is the most visual sign of courage, but in many ways it is simply the fruit of prior steps of courage. Unless we face the everyday fears that can keep us from the good in numerous small choices, it is nearly impossible to do what is right in major decisions, with which we have huge fears. In the next two sections, we will look at some common fears and suggest some positive ways of dealing with them.

For Review
- How does courage entail going for the good?

3
Have you ever loved something or someone so much that you did not mind facing all kinds of obstacles for what or whom you loved? In a paragraph, describe the good you fell in love with and the obstacles you had to deal with.

The Courage to Hang in There: The Commitment of Marriage

Committing yourself to something or someone for a lifetime takes a lot of courage. Commitment seems so risky, when the likelihood is that enormous problems and differences are going to come up somewhere down the line. This woman talks about the need for courage in a marriage, about having the courage to hang in there and to "keep your eyes on the prize" over many years:

> Now and then I hear the question: What good is a lifelong commitment? Wouldn't it be better to be able to back out of a vocation if things get difficult?
>
> My answer is an emphatic NO! Only a real, total commitment frees us to put our whole heart and soul into a project. For example, when I made a solemn vow to God on my wedding day that I would take my husband "till death do us part," I *meant* it. When times get rough, then, I don't say to myself, "If things keep going like this, I'll get a divorce." Instead, I pray to be stronger and more loving in living my wedding vow. The difficult time then turns out to be an opportunity for growth, and Russell and I end up closer than ever before. Neither of us needs to be afraid the other will simply quit trying. We are free to be ourselves, to love each other totally without holding back for fear of being hurt by the other's rejection. Yes, our marriage requires a lot of sacrifice, but the result is a joyful life together. (Paiva, "Lifetime Decisions")

- Besides a lifetime commitment, what are some other instances you see in everyday life of people having the courage to hang in there?

Above: A difficult, painful time in a marriage can be an opportunity for a couple to grow closer.

What Are We Afraid Of?

Every situation calling for courage involves the potential for harm, the possibility of assault on whatever makes us feel comfortable or secure. Fear is normally a healthy response—a warning signal of possible harm. If we are courageous, we pay attention to—rather than try to hide or deny—our fears. The virtue of courage helps us to face our fears directly. **4**

The following quotes, cases, and stories are examples of fears faced by a variety of persons. In most cases, the fear was overcome. As you read, think of how you would handle similar bouts with fear.

Rejection by Friends

The fear that we will be rejected by friends for doing something they do not like is familiar to most of us. Often we are surprised to find out that we have exaggerated the fear. Our friends, it turns out, are not nearly as hard on us as we imagine—or as we can be on ourselves. But at other times, our fear of rejection is well grounded in reality.

For instance, Adam talks about standing up to friends for what you know is right:

A lot of times your friends will be picking on some kid who's considered a geek or a nerd. You might try to get them to cut it out. Like saying, "Stop. It's not funny. That's stupid." What you get from your friends is "Tch . . . [a sound of disgust]." Or they might say: "Give me a break. It's just *Bob*. Like it really *matters*."

- In this example, what good is at stake?
- What might Adam say to himself to overcome the fear of rejection by his friends?

Boredom

The dread of boredom stands in the way of doing what is right more often than we might imagine. Here are some comments from people whose actions are being shaped by that fear:

1. You have a choice—either get stoned with everybody else or have a real dull night. What kind of choice is that?
2. When my mom told me I had to stay in and study last night, we got into this huge argument, as usual. She doesn't understand how restless I feel, like I'm in prison or something.
3. We'd been married six years, and we were all settled in with a kid. Then I started to have this desperate, trapped feeling. Life stretched out ahead of me, and all I could think of was fifty more boring years like this. I needed some excitement in my life, so I found someone who made me feel like my old self again. That was really good, for about six months.

- Why is the prospect of being bored a powerful fear for many people?
- Where does the thrill-a-minute approach to life come from? How does it get started? How is it kept up? What is a healthy alternative? **5**

Failure

The fear of failure keeps many of us from growing to our full potential. Even capable persons can be paralyzed by the fear of making a mistake, appearing stupid, or being thought of as foolish. **6**

A fifty-six-year-old woman relates what happened when her husband had to retire early because of emphysema:

4
What are your greatest fears? Make a list of ten of them. Choose your top three fears and rank them from 1 to 3, with 1 being strongest.

5
Choose one of the above three situations of fear of boredom. Then compose a piece of advice that you could give to the person involved, to help him or her cope with the dreaded situation.

6
Suppose you try something in spite of your fear of failure. Suppose also that your worst fear comes true, and you fall flat on your face. Write down a realistic message you could give yourself then.

When Clyde got sick and had to retire, I had no idea what we'd do. I hadn't had a job in thirty years, but we had to eat. The kids could help some, but they were all just getting started on their own.

Job hunting was real hard. I was scared to death they'd turn me down on first sight, especially when most of the interviewers were half my age! Without asking it directly, I could tell that all they really wanted to know was why a woman my age would try to go back to work. Nothing turned up for quite a while, and I was afraid nothing ever would. But then I got a job with Kmart. I guess they needed a "senior citizen" for their affirmative action quota. Anyway, I showed them. Now I'm assistant manager. I love it. I sure had to keep at it, though.

- Have you seen the fear of failure cramping the choices that young people make about courses in high school, further education, careers, and activities?

- Why do you suppose so many people are terrified of failing? Where does this fear come from?

■

Above, left and right: Trying anything challenging, like a sport, requires that we confront our fear of mistakes and failure.

Martin Luther King Jr.: Building Dikes of Courage

The great civil rights leader Martin Luther King Jr., a person who knew something about courage, had this to say on the subject:

> Courage and cowardice are antithetical.

> Courage is an inner resolution to go forward in spite of obstacles and frightening situations; cowardice is a submissive surrender to circumstance.

> Courage breeds creative self-affirmation; cowardice produces destructive self-abnegation.

> Courage faces fear and thereby masters it; cowardice represses fear and is thereby mastered by it.

> Courageous [persons] never lose the zest for living even though their life situation is zestless; cowardly [persons], overwhelmed by the uncertainties of life, lose the will to live.

> We must constantly build dikes of courage to hold back the flood of fear.

(A Testament of Hope, pages 512–513)

Loss of Job or Financial Security

A threat to our financial security can produce enormous fear. Great courage is required to take a needed action that could jeopardize one's job. Here is an account of Laurie's dilemma:

Laurie had to talk to someone. Ann seemed like a logical choice because she had been around the company for a long time and knew all the ins and outs.

"First," Laurie explained, "he just commented on how nice I looked, although I didn't like the way he'd raise his one eyebrow. I'd just smile and thank him. It gave me the creeps, though. That went on for a few weeks. Then he asked me out for a drink. I told him I was dating someone else, but he got pretty insistent—frowning and kind of stern."

"That stuff goes on all the time, Laurie. Sure, Jack sort of likes to come on to women, but you know, you just have to smile and flatter him a little. He'll leave you alone."

"But that's just it. Yesterday, I was working at my terminal on a brochure layout. Jack stuck his head in and said, 'Got a minute?' As he closed the door behind him, I got this eerie feeling. Well, so he was going to show me this document. Instead of handing it to me across the desk, the jerk came up and stood behind me. He bent over. His body was pressing my back. I pulled up closer to my desk, but he came on to me again. I was jammed up against the desk. I tried to stand up, but he wouldn't let the chair go back. I told him that if he didn't move, I'd scream. He backed off but said, 'You're really hyper. I didn't mean anything. If you're going to get like that, maybe we need to think about whether you really fit in here.' My phone buzzed. I picked it up fast. He left. Now what do I do? I'm not letting that creep come on to me like that."

"Well, knowing Jack, you'll be out on the streets if you cut him off completely."

"You're a lot of help, Ann. You make it sound like I should just let him do whatever."

"Oh, c'mon, don't get so upset. It's not that big of a deal. Besides, you do like your job, don't you?"

Disgusted, Laurie turned sharply and walked away without even replying to Ann's last comment.

Laurie's fury only grew as she reflected on her conversation with Ann. But she knew that Ann's attitude was common among the company's employees. She really could lose her job. Jack had the reputation of a snake. The more she thought about it, the angrier she got. She would not allow herself to be abused.

The next day Laurie set up an appointment with the personnel director. Minutes seemed like hours as she waited for the appointment. Laurie wracked her brain trying to think of some solution less drastic than accusing Jack of sexual harassment, but she couldn't. At 2:30, she nervously sat down in the personnel director's office.

"I want to report a sexual harassment incident that happened in my office. . . ."

- Short of losing her job, what else does Laurie have to fear by not being "nice" to Jack? List all the pressures on Laurie to keep her mouth shut and not make waves.
- In the LISTEN process, the S stands for "Seek insight beyond your own." Laurie did that by consulting Ann. However, she also had to weigh the value of Ann's advice, and she found it lacking. What are some examples of poor advice you have received from others?
- How can sexual harassment be prevented?
- What could a company do to reduce employees' fears about reporting sexual harassment? **7**

7
In the news or among people you know, find an example of someone who behaved courageously when faced with losing a job or financial security. Write up the example, focusing on the person's courage.

Not Being Understood

Sometimes you make a decision that you feel is good but that is put down by people you care about. The fear and the reality of not being understood can drive people from what they believe to be the best course of action. Courage stands as a shield of steadiness against a tide of misunderstanding. Here is Joe's example of this:

The summer before my senior year, my parents decided to go on a vacation to Michigan for two weeks and take my little sisters along. It was gonna be nice visiting my aunt and uncle and cousins out there. They asked me to go, too, but they knew I might be too busy with my job and all. I did want to earn a lot of money that summer, so it made sense to stay home and work. And my friends would think I was weird if I went on a family vacation instead of staying home with the house to myself. I sure didn't want to start senior year with that kind of reputation.

I was just about to tell my folks that I'd stay home when I started thinkin': This may be the last vacation we have as a family together. Next summer I'm gonna be runnin' around gettin' ready for college. And after that, who knows? It just sounded neat to be with my family. I figured I could miss two weeks of work.

My friends told me I was nuts and got on my case real bad, but I went on the trip. We had the greatest time we've ever had as a family. I'll always remember it.

- Trace the LISTEN process as Joe might have used it to make his decision.
- When no one seems to understand a decision you make, how do you know whether you're right?

The Unfamiliar

A powerful desire works to keep relationships and life patterns *the way they are*. This desire seems innocent enough, grounded as it is in the love of the familiar, the craving for security, and the need to predict what is coming. Yet because we are afraid to disturb what is familiar to us, we may cling to old patterns and ways of relating even when they are no longer good for us. **8**

■
Above, left and right: Tackling the unfamiliar may disturb our security, but it is necessary in order to grow.

8
Think of an old, familiar pattern of behaving or relating that you cling to and that gets in the way of doing what is best for you. In writing, describe that pattern and how you might be able to let go of it.

For instance, it is natural for a young person to begin a romantic relationship with another young person, to learn and grow through the relationship, and then for one reason or another, to move on and out of the relationship. This is part of the process of figuring out who you are and what you want in life. But the "moving on" phase can raise a lot of fears, prompt a lot of clutching at what once was. Overcoming the urge to cling to the familiar can be a courageous act.

Here is an account of a difficult breakup from Ben, age eighteen:

Jan and I started going out at the beginning of freshman year. We spent a whole lot of time together—movies, hiking, school dances, things like that. Pretty soon it was always Jan and Ben, like one name. We were a couple.

At the start of junior year, Jan tried out for the fall play. She got a big part and had rehearsals five days a week. So instead of doing homework with me, Jan was rehearsing. Instead of hanging out together on Saturday, she was doing homework. She was very good in the play, and I was proud of her, but she had changed so much. We were still a couple, but it was different. She had new interests, and I felt less and less connected to her.

Even so, I couldn't imagine being without her. We'd been together so long. I wasn't satisfied with the relationship, but I figured at least I had somebody—it made me nervous just to think that might change.

Finally, though, it did change. At the end of junior year, Jan told me she'd been accepted to be an intern at a summer theater in Ohio—four hundred miles away! It was really important to her. She said: "Don't feel bad, Ben. We've—I've—changed. It isn't like it was two years ago. I think I know what I want to do with my life. I'm scared to death, but I have to try it."

Well, I realized we were not a couple anymore. I'd have to move on, ready or not. It had always been comfortable knowing Jan was there, so I felt lost for a while. But moving on was the best thing for me. I've met new people and learned a lot about myself.

- Every breakup story has two sides. Imagine how Jan might have told her side.
- Compare and contrast Ben's and Jan's attitudes toward the familiar and unfamiliar.
- Letting go of the secure requires a willingness to step out into the unknown. What unknowns are Ben and Jan facing, and how is courage required?

Humiliation

In many cultures, the prospect of being shamed or humiliated is used to squelch behavior of which the culture disapproves. But fear of being shamed can also keep a person from doing what is right. In that case, it stands as an obstacle to be overcome by courage.

To be shamed or humiliated is to be told that we have no redeeming qualities or value. No one deserves such an unequivocal judgment. Thus, when someone risks being humiliated for some good decision, the words of Jesus from the Beatitudes apply especially to them:

"Blessed are they who are persecuted for the sake of righteousness,
    for theirs is the Kingdom of heaven.
Blessed are you when they insult you and persecute you and utter every kind of evil against you [falsely] because of me. Rejoice and be glad, for your reward will be great in heaven."

(Matthew 5:10–12) **9**

9
Think of a situation in which you would probably feel shamed, humiliated, or persecuted for making a good choice. Write an imaginary dialog in which you discuss your choice with the person who is humiliating you.

Here is an account of a struggle to choose what is right in the face of humiliation:

Brigid, a high school senior, comes from a well-respected, religious family. Her parents are considered pillars of her parish and the Catholic school she attends. Brigid has always made her parents proud with her straight A's and her long list of awards for extracurricular activities. Her mom and dad brag that "Brigid has never once given us a moment of trouble." And because Brigid loves and respects her parents, she has put a lot of energy into trying to be the perfect child her parents want.

At the moment, though, Brigid has confirmed her worst nightmare: she is eight weeks pregnant. It was one of those crazy things that happened when she had been drinking at a party. She barely knows the guy. He had seemed so neat. Now it's a nightmare that could become the most humiliating experience of her life.

Brigid has not confided her problem to a soul. She has been preoccupied with it all day, and has finally narrowed her choices down to two. These choices loom before her every waking moment and most of her fitful sleeping moments:

1. Carry the baby to term and give it up for adoption. This means she would be eight months pregnant at graduation. She would have to stand in front of everyone—practically parade in front of them—who had thought she was perfect. And her parents would never allow her to forget the warning they had issued when she started dating at age fifteen: "Don't you dare ever get into trouble. We couldn't live with the shame."

2. Have an abortion. Since nobody, even the guy, knows she is pregnant, she could get an abortion without anybody finding out. She could go downtown next Wednesday when they didn't have school, have the abortion done at the clinic, and pay for it out of her savings. Then she could go home and tell her parents she had cramps and needed to go to bed. It would be all over. No one would ever have to know. She knew it was wrong, but it would be over so fast that she might forget it ever happened. And she would avoid so much humiliation.

The issue of the morality of abortion will be considered in more detail in chapter 13. For now, think about this case simply as it illustrates the need for the virtue of courage:

- Which option would call for courage in Brigid?
- What images might be popping into Brigid's head when she thinks about carrying the baby to term?
- Is her fear of being humiliated by family and friends realistic?
- What are some strengths or self-learnings Brigid might develop over time if she is able to act courageously in this instance?
- How would having an abortion affect Brigid's development as a person? What tendencies would it reinforce in her?
- Think of other examples in which it is hard to face the consequences of previous ill-considered choices.

Physical Injury, Even Death

Many of us live such physically secure lives that it never occurs to us that we could be injured or even killed for the sake of something good. Others of us live in daily danger due to random violence or systematic violence in our neighborhoods. We may risk our life just to get an education—like the students described in chapter 5, who had to choose between going to school or staying safe at home, because they had a fair chance of being attacked for drug money if they did go to school.

Look Fear in the Face

Eleanor Roosevelt, a U.S. First Lady, a humanitarian, and a writer, struggled with shyness and poor self-confidence for many years. By the end of her life in 1962, she had won the admiration of the world for inspiring people to the cause of human rights and justice. Here is what she noted about courage in her book *You Learn by Living:*

You gain strength, courage and confidence by every experience in which you really stop to look fear in the face. You are able to say to yourself, "I lived through this horror. I can take the next thing that comes along." . . . You must do the thing you think you cannot do.

Soldiers in battle have always been praised for courageously risking their lives for a just cause. The early Christians esteemed martyrdom as the highest act in a life of faith. It was considered a privilege to follow the pattern of Jesus Christ. Down through the ages, thousands of martyrs have sacrificed their lives for Christ's Gospel. More recently, we have the courageous witness of people like the six Jesuit priests from El Salvador, their cook, and their cook's daughter, who were assassinated by Salvadoran armed forces in 1989.

The Jesuits had repeatedly spoken out against unjust conditions in their country, which cause hunger, misery, and early death for the majority of Salvadorans. They applied the Gospel to their country's situation, and for this they were silenced. Their deaths followed the assassinations of over ten thousand Salvadorans in the previous decade. Peasants, teachers, students, union leaders, and church people who were considered a threat to the established order were murdered—and often first tortured—to intimidate the opposition to the government. In 1980, the outspoken archbishop of San Salvador, Oscar Romero, was assassinated because of his defense of poor people in his country. Four U.S. Catholic women were also murdered in 1980 by Salvadoran National Guardsmen because of their missionary work with poor people and refugees of the civil war. **10**

In answer to the question, What are we afraid of? it appears that we have several sources of fear. Courage involves not avoiding those fears but acknowledging them and understanding where they come from.

For Review

- List and cite examples of eight fears that can be overcome by courage.

■
Above: Eleanor Roosevelt learned about courage through her own struggles with shyness and poor self-confidence.

10
Research one of the above examples of Catholics who faced injury and death for the sake of what they believed in. Find a quote or a life incident from one of these martyrs that demonstrates the courage with which the person lived.

Loosening the Grip of Fear

When children burn a finger or skin a knee, parents can help them to loosen the grip of pain by asking them to circle the hurt with one finger and to estimate the intensity of the pain on a scale of one to ten. These little behaviors help children realize that their injury is not life threatening.

Similarly, to be courageous when we are afraid requires that we loosen the grip that fear has on us. One way to think about dealing with any fear or anxiety is to remember this saying:

- **Name it. Claim it. Tame it.**

When we can identify what it is we are afraid of (name it) and recognize it as our own fear and not be ashamed of it (claim it), we are on our way to loosening the fear's grip on us (taming it). **11**

Strategies for Taming Our Fears

As you well know, facing one's fears is hardly ever easy. Courage is not something we automatically know how to put to use. Like all the other moral virtues, courage is a habit we need to cultivate and nurture through practice. Certain "tools" or strategies can be used to aid us in taming our fears. Let's look at a number of strategies as they apply to some of the previous examples, as well as others.

Seek Alternatives

Looking for alternative ways of dealing with a fearful situation can help loosen fear's grip on us. This calls for some creative imagining:

- What if I do this instead of that? Will it lessen the possibility for harm and still accomplish the good?

- Are there other ways to look at the situation that will help me to overcome my fear?

Questions like these can put us into a different frame of mind, enabling us to see that there are almost always other possibilities. When we realize that nothing is fated to turn out a certain way, our fears no longer paralyze us.

Applied to the fear of boredom, for example, the strategy of seeking alternatives can open up a whole new world. Simply asking questions like the following can get our creative juices flowing: What do I find interesting? What would I really like to do? Who else might have interests similar to mine? It takes a great deal of courage to break out of old patterns—even if they bore us to death. Imagining possibilities can help make this step into the unknown less threatening.

Be Resourceful

Being resourceful, like the previous strategy, involves looking for options. We ask: What resources can help me deal with this situation? What talents or skills do I have? Are there other people I can turn to for help? and so forth.

In the case on page 146, Brigid is trying to handle the situation of her pregnancy by herself, without consulting anyone who cares about her or shares her values about life. Perhaps a teacher at school, a counselor, or even a friend might be willing to help her bear the burden of this decision. Brigid may even be surprised to find that her parents are more sympathetic than she gives them credit for. Other agencies besides the family planning clinic may be available to Brigid as well, such as Birthright and Catholic Charities, which assist women seeking alternatives to abortion.

11
Apply the first two parts of this saying to a fear you have. Write out what you might say to yourself to name the fear and to claim it.

Plan, Plan, Plan

Being prepared decreases the anxiety caused by situations like looking for a new job. Most job-hunting manuals advise people to plan for their interviews. The manuals often offer suggestions like these:

1. Know your own skills and how your talents would apply to the job.
2. Find out as much information about the company as you can.
3. Imagine possible interview questions and how you could best answer them.

Anyone who has ever had to plan an event knows that being prepared for a variety of situations can alleviate a number of worries and embarrassing situations. Planning is essential for meeting any kind of goal, from making sure the prom is a success to fulfilling a career ambition. When we plan, we give ourselves guidelines to follow—we are not just shooting in the dark. In the process, the fear of failure is replaced with the courage to create. **12**

Challenge Yourself

Young people often do something daring as a way of preparing themselves for future situations calling for even greater nerve. For instance, one high school senior says that the reason she watches horror movies is that she wants to be a doctor someday and she needs to get used to seeing a lot of blood. This young person has the right idea in trying to challenge herself, her reasoning being: If I can handle this, then I'll probably be able to handle even-more-difficult situations later on.

However, the key to challenging ourselves is to know the difference between those things that

■
Above: To tame our fears is to loosen the grip they have on us.

12
Find an example in writing of a person—famous or not—who overcame great obstacles and went on to become highly creative.

Try a Different Perspective

Another way to loosen fear's grip on us and gain courage is to put our fears into a larger context. When compared with what someone else might be dealing with, our fears can suddenly seem quite manageable. For instance, Eric (page 138), who decided not to let his disability stand in the way of his going to college, had difficult circumstances to deal with. Eric saw how fortunate he was to still have some use of his arms, enabling him to move his wheelchair on flat places. And his mind was as sharp as ever, unaffected by the car accident. In other words, instead of seeing his glass as half-empty, he saw it as half-full. (Think for a moment about some fear you face and ask yourself how it measures up against a problem like Eric's.) Putting our fears into perspective can help us to transcend them and lessen their negative influence on our life.

Jesus' Way

In previous discussions of the virtues of Jesus, we have had a glimpse of the various challenges that Jesus encountered in his ministry. The biggest challenge that Jesus faced in his life—the greatest one most of us will face—was that of his death. This Gospel scene, aptly called "the agony in the garden," vividly conveys for us Jesus' way of grappling with immense fear.

Just before Jesus was arrested and later crucified, he went to the garden of Gethsemane to pray with his disciples:

Then he began to be filled with fear and distress. He said to them, "My heart is filled with sorrow to the point of death. Remain here and stay awake." He advanced a little and fell to the ground, praying that if it

help us to grow and those that do more harm than good. Although watching horror movies might lessen this young woman's squeamishness about blood, overexposure to violence could deaden her emotional responses, affecting her ability to be caring and sensitive—qualities also important for being a good doctor.

Meeting small, positive challenges builds our confidence and broadens our range of experiences—both of which are good resources to tap into for nurturing courage. Such testing of inner strength is a positive way to "get in shape" for life.

Above: Meeting challenges builds our confidence and broadens our range of experiences, thus nurturing courage in us.

were possible this hour might pass him by. He kept saying, "*Abba* (O Father), you have the power to do all things. Take this cup away from me. But let it be as you would have it, not as I." (Mark 14:34–36)

Jesus' companions could not stay awake with him to pray, and Peter was soon to deny he even knew him. Jesus must have felt abandoned and terrified of what was coming. One Gospel account says that Jesus was so fearful that he sweat drops of blood. In his greatest time of need, Jesus turned to God in prayer. Asking and trusting God to be with us can be a great source of courage, even in less perilous situations.

Jesus and people like the martyrs of El Salvador did not discover courage all at once when they needed it to face death. Their lives spoke continually of courage as they wrestled with the fears that accompany everyday life. Consider an action such as Jesus' defending the life of the adulterous woman before the harsh scribes and Pharisees (John 8:2–11). Jesus' courage in that instance was part of a whole life of courageous acts that prepared him to face the fear of death when the time came. The strategies presented in this chapter— even prayer—will not *eliminate* our fears. They can, however, help to loosen the grip that fear may have on us, freeing us to do what is right and good.

The Night Is Dark and Long

The following is a prayer written as a poem. It was found on a scrap of paper in a bombarded British trench in Tunisia during a World War II battle:

> Stay with me, God. The night is dark,
> The night is cold: my little spark
> Of courage dies. The night is long;
> Be with me, God, and make me strong.
> (Reprinted from *Poems from the Desert*)

For Review

- What saying can help us deal with fear or anxiety?
- Briefly describe five strategies for taming our fears.
- How did Jesus grapple with immense fear?

Above: French soldiers take cover in a trench during World War II.

An Everyday Prayer

Sometimes, getting up in the morning is an act of courage. For one or more reasons, the day looms ahead as dreadful or depressing. A person may feel overwhelmed at the thought of a test, of nerve-wracking, hated work to be done, or of a meeting that will inevitably be filled with conflict and tension. Perhaps there is nothing specific. It just may be a time in the person's life when everything looks gloomy.

This young person follows Jesus' way of finding courage:

When I know I'm going to have a really tough day—like today I had to give an oral report in history class—I sometimes lie in bed for a few minutes after the alarm goes off. I don't know if you'd call this praying or not, but I think about what I have to do that day, and I ask God to be with me and to give me the courage and strength to face things.

I also try to thank God for just giving me another day to live, and for my friends and family, and my dog, Sam. I don't think I've ever admitted to my friends that I do this—you know, pray and stuff—but it sure helps calm me down and makes me feel like I can make it through whatever I need to do. If nothing else, it makes it easier to get out of bed on mornings like this.

- What helps you to get out of bed in the morning on tough days?

Above: Prayer can help us face the day with a sense of hope and calmness.

Nothing Can Separate Us from God's Love

Saint Paul's Letter to the Romans, addressed to a community suffering many trials, speaks to us today as well:

Who will separate us from the love of Christ? Will hardship, or distress, or persecution, or famine, or nakedness, or peril, or sword? As it is written,

"For your sake we are being killed all day long;
we are accounted as sheep to be slaughtered."

No, in all these things we are more than conquerors through him who loved us. For I am convinced that neither death, nor life, nor angels, nor rulers, nor things present, nor things to come, nor powers, nor height, nor depth, nor anything else in all creation, will be able to separate us from the love of God in Christ Jesus our Lord. (Romans 8:35–39, NRSV)

We could echo Paul in our own litany of fears that would seem to defeat us: rejection by our friends, humiliation, failure, a painful breakup, a problem with alcohol or drugs, a divorce in our family, or a terrible job market with the sense that we have no future. Paul is telling us, though, that no fear, no obstacle—not even death itself—can come between us and God. God is with us for the long haul—forever. We can count on that.

Christian hope is the sense that God loves us and is with us in all things, bringing about good even in the darkest times. This hope is grounded in the Resurrection of Jesus, which assures us that life and goodness—not death or fear or any problem we can imagine—will ultimately have the last word.

Even the smallest flicker of hope can keep our courage alive in times of trouble. This truth was symbolized powerfully to thousands of people in a marvelous occurrence during the visit of Pope Paul VI to the United States in 1976.

The pope was addressing a full house at the huge Madison Square Garden in New York City on a hot, steamy day. All of a sudden, the electricity failed, causing a blackout. The whole arena was in pitch darkness. You could not see your hand in front of your face.

After a few moments of restless reaction in the crowd, someone in one corner of the vast arena lit a match. Miraculously, it seemed, you could see throughout the arena, although dimly.

A murmur went up from the crowd. The symbolic impact of the moment was clear: In the darkest hour, even one small flame of hope casts a great light. **13**

13
Recall a time that seemed to be your "darkest hour." Write a reflection describing that time, including any "small flame of hope" that helped you survive.

8

Wholeness:
Toward
Strength,
Beauty,
and Happiness

To understand wholeness, the fourth cardinal virtue, let's hear from someone who has struggled to become whole.

One Person's Struggle for Wholeness

Through her last two years of high school, Jessica, who's now nineteen, had the eating disorder called bulimia. Bulimia is characterized by binge eating followed by purging (vomiting or taking laxatives or water-loss pills to lose weight). Having been through treatment for the disorder, Jessica is now on her way to living a more balanced, healthy life.

When I was bulimic, I was really at war with myself. It wasn't just that I wanted to eat and purge. It was that in my mind, everything that went wrong had to do with my appearance. My whole life was being turned into an eating disorder. Like if a test at school didn't go well, if I couldn't come up with enough money for college, if a guy I liked didn't ask me out, I somehow blamed it all on my appearance. I wasn't perfect enough, pretty enough, thin enough.

Deep down I had the feeling no one loved me because I wasn't perfect enough. I figured that had to be why my mom got depressed so often, because I wasn't good enough, and why my dad left us when I was little.

So I was tearing myself apart trying to become perfect, but all the while I was becoming *less* perfect.

My life was wild, crazy, dangerous, scary. It was like I was in a car out of control, and I couldn't put on the brakes.

But then one day in my senior year, I finally agreed to check into the hospital for a treatment program. It was like I slid over into the passenger seat and let somebody else—the hospital staff, my doctor—get in the driver's seat for a while. And we just sat there with the car idling, letting traffic pass by, not going anyplace—just stopping the craziness for a while until I was ready to get back in the driver's seat.

When I left the hospital after a couple of months, it was like pulling out slowly into traffic and driving along carefully. I was able to drive all by myself, and I took the car off to college. And now I know how to use the brakes real well and how to steer the car so it doesn't get out of control. I know how to have self-restraint—not just with eating but with lots of things—which is what I need if I'm going to be able to set goals for myself and a direction for my life. Like I'm really excited about writing poetry. Now I have the energy to focus on that and develop my writing. I gave a couple of poetry readings this year, and one of my professors thinks I can get my poetry published!

In the treatment program I was in, I learned that what I was trying to do with the purging was, like, to get rid of all the bad in me that made me not perfect, unlovable. I found out that I can *never* be perfect. But I can be *whole* if I accept the parts of me that I don't like as part of who I am. And I learned that there really *are* people who love me for the way I am, for me, with all my faults, not for my appearance—like my grandma. She's been so important to me. **1**

The Journey to Wholeness

We are on a journey to wholeness that bears many similarities to Jessica's journey, even if it differs in specifics. Most of us do not have an eating disorder, nor do we have to contend with some of the

1
List five other life experiences a teenager might have that feel like driving an out-of-control car and not being able to put on the brakes.

difficult family circumstances that Jessica has had to face. But we are all struggling with these issues:

- finding ourselves lovable
- balancing the various parts of ourselves into a unified order
- freeing ourselves of "hooks" that seem to grab us and control us
- learning the self-restraint that allows us to set directions for ourselves and passionately invest ourselves in something worthwhile

Wholeness, Not Perfection

To be whole is not to be perfect, as Jessica discovered. Rather, the virtue of **wholeness** is the balancing of all the parts of the self to create a dynamic and harmonious order. More than any other virtue, wholeness focuses on building the beauty and strength of the self, which makes happiness possible. (In the Catholic tradition, this fourth cardinal virtue has been called *temperance*. Here it is termed *wholeness* because that word sums up better for our modern ears the rich meaning of the virtue.)

Humans are complex creatures. We are physical (biological), rational (intellectual), emotional (feeling), social, and spiritual. If we deny any of these dimensions of ourselves, or wage war against them, we become out of balance. Like Jessica, who experienced herself as a war zone, we may try to deny the goodness of our body, of some of our feelings, or of any other aspect of ourselves that seems unacceptable. Or we may deny our spiritual side—our innate longing for goodness, truth, and beauty. Or we may throw out our reasoning capacities in favor of following our impulses for physical pleasure. All these behaviors distort the self, making us less than the whole human being we are meant to be. **2**

Like novice tightrope walkers, we cannot maintain our balance for long. Weary with effort, we have to cling to a supporting post. And when life sometimes nudges the rope, we fall into the net below. We are challenged, though, to practice long and hard, and with God's help, we can attain many moments filled with the joy of wholeness.

Jesus and the Journey

An incident from Jesus' ministry illustrates how his wholeness attracted others who were seeking healing in body and spirit. Jesus was making his way through a crowd of people to the house of a man named Jairus, whose daughter was dying.

As [Jesus] went, the crowds almost crushed him. And a woman afflicted with hemorrhages for twelve years, who [had spent her whole livelihood on doctors and] was unable to be cured by anyone, came up behind him and touched the tassel on his cloak. Immediately her bleeding stopped. Jesus then asked, "Who touched me?" While all were denying it, Peter said, "Master, the crowds are pushing and pressing in upon you." But Jesus said, "Someone has touched me; for I know that power has gone out from me." When the woman realized that she had not escaped notice, she came forward trembling. Falling down before him, she explained in the presence of all the people why she had touched him and how she had been healed immediately. [Jesus] said to her, "Daughter, your faith has saved you; go in peace." (Luke 8:42–48)

In his ministry of healing and preaching, Jesus continually called people to wholeness. He recognized the connections between the health of the body and the life of the spirit, and he longed to see people come alive and feel well in every dimension

---

2
Examine a mobile whose parts are hanging in a delicate balance. See what happens when you put extra weight on one of the parts by holding it down or take off weight from one of the parts by holding it up. In a paragraph, explain how a mobile symbolizes the virtue of wholeness.

A Time for Everything

The Hebrew Scriptures contain one of the most beautiful and famous pieces of wisdom about living a balanced, whole life.

For everything there is a season, and a time for every matter under heaven:

a time to be born, and a time to die;

a time to plant, and a time to pluck up what is planted;

a time to kill, and a time to heal;

a time to break down, and a time to build up;

a time to weep, and a time to laugh;

a time to mourn, and a time to dance;

a time to throw away stones, and a time to gather stones together;

a time to embrace, and a time to refrain from embracing;

a time to seek, and a time to lose;

a time to keep, and a time to throw away;

a time to tear, and a time to sew;

a time to keep silence, and a time to speak;

a time to love, and a time to hate;

a time for war, and a time for peace.

(Ecclesiastes 3:1–8, NRSV)

- How does this passage speak to you about your life?

of their person. No doubt his own wholeness brought others—such as this woman who was not only ill but also considered unclean and untouchable because of her bleeding—to seek that same virtue for themselves. Life calls forth life. The strength of Jesus' healthy, vital self could be felt by everyone around him. **3**

This chapter will focus on three significant qualities of wholeness and the challenges and struggles of growing in these qualities:

1. **freedom**
2. **unity, order,** and **direction**
3. **self-restraint**

For Review

- What is the virtue of wholeness?
- How did Jesus' wholeness affect others?

■

Above, left and right: Jesus longs to see people come alive in every dimension of their person.

3
Do you know someone whose vitality calls forth life in other people? Describe that person in writing.

Freedom:
The Joy of Being Unhooked

Not in the Grip of Something

One meaning of freedom is that we are not "in the grip" of something or someone. Rather, we are in charge of ourselves. We can calmly consider what we are doing and make choices with our whole self.

On the other hand, when we feel compelled to act a certain way or do a certain thing, we are not free. If what compels us is a craving or an urge or a desire within, we may be "hooked." We have to ask whether we are making our decisions wholeheartedly or if some compulsion has put the rest of our deciding self out of a job. This is how Jessica felt when she had the eating disorder: "everything that went wrong had to do with my appearance."

How Do We Get Hooked?

Short-term Versus Long-term Pleasures

The problem of being hooked comes when we get stuck on a short-term pleasure that feels like the key to happiness. For instance, we discover casual sex or a drug like alcohol. Or perhaps it is new clothes, work, or television. We try it; the pleasure seems to work—that is, we feel high, or important, or loved, or pain-free, or less anxious. But the good feeling soon wears off, and we are at a loss as to how to regain it. So we try the short-term pleasure again and again. After a while, we seem to need it in order to feel just okay. The short-term pleasure takes on an excessive importance in our life.

Some people go from one short-term pleasure to another, restless to find real, lasting happiness. But this happiness escapes them because they are hooked by the short-term pleasures and have no time to discover long-term pleasures like these:

- having loving relationships
- creating and appreciating beauty
- investing yourself wholeheartedly in a challenge
- contributing your talents
- learning a skill
- helping others grow
- being true to yourself **4**

Many adults have problems with alcohol, other drugs, and casual sex. The focus on examples of teenagers here is not intended to imply that drug abuse and casual sex are primarily problems of young people. Yet the patterns for these abuses often do begin in adolescence. The hurt and tragedy that we are seeing today in the lives of many adults and their children could perhaps have been prevented if the adults had been aware of the start of abusive patterns when they were younger.

4
Select a short-term and a long-term pleasure from those listed in the text and write each one at the top of separate columns. Under each pleasure, create two narrower columns, one labeled + and one –.

Then list the benefits (+) and drawbacks (–) of the long-term and the short-term pleasure in their proper columns.

Happiness as Forgetting Your Problems?

Consider the situation of Lynn, a high school senior who tried to find happiness but instead found herself in a self-destructive pattern of behavior:

Lynn says this about happiness: "Happiness is an important part of life. . . . Usually I'm not happy. I have a bad self-image. . . . I put myself down all the time." When asked what happiness means for her, Lynn replies, "Being at clubs, lots of people around, loud music—you forget about your problems." Lynn also talks about what typically happens at parties in clubs: she gets drunk and has sex with a guy.

Recently, though, Lynn has had a different experience of happiness. She met a guy at a party. When he suggested sex, she said no. "I just didn't want it to be like it was with the last guy I dated. Sex was just another way to get high—but it messed everything up." Amazingly to Lynn, this guy was okay with her saying no: "He just put his arm around me and we cuddled. It felt so good. He cared about me. It was the first time a guy ever said okay when I said no."

Lynn is just beginning to get a handle on what has been a very unhappy life for her. She is starting treatment for her alcohol and other drug problems. Best of all, she is discovering something about self-respect.

- What do you think of Lynn's idea of happiness?
- Explain the connection between Lynn's "very bad self-image" and the things she has chosen to do in the past.
- The popular media often give the impression that casual sex is liberating, freeing. Lynn did not experience it that way. How was her freedom hampered by these sexual relationships?
- How would the LISTEN process help someone like Lynn?

Drugs and Sex: Why Do It?

This section explores some rationales that many teenagers give for getting into self-destructive habits with drugs and casual sex.

Why Alcohol and Other Drugs?

Why do teenagers use alcohol and other drugs? Here are some typical answers:

1. It makes me feel high.
2. It makes me feel sexy.
3. It relaxes me.
4. It makes me feel like an adult.
5. I want to know how it feels to be drunk. People say it's so great.
6. I want to have something to tell my friends about later on.
7. I don't want to be "out of it" at parties.
8. It's a way to show that I can make my own decisions and that I don't let my parents tell me what to do.
9. It makes it easier for me to have fun and let go with my friends.
10. It makes me think deeper.
11. It takes away my problems and worries.
12. It keeps me from being bored.
13. It helps me cope with the pain in my life.

- Have you heard any other reasons that teenagers give for using alcohol and other drugs?
- Evaluate the reasons given: What do you think of them?
- Alcohol can make a person feel high at first. Its overall effect, though, is depression. Why, then, do many depressed people use alcohol?
- What are the hazards of "moderate" drinking or use of other drugs by teenagers?

Some Cold Facts on Alcohol and Other Drugs

The following statistics come from several national research studies:

- Roughly 43 percent of all high school seniors have used illegal drugs; 87 percent have used alcohol.
- Almost 30 percent of seniors surveyed had gotten drunk during the month prior to the survey. About 1 percent of seniors get drunk daily.
- Approximately 23 percent of tenth graders and 14 percent of eighth graders admitted to having had five drinks during the two weeks prior to the survey.
- Nearly 8 percent of tenth graders surveyed first used alcohol in the fourth grade.
- About 20 percent of all high school students are suffering from their drug use to the extent that they need treatment.
- About 75 percent of teen pregnancies result from sex during intoxication.
- According to a survey, 80 percent of teenagers say they've ridden with a drunk driver.

- Over 90 percent of teen suicides occur while the person is intoxicated.
- About 50 percent of young people with a drug problem have at least one parent with a drug problem.

- Each day, nine teenagers are killed in alcohol-related automobile accidents.

Do we have a significant problem with drugs and alcohol in our society?

Above: Drunk driving can have serious legal consequences, but more important, it can be fatal.

Why Casual Sex?

A similar list of reasons could be drawn up in answer to the question Why do teenagers have casual sex?

Many of the reasons would overlap with those in the list of teenagers' reasons for using alcohol and other drugs:

- wanting to feel high, desired, adult
- wishing to escape from problems
- getting away from boredom
- being curious about what it is like
- wanting to brag to friends about it later

As one girl said, "You want so bad to feel wanted—and you want that even more when you've been drinking."

Andy, a junior, describes how peers influence one's decisions about sex, at least for boys in his high school:

Peer pressure to have sex is tremendous. You have to live up to everybody's expectations. Guys say, "Oh, I had three girls this weekend—breakfast, lunch, and dinner." It's just a lot of baloney talk. But it puts you under pressure to do it yourself to have something to talk about.

Then there's the idea that "if you're drunk, do it." It's just assumed by everybody that you'll have sex. Alcohol just gives people an excuse.

- What similarities do problems with drugs and casual sex have?
- Why do some people feel the need to brag about their sexual experiences?
- Is there a double standard for casual sex? In other words, do people think differently of girls who engage in casual sex than they do of boys?

What Sex Is Meant For

Regardless of the reasons that a person gives for having casual sex, this thinking always bypasses the real meaning of sex and sexual expression. In the Christian understanding, sexuality is a wonderful gift from God. It is intended to give us pleasure and happiness as we unite with another person. Sex *is* a high, and it is meant to be so. Christianity is not antisex or antipleasure; the Christian tradition affirms that our sexuality is beautiful and good and meant to be enjoyed.

But enjoyment of our genital sexual expression is meant to happen in a committed, lasting relation-

---

■

Above, left and right: The enjoyment of full sexual expression is meant to happen in a committed, lasting relationship, one that is truly loving and open to new life.

ship, one that is truly loving and open to new life. Sexual intercourse expresses that commitment and helps the couple build it.

Using sex casually as a short-term pleasure merely to get high or to express a passing attraction distorts the purpose of sex as a deeply human act. Besides, it may cost a person the chance to build great long-term relationships with individuals of the other gender. A person can become accustomed to seeing members of the other gender as sex objects, not as friends. Marriage requires a lot more friendship than romance, and one who intends to marry someday needs to cultivate the art of friendship more than the skills of sex. In addition, the hurt and personal wreckage that can come from treating a powerful reality like sex as a casual encounter is devastating. **5**

Between casual sex and the sex of a committed, lasting relationship, of course, lies quite a span of other kinds of sex. There is, for instance, the sex of "going together" and the sex of "we're really in love" without a pledge that this relationship will be permanent. These contexts for sex, although not casual or merely recreational, still fall short of the way that God wants us to enjoy sexual relations. A section later in this chapter presents a discussion about why marriage is the right place, the truly human place, for sexual intercourse.

Slavery That Looks Like Freedom

Self-deception:
A Necessary Skill for Being Hooked

Many forms of being hooked are approved, even encouraged, in our society. This makes it especially easy to deceive oneself about the rightness or wrongness of certain choices.

Consider the dynamic of self-deception as it relates to Ted's lifestyle:

In the cab from the airport to his home, Ted turned on his laptop computer and went over, again, the figures from the latest round of contract negotiations. He paid the driver and walked to his door. As he fumbled with his keys, he suddenly noticed that the house was completely dark.

Inside, he turned on the lights and saw the note: Marga, his wife of nine years, had taken off with their two children. The note said, "The ten seconds it'll take you to read this note equals the amount of attention you've paid to me and the kids in the last six months. I'm divorcing you because your *real* wife is your damned job. Don't worry—as if you could—we're at my parents'."

Ted became angry immediately. He stormed upstairs thinking, Doesn't she get it? I *have* to work long hours in order to get all the things I want for her and the kids! I'm working on the most important deal of my career, and that means twenty-hour days traveling all over the country. And I could close the deal a lot sooner if I could just get Dan out of the picture—I don't need him! He's a drag on the whole project. With Marga's note still in his hand, Ted brainstormed ways of getting Dan off the project.

As he turned to reach for a pen, he remembered the note. He went to the phone to call his in-laws but couldn't remember their number. Fortunately, it was programmed into the portable phone downstairs. Ted pushed the buttons, and after eight rings his father-in-law answered, half asleep.

"Lyle, this is Ted. Put Marga on please."

"She's asleep. She doesn't want to talk to you anyway. It's almost midnight, for God's sake." The phone clicked loudly.

5
Do you agree or disagree with the Catholic position that sex should not be used in a casual way or merely as recreation? Explain your answer in writing.

Ted had lost all track of time. The adrenaline had been pumping all day, and he still felt high—and angry at Marga and Lyle. But then he thought: Dan's health isn't real good. Maybe I can get him off the project because the pressure's too much for him. . . . He can't keep up with it all. . . . Ted broke into a wide grin. "Yeah!" he said out loud to the empty house, "I can hold *that* over his head!"

Ted gulped down a martini, took a shower, and went to bed. He suddenly remembered a phone call he had to make first thing in the morning. He sat up, switched on the light, and jotted a reminder on a notepad he kept on the nightstand for just that purpose. Ted always wrote down ideas and reminders on the spot, wherever he was. Some of these little notes had proven very profitable. It drove Marga nuts—she'd grumble when he'd wake up in the middle of the night to write something down. Ted thought, with a frown, If only she'd understand—it's all for her and the kids.

With the light off again, Ted tossed and turned. He thought to himself, Things will work out with Marga. I'll negotiate some new arrangement with her. We'll take a few days off and go somewhere, as soon as this deal's done. She just needs a little attention. Then Dan's face swam into Ted's imagination. What is wrong with Dan? He used to be a fire eater, wheeling and dealing. The old Dan would have really helped this deal happen. In the back of his mind, Ted was trying to pull out a memory of a conversation he had had about five years ago with his coworker Charlie. Ted had asked about the change in Dan's personality, about his loss of steam. Charlie had whispered, "It's his wife. She almost drowned in the bottom of a bottle of vodka—know what I mean? He came home one day and she was passed out, nearly dead. His kids were a mess, too. The whole family is working it all out now. So he spends a lot of time with his family. Too much, maybe—I don't know why the boss keeps him around. Dan keeps his old accounts going, but not much new. I guess that's enough, but he'll never hit the big time."

Ted knew that could never happen to him. He'd never lose his steam as a contract negotiator. And he'd win Marga back. He rolled over and checked the alarm. He had an early flight to Boston, then on to Memphis; he'd call Marga from one of the airports. Just before he nodded off, he asked God to let his big deal go through, and "Bless Marga, Tim, and Lydia."

■
Above: Self-deception plays a major part in most addictions, such as an addiction to work.

- To what is Ted hooked?
- What is the payoff for Ted? What price must he pay to hold on to it?
- What insight does Ted have that could help him see the trap he is in?
- How does Ted deceive himself?
- How do society's values reinforce Ted's problem and his self-deception?

An Addictive Society?

Many commentators have noted the tendency in North American society for people to become *addicted*—another term for being hooked. Addictions can run the gamut—from chronic overspending to having the "perfect" body at any health cost to being pumped up by caffeine.

For instance, just when North Americans are beginning to abandon cigarette smoking as the number one death-causing practice, young people in growing numbers, especially males, are taking up snuff and chewing tobacco. Health experts say that smokeless tobacco has the same addictive potential as cigarettes. Its increasing use, they assert, will lead to an oral cancer epidemic early in the next century.

Another addiction among young people is gambling. A study that surveyed 2,770 high school students predicted that gambling would become "the major form of teenage recreation in the U.S., and it also will be the major addiction" of the 1990s. The same study reported that in 1989, seven million teenagers in the United States gambled, and one million of them had serious addictive problems with their gambling.

In the United States, legalized gambling (for those eighteen years of age or older), especially in the form of lotteries and casinos, has become more and more common in recent years. TV commercials and newspaper ads encourage us to "take a chance" by buying lottery tickets and visiting casinos, leading us to believe that easy prosperity is just around the corner. In such a climate it is not surprising that young people will be tempted by the lure of big winnings, and some will develop addictive behavior. **6**

Getting Unhooked

Getting unhooked, or even better, not getting hooked in the first place, requires a courageous honesty and discipline with oneself. As discussed earlier, self-deception is a great obstacle to true freedom.

6
In writing, compare and contrast a psychological addiction like gambling or chronic overspending with a physical addiction like alcoholism. What traits do these addictions have in common? How do they differ?

Mark, now age twenty, gives us an example of the honesty and discipline that is needed to become free. He had been drinking heavily, smoking marijuana, and experimenting with many other illegal drugs for several years. Finally, after he dropped out of school in eleventh grade, Mark's parents insisted he get treatment for his addiction. Reluctantly, at the age of eighteen, Mark entered Straight, a drug rehabilitation program. The following are several of his comments·about his experiences, which appeared in an issue of *Youth Update:*

"By the 11th grade, I was just so lost. If someone would say, "Hey, let's go get high," I'd be gone. I had an addiction to peer pressure. And when you start depending on drugs for happiness, security and pleasure, or listening to peer pressure, that's when trouble starts. . . .

". . . Somehow I thought I was *really making it* away from home, when actually I was at the lowest point of my life. . . .

"[After my parents got me into treatment,] I was in Straight two years. I worked a lot on being honest. I learned about self-acceptance and dealing with guilt. After I graduated from the program, I couldn't believe I was *off* drugs. I was relieved. I knew I was going to stay off because I was ready. I had been at the bottom. I even was able to finish high school.

". . . The biggest thing I lacked was security. I was so worried about what other people thought about me. But I don't have to be scared about anything anymore because I have security in *myself.*

"When I moved out of the house recently, my parents treated me like I was an adult. That's great. I can socialize with them and be me, which is a really great feeling. I've matured a lot. And my sisters and I get along a whole lot better than we used to.

"I am Catholic; so's my family. I'm not a religious person, but I do believe in God. I don't know if he's a big reason for me staying straight. But when I have problems that could cause me not to stay straight, I go to him and they'll be answered."

After finishing treatment, Mark entered a university, an accomplishment of which he was rightfully proud.

Freedom is not realized without struggle. Often the persons who most value their freedom are the ones who have gotten trapped and have managed to become free through hard effort, the support of a community, and God's grace.

Most of us are not addicted in a medical sense. But we all have our hooks—things that grab us and seem to "make" us act in ways that are against our better judgment. Everyone has the potential to become more unhooked—to grow in freedom and therefore to become more whole. **7**

For Review

- Contrast short-term pleasures with the pleasures of long-term happiness.
- What rationales for teenagers' doing drugs are similar to those for having casual sex?
- In the Christian understanding, what is sexuality intended for?
- Give three examples of things that can hook us, besides casual sex, alcohol, and other drugs.

7
In what way do you have the potential to become unhooked and grow in freedom? In a paragraph, describe one hook you would like to be free from.

Unity, Order, and Direction: Peaceful and Purposeful

Related to the freedom of wholeness are other qualities of the self—unity, order, and direction.

Not a War Zone

Being unified means that a person is not a war zone within. The dimensions of the person—the body, the emotions, the mind, the spirit—are not at war with each other, chewing up all the energy inside the person in a useless struggle. Recall that Jessica described her eating disorder as being "at war with myself." Being unified does not mean that the person never feels inner conflict. But it does mean that the person is not continually in turmoil—out of whack. Instead, the person experiences herself or himself as living in some kind of order and harmony within.

Living in order allows the person to be focused and purposeful, to have a sense of where he or she is headed and how to get there. Those who feel only inner chaos are not able to direct their energies to a purpose single-mindedly. Without being channeled, their energies evaporate and are lost.

In Touch with One's Needs

Persons with unity are able to stay in touch with what is happening inside them. They sense how they feel and what they need to maintain their own sense of peace. They can "talk to" themselves realistically, acting as a friend to themselves. Such persons know their own boundaries—when and where they need to draw the line between their own needs and the needs (or demands or wishes) of others. This is not selfishness but legitimate self-caring. For example:

Leroy is a key player on his high school's basketball team, the top scorer. Before most games, though, he becomes quite nervous, scared that he will blow it for the team when they are depending on him so much. One thing that contributes to Leroy's nervousness is that in the ten minutes before a game starts, the coach and all the players gather in the locker room to get each other pumped up. It seems to build team spirit, all that cheering and getting wound up. But for Leroy, the cheering only makes him feel more on edge. This tension carries over into the game so that even when he scores high, by the end of most games he feels like a nervous wreck.

In the last few games of the season, Leroy has tried something different. He stays with the guys for about five minutes in their pep session before the game. But when he feels himself getting edgy, he goes off to a corner of the locker room by himself, takes some deep breaths, and says things to himself that he knows he needs to hear: "Just stay calm, Leroy. Focus on the game, not on how many points you make. Keep cool, and remember, you're not the whole team."

Leroy has found that when he gives himself permission to do this instead of staying in the pep session the whole time, he is much calmer throughout the game, he feels good afterward, and his scoring is better than ever.

- What is the difference between self-love and selfishness?
- Think of other situations that require drawing your own boundaries in a self-respecting and other-respecting way. How would you draw your boundaries? **8**

8
Write down some words you could say to yourself when you are in a situation in which you need to pay attention to your own feelings and needs.

The Long View

In order for chaos not to reign in one's life, a person needs to be able to pay attention to the long view rather than to short-term impulses. Living impulsively, without regard for what makes sense over a longer period of time, tends to add more chaos to the life of a person who already feels turmoil inside.

In the following example, Melissa finds it hard not to give in to her urge to buy things on credit.

Just before Melissa's parents got in their car to go home, her mom gave her a MasterCard with the admonition that she should use it only in an emergency. Otherwise, she should write a check from her account.

For her first month at college, Melissa followed her mother's guideline, but one day she was walking through the local mall with three of her friends. A record store had compact discs on sale. Melissa found two that she had been wanting for a month. Then, spotting another one at half-price, she picked it up. By the time she got to the cashier, she had six CDs. Realizing that she did not have sufficient cash nor enough money in her checking account right then, she decided to use the credit card. She signed the slip, promising herself that she would be more careful in the future.

Despite pledges to herself to stop buying things, Melissa ran into trouble quickly. Without telling her parents, she requested and received an extension on her credit limit from MasterCard. When she hit that limit, she applied for another credit card from a different company. Over the next three months, she piled up debts of nearly three thousand dollars.

Looking at her credit card bills, Melissa could not believe that she was in so deeply. Using the cards had seemed so painless that she had lost track of how much she was spending. She had gotten in the habit of paying just enough each month to be able to keep using the cards. However, the interest payments were mounting on top of the principal. And now Melissa could not even manage the minimum required payments.

Linda, her roommate, found Melissa sitting on her bed in the midst of the credit card bills, crying. When Melissa explained what was going on, Linda told her that she ought to call her parents.

"How did you get into such a mess?" Linda asked.

"It was so easy to buy stuff, and I just lost track. Oh, God, this is awful. My parents will kill me."

- What are the long-term effects of spending beyond your ability to pay?
- How do credit cards make it easier to live impulsively?
- When a cardholder builds up a large debt and doesn't pay it off, does the credit company benefit?
- How does overspending contribute to happiness or take away from it?
- What should Melissa do now?
- If Melissa calls her parents, what should they do?
- How can this experience benefit Melissa's development as a whole person?

Our Bodies, Ourselves

Part of the unity that characterizes whole persons is a certain peace with themselves. When we feel bad about ourselves—that is, when we find ourselves unacceptable—this poor self-esteem is often reflected in how we feel about our body and how we treat ourselves physically. Earlier in this chapter, drug addictions and casual sex were discussed

Money and the Quest for Wholeness

Olivia Mellan, a psychotherapist and author of *10 Days to Money Harmony,* told an interviewer:

> "Chronic overspenders have a kind of hole in them, which they try to fill with what money can buy. They think that money equals love, happiness or pleasure. Even if the overspender has the money to spend, an out-of-control, compulsive impulse takes . . . over. It's anesthetizing—a way to avoid facing deeper needs. In our . . . culture, we are taught instant gratification, not mature delayed gratification. That's why we have a national deficit."

The way we spend money undoubtedly affects our individual, family, and national life. The effects are most noticeable on the economic level, but the psychological and spiritual levels are also influenced. A brief look at the manner in which Christmas and Hanukkah are commonly celebrated in the United States offers us a chance to see these effects more clearly and to reflect on the "hole" we try to fill in ourselves by overspending.

On the economic level, writers Sue Halpern and Bill McKibben report the following:

> The amount of money spent on December gift-giving is large enough to make it an issue worthy of serious consideration. Although statistics are hard to come by, the average American planned to spend upward of $750 on Christmas in 1991. . . . The total value of gifts given in the December holidays exceeds $37 billion. . . . The nation's holiday gift budget is equal to the amount of money given to charities over the course of an entire year. ("Hundred Dollar Holidays")

Halpern and McKibben's concern goes beyond the economic to the psychological and spiritual influence of our holiday spending habits:

> The ways in which we celebrate Christmas and Chanukah may have a significant effect on how we come to view consumption. That is, the powerful idea given us as children that transcendent joy lies in a heaping pile of presents

may condition us to look to the shopping mall and mail-order catalogue for satisfaction and fulfillment throughout our lives.

Finding alternative ways to celebrate these holidays, Halpern and McKibben suggest, may help "point us in new directions," and they promote some possibilities:

> Holiday celebrations should be *more* joyful than they are at present, and . . . overcommercialization has done much to rob the real pleasure from the December holidays. In place of gift-buying, we are suggesting a whole range of substitute activities—church and synagogue programs, gifts of service, gift-*making*, giving coupons redeemable for a trip to the museum or a hike in the woods, etc. We are urging people to take a slower pace in an effort to make the celebration more enjoyable.

Taking these general suggestions and adapting them to our particular families and communities could provide a new way to "fill the hole" experienced by overspenders. Money, as Olivia Mellan implies, is no substitute for love, happiness, or pleasure.

as hooks that take away people's freedom. These problems are also signs that individuals are not at peace with themselves because they are willing to abuse their body for some short-term gain.

A number of other ways of physically being at war with oneself have been growing in recent years, especially among young people. Jessica's story at the beginning of the chapter involved one of those ways—bulimia.

Persons who feel bad about themselves may focus excessively on some media-promoted standard of appearance, such as being ultrathin or ultramuscular. They turn their dislike of themselves into a dangerous quest for bodily "perfection." There are several ways that some young people, and occasionally adults, can abuse themselves:

1. *Anorexia nervosa* is a pathological fear of weight gain. Anorexic persons, typically females but also increasingly males, have a distorted picture of themselves. They may look like a skeleton but see themselves as fat. Starvation slows down the body's respiration and pulse rate, damages organs, and can lead to death.

2. *Bulimia,* Jessica's problem, is a more common eating disorder, but it can accompany anorexia. Bulimics, typically females but some males as well, find themselves obsessed with food; they go on eating binges. Then they purge themselves to get rid of the weight by vomiting or taking laxatives or water-loss pills. Such purging can cause permanent damage to the body and, in some cases, lead to death.

3. *Hypergymnasia* is a relatively new disorder in response to the social pressure to have a body that looks in perfect physical shape. A person will eat and then dangerously overdo physical exercise in an attempt to burn off whatever is eaten. These persons go to extremes to prove they can be ultrathin and perfectly healthy at the same time.

4. *Anabolic steroids* are currently used by about one in fifteen male high school seniors. These powerful drugs are taken to give one the "he man" muscular look and to boost performance in athletics. Their effects are temporary; as soon as a boy or a man stops taking them, his muscles begin to shrink. Serious, even fatal, side effects—including liver tumors, blood disorders, sterility, and aggressive behavior—can result from taking anabolic steroids.

Harming ourselves in any of these ways is a serious matter. These behaviors and less extreme methods, like constant fad dieting, are indicators that young people in our society are being pressured not to accept themselves and their imperfect but wonderful bodies. In many cases, the roots of this self-loathing go deep and require psychological help. **9**

Those who cherish their body will not punish it by filling up on junk food, overeating, smoking, abusing alcohol and other drugs, getting little sleep, and not exercising. Caring for ourselves means giving our body good treatment: a balanced diet, the right amount of rest, regular exercise, and relaxation.

Being at peace with ourselves frees us up to put energy into our life goals and dreams instead of into an inner war.

For Review

- Why is order and harmony within a person necessary?
- Define anorexia nervosa, bulimia, hypergymnasia, and anabolic steroid abuse.

9
From a popular magazine for teens, select an ad that promotes the quest for bodily perfection. Write a critique of the ad from the perspective of the virtue of wholeness.

Self-restraint: Tending the Fire Within

Self-restraint is the right channeling and controlling of our drives and impulses—whether biological, emotional, or intellectual. This is not a popular concept in our society. Restraining ourselves, after all, means possibly missing out on something important, some wonderful experience that we long to have. Young people especially do not want to slip into dullness. So the message is out: Go with your impulses! Follow those drives! Be passionate about life, not dull! Why hold back when you can experience it all now?

According to that backdrop of voices in our society, self-restraint sounds like the opposite of living passionately.

Being Truly Passionate

Restraint and Passion

Recall what Jessica (in the opening of this chapter) had to say about self-restraint. For her, learning how to "put on the brakes" was the first step in calming down and gradually being able to "drive the car" again. Her impulses had been out of control. Until Jessica could get her racing impulses to settle down, she could not set her own goals and directions. With self-restraint, she was eventually able to become truly passionate about her poetry and excited about life. Jessica had energy to invest in life because her energy was not sapped by impulses gone reckless.

Rather than throwing a wet blanket on passionate living, self-restraint frees us to pour our heart into something because our efforts are not recklessly scattered among impulses.

Paper Blaze or Hot Coals?

An analogy may help to clarify the meaning of self-restraint and its relationship to living passionately.

If you have ever had experience with campfires, you know the difference between a newspaper blaze and a fire of hot coals. Think about each of these types of fires:

- Which type of fire is easier to get going? looks more spectacular in the beginning? goes out more quickly?

- Which type of fire takes more tending and careful preparation to build?
- Which fire provides more warmth? might last through the night? can be used for cooking?
- Which one is more likely to go out if a little wind comes up?

Self-restraint is "tending the fire within." We are all blessed with the "fuel" of life's energy within us—our emotions, our drives and urges, our longings for pleasure. This wonderful fuel is called the "passions" in Catholic tradition. But we have to resist our impulse to get an instant big blaze going with this fuel, or it will burn out like a newspaper fire. In other words, we have to master self-restraint—not giving in to our passions on demand. Then we will be able to build up our inner fire, tending it carefully and patiently until we become persons of depth whose passion, like hot coals, warms and lights ourselves and the world around us for a lifetime. **10**

Being able to practice self-restraint makes a lot of sense when we look at our life as a long-term project of building our character. As discussed throughout this text, the key question for every human being is this: What kind of person do I want to be and become? Do I want to be a person who can "tend the fire within" for the sake of something worthwhile? Self-restraint is required to achieve anything of enduring value—like a loving relationship, an education, or the raising of children.

For the Sake of Life Today

Being able to practice self-restraint is crucial for our long-term development as persons of depth and character. But, as experience shows over and over again, self-restraint is also necessary to prevent shorter-term consequences that can be devastating, even fatal.

We are all familiar with the hazards associated with not practicing self-restraint. Here are just a few examples:

- pregnancy out of marriage
- venereal disease and AIDS
- flunking out of school
- going bankrupt
- criminal arrest and jail terms
- alcohol and other drug addiction
- accidents and injuries due to drunk driving
- family violence and abuse

In the immediate situation, many people think they are invulnerable and immortal: "*I could not become pregnant, or get caught, or become addicted, or get in an accident. That's what happens to other people.*"

Here is an account of a tragedy that came about through just such an outlook:

"More! More! More!" The whole bar seemed to be yelling at Doug to down one more shot. His head was swimming already, but what the hell, he thought, it's my birthday. He held up the glass. The crowd cheered and started singing "Happy Birthday" again. Putting the glass to his mouth, Doug tossed the hot whiskey down the hatch.

The chants started again. His glass got filled again. By now, Doug had lost track of how many drinks he'd had. People kept buying, the chants were getting louder, and Doug was tossing back his head and swallowing the drinks.

After a while, Doug slumped to the floor. His friends cheered and jeered, carrying his limp body out of the bar. By the time they pulled into their dormitory parking lot, Les and Mike had sobered up enough to be

---

10
Apply the analogy of paper blaze and hot coals to a situation in which a person might need to practice self-restraint. In writing, describe which behaviors in that situation are like lighting a newspaper blaze and which behaviors are like patiently tending a campfire until the coals become red-hot.

scared. Doug's eyes were rolled back, and he had turned white.

After getting Doug to bed, Mike roused the resident hall director. She took one look at Doug and called the paramedics. When they finally arrived she had been doing CPR for nearly ten minutes, knowing without wanting to admit it that Doug was dead.

Some of the students didn't want to believe that anyone could die of alcohol poisoning. But it had really happened, here, to one of their own. A pall spread over the campus.

- Why did Doug drink so much that night?
- What effect did his initial drinks have on his judgment and his sense of self-restraint?
- What responsibility, if any, did the crowd at the bar have for Doug's death?
- After a tragedy like this, do people who know what happened generally change their ways? for a short time? permanently? Why or why not?

Why Wait for Sex?

The Call to Chastity

Earlier in this chapter, casual sex was described as wrong because it is destructive to persons and distorts the intended meaning of sexual intercourse. In terms of sexuality, the call for self-restraint in our life is known as **chastity**. In a chaste lifestyle, a person's sexual desires are lived out in a way that is in harmony with her or his state in life—single, engaged, married, and so on. Decisions about sexual behavior are made with a clear understanding of the meaning of sexual intercourse: it is intended to express and promote the bond of mutual giving and receiving between a man and a woman who are committed to each other permanently, in a relationship that is loving and open to new life.

Above: Pregnancy out of marriage can be a difficult consequence of not practicing self-restraint.

The Catholic church affirms that marriage is the context in which this kind of bond can happen. Outside of marriage, a man and a woman may love each other deeply and feel committed, but they have not sealed their love with a permanent pledge to a shared destiny for life. They have not promised to accept and deal with whatever life brings, blessings as well as hardships—together. They have not confirmed their commitment by declaring to their family, friends, and community: "We are in this together—for life. We are ready to be parents if children come our way. We are a family."

Recall Marie and Vince, the couple in chapter 4 who decided to wait until marriage to fully express their love sexually. They talked about a number of reasons for their decision. In this light, also consider the case of Steve, described by the campus minister of a major Catholic university:

I will never forget an encounter I had recently with a bright, athletic and attractive student named Steve, who confided in me that he decided to maintain his chastity until he marries, at which time he assured me laughingly that he will "go wild"! Steve's appreciation for the goodness of sexuality is strong, but he is courageously waiting for its fullest expression in marriage. His peers would be surprised at his determination to be chaste, because they know he loves to party. (Fourqurean, "Chastity as Shared Strength")

In a society where sex outside of marriage is increasingly accepted and even expected, these decisions might seem old-fashioned. But more and more psychologists and health experts are recognizing with the church the wisdom of saving sexual intercourse for marriage. This is partly because of the epidemics of venereal disease and AIDS in young people and the increasing rate of teenage

pregnancy. But there are many other solid reasons for the experts' advocacy of premarital abstinence.

When two persons are in the midst of an intense relationship, however, it is often difficult to think about waiting. Considerations of the value of abstaining before marriage, if they are there at all,

■

Above: Babies need families where the parents can give them what they need to thrive—particularly the parents' mature, nurturing presence.

may tend to float right out the window. For a couple in love, having sex may seem like the most natural thing in the world to do.

Falling in love is a wonderful experience, one of life's great gifts. And teenagers truly can fall in love. However, that experience of falling in love, beautiful and pleasurable as it is, should not be mistaken for the enduring love that long-term commitments are made of. **11**

Let's consider the church's rationale and the reasons proposed by psychologists and health experts for waiting for sex until marriage.

Babies Need Families

The most obvious reason for saving sex until marriage is that sex is the cause of pregnancy—and babies deserve to be born and raised in a stable family. Children need a mother and a father who share in the tasks of raising and loving them. No matter how good her intentions, an unmarried teenage mother simply cannot give a baby everything that the child needs to thrive. The young woman needs to become more mature herself before she can cope with the demands of mothering. And when teenagers marry because of a pregnancy, new problems often arise. Most of these marriages do not last.

In a small but significant number of cases, unmarried teenage girls choose to become pregnant. Their motivation, however, is often inappropriate: they expect that by having a baby to love and be loved by they will develop greater self-worth. Such a motive places an unfair burden on the mother and child and can impede the emotional development of both.

The availability of birth control has not helped solve the problem of teen pregnancy. It is a widely held belief that by making "family planning" clinics accessible to teenagers, the number of teen pregnancies will be reduced. This is not the case, however, according to research reported in the *Wall Street Journal:* "As the number and proportion of teen-age family planning clients increased, we observe a corresponding increase in teen-age pregnancy and abortion rates. The original problems appear to have grown worse." More than a million teenagers become pregnant each year, and that number continues to grow.

- Why do you think the rate of teenage pregnancy is going up so alarmingly?
- Do you think the availability of contraceptives for teenagers is a solution to the problem or part of the problem?

The Hazard of Premature Bonding

One of the greatest psychological problems with teenagers engaging in sexual intercourse is that in the emotional hothouse of sexual intimacy, a young man and a young woman tend to merge their personalities before they have had a chance to form their own individual identities. This is called premature bonding. The bonding of marriage is fine for two mature persons who are able to keep their own separate identities. But for a young person who is still forming an identity, genital sexual involvement is too much to handle. The couple may isolate themselves from family and friends. They may short-circuit all the other important ways that they need to develop as they pour themselves into their intense relationship. As one young man remarks, "I have a good friend who's having sex with his girlfriend, and it seems like that's all they ever focus on. Their relationship is real narrow."

11
Make three columns, headed "Falling in Love"; "Committed, Long-term Love"; and "Using the Other, Not Love." Beneath each heading, write as many behaviors, feelings, and thoughts as you can think of that are characteristic of that experience.

A related problem is that the bonding experienced is sometimes one-sided. In other words, only one partner acknowledges that the sexual activity is meaningful, while the other pulls away from the relationship or continues it only to take advantage of the sexual activity. A fifteen-year-old girl, bitter and heartbroken, summed up her former relationship: "I guess he got what he wanted. I thought he loved me, and I said yes to sex because of that. But once I said yes I was history." As with premature bonding, an experience of this nature can damage a young person's growth to maturity.

The Illusion of Forever
The flush of being in love can easily feel like a total commitment: "We'll always be together. I can't imagine life without you." The joy of getting so close to another person, feeling so wanted, accepted, and understood, all mixed together with the surge of hormones, makes the experience *seem* ultimate and destined to last forever.

Usually, however, being in love does not last forever. "In love" feelings tend to be temporary. That is normal and expected in human development, although sad for those enduring a breakup. When a couple seal a temporary "in love" relationship with sexual intercourse, any of several results can come about for the persons involved:

Clouded judgment. Sexual intercourse clouds the individuals' judgment about the relationship. It creates pressure to stay together when the relationship may not be healthy or happy.

A setup for being hurt. A sexual relationship creates expectations of long-term commitment that realistically cannot be met. It sets up persons for later hurt—moral, emotional, and psychological.

Artificial intimacy. Engaging in sexual intercourse artificially speeds up the development of intimacy. Physical intimacy, which is relatively easy to achieve, then substitutes for all the other kinds of intimacy that take a long time to develop and cannot be rushed. Many teenagers, no longer given the hugs and cuddles of childhood, are hungry for touch. They may easily jump into a physical relationship because they feel deprived of the warmth of human touch.

"Tending the fire" carefully and patiently will give you warmth and light for a lifetime. Growing in genuine friendship develops your character toward becoming a person of depth, someone who warms and lights yourself and the world around you. Having only physical intimacy does not lead you in that direction. **12**

The Goodness of Learning to Be Lovers Together
Finally, hear from a man who decided to save sex for marriage. He said the following in a letter:

"My wife and I waited until we were married to have sex, which was a different decision than many people nowadays make. But I think it was a good one. Maybe if we'd had sex with other people or with each other before we were married, we'd have been more experienced or knowledgeable. But learning about sex together . . . made it that much more special. Also, we didn't have to worry if either of us was "as good" as the other lovers either of us might have had before. . . .

"By being willing to wait until we were married, I felt I was showing [my wife] that it wasn't just sex that I wanted from her but real, true love and lifelong commitment. And she was showing me the same thing. . . . We really trusted each other, and that

---

12
In the Catholic church's rationale for waiting for sex until marriage, which reasons seem most strong or convincing to you? Explain your answer in writing. If none of the reasons seems convincing, explain why.

made us feel safe enough for us to really 'let go.' We didn't have to worry that if we did it 'wrong' or it wasn't great the first time that it would all be over. And, really, it wasn't so great the first time. It was kind of awkward and embarrassing. But I knew and she knew that we'd both be around tomorrow. . . . This trusting and promising made us able to grow to be better lovers than we might have otherwise." (Quoted in Madaras, *The What's Happening to My Body? Book for Boys,* page 167)

- How do you react to what this man says about saving sex for marriage?
- How do trust and commitment enable persons to become better lovers?

For Review

- What is the relationship between self-restraint and being passionate about life?
- Summarize the Catholic church's rationale for waiting until marriage for sex.

You Are Immensely Valuable and Worthy

This chapter began with Jessica's account of how she sought wholeness while trying to overcome the eating disorder of bulimia. From there, the chapter has ranged far and wide in looking at the many ways that people's lives need to become more whole. Freedom; unity, order, and direction; and self-restraint are dimensions of wholeness that encompass a great variety of important life issues.

Perhaps the most significant message you can take from this chapter is this: *You* are immensely valuable and worthy, no matter how broken, unfree, divided, or out of control you have ever been. People can begin again, and often they become better persons for having learned from mistakes and heartaches.

It is important to know, too, that Jesus is the one calling you to wholeness. He will not leave you alone in your search for your own strength, beauty, and happiness.

■

Above: Knowing that you are of immense value and worth can strengthen you in your quest for wholeness.

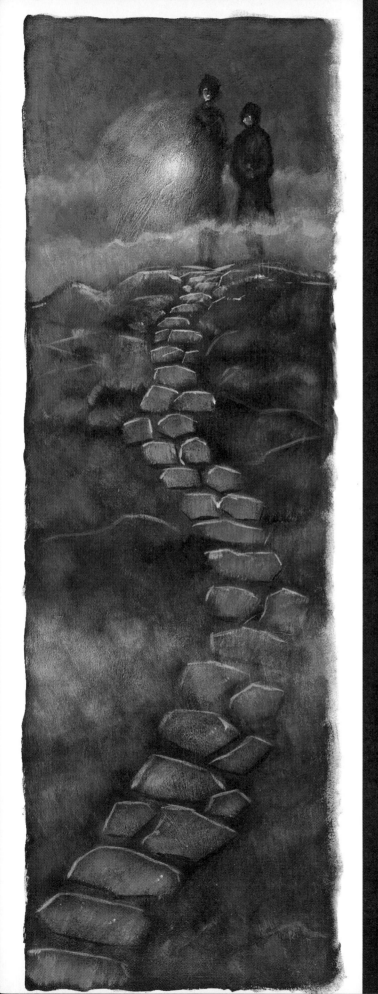

9

Honesty:
Creating Trust

ONE young man's experience with honesty offers us an introduction to this virtue:

The Turnaround

Jim, age nineteen, has lived with honesty and dishonesty, and he is glad to say that "honesty is better." Like many people, Jim got into a pattern of lying in his younger years—in his case, to his parents. By the time he was thirteen, Jim was regularly taking substantial amounts of money from his parents' wallets and lying to cover it up when they confronted him. He was lying about where he was going, who he was going with, and so on. Here Jim talks about his experiences:

At first it didn't seem like much, but after a while I thought about it and got upset. I was lying to cover up lies. And I was always afraid of my parents; I couldn't face them because I knew they knew I was lying, but they couldn't prove it. I felt so guilty and insecure and afraid, and I didn't know what to do about it.

When you're in that situation, owning up to all the lies just never occurs to you; it never enters your mind as a possibility. All you can think of is, How can I get through this lie without them finding out about all the others? It becomes easier to be dishonest. You learn how to deal with your guilty feelings, how to lie better.

At age fourteen, Jim had a turnaround. Caught in the act of stealing, he could no longer deny his dishonesty. So he did the "unthinkable"; he confessed to all the lying and stealing he had done over the previous years.

The best solution—the only solution for me—was to cleanse myself of what I had done. I had to make a clean break, start over, ask my parents' forgiveness, and then slowly build up their trust in me. If I had gotten away with the stealing, it would have been worse. Dealing with the guilt inside you is harder to take than any punishment.

After that, I felt free inside. It's been five years since I turned around, and I've learned that honesty is an extremely strong base to build a relationship on. Now I have a real, solid relationship with my parents, built on trust. With honesty and trust, you can share experiences and feelings with another person. Without honesty, there's distrust and the relationship disintegrates. That's true with friends and true with parents. Honesty in a relationship is my highest ideal. **1**

1
What was Jim's greatest fear about owning up to his previous dishonesty? Write a paragraph describing that fear and how Jim's honesty with his parents required the virtue of courage.

■
Above: A solid relationship with one's parents is built on trust.

179

What's So Great About Honesty?

"The Truth Will Set You Free"

The virtue of **honesty** is the ability to seek and uphold the truth. As limited persons, we cannot know the truth completely or fully, but we can consistently strive for greater clarity and understanding. So honesty is not only the absence of lying but also a sincere devotion to truthfulness as a value in itself. An honest person seeks the truth with an open mind and tries to clearly communicate that truth. Honest persons are trustworthy: they can be relied upon to be who they claim to be, to mean what they say, and to keep their word.

For Jim, a love for honesty did not come overnight. He came to value truthfulness by first feeling the destructive effects of deception. Then, over a number of years, he saw what good can come of being truthful, even when it hurts.

Jim is now devoted to the truth and sees honesty as his highest ideal. The words of Jesus now have living reality for Jim: "'You will know the truth, and the truth will set you free'" (John 8:32).

Jesus loved the truth with his whole being and lived the truth of God's love every day of his life:

"For this I was born and for this I came into the world, to testify to the truth. Everyone who belongs to the truth listens to my voice." (John 18:37)

Jim did not have to die for the truth as Jesus did. But Jim does know something about suffering for the truth. No doubt great challenges will come his way in life because of his commitment to honesty.

Why Be Honest?

In a world where dishonesty seems almost commonplace and is often expected of people as part of "getting ahead," why should a person be honest? Like all the other virtues, the seeking and upholding of truth enables persons to live a more fully human life. How is this so?

Living in the Real World

First and foremost, honest persons wish to live in the real world, a world so complex that none of us knows it entirely. We need the best insights of others—living and dead—to make sense of this world. (Recall the discussions about reality on page 78 in chapter 4.) After his turnaround, Jim found out that sticking to reality by being honest gives people a common reference point: they have more to share because they live in the same world.

Above: "The truth will set you free."

Dishonest people, on the other hand, often live in their own make-believe world, out of touch with what is really going on. And the more lies they tell, the further away from reality they get. In an unreal world, trust has no basis. Yet trust is essential for positive, healthy relationships within society, with friends and relatives, and even with oneself.

Society's Dependence on Honesty

A healthy human society depends on honest deeds and communication. To accomplish even the simplest task, we need to have information we can count on. For example:

- The store will close at 9:00 p.m., as the ad says, not at 5:00 p.m.
- Your teacher will test you on the seventh chapter, not the eighth.
- Your part-time job will pay $5.50 per hour, not $4.85.
- The mechanic will actually fix the faulty brakes on your family car.

Without honesty in our communications and actions, human society would grind to a halt, with everyone paralyzed by a lack of trust and by the fear that what looks real is just a sham. **2**

In light of the need for honesty in society, consider the following example:

At lunch time I went to my locker to drop off my books, and about ten lockers away was a small crowd. They were looking in a box that this one guy had pulled out of his locker. The box was filled with new CDs—recent stuff—and the guy was selling them for five dollars each. They were stolen, obviously. I could see the name of the store on the side of the box. I'd like to save money on CDs too, but it just didn't seem right. I'll probably go to the store and tell them what I saw—not the kid's name, but they should do something about security.

- How would you answer someone who thinks that theft or buying stolen goods is not serious because "the business has plenty to spare"?
- Who ends up paying for theft from businesses?

A Basis for Personal Relationships

By generating trust, honesty forms a basis for relationships at the personal level as well as the societal level—friendships, marriages, parent-child relationships, and other close ties.

A source of hurt frequently mentioned by high school students is gossip. Gossip, rumors, and slander can ruin a person's reputation, devastate self-esteem, and wreck friendships. Besides hurting the individual, gossip creates feelings of insecurity and mistrust that poison the atmosphere and make everyone begin to feel at risk. For example, a seventeen-year-old comments:

Gossip can be awful. I hear people stabbing their friends in the back all the time. It makes it hard to trust anyone.

- Why do people gossip and spread rumors about others?

Gossiping, backbiting, and manipulating others with half-truths create a world of distrust in which people feel threatened and insecure and cannot thrive as human beings. **3**

Freedom from a Web of Deceit

In the opening example of this chapter, Jim spoke of feeling free inside when he came clean about his web of lies, a web spun by inventing more lies to cover up previous lies. The web of lies, however, is not really a protection or a way out; it is a trap. "A liar must have a perfect memory," as the saying goes. Consider the predicament Olivia is facing:

2
Jot down examples of information that you have to count on as true; in other words, if this information were false, your life or your plans would be messed up.

3
Compose a remark you could use when you hear someone gossiping—a comment that would accurately and tactfully express your feelings about gossip.

After a while, my head buzzed and hurt from trying to figure out the mess I'd gotten myself into. First I had told Luke that I couldn't stand Patrick because he bragged a lot and acted like a big shot, but when Patrick asked me if I wanted to go to Beth's party with him, I jumped at the chance. I hadn't realized that Patrick was really interested in me. Then Patrick got angry at me because Luke told him what I had said about him. But I liked Patrick and wanted to keep going out with him, so I called Luke a liar, saying that I had never said any such thing. Now Luke won't even look at me.

Even if the deception goes undiscovered, persons who lie still have to live with anxiety, guilt, and fear. Perhaps worst of all, they must live with the knowledge that they have become the kind of person who can lie skillfully and successfully. **4**

A Sense of Integrity

People caught in the web of deceit deprive themselves of integrity—even identity. They become citizens of an unreal world. Honest persons, consistently seeking and upholding the truth, are rewarded with a sense of being faithful to who they are.

Here is an example of how the lessons of honesty's rewards are passed down through generations:

[A woman] recalled a shopping trip made with her grandfather and the discovery on return to their home that the clerk had made a mistake and given them more than they were entitled to. Her grandfather told her they would return the items.

She remembers protesting that the store wouldn't know. And she remembers her grandfather's reply: "Yes. But we would."

The memory stayed with her. Once, shopping for clothes with a daughter who would soon be going to college, they were inadvertently given an expensive pair of shoes. The very next day they returned the shoes even though the store was a good distance away. The manager was astounded. "Why did you do it?" he asked. "The store would probably never know."

"Yes, but we would," the daughter said, with a knowing look at her mother. ("Honesty Is Still in Style," *Christopher News Notes*)

- What are some other examples of persons being honest when no one would know otherwise? **5**

Honesty does the following:
- **enables people to live in the real world**
- **keeps human society working**
- **forms a basis for personal relationships**
- **gives people a sense of inner freedom**
- **endows persons with a sense of integrity**

For Review

- Define the virtue of honesty.
- Give five reasons that a person should be honest.

4
Write about an incident in which a web of lies was spun, either in your own life or someone else's. Did the web become a trap for the person telling the lies? If so, how?

5
Think of an incident when someone you knew was honest out of a sense of honor, like the grandfather and the daughter in the above account. Based on this experience, write a letter to your future son or daughter, giving advice about how to be a person of integrity and honor.

"Plant an Act . . ."

This wise old saying, first given in chapter 1, bears repeating in light of the virtue of honesty:

Plant an act; reap a habit.
Plant a habit; reap a virtue or a vice.
Plant a virtue or a vice; reap a character.
Plant a character; reap a destiny.

The Starting Place: Honesty with Self

Staying in Tune with Yourself

Honest persons tend to be first of all honest with themselves. They are skilled at listening to what is going on inside them—what they are really thinking and feeling. They see the truth about themselves and their own motives; they do not put a smoke screen over their awareness of self. They stay in tune with who they really are and, more important, with what kind of person they want to become.

Consider the following situation as it relates to honesty with self:

Danny walked into the locker room, knowing that he'd had enough of grunting and sweating, running wind sprints, and knocking heads on the football field. "Hell Week" was over. The coach as much as told Danny that he would start at center. Even so, Danny just wanted out of the game he had come to loathe.

Danny had thought long and hard about his decision, and he still wasn't completely sure why he had started to hate playing. He was strong and reasonably quick for a junior who weighed 217. Indeed, he was the biggest player on the team. Part of what made him rebel against playing this year was his anger. To get psyched before or during a game, he had to get mad. Last season he had broken a guy's leg. The hit was legal, but Danny had been playing mean. When Danny heard the guy's bone snap, it was as if something had snapped inside him. During the off-season, one question nagged at Danny: "Is any game worth all this?" His friends said yes. They couldn't understand the question. His parents just murmured, "Do whatever you want."

The mindless drills, barking coaches, vomiting players, and the sheer pain of Hell Week convinced Danny that he couldn't fake interest any longer. Yet he dreaded telling his head coach, a man not known for his understanding and listening skills. But Danny took a series of deep breaths, knocked on the door, and walked into the coach's office.

"I've turned my pads and stuff in at the equipment room. I don't want to play this year. My parents say it's okay. I want to spend more time on my studies." Inside, Danny winced, acknowledging that schoolwork was hardly any part of his decision. He didn't want to start weaseling with the truth.

"You can't quit." Coach Miller glared at him and then fiddled with his whistle.

"What do you mean?"

"Steiner, you're the biggest guy we've got out there. What is this, some kind of joke? I don't have time for this garbage."

"No joke, Coach. I just don't want to play." His words came out calmly, but inside Danny's stomach was churning like a concrete mixer.

"Look, Hell Week's over. Why did you even come out? The team needs you. What the hell kind of reason is 'I don't wanna play'? Besides, what are people gonna think? Do you want to be a quitter? I mean, did you turn into a wimp this summer or something?" Miller's face turned scarlet. Instead of fiddling with his whistle, he started jerking hard on it.

"I don't know all the reasons, but that's it. I'm quitting." Danny opened the door and began backing out. "I may even do debate this year." He tossed this

in, remembering some of Miller's sneering comments about debaters. Actually, he liked debate. Maybe he would try it.

As Danny walked into the locker room, the release that he thought he would feel, the sense of freedom, did not immediately come to him. In fact, Danny suddenly wondered what the other guys would say. He felt alone and different as he stood at his locker, collecting his personal gear. The other guys talked about practice and traded jabs. This was no longer his world.

Danny wondered if he had done the right thing, but then a guy snapped a towel at someone's rear end. The sound hit Danny like the snap of the guy's broken leg last year. Although he realized that quitting football would sit uneasily with him for a while, he also sensed that deep inside he felt right, honest. Playing football might please Coach Miller, the guys on the team, the fans, and maybe even his parents, but it wouldn't please him. That had to count for something.

- How does the LISTEN process apply to Danny's decision? Which part of the process is especially important in being honest with yourself?
- When people recognize something about their needs and wants that will be hard for others to accept, what do they tend to do?
- What are the costs and the rewards of being true to yourself?

Self-deception: Companion to Other-deception

Persons who are out of touch with themselves do not reflect clearly on the reality of what is going on inside them—how they are feeling, why they are reacting or thinking a certain way. Such persons are more prone than others to self-deception. They are good at "kidding" themselves; they can more easily tell themselves that something really does not matter when in fact it *does* matter.

Self-deception in some form typically accompanies the deception of others. Clouding reality helps the dishonest person to feel less guilty about what she or he is doing. As discussed under the virtue of wise judgment (chapter 5), deception of self and others commonly takes place through rationalizations. Here are some additional examples of rationalizations, showing how easily deception comes to us:

1. I won't tell my daughter [age four] that I'm leaving tonight and will be gone for a week, because I know she'll get all worked up and won't be able to sleep. So I'll say I'm going out for the evening. Grandma can tell her in the morning that I'll be gone for a week, and she'll have time to calm down before bed.
2. With the state of distraction I'm in, I wouldn't be any good to them at work today. I'll call in sick.
3. Melita is so sensitive that I shouldn't tell her I want to do something with some other friends tonight. I'll just say I'm grounded.
4. When the Congressional Investigating Committee asks me about that memo, I'll have to keep it from them. It's a matter of national security, and they don't have an appreciation of that.

- How is the individual in each of these situations deceiving herself or himself? What is the likely truth that the person does not admit? **6**

6
Write down something you have told yourself in the past that you now recognize as a rationalization. Explain why you think you felt the need to fool yourself in this way.

Becoming Strong Enough to Welcome the Truth

None of us is totally honest with ourselves all the time. Everyone engages in self-deception, rationalization, and inner smoke screening on certain occasions or in particular areas of life where reality is hard to face. Everyone has room to grow in honesty with self. Maturity is marked by such growth.

Becoming more honest with oneself does not come automatically or instantaneously, however. Muscles become strong only with use—and then only gradually. To become strong in the virtue of honesty, we need ways to help us become strong enough to welcome the truth, not fear it. Here are some suggestions on how to become more honest with yourself:

Journal writing. It is hard to be honest with yourself if you believe that what you feel is bad or unacceptable. Feelings are neither good nor bad; they just *are.* Journal writing—getting your feelings and thoughts down on paper for your own reflec-

tion—can be a safe way to get in touch with your real self. Try to get to the heart of your emotions or reactions without judging them as acceptable or unacceptable. Over time, this practice helps you to become more reflective about yourself and accepting of yourself, and therefore, more honest with yourself and others. **7**

Sharing feelings with others. Sharing your feelings and thoughts with a friend who accepts you and can be a sounding board for you is critical to growing in self-honesty. In journal writing, you pour things out to yourself. In talking with a friend or adviser who cares about you and does not judge you, you become clearer about your reactions and their causes. If you are not used to sharing your feelings with others, at first just try being honest with one person whom you feel you can trust. It is okay to test the water before jumping in.

Praying. Prayer can be a way of pouring out your feelings to God. Because God accepts you completely, it is safe to express yourself freely with God, even with feelings like anger, despair, sorrow, revenge, or jealousy.

Communicating what is inside us to persons who love us, including God, encourages growth in self-honesty. Honesty with self forms a necessary foundation for honesty with others, especially when honesty exacts a high price from us.

For Review

- How is self-deception related to deceiving others?
- What are three ways to become more honest with oneself?

■
Above: A retreat can help us to become more honest with ourselves by giving us the chance to reflect on what is going on in us and to share our feelings with others and with God.

7
List three concerns that you may choose to write about in a private journal.

Pouring Out Your Soul to God

In their prayer, the ancient Israelites did not hold back anything of themselves. They poured out their souls to God, expressing their distress, sorrow, and anger. In Psalm 137, the people tell God exactly how they are feeling about being held captive in Babylon, where they were exiled after the destruction of their beloved city Jerusalem and their Temple.

By the rivers of Babylon
we sat and wept, remembering Zion.
On the poplars of that land
we hung up our harps;
there our captors asked of us
the lyrics of our songs
and urged us to be joyous:
"Sing for us one of the songs of Zion!" they said.
How could we sing a song of Yahweh
while in a foreign land?
If I forget you, Jerusalem,
may my right hand forget its skill!
May my tongue cleave to the roof of my mouth
if I forget you,
if I do not consider Jerusalem
my greatest joy.
Remember, Yahweh, what the Edomites did
that day in Jerusalem.
When they said "Tear it down,
tear it down to its foundations!"
O daughter of Babylon—you destroyer—
happy those who shall repay you
the evil you have done us! **8**

(Psalm 137:1–8)

8
Respond in writing to these questions: What emotions are the people expressing in this psalm? Are you surprised at any of the sentiments in the psalm? Would such a prayer help the people to be more honest with themselves?

Costly Honesty

Earlier in this chapter, Jesus' words were quoted in connection with Jim's turnaround from a pattern of lying: "'You will know the truth, and the truth will set you free'" (John 8:32). A Christian preacher once humorously adapted Jesus' words to fit our typical experience with honesty in difficult situations: "'You shall know the truth and the truth shall make you flinch before it makes you free'" (quoted in *Context*). Jim would no doubt have agreed with that, and Jesus probably would have too.

The reality is that honesty often costs us something. But lies have their costs as well. Thus, one question we have to wrestle with is, Which costs are we willing to live with? However, honesty is not just about costs. Being honest frees us, because it keeps us living in the real world, where possibilities for growth and goodness exist. These are gains that dishonesty cannot buy.

As we look at some situations in which honesty exacts a price that can be hard to pay, search out the possible gains that honesty can bring.

Facing Blame in a Tight Squeeze

The tight-squeeze situation is one in which a person or a group will have to face blame, criticism, and possibly punishment if their actions are found out by others—like Jim's situation from the first part of this chapter.

Familiar Tight Squeezes
Besides the following situations, you can probably come up with numerous other examples of tight squeezes:

1. Sarah comes home three hours after her curfew. Her parents are waiting up and want to know why she is late.
2. Rob started a false rumor that Janice had sex with him after a party. Now it is all over school. Janice is devastated, and she confronts Rob, wanting to know how the rumor got started.
3. Avery realizes he forgot to send an important document to one of his company's clients. Now it seems that the client will lose thousands of dollars because of Avery's carelessness. He has to meet with the client and explain the client's impending loss.

- For each of these tight-squeeze situations, think of two responses that the person in the squeeze could give: *(a)* a dishonest response, and *(b)* an honest response.
- What costs accompany the dishonest response? What does the person gain?
- What costs come with the honest response? What gains?

Telling a lie to get out of a tight-squeeze situation is appealing because it often "works." That is, people buy the lie and the dishonest person escapes blame, criticism, or punishment. The problem is "solved," at least in the short term, at seemingly little or no cost to the liar. But, as the saying goes, "What goes around comes around." Lies usually come back to haunt their teller sooner or later. **9**

Obscure Language in a Tight Squeeze
The mentality that "if it works, do it" appears so commonly in our world that it is almost unquestioned. Government officials regularly hide facts from the public in order to smooth the way for policies that would otherwise meet with resistance.

9
Think of a tight-squeeze situation that one of your friends might be in. Write an imaginary dialog in which you try to convince your friend that telling the truth would be the wiser choice.

units" as a measure of nuclear radiation—until public ridicule forced it to be dropped.

Speaking so as to obscure real meanings and intentions is a dishonest way of getting out of a tight squeeze, whether it is done by government agencies, groups, corporations, or individuals. **10**

Accepting the Possibility of Failure

Another cost of honesty can be the possibility of failure. For instance, cheating on tests and homework is done partly because people are reluctant to study hard enough. But another motive is the fear of failing or of not performing highly enough to "make it"—get into the right college, get on the dean's list, get into medical school, and so on.

The following is a discussion among several high school students about the morality of cheating in school:

Joanne: One time I was all ready to cheat on a math quiz, with the formulas all written on my arm, but I got so nervous. I failed anyway, and I still don't know how to do those problems.

Jerry: I can't stand my math teacher, so if I cheat in his class it's no big deal. But in English I like my teacher, so one time when I cheated I felt really guilty about it.

Dave: But sometimes it's okay to cheat.

Mario: Come on, it's being dishonest with yourself.

Dave: No, it's only dishonest with yourself if you cheat and think you know your stuff. But if you cheat and still admit that all you got out of it was a better grade, then you're not lying to yourself.

Danielle: But guys, it's still dishonest. Somebody else might have studied all night and really learned it, but they get the same grade as you. It's dishonest to think that what you did was okay.

When agencies, campaigns, or corporations blunder badly, they may refer to hiding the mistakes or disasters from the public as "damage control." Even when outright lying does not occur, often the facts are obscured in foggy language or euphemisms that are intended to mislead or to make unpleasant facts seem pleasant.

As an extreme example, the attempt by the Nazi government to wipe out all Jews was termed the "final solution" to the "Jewish problem." But the Nazis did not have a monopoly on deceptive language. U.S. officials in the Vietnam war referred to the wiping out of resistance in the countryside through the bombing of villages as the "pacification program." The term used by the U.S. Central Intelligence Agency (CIA) for assassination carried out by the agency is "termination with extreme prejudice." The Pentagon used the term "sunshine

---

■
Above: As a "damage control" strategy, disturbing facts are often obscured in foggy language that is intended to mislead.

10
On paper, brainstorm examples you have heard of phrases that obscure the facts. For each example, translate the foggy phrases into clear phrases.

Dave: If you get caught, it's dishonest. If you get away with it, honesty's not a problem.

Melinda: If I have to cheat for a grade then something's wrong—no grade should be so important that I'd cheat for it. I wouldn't be very happy with myself if I had to look at someone else's paper to get an answer. I don't cheat because I don't want to feel guilty. I want to feel good about myself, and I want God to be happy with me. I admit, I've cheated. But only when I was too proud to face the fact that I'd come up short otherwise.

Jerry: Sometimes you have to cheat if you want to get anywhere in life.

- Evaluate the different arguments made by the students in this discussion.
- Suppose you must choose between cheating on an exam or failing an important course. Use the LISTEN process to evaluate your situation.
- What are the costs of not cheating to students who prefer to be honest? What do honest students gain?
- What is the connection between cheating in school and cheating in business as an adult? **11**

Losing Power and Control

The price of honesty may at times be that we do not stay in control of a situation, that we cannot have our way or do what we want. In business, the attempt to stay in control motivates many unsafe, if not illegal, practices. For example:

In 1990, a U.S. federal grand jury indicted a major airline and several of its employees on sixty counts, charging that over a period of four years, they deliberately falsified maintenance records on airplanes. The planes should have been kept on the ground for scheduled service or repairs. According to the indictment, officials of the airline were involved in a criminal conspiracy that relied on intimidation and coercion of employees to fake the maintenance records. The motive behind falsifying the records was to avoid flight delays and cancellations. (Summarized from an article in *U.S. News and World Report*)

- What are some possible consequences of keeping a plane in the air when it needs to be serviced or repaired? Why might an airline take such a risk?
- If the airline is indeed guilty as charged, what role would self-deception have likely played in the officials who gave the orders? in the employees who carried out the orders?
- What would be the costs to the airline of keeping honest maintenance records? What would be the gains?
- What would be the costs to an employee who refused to go along with a dishonest practice? What would this employee gain?

Honesty can cost a great deal: blame, criticism, and punishment; failure; and loss of power and control. It can cost you your job and even your life, as Jesus' example shows us. Ultimately, however, honesty buys more than it costs because honesty creates an atmosphere of truth and trust that allows human beings and society to flourish.

For Review
- Contrast the costs of honesty with its gains.
- Give two examples of obscure language used to hide facts or mistakes from the public.

11
Write a one-page essay describing cheating in your school (if it occurs) and the effects it has on your own and others' motivation to learn.

Is a "White Lie" Okay?

We are all used to hearing "white lies"—supposedly innocent untruths that do not seem to hurt anyone but that make things run pleasantly or more smoothly. Because they seem to help more than hurt, they must be okay, right?

Some Examples

Before judging the morality of white lies, let's take a look at some typical examples:

1. "Tell them I'm not home." (You don't want to talk to some unpleasant visitors.)
2. "He is one of the most outstanding students I have ever taught. I highly recommend him for the position." (He's actually a mediocre student who asked you to give him a good recommendation.)
3. "What a neat haircut! I love it." (You hate it.)
4. "Your mommy and daddy still love each other, honey. It's just that we think it's best if we don't live together." (You don't want your child to know what is really behind the divorce.)
5. "You'll be bouncing back before long, Helen. Just keep your spirits up." (You think that telling your patient she is dying would be too depressing for her.)

• Do you think any of the above white lies are morally acceptable? Explain your answers.

Problems with White Lies

So what is the problem with white lies? A number of problems make these deceptions morally questionable. When we look beneath the surface, white lies are not the innocent communications that they seem to be. Like other lies, ultimately they eat away at trust among persons. Here are some of the specific reasons that white lies are not so innocent after all.

Above: White lies cloud and ultimately destroy trust and make genuine communication more difficult, not less.

Harmless in Whose Eyes?

Often when we tell a white lie, we justify it by saying we did it for the other person's benefit. But look at a white lie from the perspective of the person deceived. In most cases, people who have been told a white lie would view that lie not as harmless but as hurtful. If they knew about it, they would feel used, manipulated, foolish, and patronized. They would reason correctly that the other person did not respect them enough to give them the truth in a tactful way. Some people, of course, do not want to know the truth. Even so, it is demeaning and disrespectful to lie to them. In more serious situations, such as cases 4 and 5 in the previous examples, grave injustice and harm can be done by lying, even when the person on the receiving end would rather hear a lie than the truth. **12**

Cheap Communication

The difficulty with flattering or excuse-giving white lies is that they cheapen communication. When these lies are commonplace, it becomes harder and harder to trust the word or opinions of others. For example, people who really are pesky visitors never get even a hint that their behavior is irritating. A person whose haircut looks ridiculous hears only praise for it. Letters of recommendation cannot be trusted by employers or colleges because all the letters speak in such glowing terms about the applicants. The meanings of words become blurred. Does "outstanding" really mean "average," and "average" mean "poor"?

Part of a Deceptive Pattern

If we consider a single white lie, usually it looks innocent enough: The effects of the lie do not seem that harmful, and they may even seem bene-ficial. However, it is a mistake to look only at the single lie and to miss the bigger picture. Small, seemingly harmless lies pave the way for bigger, more serious lies. And sometimes bigger lies are necessary in order to save face from previous, smaller lies. Lies multiply and reinforce one another. Lying can become a habit and a part of one's character.

Nothing but the Truth?

Not the *Whole* Truth

The obligation to be honest, though, does not require us to tell the *whole* truth at all times. Things can be left unsaid or only partly said—with tact and sensitivity—and still be truthful. For instance:

- Irritating visitors can be told, "My mom is busy now. Can she call you later?" rather than "My mom says you people stay too long. She doesn't want to see you."

12
Think of a hypothetical white lie that someone might tell you. In writing, reflect on how you might feel if you found out that the person was lying to you.

 Above: Small, seemingly harmless lies may lead us into a sticky web of bigger, more serious lies from which it is hard to break free.

- A dying woman can be told, "Your condition is very serious. I'm really concerned about you," rather than "You are dying and probably won't live six more months." The first response will give the patient an opening to ask more about her condition, and the doctor might then respond, "We can shrink this tumor with treatment, but it has gone too far to be gotten rid of. The cancer has also spread to other systems, so it is unlikely that it can be controlled."
- A child of divorcing parents can be told, "Mommy and Daddy are having so much trouble getting along that we think it's hurting all of us too much," rather than "Mommy and Daddy hate each other." **13**

Withholding Facts from Those Who Have No Right to Them

We are not obligated to tell the *whole* truth at all times. For the purposes of tact or compassion, we may tell only part of the information that is true.

To prevent serious harm from happening, in certain situations we may have to withhold information entirely from someone who has no right to it. For instance, during World War II many heroic citizens of France and the Netherlands hid Jews in their homes to prevent them from being taken prisoner by Nazi officials, sent to concentration camps, and executed. The citizens' refusals to disclose the whereabouts of the Jews were not actually lies, because the Nazis had no right to that information. Lying is always wrong, but keeping facts from those who are bent on using those facts for evil purposes is not lying. In such cases of being questioned, to give an evasive answer or an answer that could easily be interpreted another way is the moral thing to do.

This necessary withholding of information, however, should not be confused with telling white lies. White lies, as discussed earlier, are really not so innocent because they *are* lies.

Yet what about in situations a little closer to home and not so extreme? For example:

A sixteen-year-old girl is applying for her first job. When she gets to the question *Have you ever been arrested?* she freezes with anxiety. The truth is that she was once arrested. At age thirteen, she was at a party where the police arrested everyone for drinking. Her dilemma: if she says she was arrested, she thinks she will be automatically out of the running for this job, even though she does not drink anymore.

- What morally right choice could this person make?

The issue of white lies highlights the mentality of "if it works for me, do it." These supposedly well-intentioned deceptions are tempting to fall into because they seem to work so well, making things run more pleasantly and conveniently, at least temporarily. But these lies help create a shadowy world in which reality is hard to find.

For Review

- What are three problems with white lies?
- Is a lie ever morally permissible?

13
For three days, keep track on paper of the situations in which telling a white lie seems like the obvious or easiest thing for you to do. Next to each situation, explain what you actually did or said.

"Kindness and Truth Shall Meet"

Many people fall into the habit of hiding the truth because they are genuinely afraid of hurting other people, and they think that people are too delicate to handle honest communication. This can result not only in telling white lies but in being backed into choices that in the larger picture are more harmful than being truthful.

Not an Easy Combination

Combining care for another person with honesty is often not easy to do. But for Christians, the ideal is that "kindness and truth shall meet" (Psalm 85:11). In other words, honesty should not be used as a weapon to sting and wound another person. We are always called to speak the truth *in love,* never intending to hurt with our words. Occasionally, however, we must say things that need to be said but that the other person does not want to hear. Kindness does not mean keeping our mouth shut in these instances. Rather, it means caring enough about ourselves, the other person, and the integrity of the relationship to speak the truth in a respectful way.

We need to keep in mind that speaking the truth does not equal blurting out everything that is on our mind. Discretion, sensitivity, and proper timing are needed. **14**

A Hard Truth to Tell

In the following situation, Deanne struggles to bring together kindness and truth in her communications:

Deanne answered the phone, somehow sensing that she'd hear Julie's voice at the other end.

"Dee, this is Julie. I got accepted into the Residential College, too. Now we can room together." Julie's enthusiasm burst through the phone.

Deanne hesitated. She didn't want to room with Julie. Julie was so hyper and then so down—like a roller coaster—all the time, that living with Julie would drive her bonkers. Yes, she liked Julie, but she could only take her in small doses. Julie's study habits followed her moods. Deanne knew that she would have to study hard if she wanted to get into law school, so she couldn't afford to be tossed about in the wake of Julie's erratic emotions. Besides, Julie smoked. Deanne hated the smell of smoke on her clothes and in her hair.

"Dee, you there? What do you think? Should we do our housing applications together?"

"Julie, I've been thinking. I kind of need more space next year. I think that it would be good for me to room with someone new. We could still spend lots of time together."

"You don't like my smoking. I knew it. But I would never smoke in the room."

Deanne had heard smoking pledges like this from Julie before, pledges that Julie promptly forgot.

"You shouldn't have to live by my rules, and I can't handle smoke."

"How come you don't want to room with me? Really."

"Like I said, I just think that I need to be exposed to new people. We'll be in the same dorm. If we roomed together, we'd be less likely to meet new people."

"You could still end up with a roommate you don't like—then what? And I could too."

"It's possible."

14
Interview someone you consider tactful. Find out some of the dilemmas this person has faced in trying to combine kindness and truth. Write up the results of your interview but do not identify the person by name.

"You mean you're willing to take a chance with somebody you don't know rather than room with me? I didn't know you disliked me that much. I always thought we were friends."

Deanne gritted her teeth, holding back a number of nasty retorts. "I'm sorry if it seems that way, Julie. I'm trying to be honest with you and with myself. I like you, and I want to spend time with you next year—but not as roommates. You're very adaptable. You'll do fine."

"Well, good-bye," Julie snapped and slammed down the receiver.

Deanne grimaced. She didn't want to hurt Julie, but she didn't want to room with her either.

- How well did Deanne combine kindness and truth? What did you like about how she expressed herself? Was anything missing?
- Should Deanne have told Julie that it would be hard to live with Julie's emotional ups and downs?
- As this story illustrates, trying to combine kindness and truth does not always leave people feeling happy with you. What responsibility does Deanne have for Julie's hurt feelings, if any? What should Deanne do now?
- If Deanne had been concerned only about kindness and not about truth, what might have happened? Or if she had been concerned only about truth and not about kindness, what then?

For Review

- Explain the ideal that "kindness and truth shall meet." How does this happen in everyday life?

Honesty: Sincerity and Skill

At the beginning of this chapter it was noted that honesty is the sincere devotion to truthfulness. That, of course, is where honesty begins. But it does not end there. We can intend to be truthful, but we can be unskilled in *looking for truth.* That is, we can operate with a closed mind—a mind that fixes on one understanding of things and refuses to look beyond that understanding.

Honesty requires both the intent to be honest and a habit of seeking truth—refusing to shut down our mind or harden our heart. The honest person does not live in a vacuum, however. We need others to help us figure out what is true, what is real. Admitting that we do not know it all and that much remains uncertain is a healthy part of developing an honest character.

Above: Being skilled in looking for truth means that we seek the light of others' insights and understandings as well as our own.

10

Respect
for Persons:
Looking Again

Images of Respect

- "What I like about Mr. Nielson is that when he talks with you, you feel like you're worth something. You walk out of his classroom feeling like somebody. I don't know how he does it, he just does."

- "Marcy doesn't make fun of people behind their back, even when everyone else is having a big laugh. She has a good sense of humor, but not at someone else's expense. I respect and admire her for that."

- "I can tell that Ricardo respects me, because he really listens to what I say; he doesn't just blow it off like it's nothing."

- "The neat thing about Maura is that she has all different kinds of friends. Kids from groups that hardly talk to each other—maybe because of their taste in music, or their race, or the way they dress, or how much money they have— they're all friends with Maura. She just doesn't let those differences get in the way."

To have **respect for persons**, a dimension of the virtue of justice (studied in chapter 6), is to recognize and honor the essential goodness of each person. Respect communicates, "You are valuable. Your thoughts and feelings matter. You count." Disrespect for persons, on the other hand, communicates, "You are valuable only if I can get something I want from you. Your thoughts and feelings are of little importance. You don't count much." **1**

Christian Faith: "Everyone Counts"

Look Again: Seeing with God's Eyes

In the Christian vision, every person counts. Absolutely no one is outside the scope of God's love. In everyday life, though, a different understanding of respect often holds: We believe that we should respect only those people who *deserve* our respect. People must earn our respect by being "nice" people. Fortunately, God, who is the source of all goodness, does not view us that way.

The Latin roots of the word *respect* mean, literally, "to look again." To respect the essential goodness of each person is to take another look, a deeper look, in order to find the person that God loves. From the view of justice, respect of this kind is a basic human right (see page 114 of chapter 6).

The Example of Jesus

A minister from Illinois expresses how Jesus saw the person God loves in everyone he encountered:

"Don't most of us carry around a little unwritten, maybe subconscious, list of people for whom we believe God has no use? How about the guy who peddles dope to elementary school children? Child pornographers? Bribe-taking attorneys? Crooked politicians? Greedy stockbrokers?

1
In a paragraph, describe someone who makes you feel respected. How does that person communicate respect?

"The fact is we're all wrong. Jesus spent a lot of time with people just like that: irreligious people, undesirables, the unconvinced, the spiritually confused, the morally bankrupt." (Quoted in *Youthworker Update*)

Recall the story from the beginning of chapter 2 about Jesus, Simon the Pharisee, and the "woman with the bad reputation." The whole thrust of Jesus' behavior in that incident at the dinner party and in many others like it was to show that God's love encompasses everyone.

The Example of Saints

Francis of Assisi, the thirteenth-century saint popularly known for his love of nature and for his life of simplicity and poverty, took on the perspective of God in his attitude toward all of creation, especially human beings. One of his biographers, G. K. Chesterton, gives us this vivid portrait of Francis's respect for persons:

From the Pope to the beggar, from the sultan of Syria in his pavilion to the ragged robbers crawling out of the wood, there was never a man who looked into those brown burning eyes without being certain that Francis Bernadone was really interested in *him;* in his own inner individual life from the cradle to the grave; that he himself was being valued and taken seriously, and not merely added to the spoils of some social policy or the names in some clerical document. . . . He treated the whole mob of men as a mob of Kings. (*St. Francis of Assisi,* page 142)

In our era, those who have visited with Mother Teresa of Calcutta say that she communicates the same respect that Francis gave to everyone he met. What Jesus, Francis of Assisi, and Mother Teresa were doing when they treated each person they met as sacred, worthy, and valuable was seeing those people with "God's eyes." **2**

The Dynamics of Respect

The Golden Rule

One way of describing respect is to point to the Golden Rule: "'Do to others whatever you would have them do to you'" (Matthew 7:12).

With its grounding in the Golden Rule, respect for persons builds upon a basic human capacity, empathy. **Empathy** is the ability to understand another's feelings, thoughts, and experiences from that person's point of view. Most often, empathetic persons draw upon their own experiences. They remember how it felt to be treated a certain way and realize that if they felt that way, so might others. But even more than that, empathetic persons desire for others the same treatment that they desire for themselves.

At other times, empathizing requires that we use our gift of imagination, as the college student in the following example did. The story comes to us from the student's teacher:

Several rapes had been reported on campus within a month's time, so I decided we ought to discuss the crime in class. The next day a big guy named Bill, usually an enthusiastic participant, was very quiet. After class that day I asked him why he was so silent. Bill explained to me that during the discussion on rape he had really had a tough time relating to such an experience and that bothered him. So he spent a long time that night trying to imagine being raped—with its fear and pain, its shame, anger, and hate—and when he got through to the experience, he broke down weeping.

Obviously, in order to have empathy for others, we have to be able to recognize our own goodness and worth. We need to see that we, too, have the right to be treated with respect. The virtue of re-

---

2
Focus on a category of persons who, in the eyes of most people, do not deserve respect. Write two descriptions of a person in that category: one as seen through the eyes of "most people" and another as seen through "God's eyes."

specting persons gets at the essence of the command to love. **3**

When we are empathetic, we find that other people, like ourselves, want these things in relationships:

- **to be treated as valuable in ourselves, not simply to be used by other people**
- **to be treated with care, not violence**
- **to be accepted as individuals, not put down for belonging to a certain group or category of persons**

In the remainder of this chapter, we will look at how these aspects of respect are seen, and sometimes are not seen, in everyday life.

For Review

- Define the virtue of respect for persons.
- Why respect all persons, even those who do not seem to deserve our respect?
- What is empathy?

■
Above, left and right: In the Christian vision, all persons deserve to be treated as worthy, as valuable in themselves.

3
Imagine yourself in the shoes of a person of a race, class, or culture different from your own. Pretending you are that person, write a one-page description of an experience in which you were not treated with respect.

To Be Valued, Not Used

Being Used: A Bitter Experience

No one likes the feeling of being used or manipulated for someone else's purposes. Here is one unhappy possibility:

Ginny and Victoria have struck up quite a friendship over the last two weeks. Ginny is delighted because she has not had a close friend since she started coming to this high school a couple of years ago. One day, though, she overhears Victoria speaking to another girl: "Yeah, I know she's kind of weird. But her father's the manager at the country club, you know, and I need a job this summer!" With a shiver, Ginny realizes that Victoria is talking about her.

- In what ways has Ginny been used? How would you react if you were in her situation?
- What harm does Victoria do to herself by using Ginny?
- What role, if any, does self-deception play in the above case—either in the "user" or the "used"?
- Think of other similar situations in which one person uses or manipulates another. How are both persons hurt?

Being Useful Versus Being Used

Christians are challenged to form relationships based on valuing other persons as worthy and wonderful *in themselves,* apart from what they can *do* for us. Of course, people can be and are useful to one another: your friend helps you with math; your teacher lets the coach know that you have a lot of pressure from classwork this week; your supervisor puts in a good word for you to the boss; your friend gives you rides all the time because you do not have a car.

Valuing what other people do for us is not wrong. The moral problem develops when persons look at relationships only, or mostly, in terms of getting something for themselves rather than showing concern for the other people involved. Valuing what a person does for us should not be confused with valuing the person.

"What Profit Does it Show . . . ?"

Manipulation is another destructive way of using people. It can be subtle or obvious. For instance, some manipulators try to make other people feel guilty in order to get them to do whatever they want. Others will try to make another person look bad or foolish or incompetent in order to make themselves look better.

As with other bad habits, the tendency to use and manipulate others can develop into a way of life. After a while, the manipulator does not even realize that he or she is constantly using others to get something. Sadly, a person with a manipulative character loses the capacity for genuine friendship. For such individuals, Jesus' words have particular meaning: "'What profit would a man show if he were to gain the whole world and destroy himself in the process? What can a man offer in exchange for his very self?'" (Matthew 16:26). **4**

For Review

- How is being useful to someone different from being used?

4
Recall two experiences you have had: one of being valued for who you are as a person, and another of being used or manipulated by another person. In writing, contrast your reactions to these two experiences.

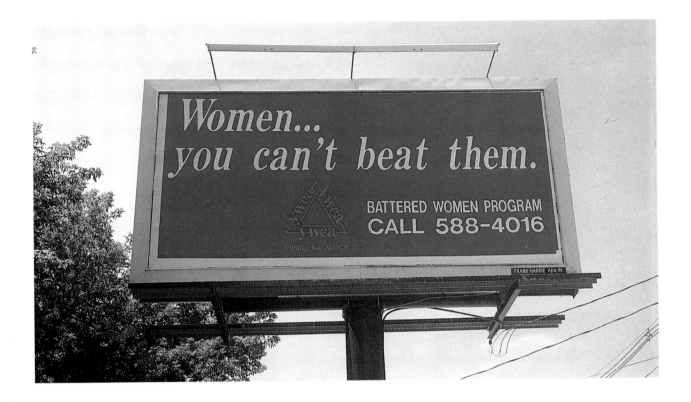

To Be Treated with Care, Not Violence

Violence—whether physical, emotional, or psychological—is perhaps the worst form of disrespect for persons. Being treated without violence is the bare minimum in terms of respect.

Domestic Violence

Increasingly in the family—the place where the fundamental experiences of respect should be happening—persons are being hurt. Domestic violence occurs in wife or husband battering, in physical or sexual abuse of children, and in verbal abuse that damages people emotionally and psychologically.

Greater Danger at Home

Unfortunately, for many people, the chances of being assaulted, beaten, or even killed are much greater in their own home, at the hands of a loved one, than on the streets, by a stranger. Here are some startling U.S. statistics:

1. In the United States, a woman is battered every fifteen seconds. It is estimated that two to four million women are physically abused each year.
2. In 1991, nearly 30 percent of all female victims of murder were killed by their husbands or boyfriends.

3. In 1991, there were 2,694,000 reports of child abuse—40 percent more than in 1985.
4. In 1992, nearly 1,400 children died from abuse and neglect—54 percent more than in 1985.
5. Most sexual abuse offenders are persons known and trusted by the abused child.
6. Approximately 4 percent of elderly Americans are victims of abuse.

Domestic violence often spills over into other relationships. For example, violence is becoming common in dating relationships of high school and college students. *Teacher* magazine reports that 41 percent of high school students have been involved in dating violence—usually in long-term dating relationships. Researchers are finding that the patterns of violence in a dating relationship tend to follow the patterns of violence that the young person in the relationship experienced or witnessed as a child with her or his parents.

Emotional Abuse

Of course, abuse need not be physical to be destructive. It can be emotional, such as in the case of a parent or guardian who continually tells a child—in words, behaviors, or neglect—how unlovable he or she is. These forms of psychological violence also spill over into other relationships. At one extreme are persons who turn their own experiences of being put down into constant put-downs of others. At the other extreme are those who become so numbed by emotional abuse that they tolerate it in their other relationships. **5**

Reasons for Violence at Home

Why do people hurt the ones they live with and supposedly love? A high school junior who has witnessed domestic violence suggests one possible reason:

Frustration. People who are unhappy and unsatisfied with themselves and their lives can get so frustrated and tied up inside that they just reach a breaking point and become violent.

Several years ago my oldest sister was a victim of domestic violence. Her husband was a very frustrated person—his life hadn't turned out anything like he'd expected, and my sister was close by and vulnerable, and he took it out on her. Fortunately, she escaped that relationship. She still has visible scars. I have scars, too, but not visible—scars that make it hard for me to trust others, even if they say they love me.

- What do you think of this explanation of the reason for violence?

Patterns of abuse may be passed on from one generation to the next. If we have such tendencies, we need to examine where they might have come from and try to change them. We all grow up with a certain amount of negative emotional baggage, but that does not relieve us of the responsibility to become persons who give and expect respect.

A look at domestic violence from a broader view reveals that violence at home is fed by violence in society. Many movies and TV programs glorify violence. In addition, racial prejudice and greed breed unjust social, economic, and political systems. These systems in turn foster situations such as poverty and unemployment, thus putting on people pressures that can magnify a tendency toward violence. Feelings of powerlessness, frustration, and hopelessness also lead to alcohol and other drug abuse, which often figures prominently in domestic abuse. **6**

5
Do you know of anyone who has been a victim of domestic abuse? If so, list the effects you think the abuse has had on the person.

6
Do you agree or disagree with this statement?
- Music recordings and music videos with violent themes foster violence toward persons in real life.

Support your answer in a one-page essay.

Reflections of a Battered Wife

Read the words of a woman who offered her reflections anonymously:

> In the beginning, I was young . . . he was handsome. He said I was beautiful, smart, worthy of love . . . made me feel that way. And so we were married, walking joyfully together down a church aisle, our union blessed by God.
>
> Then came the angry words . . . the verbal tearing apart of me . . . the same me who my father had said was special . . . created by God for a purpose. . . . Now I was made to feel ugly, unintelligent, unworthy of any love, God's or man's. And so I crawled helplessly, night after night, into the corner of our bedroom and cried.
>
> Next came the beatings . . . unrelenting violence . . . unceasing pain. I shouldn't stay, but this is my husband. . . . I promised forever. He says I deserve it . . . maybe I do . . . if I could just be good. I feel so alone . . . doesn't God hear me when I cry out silently as I lie in bed each night?
>
> Finally came the release, the realization. It's not me . . . it's him. . . . I am worthy of love, God's and man's. One spring morning, my heart was filled with hope and with fear now only of starting over on my own. And so again I walked . . . down the hallway of our apartment building . . . never again to be silent . . . never again to live with that kind of violence, to suffer that kind of pain. ("When Home Is Where the Hurt Is," *Christopher News Notes*)

Sex and Violence

Another example of violence in our society is the linkage of sex with violence in the media and in the real world of people's experiences. Sex, a wonderful gift in our human nature, is meant to be associated with love, intimacy, respect, pleasure, and joy—not with violence, which destroys all of those. Sex and violence are combined in cases of rape, sexual abuse, and pornography.

Rape

Whenever a person is forced to have sexual intercourse with another, that act is a rape. It does not matter whether the persons are strangers to each other, on a first date, going together steadily, or married. Rape is one of the most extreme violations of body and psyche a person can experience; it must never be dismissed casually no matter what the relationship of the persons involved. (While women are the primary victims of rape, rape can and does happen to men.)

A significant portion of the violence in dating relationships (discussed earlier under domestic violence) comes in the form of date or acquaintance rape. In small but growing numbers, victims of date rape are finding the courage to come forward and report that they have been raped on a date or by a steady boyfriend. Unfortunately, until recently, the climate in our society has not been receptive to hearing about such matters. Even today, the victim is often blamed rather than supported. The assumption seems to be that the man has a "right" to have sex with a woman if he has invested anything in her at all, as if she is thereby his property.

Even among young people, this notion holds. In a survey conducted by the Rhode Island Rape Crisis Center of 1,700 sixth-to-ninth graders, nearly 25 percent of the boys and 17 percent of the girls said it is okay for a man to force a woman to have sex with him if he spent money on her. Even more discouraging, the study found that 65 percent of the boys and 57 percent of the girls said it is okay for a man to force a woman to have sex with him if they have been dating each other for more than six months. **7**

Persons who have been raped under any conditions need help to cope with the trauma. And those who force someone to have sex, no matter what the conditions, need to understand their own behavior as violent and criminal, not sexy.

- Why does our society tend to blame rape victims?
- Discuss the statement, "A person always has the right to say no."
- How can society and individuals discourage the attitudes that underlie rape? How can they be more supportive to rape victims?

Sexual Abuse of Young People

Although sexual abuse can be considered to fall under the category of domestic abuse, it frequently occurs outside the family as well as within it. Sexual abuse is violence, because even when it takes the form of getting a child to "agree" to sex rather than physically forcing it, sexual abuse does grave damage to children in their growing years. In addition to possible physical harm, sexual abuse often causes serious immediate and long-term psychological damage, including the impairment of the person's ability to trust in relationships.

The evidence of sexual abuse of children from recent research shows it to be more widespread than most people, including psychologists, ever imag-

---

7
Explain in writing why you think the above survey turned up the results it did.

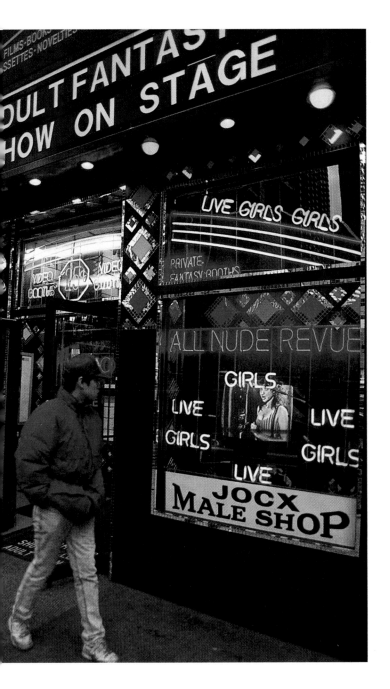

ined. In large-scale community surveys, 20 to 30 percent of adult females report that they were sexually abused before the age of fourteen (most between ages five and eight). About 10 percent of adult males report that they were sexually abused as children. Often an abusive situation does not become known to others until much later, when the victim is an adult, because she or he was told to keep it a secret by the abusing parent or stepparent, other relative, or neighbor. Also, the shame and the mistaken belief that the abuse is the child's fault are often so intense that the child represses all memory of it until years later. **8**

Like spouse or child battering, sexual abuse is a legacy passed down from generation to generation. People who commit sex crimes as adults were usually abused as children. Those who have the courage to get help in these situations—whether as a victim or a victimizer, whether as a child or an adult survivor—are breaking the cycle of a terribly unjust and hurtful legacy.

Pornography

The problem with pornography is not that it is concerned with sex or nakedness, nor that a person looking at it might experience sexual feelings. By creating us as sexual creatures, God affirmed the goodness of sex, our bodies, and our sexual feelings. The problem with pornography in films, magazines, and music videos and lyrics is the way in which sex is portrayed and promoted—as linked with exploitation and violence. These kinds of materials promote physical, sexual, and emotional abuse. Pornography is not about how wonderful sex can be but about how inhuman it can be, and such inhumanity is glorified by the assumption that it is appealing.

■
Above: Pornography is not about how wonderful sex can be but about how inhuman it can be when linked with exploitation and violence.

8
List some thoughts that could prevent a child or a teenager from disclosing incidents of sexual abuse. Answer those thoughts with your own responses.

Christine Gudorf, a writer and theologian, makes these comments about pornography and provides a helpful analogy:

Pornography . . . is sexual depictions of persons in ways that imply or encourage the denial of their full humanity. Pornography is not simply depictions of some sinful thing or activity but the twisting of something good (sexuality) to less than human ends. . . .

Pornography insists that sexuality is essentially a mechanical activity done by one person to another in order to satisfy a physical appetite. This is what makes it ultimately boring, unsatisfying, and dangerous to our humanity. Imagine watching a couple eat one meal after another if those meals conveyed only the mechanics of eating and never reflected the tangle of emotions and needs satisfied in eating, the ability of shared meals to bind persons together, or the subtle interactions of context and personality with food sharing. ("Teach Your Kids to Look Past the Pictures")

- React to Gudorf's statements and her comparison between sexuality and the sharing of food.
- If a young person's earliest "information" about sexuality is from dehumanizing, violent pornography, what effect might that have on that person's capacity to develop caring sexual relationships?

Getting Help Is Crucial

Fortunately, for victims of violence and abuse, help exists in the form of counseling, support groups, and shelters for battered women and children, although more is needed. Anyone who is being abused physically or sexually definitely needs to seek out help immediately from some trusted person—a pastor, teacher, relative, or friend—in order to figure out what to do about it. In some cases, calling the police is the only solution.

Increasingly, too, there is hope for persons who recognize their own abusive behavior or their potential for it and want to get help to end it. In many communities, special programs of individual and group counseling now offer abusers the chance to learn how to handle problems without violence. Emergency telephone hot lines and organizations such as Parents Anonymous give spouses or parents who are struggling with their own tendencies toward violence the support they need to prevent further abuse from happening. **9**

- How might the LISTEN process empower abuse victims to seek help? empower abusers to seek help?

For Review

- What is the bare minimum in terms of respectful behavior?
- How do abusive relationships—whether physical, emotional, or psychological—create further harm and abuse?
- Define rape. What common assumption in society tends to support date rape?
- Why is pornography harmful?
- How can a victim of abuse try to become free of the abuse?

9
Investigate and then make a list of some agencies or individuals in your community that can help victims of abuse or abusers themselves.

To Be Accepted, Not Stereotyped

Another important quality of respectful relationships involves accepting persons as individuals, not putting them down because they belong to a certain group or category. Consider this example:

Rudy Mendez filled out the job application quickly. He knew that the Snelling Company hired summer workers to fill the huge volume of orders hitting them during their prime season. Rudy walked up to the desk of the personnel officer, and when she finally looked up, he handed her his application. She looked over his application.

"You have a work permit?" she snapped.

"What do you mean?"

"What I *mean* is, do you have a work permit?"

Recognition suddenly struck Rudy. The woman thought that he was an illegal alien from Mexico. To her, all people with Hispanic names were illegals.

"Look, it says here I was born in Carmel. My parents were born in Carmel."

"Prove it."

"Why should I have to prove it? You didn't make that blond guy who was just up here before me prove it." Rudy's anger and embarrassment boiled.

"Listen, Mr. Mendez," she snapped, "his name wasn't Mexican. We can't afford to hire illegal aliens. So you either show me some ID that proves what you wrote here, or I tear this application up."

In this instance, Rudy is the victim of stereotyping. Because of his Hispanic surname, it is assumed that he is an illegal alien.

• How might companies handle the question of identifying illegal residents in a way that is respectful to everyone who applies?

■
Above, top and bottom: Persons want to be accepted as individuals, not put down because they belong to a certain group or category.

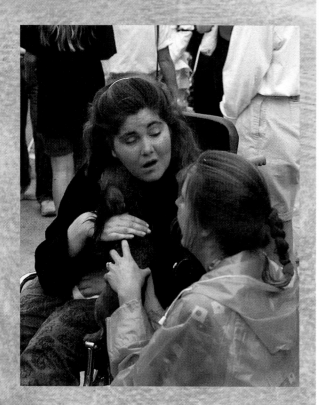

"Don't Label Me"

Don't label me.
Dare to be with the uncomfortable moment of
    not knowing.
Be with me with open eyes and an open heart
    and share this moment with me.
See me for who I am—a part of creation;
    ever evolving, ever changing.
But please don't label me. For by labeling me
    you limit me. You limit the gifts and surprises
        that I have to share.
If you must put a label on me, to deal with me,
    label me with love, with dignity and with
        compassion.
For it is out of these labels that you will begin
    to see who I am.

                              Melody Martin

Stereotypes and Prejudice

A **stereotype** is a mental label applied to the members of a group, an oversimplified "picture" of who they are based on assumptions about the group as a whole that may have little or no basis in fact. Often, the assumptions are negative. For example:
- "People on welfare are lazy and don't want to work."
- "Orientals are trying to take over the United States."
- "Jews are tight with money."
- "Jocks think they're better than everybody else."
- "White people will screw you over any chance they get."
- "Girls don't have the ability to lead."
- "Old people are boring."
- "Teenagers are selfish and materialistic."

When we carry such assumptions into our interactions or dealings with members of various groups, we communicate disrespect. We say, in effect, "I already know what you're about. You can't tell me anything new about yourself." **Prejudice**—prejudging people without knowing them as individuals—is at the heart of stereotyping. **10**

Words and Attitudes That Hurt

One of the most common ways that prejudice lives on in society is through racial and ethnic jokes and slurs. Persons who engage in such verbal abuse tell themselves that they are doing no harm because the objects of their laughter and name calling are not around to hear. But by speaking in this way and by telling and laughing at such jokes, these persons perpetuate a poisonous climate of put-downs and disrespect toward members of other races or groups.

10
Focus on a category of people you belong to, for example, teenagers, people of a certain race or ethnic group, people from a particular neighborhood, people who listen to a certain type of music. List five stereotypes or prejudices that many people hold about that category. Then respond to those stereotypes in an open letter to those who hold them.

The U.S. Catholic bishops describe the current climate of racism in this way:

Crude and blatant expressions of racist sentiment, though they occasionally exist, are today considered bad form. Yet racism itself persists in covert ways. Under the guise of other motives, it is manifest in the tendency to stereotype and marginalize whole segments of the population whose presence is perceived as a threat. It is manifest also in the indifference that replaces open hatred. The minority poor are seen as . . . expendable. Many times the new face of racism is the computer print-out, the graph of profits and losses, the pink slip, the nameless statistic. (*Brothers and Sisters to Us,* page 6)

- Discuss the bishops' statement.
- In what ways does racism exist in your school or community?

Actions: Even Louder Than Words

Though the prejudice communicated in words and attitudes can do significant harm, many times our actions say much more. The decisions we make, the priorities we set, the money we allocate to certain groups can spell out prejudice as well. Certainly this is true with government affairs and in corporations, but it is also true in families and other communities, such as schools.

Consider the following discussion taking place at a high school's student council meeting:

"Buck, I don't believe you!" Michelle's fury was fulltilt now. "If the *boys* were going to regionals, we'd pay for buses for everybody."

"Nobody wants to see a bunch of girls play basketball," Buck retorted.

"Hold it." Christopher wanted to calm things down. "Look, we're getting nowhere. Let's go back to

Michelle's proposal. How many buses can the Student Council afford to charter for the girls' regionals?"

"If us guys were going to regionals, the school'd send the pep band, the cheerleaders, and just about anybody who could pay to go. We'd have a pep rally, too." Everyone listened to José, not only because he stood 6'7", but because he never said anything.

"Right, that's what I mean," Michelle nodded. "We should have a pep rally, too, just for the girls' team."

"We've only had one rally for basketball all season. The girls were introduced then."

"Yeah, *after* the boys, who are five-and-thirteen." Sandra stared coldly at Buck.

"How about just sending the cheerleaders and letting anybody else who wants to go sign up?" Shelly offered this as captain of the cheerleaders, although she hated going to girls' games.

"Shelly, what are you talking about?" Michelle gasped. "You ought to be *defending* the girls' team's rights, not giving 'em away!"

■
Above: Decisions about how resources are spent in a community, such as in a school, can speak louder than words.

"I say we take some of the athletic budget and some of the profits from the last dance and send the cheerleaders and the pep band. Then let's sell tickets to anybody else who wants to go. And let's have a pep rally." José's voice had an angry edge to it, even if he appeared calm.

"No way. Not enough people care about the girls' team to justify it. Besides, we've got two wrestlers going to regionals. Why not a pep rally for them? Shouldn't we send fans with them?"

"Cut it, Buck." Christopher was getting weary of this debate. "Let's vote on José's motion. I have to get to work. All in favor, raise your hands."

- What message will be communicated to the girls' basketball team if the Student Council votes against José's motion? What if the council votes in favor of José's motion?
- What stereotypes about girls and girls' sports are operating in the debate?
- How might the stereotypical attitudes expressed in the meeting spill over into other aspects of the students' lives? **11**

Melting the Prejudice Barrier

Most prejudice is rooted in fear, which in turn often stems from ignorance: We fear what we do not know. The fear that leads to prejudice can also grow out of insecurity about oneself. For example, people with a poor self-image often put down others in an attempt to feel better about themselves. All of us have pockets of fear that lead to some areas of prejudgment in our attitudes. Overcoming the barrier of prejudice that divides us from persons different from ourselves requires that we first recognize our own prejudice. But this barrier within us is more likely to yield to "melting" than to

"smashing." Attitudes ingrained in us for many years take time and patience to change.

The most direct and effective approach to dissolving these barriers of prejudice is to get to know persons in the group that is feared or stereotyped. Knowledge of real individuals brings understanding. When we refuse to go along with the prevailing stereotypes about particular groups, we accept persons in those groups as unique individuals. We are open to them, ready to let them show us who they are. This is an attitude of respect that also enables the respectful person to grow.

Swapping Stories Across the Generations

In the following example of melting barriers, a youth minister tells about how the young people of his parish took the initiative to get to know older people who live in a retirement residence in their community:

Our intent was to have an evening just to swap stories between the generations . . . a kind of "hanging out together." . . .

. . . About fifteen young people were present [and about a dozen older people]. . . . Several teens started, then several elders, then several more teens, and the exchange rolled along with great gusto. We heard stories from ski trips and from the workplace. We heard about potential fight situations handled with prayer. And we heard stories about learning to milk cows . . . and about the temptation to use drugs. We heard school stories and love stories. . . . Many laughs and a lot of drama emerged from the things we told one another. . . .

. . . For the young people, their stereotype of "the old person" gave way to a recognition of distinct personalities:

11
Describe in writing how attitudes toward men and women are expressed in the practices of an organization at your school.

Let Go and Soar

Besides doing an injustice to the person who is so labeled, prejudice also harms the growth and integrity of the one who carries the prejudice. As noted African American singer Marian Anderson said, "As long as you keep a person down, some part of you has to be down there to hold him down, so it means you cannot soar as you otherwise might."

- "This one is such a character."
- "That one had such a short fuse."
- "This one was really into what we were saying."
- "That one is such a love."

And for the older people, a kind of compassionate shock wave hit them as they picked up on the kind of pressures today's youth have to cope with. The teens felt that they had really been heard and understood. (Doolittle, *Be Alive in Christ,* pages 91–92)

- What are some stereotypes that many teenagers have of older people? What stereotypes do many older people have of teenagers? Why are these stereotypes so popular?
- Why did the story-sharing activity work so well for both the younger and the older people? **12**

"A Gift from God About to Happen"

Persons with physical or mental disabilities know well the sting of discrimination that comes with stereotypes and prejudgments. As one young woman put it:

I am not my arm. It is only one part of me. It's natural for people to be curious, for them to notice my arm—even I look twice at it myself sometimes. The fact is, though, we all have differences. Some people's are just more noticeable than others'. But those differences don't make one person better than or superior to another.

As with other forms of prejudice, melting the fear-based barriers of prejudice toward persons with disabilities happens by getting to know the person

12
Imagine a similar get-together in a school between two racial groups that until now have had very little contact with each other. Explain in writing what you would do to foster mutual understanding if you were leading the get-together.

as an individual. Here are some suggestions that can help this process:

1. **Ask questions.** Asking questions is often the best way to break the ice:
- What classes are you taking?
- What are your hobbies?
- How many brothers and sisters do you have?
- Where do you live?

Try to see past the differences and get to know people with disabilities as you would anyone else.

2. **Find out more about the particular disability itself.** Basic knowledge about a particular disability can serve as preventive medicine against stereotyping and prejudice. For example, cerebral palsy impairs people's ability to control their muscles, making such things as talking, eating, or walking difficult. Too often persons with cerebral palsy are presumed to be mentally retarded when in fact their disability has nothing to do with intelligence or mental development. **13**

3. **Recognize the gifts that persons with disabilities have to offer.** Respecting persons involves being open to the gifts others have to offer us. This is especially important to remember with regard to persons with disabilities because it is often too easy to focus on their "deficiencies." Echoing this suggestion, a woman who works with mentally retarded persons brings this attitude to her work: "When I approach a new person I am about to work with, I see the encounter as a gift from God about to happen."

Healing Actions

An earlier discussion addressed how actions often cause even more harm than words. But the power of actions over words can work in positive ways as well—ways that melt walls of prejudice. For example, sometimes one person's actions can bring healing into blatantly racist situations:

- When a black family was burned out of its Brooklyn home by racists, neighbors took up a collection and offered words of support. One white woman reassured the family: "We're with you."

- In Philadelphia a 13-year-old white youth [testified] in court against a youth who spray-painted "We don't want no niggers" on a house a black family was considering buying.

- In 1947 when Jackie Robinson became the first black man to play Major League baseball he faced venom nearly everywhere. During a game in Boston, the taunts prompted one of his teammates, Pee Wee Reese, a Southern white, to call timeout and walk over to Robinson, put his arm around his shoulder, and stand there with him. The gesture said: "This man is my friend."

- At Temple Beth Shalom in Manalapan, N.J., groups of children scrubbed away at the anti-Semitic slogans painted on the temple's outside wall until there was hardly a trace of the markings left. Adam Davis, 11, a Catholic, came to the cleanup with his mother, father and brother.

  "My mom told me before we got here that we are the future of the world," the young boy explained. "We should live in peace not prejudice." ("Healing the Hate," *Christopher News Notes*)

- On December 7, 1941, Japanese planes bombed the U.S. Pacific Fleet in Pearl Harbor, Hawaii. The action propelled the United States into the Second World War. It also fueled mistrust and hatred of Japanese Americans, 120,000 of whom were unconstitutionally placed in internment camps on the west coast.

13
Do some research on a disability you would like to know more about. Write down some facts about the disability that, if understood, would enable a person to relate more easily to someone who has that disability.

Even Japanese Americans who served in the U.S. Armed Forces were not exempt from prejudice. Mitsuo Usui tells of an experience of prejudice which, in this case, is answered by a healing action:

"Coming home, I was boarding a bus on Olympic Boulevard. A lady sitting in the front row of the bus, saw me and said, 'Damn Jap.' Here I was a proud American soldier, just coming back with my new uniform and new paratrooper boots, with all my campaign medals and awards, proudly displayed on my chest, and this? The bus driver, upon hearing this remark, stopped the bus and said, 'Lady, apologize to this American soldier or get off my bus.' She got off the bus." (Quoted in Brimner, *Voices from the Camps,* page 68) **14**

For Review

- Define a stereotype. How is prejudice related to stereotyping?
- Give examples of words, attitudes, and actions that express prejudice.
- What is the most effective approach to melting the prejudice barrier?

"When the Truth of God's Love Grips You"

Most Christians would agree with the insights about respect expressed in this chapter. However, putting these principles for respect into practice on a daily basis can be quite a challenge. As with all of the Christian virtues covered in this course, we do not face the challenge alone. As we grow in our ability to be respectful of all God's children, communities and relationships of support are within our reach. Most of all, we have the example of Jesus and the gift of God's grace to fortify us along our journey to becoming respectful persons.

As the minister from Illinois who was quoted earlier in the chapter reminds us:

"You have never looked into the eyes of a human
  being who does not matter to God.
No, not even when you looked in the mirror.
When that truth grips you at the core of your being,
  you will never be the same.
You will live in awe of the scope and depth and
  breadth of God's love,
  and you will treat people differently."
                    (Quoted in *Youthworker Update*)

14
In writing, explain an action that could help heal the wounds caused by prejudice against minorities in your city, community, or school.

"You have never looked into the eyes of a human being who does not matter to God."
Above: A Maryknoll lay missioner in Venezuela finds a friend.

11

Compassion:
Solidarity
with Those
Who Suffer

A Matter of the Heart

The Compassionate Friend

Justin, age sixteen, talks about a significant friendship in his life:

Darrell is the kind of friend you can tell anything. We joke a lot with each other and give each other a hard time sometimes. But I know if I really need a friend to spill my guts to, Darrell's the guy. I know 'cause I've done that a lot this past year or so. And he listens like he's not tired of hearing it. It's not that he has this great advice to give or anything. Mostly he just lets me know he understands and that I'm not *alone*. That helps me hang in there.

At the end of last year, I was seriously depressed. I was even thinking about suicide, but I didn't tell anyone about it. Well, Darrell picked up on how bad I was doing, and he figured out that I was suicidal. And he pulled me out of it. He talked me through it, and he helped me get the nerve to talk to one of the counselors at school.

Everyone should have a friend like Darrell. I hope that I can be that sort of person for other people.

If we are fortunate, we have felt the compassion of others many times in our life. Without the compassion of someone to help us through pain and difficulty, life can seem unbearable at times. Like Justin, we all need someone in our life to be there with us when we are low. Even just the presence of a compassionate person is sometimes enough to relieve us for a while of the heaviness of our burdens and help us put things into perspective. **1**

Moved to Alleviate Suffering

Why does a compassionate person have such a powerful presence? The answer becomes evident in the definition of compassion: The virtue of **compassion** is the ability to be conscious of the suffering of others, to be moved by their distress, and to desire to alleviate their suffering. (The word *compassion* comes from two Latin words: *pati*, meaning "to suffer," and *com*, meaning "with.")

By listening intently, Darrell communicated to Justin the message that he was truly with him. In a way, Darrell bore Justin's pain with him, and that lightened the load for Justin. Darrell also knew when it was appropriate to give advice and when it was not. For instance, when Justin was suicidal, Darrell was able to steer him out of his depression enough to enable him to get the help he needed. Simply listening would not have been enough. **2**

Compassion for others often builds upon our own personal experiences of suffering. We know what others are going through, and we want to do what we can to help lessen their pain. But compassion is also possible in situations where the suffering of the other person far exceeds anything we have ever been through. Here the suffering may be so great that we cannot help but be touched and moved by it. Obviously, compassion requires a lot of empathy (see page 198 in chapter 10)—the ability to put oneself in another's place.

Mercy is another word often associated with compassion. Sometimes mercy carries the meaning of forgiveness. For example, God's mercy for us includes an unlimited supply of forgiveness. In many

---

1
Recall a time when you felt the compassionate presence of another person. In a paragraph, describe how that person's presence affected you.

2
List at least three guidelines that could help you decide whether to give strong advice to a friend who is hurting emotionally.

The Works of Compassion

In the Catholic tradition, the works of compassion listed here (historically called the corporal and spiritual works of mercy) are of central importance in the life of a Christian. **3**

- To feed the hungry
- To give drink to the thirsty
- To clothe the naked
- To visit the imprisoned
- To shelter the homeless
- To visit the sick
- To bury the dead

- To admonish the sinner
- To instruct the ignorant
- To counsel the doubtful
- To comfort the sorrowful
- To forgive all injuries
- To bear wrongs patiently
- To pray for the living and the dead

cases, however, the two words *mercy* and *compassion* are used to mean the same thing. So for the purposes of this course, we will be considering them the same virtue.

Compassion, then, is a sign of solidarity among persons. It indicates a capacity to be with others in a supportive but equal way, rather than against them, in competition with them, or in a superior position to them. Above all, compassion comes from a heart that can be moved—a heart of flesh and blood, not a hard, cold, stony heart. This is the kind of heart God wants us to have:

"I shall pour clean water over you and you will be cleansed. . . . I shall give you a new heart, and put a new spirit in you; I shall remove the heart of stone from your bodies and give you a heart of flesh instead." (Ezekiel 36:25–26, NJB) **4**

For Review

- Define the virtue of compassion.

■
Above: Christ in the Breadline, a woodcut by twentieth-century artist Fritz Eichenberg, depicts Jesus among the destitute masses that were a common sight during the Great Depression of the 1930s.

3
Write an example of how a young person might do any of the above works of compassion.

4
In writing, contrast a "heart of stone" with a "heart of flesh." Give some examples of words, attitudes, and actions that characterize each type of heart.

Compassion:
A Two-way Street

The Story of the Last Judgment

Read Jesus' account of the last judgment from Matthew's Gospel and think about the significance Jesus places on acts of compassion:

"When the Son of Man comes in his glory, and all the angels with him, then he will sit on the throne of his glory. All the nations will be gathered before him, and he will separate people one from another as a shepherd separates the sheep from the goats, and he will put the sheep at his right hand and the goats at the left. Then the king will say to those at his right hand, 'Come, you that are blessed by my Father, inherit the kingdom prepared for you from the foundation of the world; for I was hungry and you gave me food, I was thirsty and you gave me something to drink, I was a stranger and you welcomed me, I was naked and you gave me clothing, I was sick and you took care of me, I was in prison and you visited me.' Then the righteous will answer him, 'Lord, when was it that we saw you hungry and gave you food, or thirsty and gave you something to drink? And when was it that we saw you a stranger and welcomed you, or naked and gave you clothing? And when was it that we saw you sick or in prison and visited you?' And the king will answer them, 'Truly I tell you, just as you did it to one of the least of these who are members of my family, you did it to me.' Then he will say to those at his left hand, 'You that are accursed, depart from me into the eternal fire prepared for the devil and his angels; for I was hungry and you gave me no food, I was thirsty and you gave me nothing to drink, I was a stranger and you did not welcome me, naked and you did not give me clothing, sick and in prison and you did not visit me.' Then they also will answer, 'Lord, when was it that we saw you hungry or thirsty or a stranger or naked or sick or in prison, and did not take care of you?' Then he will answer them, 'Truly I tell you, just as you did not do it to one of the least of these, you did not do it to me.'" (Matthew 25:31– 45, NRSV)

- In Jesus' teaching, what is the basis for God's judgment of a person's life?
- With whom does "the king" (Jesus) identify himself?

Where Is God Hiding?

Many people think that God only "hangs around with good people" or is present in their own life only when things are going well. Even faith-filled persons sometimes question where God can be found in a world in which so many people suffer— from hunger, homelessness, war, or sickness, but also from the psychic pain of depression, loneliness, or low self-esteem. **5**

Jesus gives a surprising answer in his story of the last judgment: God is *not absent* from the lives of those who suffer. Just the contrary: God is present to them in the depths of their need. And when we act compassionately, we participate in God's compassion, allowing God's love to flow through us.

Gifts to Share

Jesus teaches another important lesson concerning the suffering persons we care for out of compassion: They too have their own gifts to share. A compassionate individual appreciates the gifts that the suffering person carries. Thus, you may often hear a person of compassion saying, "Oh, I really

5
Have you ever questioned the love, or even the existence, of God because of the suffering you see or experience in the world? If so, describe your doubt in writing.

Portraits of Compassion

The best way to understand compassion is to see it in action. The following accounts offer some portraits of what compassion looks like.

In the Soupline

In this essay from the *Christian Science Monitor* entitled "Johnny's Holiday," a teenage girl named Jill recalls an incident that gave her new insight into the meaning of compassion:

The line outside the soup kitchen in the heart of the Tenderloin of San Francisco was already around the block when I arrived. I got off the bus with my friend Michelle, and as we walked past the line the stench of urine, sour wine, and cheap tobacco overpowered the air, making my eyes water. I realized as I looked around me that at the age of 16 I had more than most of these people ever had, or ever will have. Suddenly, guilt overpowered me. I wished I could trade all that I had to help these people.

I walked through the door and was handed a starched white apron and a ladle. Despite the odor outside, the air in the hall was filled with cooked turkey, rolls, gravy, and chocolate brownies.

I was put in charge of dishing out the large tub of gravy. I stuck my ladle in the muddy water they called gravy and looked around. The man next to me stood close to 6 feet, 5. His face was covered with a poorly manicured beard and mustache. His clothes consisted of a baggy shirt and baggy pants, both a dingy gray, making them look more like a uniform. As I looked down, I noticed that a pair of handcuffs held his hands together, making his veins bulge underneath his many tattoos. Quickly I looked up at his face, feeling the same guilt as I had when I walked by the line outside. His large black eyes caught mine and he gave me a huge, toothless smile.

receive from these people more than I give." The gift may be gratitude and a smile, or a model of personal strength in the midst of extreme hardship. On the other hand, the person being helped may be too bitter to feel grateful or strong and may even react hostilely to help. Perhaps the suffering person's gift that day is a living lesson in how poverty, injustice, or rejection can grind down a human being's spirit. Compassion is a two-way street: giving and receiving goes both directions. **6**

■
Above: Homeless men try to warm themselves near steam grates on the streets of Washington, D.C.

6
Besides the gifts mentioned above, list five or more gifts that suffering people might share with those who care for them.

"Kinda a drag," he said, holding up his cuffed hands. "At least I'm out for a day, ya know." He was still smiling.

Johnny and I stood, slopping food on trays and talking. He told me of stabbing his [drug] dealer four years ago, and of prison life. "But now I's found the God Almighty 'n he's gonna save my soul." As he talked, he looked up at the water-stained ceiling. The large stainless-steel cross around his neck hung just above his heart.

Finally, everyone was fed, and all but four of the twenty turkeys were gone. The guard that had been watching Johnny all day began to walk toward us. Johnny turned to me, facing me for the first time. Quickly, he grabbed my hand, looking me in the eyes.

"I'll pray for you, Jill. Take care of youselve." He squeezed my small hand in his and walked away, closely followed by the guard.

I got back on the bus. The smells that at first I found repulsive now saturated my clothes. Johnny's words swirled in my head: "I'll pray for you, Jill." I knew if Johnny did pray for me, I would be all right and so would he.

- Describe the change that occurred in Jill's attitude about volunteering at the soup kitchen.
- What was the gift that Jill was given during her afternoon of service? **7**

In My Own Backyard

Scott talks about his gesture of compassion to an elderly neighbor whose husband had recently died:

I don't know why I started dropping in on Mrs. Carey. I guess I just remember Mom talking about how lonely my own grandma was when Grandpa died. I've been stopping by a couple of times a week for about four months now. Sometimes I do stuff for her around the house or in the yard, other times we just sit and visit—I can't resist her chocolate-chip cookies! I know my visits mean a lot to her, but they've come to mean a lot to me, too. She's a sensitive, wonderful person. I've learned a lot from her.

- How might Scott's experience with Mrs. Carey help him to be compassionate in other situations?

In a Healing Place for the Homeless

Christ House in Washington, D.C., offers homeless persons a place to rest and recover when they are too sick to be on the streets but not sick enough to be in the hospital. Janelle Goetcheus is a physician and the founder of Christ House. She also coordinates an outreach health program from Christ House. The outreach program focuses on getting medical help to people living on the streets or in the often frightening, dirty conditions of the shelters.

Testimony to the compassionate care given by Christ House staff comes from Sylvester Dean. This man was twice a guest there. The first time that Janelle Goetcheus discovered him ill in a shelter, Sylvester remembers, "I had a swollen liver, a broken wrist, and heart trouble. They took good care of me here [Christ House]. They gave me the attention nobody ever gave me in my life." But after a promising send-off to a rooming house and two jobs, Sylvester fell back into his old drinking problems, lost his jobs, and ended up back in the shelter. He recalls:

"Dr. Goetcheus saw me again, and she was shocked at how I looked. She was so disappointed, I felt like crying. I had lost weight, and I was down there fighting, and my eyes were black and swollen up. It really hurts when somebody cares about you and they see you that way. I . . . just started crying.

7
Describe in writing how the incident at the soup kitchen might have developed if Jill had not been open to the gift offered by Johnny.

About her visits to the large shelters where she gives medical care, Janelle Goetcheus says this:

Someone may come to me with a sore throat, and that is the very least of all that they are going to have to face that day—what they have to face in terms of living in a shelter, figuring out where they are going to eat, and dealing with basic issues about how they are going to stay alive. And all I have to offer is the time I can be with them when they come to see me.

But I find that just being with them is a gift to my soul. I feel a deep gratitude for what they share with me.

That doesn't mean I don't ache. My inner self just aches when I come out of a shelter. But in the midst of the aching, I know that it is still good to be there. And I want to be there. ("Rest for the Weary")

• How is it possible for compassionate persons to feel gratitude and joy when they are surrounded by suffering and misery?

All of these portraits of compassion illustrate that compassion is a two-way street. The giver receives and the recipient gives. In the eyes of Christian faith, those who are compassionate participate in the compassion of God. God's love flows through them. And those who receive mercy and compassion offer to the ones who care for them the gift of Jesus himself.

"I was kind of ashamed to come back up here, but Dr. Goetcheus told me don't feel like that. She said, 'Christ House is always open for you, Sylvester.'

"I've seen people come in here like they lost their last hope; and I've seen people walk out with a smile on their face. It's not all in the medicine, it's the way they treat you, and make you feel like part of society. . . .

". . . Dr. Goetcheus and Sister Lenora saw it in me; they said, hey, this man is worth something. And they didn't give up on me." ("Rest for the Weary") **8**

From Christ House, Sylvester later moved to Samaritan Inn, a small group home affiliated with Christ House, and held a steady job.

Sylvester Dean's gratitude is matched in the staff by the sense of being gifted by those they serve.

For Review

• What is Jesus' answer to the question, Where can God be found in a world in which so many people suffer?
• Explain this statement: Compassion is a two-way street.

■
Above: Dr. Janelle Goetcheus of Christ House, working from an outreach van on the streets of Washington, D.C., gives medical care to a homeless man.

8
How did Sylvester get the message that he was "worth something" at Christ House? List some possible ways—whether house policies, physical features of the house, or staff actions—that would have communicated respect for the dignity of each resident.

On the Way to Compassion

Becoming a person of compassion is a lifelong process that involves these dimensions:

- **imitating the example of Jesus**
- **turning our own suffering into opportunities for becoming more sensitive to the pain of others**
- **actively seeking out opportunities for compassion**

Jesus, the Model

The Gospels speak often of Jesus' compassion:

- "When he saw the crowds, he had compassion for them, because they were harassed and helpless, like sheep without a shepherd" (Matthew 9:36, NRSV).
- "When he went ashore, he saw a great crowd; and he had compassion for them and cured their sick" (Matthew 14:14, NRSV).
- "In those days when there was again a great crowd without anything to eat, he called his disciples and said to them, 'I have compassion for the crowd, because they have been with me now for three days and have nothing to eat. If I send them away hungry to their homes, they will faint on the way—and some of them have come from a great distance'" (Mark 8:1–3, NRSV).
- "A man who had died was being carried out. He was his mother's only son, and she was a widow; and with her was a large crowd from the town. When the Lord saw her, he had compassion for her and said to her, 'Do not weep'" (Luke 7:12–13, NRSV).

Jesus' entire life expressed compassion. He felt acutely the sorrows of others, and he spent much of his ministry trying to alleviate suffering. Jesus was and remains the fullest human embodiment of God's compassion. As our model of full humanity, Jesus reminds all of us, who are creatures made in God's image, that we also are to reflect God's compassion in the world.

Pain Can Be Gain

One way to follow the example of Jesus is to allow the suffering in our own life to become the seeds of compassion for others. This does not mean that suffering should be sought after by us as a means to becoming more compassionate. (Enough suffering happens to us in life's course of events to give us plenty of fuel for compassion. Life can be hard, and God does not want us to go looking for ways to make it harder.) The point is, though, that the troubles and pain that do come our way, unwelcome as they are, can have the effect of softening us, sensitizing us to the problems of others. In other words, our own difficulties can be opportunities for insight, growth, and compassion. This is what Jesus meant when he said:

"Amen, amen, I say to you,
unless a grain of wheat falls to the ground and dies,
it remains just a grain of wheat;
but if it dies,
it produces much fruit."

(John 12:24)

It Can Go Either Way

Yet suffering in itself does not make a person become compassionate. Some people who have suffered a lot become bitter, closed, hardened. Others, for some reason, turn their suffering into a kind of rebirth. They become deeper, wiser, and more generous and caring. For instance, a young person experiencing peer rejection might become particularly sensitive to the feelings of a new student who is finding it difficult to fit in. But, the opposite is also possible: a person rejected by peers might try to pump up her or his own ego by putting down someone else. Suffering can make us more sensitive to others—or less sensitive. **9**

What accounts for the difference? Christians believe that suffering can lead to compassion because of God's ever present grace and a person's openness to that grace. Individuals may not even recognize the movement within them as grace, as God's presence, but they are nonetheless open to it. That is what makes the difference between suffering that turns to bitterness and suffering that turns to compassion.

A Story of Forgiveness

A man tells the story of how, as a young student brother of a religious order, he experienced the compassion of a woman who had plenty of reason to be bitter:

During the summer of 1966, I helped organize a rent strike against a slum landlord in Chicago. We didn't know it at the time, but our efforts eventually paid off. Rents were reduced, and the landlord began fixing up the buildings. I was entering my junior year of college and feeling the fervor of the civil rights movement. Dr. Martin Luther King Jr. was leading marches all over the South. The Black Panthers were taking a more militant stance. Well anyway, here I was, a pretty naive white guy, born and raised in the South, knocking on doors in the slums of Chicago's west side.

When I look back, guilt at my own racism had a lot to do with my motivation. I'd begun to realize how prejudiced I had been—thanks to the racist culture I'd been raised in. My zeal to get this slum landlord out of business had an angry edge to it. I didn't understand how intolerant I was of intolerance or how unforgiving I was of my own past. Then I encountered Mrs. Higgins.

I'd been prowling through these decaying buildings, getting signatures to support the rent strike. In those days, we all wore suits. The heat wilted me every day and put me on edge. Mrs. Higgins' apartment was up three long flights of graffiti-smeared stairs that smelled of urine and stale cooking odors.

When I knocked on the door I almost hoped that nobody would be home so that I could quit for the day. Then I heard someone unlatching about four different locks. Finally the wrinkled face of a small, old woman peered out of the apartment.

"Hello," she smiled. "Can I help you?"

I delivered my spiel about organizing the rent strike against the exploitation by the landlord. Her kind eyes never left my face. She appeared to listen intently.

When I finished my pitch, she said, "You look real hot. Would you like some lemonade? It'll make you feel lots better. Come in, won't you, and sit down."

Surprised and relieved, I assented. I was desperately thirsty, and Mrs. Higgins had an indefinable quality about her that made me feel comfortable and at home. Most of the paint had peeled off the walls. The ancient furniture was threadbare. Even so, everything had a well-scrubbed cleanliness about it.

Mrs. Higgins asked me where I was from. I haltingly replied, "Memphis." I suppose I feared that she would lump me together with the KKK (Ku Klux Klan) and the segregationists who, at the time, still led fierce opposition to integration.

Instead, Mrs. Higgins smiled. "I come from a sharecropper's farm down near Tunica, Mississippi, not far from Memphis."

9
Describe in writing a person you know whose pain or suffering seems to have made her or him more sensitive to others. Explain why you think that person became more sensitive rather than bitter.

We talked about southern places and things for a while and then about the civil rights movement, which Mrs. Higgins took keen interest in.

Then she said, "You know, I understand why so many of these black kids are so angry." Her voice became somber, and her eyes looked beyond me into a long distant past.

"I used to hate white people. For years I did. You see, when I was a little girl we'd all go out to chop cotton—my momma, sisters, and brothers. This one day, the sun just about was killing everybody, but we had to keep working. The landowner drove up in his truck. He was a bad man. He came over to my momma and started yelling and grabbing at her arm. I couldn't hear what they said because I was too far away. My momma was a proud woman and didn't take shoving from nobody. The next thing I know, that white man had snatched up the hoe she'd been using and was hitting her. I yelled and started running to her. Some of the other people jumped on the man, but it was too late."

Her mother lingered for a day before she died. The killer was never charged. Mrs. Higgins paused and breathed deeply, as if the effort of the telling had worn her out.

"Well, I held to my hate like a junkie holds on to his drugs. Then about twenty years ago, I finally heard the words of Jesus about forgiveness and love. I'd been so sour on the world; I'd been miserable in my own self. Then and there I pledged to Jesus that I better stop hating white people. Let me get you some more lemonade."

As she went into her tiny kitchen, I sat stunned. This old, poor woman forgave her mother's murderer. I can't completely explain it, but somehow I felt forgiven too. I left there, strike petition forgotten, realizing that Mrs. Higgins had given me something of infinitely more value than her signature.

- Of what was the young brother guilty?
- Reflect on Mrs. Higgins's compassion. How did she become that way? Do you think it was easy for her to turn her hate into love, or was it a daily struggle? What helped her?
- What might the impact of this encounter have been on the brother's capacity for compassion in the future? How do you think it might have affected his approach to the slum landlord, which he said had an "angry edge" to it?

When we receive the compassion and mercy of another human being, or of God, we become more compassionate ourselves. The compassion of Jesus has brought forth heroic love in thousands, even millions, of his followers over the centuries. That is how it goes—goodness brings forth more goodness. **10**

Seek and You Shall Find

Compassion also comes to those who seek it, to those who willingly open up their heart to other people in a time of need. Opportunities for compassion are many—in the life and career choices we make, through involvement in service organizations and projects, as well as in day-to-day living. But as with the other virtues studied in this course, growth in compassion is not something we do all on our own. Compassionate persons know they need the support of a community.

"A Different Spirit in This Home"

Recall Janelle Goetcheus of Christ House, who works with homeless people. On the subject of community, she says this:

Certainly to do this work on one's own would be very difficult. But I am with others who share the same experiences, and we can talk together about the things that have happened in a day, and pray and laugh together. That's part of what gives me joy. ("Rest for the Weary")

Alone, it is nearly impossible to face human misery day after day. For that reason, the founding members of Christ House chose to have the staff and their families (including children) live on the third and fourth floors of the house.

"We didn't want to be just doctors," [Janelle] explains. "We wanted to be with people in deeper ways. There's a different spirit here in this home, because it is our home, too, and we want it to be a good home for the guests." (Hollyday, "Rest for the Weary")

- Imagine what it might be like living in Christ House as a staff member.

Support in a Youth Group or Class

Most persons' compassion does not lead them to the kind of commitment made by the staff of Christ House. However, for the more ordinary ways of giving service, people also need a community of support.

A Catholic youth group in Reading, Massachusetts, is a good example of a support community for persons involved in service. The group was given a regular slot every few months at a busy Episcopalian soup kitchen in downtown Boston. On their appointed evening, they were responsible to cook and bring and then to heat and serve 225 dinners to hungry people. Their youth minister writes:

Our effort was headed up by a high school senior working with one college-age adult and a team of five other planners. They mobilized the cooking efforts of about forty-four parish families and the serving efforts of about fifteen adventuresome group members.

The bags, cans, and coolers of food were gathered and loaded into our cars. When everything was loaded and ready, we stood in a circle and prayed with great anxiety and excitement. We asked for extra helpings of love to take with us.

When we got to Saint John the Evangelist Church, we hit the ground running. There were tables to set, salads to serve, casseroles to heat, and so on. The work went on at a frantic pace. The guests were not-so-patiently waiting, and soon the platefuls of good food were pouring out of the kitchen at amazing speeds. There were many grateful and affirming comments, some obnoxious and demanding comments,

10
Bring in an account from a newspaper or magazine of how one person's goodness brought forth goodness in others.

"Let Them Know They've Been Loved": One Family's Compassion

The following account shows how one family responded to the challenge to be a community of compassion by welcoming foster children:

The Alis [Irene and Khalif] live in a rambling, comfortably cozy home in West Babylon, Long Island, where, in addition to their 11-year-old daughter, Desiree, there are two infants with AIDS, Kenneth, eleven months, and Jerome, four months old. Another four-month-old infant with AIDS had been with them only a short time when he died. . . .

There have been times also in recent months when Kenneth has been very sick and when he has obviously regressed. Lately, he has not been able to crawl or pull himself up. He has had pneumonia, and there is fluid and a cyst on his brain. And on nights when he has had to stay overnight at North Shore University Hospital, Irene and Khalif have taken turns staying with him and sleeping on a chair in his room. . . .

Why, with their own family to raise, would the Alis want to open their home to infants some people might consider a risk, a danger, a hazard to their health? Why, with so many children in need of homes, would the Alis single out a few infants whose future does not stretch very much into the year or even the next couple of months?

"Look at the children's faces," Khalif Ali responded quietly, eloquently, pointing to Kenneth and Jerome smiling up at him and his wife.

"No one wants to leave this earth alone," Irene added, picking up Kenneth and holding him against her. "If you just hold someone, at least they know they're loved and are not alone and can go in peace. They're so innocent, and they had no choice in any of this." . . .

"We wanted the opportunity to give them a family and a home before they passed away," Irene said softly. "That's all it was, someone to hold them and let them know they've been loved."

That is all. As incredibly, stunningly simple as all that. (Ryan, "Foster Parents of Special Breed")

■
Above: Irene and Khalif Ali and their daughter, Desiree, have opened their home to infants with AIDS.

several tender moments, and a few difficult moments. All in all, it was a challenging night.

When the last guest was gone and the last bit of cleanup was complete, we sat in a circle and debriefed . . . :

- "They looked normal."
- "They looked so sad."
- "I loved it."
- "I was scared."
- "I got proposed to."
- "I got pinched."
- "I feel funny going back to a home where I have everything I need."
- "I feel grateful going back to a home where I have everything I need."

Serving that meal was a first for us. In three months we will get another slot, and we really want it. More of the group wants to be involved the next time. The experience really affected the whole group; it impacted our hearts. The impacts were heavy but healthy. (Doolittle, *Be Alive in Christ*, pages 81–82)

- How important is it for people to be able to "debrief" after their experiences of giving service?

In many Catholic high schools, community service is required or offered as an elective religion course. Parishes often require community service as a part of preparation for receiving the Sacrament of Confirmation. The young people may tutor in schools, help at a shelter, assist at a day care, do activities with residents at a retirement home, and so on. The community service class can function as a support group and a faith community; members can encourage each other and share their experiences in regular class meetings. **11**

Having a support community with whom to share the anxieties, the frustrations, the satisfactions, and sometimes the work itself, makes the job lighter—and even joyful. It enables people who are trying to be compassionate to know that they are participating in something greater than their own efforts. With Christian faith, people can come to realize that their service is part of God's compassion for the whole world.

Day by Day

The examples in this chapter, for the most part, have focused on persons involved in service projects or programs. However, many opportunities for compassion are woven into everyday life as well:

- helping someone pick up their dropped books and papers
- consoling someone who has been unjustly criticized
- listening to a friend who is having a tough day
- befriending a new person at school
- sharing your lunch with someone who forgot theirs **12**

For Review

- How did Jesus show compassion?
- How can people's own suffering help them to become more compassionate?
- Why do persons who are trying to be compassionate need a community of support?

11
Interview someone in your school or parish who is involved in a community service project. Find out what the service has meant to the person and what kind of group support, if any, was available for those giving the service. Summarize the results of your interview in writing.

12
From your own experience, add to the above list some everyday opportunities for showing compassion.

Mercy in the Sand

A family of five were enjoying their day at the beach. The children were bathing in the ocean and making castles in the sand when in the distance a little old lady appeared. Her gray hair was blowing in the wind and her clothes were dirty and ragged. She was muttering something to herself as she picked up things from the beach and put them into a bag.

The parents called the children to their side and told them to stay away from the old lady. As she passed by, bending down every now and then to pick things up, she smiled at the family. But her greeting wasn't returned.

Many weeks later they learned that the little old lady had made it her lifelong crusade to pick up bits of glass from the beach so children wouldn't cut their feet. (De Mello, *Taking Flight*, page 124)

One Body in Christ

Compassion is a way of seeing ourselves as part of (or one with) all of humanity. In solidarity with other human beings, we see their joys as our joys, their pain as our pain. We see other human beings as offering something of themselves to us, as well as receiving from us. This can happen between brothers and sisters, spouses, parents and children, friends, and coworkers, not just with those who need the kinds of service described in this chapter. Solidarity can even happen with strangers to whom we have no apparent connection.

Saint Paul summed up the solidarity of compassion in the First Letter to the Corinthians. In this letter, he compared a physical body with the community of human beings united in Christ, the "Mystical Body of Christ":

For just as the body is one and has many members, and all the members of the body, though many, are one body, so it is with Christ. For in the one Spirit we were all baptized into one body—Jews or Greeks, slaves or free—and we were all made to drink of one Spirit.

Indeed, the body does not consist of one member but of many. If the foot would say, "Because I am not a hand, I do not belong to the body," that would not make it any less a part of the body. . . . As it is, there are many members, yet one body. The eye cannot say to the hand, "I have no need of you," nor again the head to the feet, "I have no need of you." . . . But God has so arranged the body . . . that there may be no dissension within the body, but the members may have the same care for one another. If one member suffers, all suffer together with it; if one member is honored, all rejoice together with it. (1 Corinthians 12:12–26, NRSV)

12

Respect for Creation: The Earth as God's

"It's a Part of Me"

When asked what motivated his involvement in many of the environmental awareness projects at his high school, Wes, a senior from a Minneapolis, Minnesota, suburb, gave this response:

When we first moved to Golden Valley last year, I would get this feeling sometimes like a part of me was missing—like I left some part of me behind. I grew up near Grand Marais on the North Shore of Lake Superior. At first I couldn't figure out what was missing, but then when summer came and my new friends and I started hanging around the lakes here in Minneapolis, it dawned on me. The part of me that was missing was Lake Superior. The lakes here are nice and all, but just not the same as Lake Superior.

All the tourists who go up to the North Shore for vacations always go on and on about how beautiful the shoreline and the forests are. And it is spectacular, but a lot of the tourists are really scared by Lake Superior itself—it's so cold all the time, and it's known for its storms and shipwrecks. But to me the lake always had this great, powerful presence that I felt drawn to—like I could get strength from it. I loved to go down by the lake in the winter when it was snowing. The clouds were so thick, and they'd just hang there right over the water, and that water was so choppy and cold. And these huge waves would slap up against the cliffs on the shore. The cliffs were real rocky and the ice made the strangest, neatest formations. I would just stand there awestricken and try to soak up as much of the lake's power as I could—before I got too cold!

I miss the lake, but I also realize that it will always be a part of me, a part of who I am. Doing things to help the environment is my way to make sure the lake part of me never disappears. Next year at the university, I'm hoping to declare a major in fisheries and wildlife management. Eventually, I'd like to work for the Department of Natural Resources up near home. That lake gave me a lot while I was growing up. I just feel I ought to give something back.

- Have you ever had an experience of feeling connected to some nonhuman part of creation? If so, take some time to reflect on that experience.
- What motivates young people to help out with environmental projects?

Respect for creation happens in much the same way as respect for persons: we are more respectful of creation when we get to know it better, when we take the time to foster a relationship with other creatures and the earth.

For Wes, his relationship with Lake Superior was important and life shaping. He recognized that he himself was a part of this creation, and it was a part of him. Out of such a strong sense of connectedness grew a deeper understanding of, and appreciation for, the created world, as well as the desire to help care for its well-being. **1**

The virtue of **respect for creation** is the ability to see all created beings—human and nonhuman, living and nonliving—as good in themselves, and as having basic needs that must be met. This respect is shown in these ways:
- **understanding how creation works**
- **appreciating creation**
- **taking care of creation**

Before discussing these three aspects of respect for creation, however, let's look at the biblical teachings about creation that provide the foundation for this virtue.

1
Focus on some part of nonhuman creation that you feel connected to—for example, a tree, a dog, a field of grass, the sky. In writing, describe this part of creation and your feelings about it.

The Biblical View: The Earth Is Good

Deeply rooted in the biblical tradition of Jews and Christians is the fundamental belief that all creation—the earth and the whole universe—is good. "God looked at everything he had made, and he found it very good" (Genesis 1:31). Over and over, the ancient Jews reminded themselves that the earth in all its goodness belongs to God, praying in psalms like this one:

The earth is the LORD's and all that is in it,
  the world, and those who live in it;
for he has founded it on the seas,
  and established it on the rivers.

(Psalm 24:1–2, NRSV)

In other words, the earth is God's, not ours. We need the humility to see that we are not created to rule over the earth but to care for it. **2**

Human Beings as Stewards of Creation

The biblical view of creation is mindful of the fact that human beings are part of the created world, that we are made of the same stuff as the plants and the animals, the land, the water, and the air. But the Scriptures also say that human beings are created in God's image. As part of creation, humans are to reflect God to the rest of creation, to care for and tend this amazing and beautiful world as God would, because creation is beloved to God. This caretaking, called stewardship, requires that we value the rest of creation as good *in itself,* not simply because it is useful to us.

Thus, God, human beings, and all of creation are meant to live in a grace-filled, respectful relationship with one another. That was the situation described in the Genesis story of Adam and Eve living harmoniously with all the other creatures in the Garden of Eden.

2
Go back to the part of nonhuman creation focused on in activity 1. Describe some ways you can care for that part of creation, recognizing it as God's, not ours to do with as we please.

Exploitation and Abuse

Since the beginning of human history, though, we human beings have gotten farther and farther away from our God-given role as stewards of creation. Progressively, we have forgotten our connectedness to and dependence on the earth. In a number of ways, we have become abusers and exploiters of the earth. Even in biblical times, abuse of the land was common. Wealthy people tried to amass land so they could make fortunes off its produce. Also, defilement of the land (understood in modern terms as pollution) brought death to crops, animals, and people—not the life of abundant harvests.

Prophets such as Isaiah, Jeremiah, Ezekiel, and Hosea cried out against the abuse of the land by human beings. Their message was clear: The earth must not be exploited; it must be cared for. There can be no justice for people on the land without justice for the land itself. **3**

• How does harming the land cause injustice to the people who depend on the land for their well-being?

A Sabbath for All of Creation

The biblical belief in the importance of the Sabbath relates to justice for all of creation, not just human beings. On the Sabbath day, according to God's law given to the ancient Israelites, persons were to rest but also to allow the animals that worked for them to rest. No creature was to be exploited, whether human or nonhuman.

Likewise, the land itself periodically needed a break from producing. So Sabbath law required that every seven years one's farmland must be given a year to rest and lie fallow. In addition, every

Principles for Land Stewardship

In *Strangers and Guests,* a 1980 statement on land issues, the Catholic bishops of twelve midwestern states outlined ten principles for stewardship of the land, gleaned from the Scriptures and the teaching tradition of the church:

1. The land is God's.
2. People are God's stewards on the land.
3. The land's benefits are for everyone.
4. The land should be distributed equitably.
5. The land should be conserved and restored.
6. Land use planning must consider social and environmental impacts.
7. Land use should be appropriate to land quality.
8. The land should provide a moderate livelihood.
9. The land's workers should be able to become the land's owners.
10. The land's mineral wealth should be shared.

(No. 50)

3
List several examples of the ways humans currently pollute and abuse the earth. Then come up with some suggestions for stopping these destructive practices.

■
Above: Soil erosion can be prevented by planting crops in contour strips. This method is one way to practice stewardship of the land.

fifty years, in what was called the Jubilee year, all pieces of property that had been accumulated were to be returned to their original owners. This law was designed to break up land monopolies run by profiteers who took what they wanted from the land and put nothing into it. The land would then be back in the hands of people who were entrusted with caring for it.

Giving and Receiving

The biblical vision of how we ought to treat creation contains much practical and ethical wisdom for modern people as well as the ancients. For instance, today's advocates of ecologically sound farming would agree with the wisdom of giving the soil a periodic rest. Also, smaller family-owned farms tend to foster a more intimate relationship with the land than do huge agribusiness farms; thus, family farmers are more likely to care for and not abuse the land. **4**

The Jewish and Christian tradition, then, affirms that the relationship between the earth and humans, like the relationship between persons, must be one of mutual giving and receiving. It cannot be a one-way street. That is, the earth gives us humans what we need to sustain us, but we must also give back to the earth what it needs to sustain its own life and to be what it was created to be. This is a matter of ecological justice, a dimension of justice first referred to in chapter 6.

Jesus:
A Jewish Outlook on Creation

Jesus grew up with this biblical wisdom about creation. Certainly he must have prayed the Psalms, like Psalm 24, quoted on page 230, many times

and been moved by his awareness of God's love for creation. This is why he often referred to God's care for the earth's creatures:

"Look at the birds of the air; they neither sow nor reap nor gather into barns, and yet your heavenly Father feeds them. Are you not of more value than they? . . . And why do you worry about clothing? Consider the lilies of the field, how they grow; they neither toil nor spin, yet I tell you, even Solomon in all his glory was not clothed like one of these." (Matthew 6:26,28–29, NRSV)

Jesus saw God's providence and wisdom in the natural world. Jesus' own loving embrace extended to all of creation, not just to humans. The Reign of God that he announced as "already in your midst" means that God's justice and peace are to reign in all relationships—human beings with God, human beings with each other, and human beings with the rest of creation.

For Review
- Define the virtue of respect for creation.
- What is the fundamental biblical belief about creation?
- Define stewardship of creation.
- How did Jewish Sabbath law relate to justice for all of creation?
- Explain this statement: The relationship between the earth and humans must be one of mutual giving and receiving.

4
Research modern farming practices to find out which are harmful to the land and which are beneficial. Write up your findings in a brief report.

Understanding How Creation Works

The first step toward respecting creation is learning how creation works. Learning the ways of creation leads to understanding its needs and therefore its rights.

A Networked World

The most important lesson we learn from creation is that it is all interconnected. Everything depends on everything else. This networking happens globally as well as in a local environment like a pond or a forest. Over millions, even billions, of years, all the connections in the earth's ecosystems (living communities) have developed into a dynamic balance—a delicate yet strong, flexible yet stable, network. This is the wonder of creation. **5**

Human beings have long watched and listened to our world, and learned about its intricate workings. But now we know we must learn from the wisdom of the earth how to work *with* its natural systems, not *against* them.

An Illustration: The Problem of Global Climatic Change

To illustrate the interconnectedness of creation, let's examine one environmental problem that is often in the news. The problem is that of global climatic change, whether toward warmer or cooler temperatures. Large-scale changes in the global climate, which scientists are foreseeing given current temperature trends, can have disastrous effects on the planet and on life as we know it.

To get at the problem of global climatic change, we need to understand the connections between the earth's atmosphere and the life that inhabits the earth's surface.

Earth as Air Purifier

Our air is a remarkably stable mixture of gases in proportions that support life—and meet our own specific requirements as humans. How do the gases in the atmosphere stay in the correct proportions? The earth itself, or rather the thin sheath of living organisms covering the surface of our planet (the ozone layer), acts like an air purifier. The biological activity on the earth's surface works like

---

■

Above: The earth as air purifier becomes overloaded when human beings add too much carbon to the atmosphere and crowd out biological activity from the earth.

5

Think again about the part of creation focused on in activities 1 and 2. List ten ways this part is interconnected with the rest of creation—that is, how it depends on and is depended upon by other parts of creation.

breathing—taking in "old" air, purifying it, and letting it out again.

The earth's life, then, is the purifier and regulator of the atmosphere. And that life consists of the continuing processes of birth, life, death, and decay of organisms. Believe it or not, the death and decay of organisms is vital to keeping *us* and all living things alive!

Earth on Overload

When the earth's living surface, the "air purifier" just described, is overloaded with work to do (dirty air to purify), the atmosphere gets messed up. Global warming and other strange climatic changes already occurring worldwide are symptoms that the earth as air purifier cannot handle the workload.

The earth as air purifier becomes overloaded in one of two main ways:

1. **Too much carbon.** Human beings release too much carbon, through burning fossil fuels like gasoline, coal, and heating oil, and through burning organic matter like dead leaves and grasses rather than letting them decay and become part of the soil.

2. **Loss of living organisms.** Human actions—such as wiping out whole local ecosystems to build a shopping center, letting soils erode, or polluting—bring about great losses of biological activity and diversity on land and in water. Masses of plants, animals, living soils, and thousands of species are being threatened or wiped out through human actions. Called desertification, this process does not refer only to the making of deserts. It means a great loss of diverse living things in waterways, rain forests, grasslands, scrublands, hardwood forests, or even in your own backyard. This loss of living organisms makes the earth's purification efforts that much less effective because those efforts depend on the processes of life, death, and decay.

Thus, many human activities have been adding excess carbon to the atmosphere while also crowding out other species and their biological activity from the earth. These activities disrupt the ingenious system that seems to know what we need to live, a system that supports human life by regulating the air we breathe. Global climatic change is a sign that the earth is working overtime at its job of purifying. Many concerned people worldwide are urging humankind to give the earth—and ourselves—a break. **6**

• Imagine using the LISTEN process to work out ethical solutions to problems like desertification. Which part of the LISTEN process relies on understanding how creation works?

6
Find an article on the problem of global warming or another large-scale climatic change. Explain in a one-page report the harm to humans that this change could bring about if it continues.

A Sense of Wonder

When we listen carefully to a friend—to the person's voiced words but also to her or his gestures, expressions, and unspoken words—we begin to understand our friend more intimately. Learning some new dimension of our friend, or just reflecting on who the person is, can lead to a sense of wonder, even reverence, at the beauty and complexity of our friend.

Like tuning in to a friend, we can also listen closely to the sign language of creation to try to understand it more intimately. The study of science is a great help. Getting closer to the earth and simply observing it is also a way of listening. Reflecting on the intricate, delicate, marvelous workings of the created order—such as in the example of how the earth purifies our atmosphere—can bring us to a similar sense of wonder at how it all works and a desire to cooperate with that order, not destroy it.

For Review

- What is the most important lesson we learn from creation?
- Why is the earth's air-purifying system becoming overloaded?

Appreciating Creation

The sense of wonder that comes with understanding some of the genius of the created order often blossoms into appreciation for creation. But appreciation requires more than wonder; it involves developing our own relationship with creation. How can we do this?

Getting Closer to Living Things

How do you develop a relationship with a person you never see, talk with, or spend any time with? It isn't easy. If we never make contact with the natural world—other than contacts with humans—we will have a tough time appreciating nature.

Go Out to the Natural World

Persons who live in the country or in small towns, of course, have an easier time developing a relationship with the earth than those who live in cities and in many suburbs. However, cities still have parks and trees and animals.

Camping, picnicking, and hiking in state parks outside the urban and suburban environment are other ways to strike up a relationship with the earth. Even just leaving your house to gaze at the stars on a clear night or to watch the varied kinds of clouds by day can give you a sense of perspective like nothing else can. **7**

A young person named Charles tells of appreciating creation while riding along in a car:

One day I was with the family in the car coming back from somewhere. I don't remember where we went, but it must have been last year because I was reading a chemistry assignment about atoms. I remember suddenly realizing that those tiny little structures were in everything, and that anything around me was made up of millions of them.

I looked out the car window and watched as thousands of trees went by my window every second and stretched all the way to the horizon. (We must have been driving through the mountains in some vast open state.) I watched one tree go by and tried to concentrate on one leaf, trying to imagine that it contained countless little things in it. I realized that God had created every single atom in that leaf—an incredible, unbelievable feat in itself. And then I looked around at the whole forest around it, and I realized that God created all that, too—God created every atom; . . . and I saw how vast the rest of the universe was compared with that single leaf—and God created everything.

I suddenly felt God's power and care. Everything that God made must have been important enough that it was put together out of so many complex pieces. It helped me to realize how petty the little everyday problems were, the problems that we allow to weigh us down and distract us from the amazing beauty all around us. (Koch, ed., *Dreams Alive*, page 73)

Bring the Natural World In

Another way to get closer to creation is to bring the natural world into a room at home or a classroom. A room can be completely transformed by bringing in plants and pets. People are frequently amazed at how different they feel when surrounded by these living things, and how cold and sterile a room seems when all the plants and animals are removed. For many of us, a pet like a dog or a cat becomes an integral part of our life—brightening it with genuine affection and shared fun. Bringing in the natural world also gives us a chance to learn how to care for these living things.

7
Go to a place in your neighborhood, city, or region where you can spend time developing your relationship with the natural world. Then reflect on the experience in writing.

■
Facing page: Cathrine Sneed, who found new ways to connect people and nature, has helped transform many lives.

Caring for Creation: A City Story

The thought of appreciating creation often inspires images of majestic mountains, rich farmland, and beautiful forests, lakes, and rivers. Rarely does it bring to mind images of cities with tall buildings, tenements, and crumbling sidewalks. But the need to respect creation is as much an urban reality as a rural one. Cathrine Sneed and the Garden Project demonstrate that such care is appropriate and vital in the city.

Sneed was a special assistant to the sheriff of San Francisco County when she and a few inmates began to clean up a piece of land on county jail property. In 1984, they were ready to plant seeds. Ten years later, 160 prisoners were working each day in the garden, which had grown to eight acres. Produce from the garden was given away— to soup kitchens, to projects that feed senior citizens, to homeless people, and to people suffering from AIDS.

Growing food and sharing it with those in need gives the prisoners a chance to feel good about themselves. It gives them a sense of power: they, who had done wrong, could now see that the work of their own hands could make something good. On another level, the garden gives prisoners a direct and transformative experience of nature. Cathrine Sneed describes Forrest, a prisoner with a criminal record spanning thirty years. When she first met him, Sneed says, Forrest could not have been described as a "nice guy." But people change:

Now he is the first person to come up to you in the garden. At first, it is kind of menacing, because he looks kind of menacing. He's got tattoos everywhere, but what he wants to do is give you a bouquet of flowers, because he is very proud of the flowers. That is transformation.

After starting the prison garden, Sneed realized that the project needed to expand to the outside community. Starting with an empty lot behind a bakery, she began the Garden Project, a program that employs people after they have been released from jail. The Garden Project's produce is sold to area restaurants, including the famous and fancy Chez Panisse. Another offshoot of Sneed's original prison garden is the Tree Corps. Employees plant and maintain trees throughout the city, adding to the beauty of their surroundings *and* helping to fight global warming. Neighborhood people sense a connection to the new trees, says Sneed: "People know that this tree in the ground means that their uncle, or brother, or sister has a job and so they protect the tree."

The success of these projects has many dimensions. The gardens themselves bring beauty to city neighborhoods and provide food for many who are in need. They create dignified, satisfying work for former inmates, decreasing the chance that they will fall back on criminal behavior and return to jail. They encourage education—workers who are curious to know more about the way a garden works have a strong reason to improve their reading and comprehension skills. And they increase the respect that participants have for creation. As Cathrine Sneed puts it, "What we're doing is finding ways to connect nature and people." (Based on "These Green Things")

Becoming Familiar with the Rhythms of Life and Death

Persons who appreciate creation become familiar with the rhythms of birth, life, death, and decay that all living things go through and that are necessary to continue life over generations.

Watching the change of seasons can help us meditate on the life cycle that is essential to all natural things. We see the promising greens of spring become the deep greens and golds of summer. Then we observe the golds, browns, oranges, and reds of the autumn leaves giving their last offering of color before they fall and die. Then we witness the apparent black-and-white barrenness of winter—before the spring bursts again. From the changing seasons, we are constantly reminded that new growth comes from the rich soil of decaying organisms and that life cannot continue without death. We learn that the precious gift of physical life, even our own physical life, is part of a cyclical process that is immensely bigger and wiser than ourselves. **8**

Letting Creation Renew You

Finally, appreciating creation means that we allow the natural world to renew us and, in a sense, nurture us. Good friends give to and receive from each other. Like the best of friends, the earth and the whole universe are constantly there for us, reaching out to us with their healing energies. We need to stop long enough in our busy life to notice and welcome creation's presence.

Saint Francis of Assisi, known for his appreciation of and love for the natural world, thought of the elements of creation as family members with whom he had a deep personal connection. In his "Canticle to the Sun," Francis praised God for his "brothers and sisters" who renewed him every day:

Praised be thou, my Lord, with all thy creatures,
Especially the honored Brother Sun,
Who makes the day and illumines through thee. . . .

Praised be thou, my Lord, for Sister Moon and the
stars,
Thou hast formed them in heaven clear and precious
and beautiful.

Praised be thou, my Lord, for Brother Wind,
And for the air and cloudy and clear and every
weather, by which thou givest sustenance to thy
creatures.

Praised be thou, my Lord, for Sister Water,
Who is very useful and humble and precious and
chaste.

Praised be thou, my Lord, for Brother Fire,
By whom thou lightest the night,
And he is beautiful and [merry] and robust and
strong.

Praised be thou, my Lord, for our sister Mother Earth,
Who sustains and directs us,
And produces various fruits with colored flowers and
herbage.

Praise and bless my Lord and give him thanks
And serve him with great humility.

When we begin to appreciate all the natural wonders of creation, we become changed, more genuinely human. **9**

For Review
- What can we learn about life from watching the change of seasons?

8
Write a personal reflection on this statement:
- Life cannot continue without death.
In what sense have you known this statement to be true?

9
Develop a list of things your class or school could do to foster appreciation for the nonhuman natural world.

"Praised be thou, my Lord, for our
sister Mother Earth, who sustains
and directs us."
Above: The earth as viewed from
the *Apollo 17* spacecraft. The view
extends from the Mediterranean Sea
area to the Antarctic Circle.

Caretaking of Creation

The responsibility to be stewards, or caretakers, of the earth can appear to be an overwhelming task. The damage to the earth caused by human actions continues, despite loud outcries from every corner of the world.

This book is not the place to describe all the environmental afflictions the earth is trying to contend with. Many science classes and a multitude of news shows, articles, and books focus on the environmental crisis. This section of the chapter, however, highlights actions of specific individuals or groups who are concerned about the well-being and integrity of God's creation. Even small actions, done by millions of people, can make a huge impact on the future of our earth.

Smog-resistant Trees

Planting trees is one small action that offers much hope in the task of helping the earth's air-purifying system do its job. One young man went an extra mile in his efforts to help preserve the earth:

As a teenager, Andy Lipkis heard his camp counselor talking about trees dying in his hometown, Los Angeles, from smog. Years later, with research, he found a tree resistant to smog. Now his organization, The Tree People, plants seedlings of that tree in Los Angeles and surrounding areas. ("What on Earth Can I Do?" *Christopher News Notes*)

Greatly reducing the cause of smog, or pollution released into the atmosphere, is necessary too. But while government and industry people are working on that end of the problem, ordinary people like Andy Lipkis can do their part to help the earth.

Operation Brown Bags

Students all over North America have become involved in projects to increase awareness about environmental issues in their local communities. A teacher from Sweetwater, Texas, tells about her class's paper recycling campaign:

While studying our vanishing rain forests, my sixth-grade class . . . conducted some research into trees and paper waste and discovered that the U.S. ranks second behind Japan as the world's largest consumer of tropical hardwoods used for paper. They decided to visit the local grocers to find out how many paper sacks they used. They discovered that large sacks ([at the time] always made from virgin pulp, not recycled paper) cost almost five cents apiece and 1,000 per day were used, which added up to $52,000 a year. . . .

Following that experience, the students started a local campaign called Operation Brown Bags. They . . . asked [themselves], "How might we motivate the people of Sweetwater, Texas to take their sacks back to the grocery store and reuse them in order to save paper and eventually save trees?"

After brainstorming possible solutions, a plan of action emerged. Signs, flyers, newspaper stories, puppet shows, radio spots, television appearances, and plain old footwork—door to door—became part of their plan to get the word out.

A survey to monitor success revealed that the response had been tremendous. Piles of sacks could be found at the grocery stores. Knowing this was against health regulations, the students had to replan and stress that people should reuse their own sacks and not leave them at the stores.

A final boost for the project came recently when one store began paying five cents for each large grocery sack returned for reuse and crediting it to the purchase. (Maddox, "Operation Brown Bags") **10**

10
Find out what efforts exist in your community to recycle paper, plastic, aluminum, tin, and glass. Describe those efforts in writing, and offer suggestions for improving the effectiveness of your community's recycling efforts.

Deeds of Respect

1. Save energy and natural resources.
2. Sort trash and recycle as much as you can.
3. Avoid disposables, like plastic and Styrofoam throwaway items.
4. Plant a garden.
5. Plant a tree.
6. Substitute other products for aerosols, which destroy the earth's protective ozone layer.
7. Join group projects that help the environment.
8. Write to government representatives about your concerns for the earth.
9. Live *more* with *less*.
10. Pray for creation.

Above: Sorting trash and recycling as much as you can shows respect for the earth and all who depend on the earth.

In Prayer and Protest

Sunday, 6 August 1995, marked the fiftieth anniversary of the atomic bombing of Hiroshima, Japan. On that anniversary morning, more than five hundred people gathered outside the Nevada Test Site—a place where hundreds of nuclear explosions have taken place since the dawn of the nuclear age. The demonstrators gathered to pray, and made their prayer visible with a number of sacred symbols: a "mindfulness bell" made by Buddhist monks from bombs left by the U.S. armed forces in Thailand following the Vietnam war; a thousand painted and glittering folded paper cranes, a Japanese symbol of peace; prayer sticks made by Shoshone Native Americans; and a colorful tallit, or prayer shawl, from the Jewish tradition.

The participants then listened to talks about peace and the environment by a Jewish rabbi, a Shoshone spiritual leader, two Methodist bishops, a representative from the United Farm Workers labor union, and the grandson of India's Mahatma Gandhi.

Finally, everyone present formed a huge circle while 184 of the participants walked onto the test site property and were arrested for trespassing. Rooted in prayer, they had performed an act of nonviolent civil disobedience.

This act of prayer and protest was one of many sponsored throughout the years by the Nevada Desert Experience program of the Franciscan friars of California. The protesters demonstrated solidarity with all victims of atomic warfare and nuclear weapons testing—the quarter of a million people who are estimated to have died in the bombings of Hiroshima and Nagasaki, Japan, and countless others whose exposure to radiation released by nuclear tests has caused cancer and other severe health problems. The protesters also displayed solidarity with creation. Corbin Harney of the Western Shoshone Nation spoke to his fellow protesters about environmental destruction and harm caused by weapons testing: "'Together we can do wonderful things for our mother. We only have one mother—Mother Earth—and the blood of our mother is drying up'" (Quoted in Rogers, "Anti-nuclear Activists Stage Protest").

Voices raised in protest, along with changes in global politics, have had an effect on nuclear weapons policies. At the time of the August 1995 commemoration and protest, the United States was observing a testing moratorium—no U.S. nuclear weapons had been exploded in nearly three years. However, other nations continue to develop and test nuclear weapons, and the Nevada Test Site stands ready to resume testing—and to resume harm to human beings and the environment—if the U.S. government decides tests are once again necessary.

Much still needs to be done to make and keep the environment and human life safe from the destructive capabilities of nuclear weapons. But the Nevada Desert Experience program proves that prayer can play a vital role in attempts to make changes that benefit society and all of creation.

- Is breaking the law, such as trespassing, a morally acceptable way to fight for justice for the earth and its people?
- Some individuals use potentially dangerous tactics to protect the environment. For instance, they might pound metal spikes into trees or put water in the fuel tanks of bulldozers to prevent loggers from cutting down ancient trees like the giant redwoods. How would you judge whether practices such as these are morally acceptable?

- How might the LISTEN process help a person decide where and how to help with environmental issues? **11**

For Review

- Give five examples of ways we can care for the earth.

Building God's Reign

As discussed in chapter 6 on justice, people can become overwhelmed and paralyzed when they realize the extent of injustice in the world. Indeed, examples of disrespect for creation abound. Yet Christians working for ecological justice must realize that their efforts are part of a greater project, that is, God's work for justice. Jesus spoke much about God's work for justice, about the Reign of God, which comes about gradually and quietly through small human efforts:

"The reign of God is like a mustard seed which someone took and sowed in his field. It is the smallest seed of all, yet when full-grown it is the largest of plants. It becomes so big a shrub that the birds of the sky come and build their nests in its branches." (Matthew 13:31–32)

"The reign of God is like yeast which a woman took and kneaded into three measures of flour. Eventually the whole mass of dough began to rise." (Matthew 13:33)

Respect for creation is not an option for the people of God. As a dimension of justice, careful human stewardship of all creation is as essential to building the Reign of God as is loving our neighbor. God wills that justice and love govern *all* relationships, on earth as in heaven. Then,

The wilderness and the dry land shall be glad,
    the desert shall rejoice and blossom;
like the crocus it shall blossom abundantly,
    and rejoice with joy and singing.
. . . .
They shall see the glory of the LORD,
    the majesty of our God.

(Isaiah 35:1–2, NRSV)

11
Is there a potential source of environmental damage in your region that is being protested or ought to be protested? If so, write about what citizens are doing or could be doing to try to stop the damage.

13

Reverence for Human Life: Cherishing the Gift

"So Life Would Be Precious"

In Chaim Potok's novel *My Name Is Asher Lev*, Asher, raised in an Orthodox Jewish family, recalls an incident from his childhood that gives us a starting point for considering the virtue of reverence for life. He remembers one day, walking in their neighborhood, he and his father saw a bird lying on its side against the curb.

"Is it dead, Papa?" I was six and could not bring myself to look at it.

"Yes," I heard him say in a sad and distant way.

"Why did it die?"

"Everything that lives must die."

"Everything?"

"Yes."

"You, too, Papa? And Mama?"

"Yes."

"And me?"

"Yes," he said. Then he added in Yiddish, "But may it be only after you live a long and good life, my Asher."

I couldn't grasp it. I forced myself to look at the bird. Everything alive would one day be as still as that bird?

"Why?" I asked.

"That's the way the Ribbono Shel Olom [God] made His world, Asher."

"Why?"

"So life would be precious, Asher. Something that is yours forever is never precious."

"I'm frightened, Papa."

"Come. We'll go home and have our Shabbos [Sabbath] meal and sing zemiros [songs] to the Ribbono Shel Olom." (Pages 156–157) **1**

The Precious Gift of Life

In the previous incident, Asher learns a profound truth: Life is a precious gift that we should cherish while we have it, but we must not cling to physical life as if we can keep it from ending. This wisdom of Jewish and Christian tradition lies behind the virtue of reverence for human life. In fact, much of the Catholic church's rich heritage of teachings on respect for human life operates on this basic insight.

The virtue of **reverence for human life,** then, holds human life as a sacred gift to be cared for by us until physical life reaches its natural end. This virtue sees God, not humankind, as the author of life and death. Creatures participate in the ongoing process of generating new life, but ultimately God

---

1
Recall an early awareness you had of death. Describe in writing how you reacted to the reality of death and how adults in your life responded to your reaction.

is the one who brings human beings, and all other living things, to life and who allows physical life to end. Our responsibility is to care for human life once it begins and to do nothing that would intentionally harm that life. As noted in the previous chapter on respect for creation, all life—human and nonhuman—is from God and is sacred to God. In this chapter, however, we will limit our discussion to issues of reverencing human life.

Jesus: A Man Who Loved Life

In the Gospels, we find a portrait of a man who loved life and nourished life. Jesus was always trying to make people's experience of life full and rich. When thousands of people were hungry, he fed them. When they were sick, he healed those who came to him in trust. He stood up coura-geously for people when they were suffering or persecuted by others. At a wedding, when the wine ran out, he produced more wine, and of a better quality, so that the bride and groom could continue to celebrate with their relatives and friends. And Jesus taught the way of nonviolence, urging his followers to love, not harm, their enemies.

Jesus' whole ministry was an affirmation of the goodness of life. However, his love for life did not make him deny the reality of death. Despite the power Jesus had been given by God to cure others and overcome suffering, he did not try to turn back his own impending death. Facing crucifixion, he told the Apostle Peter to put away his sword and not strike at those who were about to have him killed. Jesus loved life, but he did not clutch desperately at his physical life when the time of his own death came. **2**

■
Above, left and right: The Catholic church holds that all human life, from its beginnings to its endings, deserves protection and care.

2
List some ways that people in our society deny the reality of death.

The Catholic Church: A Consistent Ethic of Life

The Catholic church responds to many threats to human life with a **"consistent ethic of life."** That is, the church holds that *all* human life, from womb to tomb, is sacred and therefore deserves protection and care.

This means that the Catholic church's pro-life concern is not focused on a single issue but extends to a multitude of human-life issues: certainly abortion and euthanasia, but also the death penalty, genetic engineering, torture, modern warfare, genocide, hunger, homelessness, inadequate health care and nutrition for pregnant mothers and their babies, and so on. **3**

Pope John Paul II has voiced the church's commitment to a consistent ethic of life on numerous occasions. In his encyclical *The Gospel of Life,* he said:

The Gospel of life is for the whole of human society. To be actively pro-life is to contribute to the renewal of society through the promotion of the common good. It is impossible to further the common good without acknowledging and defending the right to life, upon which all the other inalienable rights of individuals are founded and from which they develop. A society lacks solid foundations when, on the one hand, it asserts values such as the dignity of the person, justice and peace, but then, on the other hand, radically acts to the contrary by allowing or tolerating a variety of ways in which human life is devalued and violated, especially where it is weak or marginalized. Only respect for life can be the foundation and guarantee of the most precious and essential goods of society such as democracy and peace. (Number 101)

Dilemmas of Technology

The Catholic church's concern for human life has prompted it to speak out regarding developments in medical technology. Advances in medical technology have opened up promising possibilities for human life:

- Just a few decades ago, transplanting organs (for example, the heart, the kidneys, the liver) from one human being to another was unheard of. These transplants now save thousands of lives each year.
- When a person's lungs cannot function, that person's heartbeat soon stops. The definition of death used to be the ceasing of breathing and heartbeat, and persons in this condition were declared dead. Now such a person can be kept alive by a respirator, which artificially breathes for her or him until normal breathing can be resumed.
- You may have been treated for an illness with antibiotics like penicillin several times in your life and thought nothing of it; it was routine treatment. But if you had lived fifty or so years ago, you may have died from the same illness, because antibiotics were not yet available.
- Couples who previously could not conceive a child for medical reasons now have the benefit of many advances in fertility research.

Thus, medical technology has greatly improved human beings' chances for a long life, and a life with less suffering. Medical advances have enormously benefited humankind. But we are in the midst of moral dilemmas in medical technology. Consider these developments:

1. Tests can be done on a fetus in the womb to determine whether the baby has genetic defects and to determine its gender.

3
Respond in writing to the consistency of the Roman Catholic church's teaching on human-life issues. Do you agree that the above issues belong together in an ethic of life?

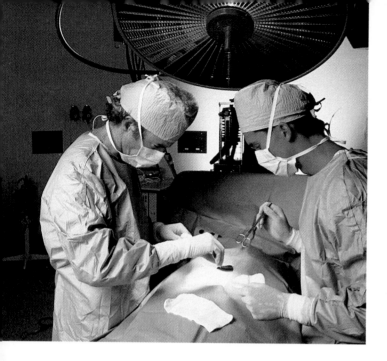

2. Genes, through which biological heritage is passed down, can sometimes be transplanted, thus altering the original genetic makeup.

3. An egg can be fertilized by a sperm in a test tube, and then it can be implanted in the mother's or another woman's womb.

4. Entirely new forms of life can be produced in the laboratory by cutting up genetic material and recombining it to make organisms that have never existed. Even the potential to combine human and animal genetic material exists.

- What might be the benefits of each of these technologies?
- Consider how each of these technologies could be used destructively or without concern for human dignity.

Raising a moral concern over scientific developments such as these does not imply that technologies to make things better for human beings should never be sought. Rather, the concern is over the issue of limits: How much control should humans seek over matters of life and death? And which humans are to decide what these limits

should be? Life and death are ultimately the dominion of God, not human beings. But many of today's technologies place in human hands more and more control over *how* and *when* life begins and ends, *which* lives begin and end, and *which* human traits will be carried on to other generations.

The danger is that such technological advances increase the temptation for humans to "play God." The reality is, however, that we human beings cannot possibly foresee all the effects of our choices. And all too often, we choose to downplay or ignore the negative effects—both short-term and long-term ones. Technological developments need to be approached with extreme caution and ethical vigilance about their possible dangers or misuse. It is crucial that we repeatedly ask ourselves as a society, Just because we *can* do something, does that mean we *should* do it? **4**

The Catholic ethic of life is concerned with what supports or threatens human life in all its stages. Because life is most fragile and vulnerable at its "edges," this chapter first focuses on reverence for human life as it pertains to life's beginnings and endings. Then the chapter turns to several issues that threaten the sacredness of human life in its middle stages.

For Review

- What is the virtue of reverence for human life?
- How did Jesus reverence life?
- What is meant by the Catholic church's "consistent ethic of life"?
- Briefly describe the moral dilemma presented by advances in medical technology.

■

Above: Sophisticated advances in medicine save thousands of lives each year. But these advances can raise moral dilemmas for us.

4

Focus on one of the developments in medical technology listed above. In writing, try to answer this question about it:
- Just because we can do this new thing, does that mean we should do it?

At Life's Beginning

Three issues are particularly important to consider for those who may one day bring new life into the world: **abortion, birth control,** and **new birth technologies.**

Abortion

Ever since the 1973 U.S. Supreme Court decision *Roe versus Wade* made abortion legal in the United States, abortion rates have climbed. According to Planned Parenthood statistics, about 1.6 million abortions are performed each year in the United States, many of them on teenagers. A United Nations study reports that U.S. teenagers have abortions at more than twice the rate of their peers in other developed countries such as in Europe. For both teenage and adult women, abortions are chosen under a variety of difficult and even tragic circumstances. **5**

Difficult Situations

Here are a few examples of situations that lead people to seek abortions:

1. Jana is fifteen when she finds out she is pregnant by her boyfriend, Matt. The prospect of facing the shame and her parents' anger, and possibly not finishing school, is just too much for her. Also, Matt wants her to have an abortion.

2. Erin, age seventeen, lives in a desperately poor family, consisting of her mother, herself, and her four brothers. Her mom has never been married and supports the family on welfare. Erin, now pregnant by a guy who doesn't want to see her anymore, fears that having a baby would set her on a path to poverty and hardship just like the one her mother has been on.

3. Caitlin is well into a career as a buyer for a major department store chain when she realizes she is pregnant. She cares about Jeff, the father, but getting married and having children is just not in her life plans.

4. Susannah and Greg have been married for ten years and have two children, ages eight and six, when they discover Susannah is pregnant again. Finances were just beginning to look up for them, as Susannah now works full-time. The couple enjoy the freedom of having school-age kids, and the prospect of changing all that has them depressed and tense.

5. Greta was raped by Cliff on a date a couple of months ago, and she became pregnant. She is horrified at the thought of carrying a baby that was conceived in a traumatic attack in which she was the victim. She hates Cliff and cannot bear to think that his action could wreck her life.

6. Jim and Cynthia were excited to discover they would have a baby. Just to make sure everything is fine, they have an amniocentesis test done on the baby in the womb. The bad news is that the test indicates the baby has Down's syndrome. The child will be mentally retarded and will have physical abnormalities as well. Jim and Cynthia were counting so much on having a normal, happy family, and now they are afraid they will not be able to cope with this child.

- For each situation above, consider what could happen if (1) the woman did have an abortion and (2) the woman did *not* have an abortion.
- Choose one situation and reflect on how the principal characters might use the LISTEN process of decision making.

5
In a one-page essay, give some possible explanations for why U.S. teenagers are having abortions at twice the rate of their peers in other developed countries.

The Church's Position

All the situations just described are hard to deal with and entail their own unique suffering. But according to the vision of morality that has been discussed in this text, none of these hardships, even being pregnant due to rape or incest, gives a woman reason to have an abortion. The teaching of the Catholic church is clear: Direct abortion is not morally acceptable in any circumstances because it is the taking of innocent human life, which is always wrong. (Indirect abortion may occur as a result of efforts to save a pregnant mother's life, for instance, through removal of a cancerous uterus. Here the indirect abortion may be morally acceptable because the ending of the fetus's life was not the intended goal of the surgery. Instead, it was a tragic, undesired side effect of saving the mother's life.)

Freedom of choice is not the issue in abortion, as pro-choice activists claim. The pro-choice position is that a woman has the right to choose what happens to her body, that it is a matter of privacy to choose whether to carry a baby to term. But the right to privacy does not give one the right to take another's life. The fetus, the baby in the early stages of life, is not a woman's property, nor just another part of her body. A fetus is a human being sacred to God.

Neither poverty, nor the fact that the parents are unmarried, nor the interruption of the parents' life plans, nor the certainty that the child will be physically or mentally disabled gives sufficient cause for killing the child in the womb. Even the way in which a child is conceived—such as by a horrible crime like rape or incest—does not alter the sacredness of that child's life or its right to be loved and cared for. (In situations of rape or incest, the Catholic church does firmly uphold a woman's right to prevent conception from happening. A number of considerations must be taken into account, but chief among them would be this: If it is known that she is not already pregnant, a woman who has been raped or a victim of incest may seek immediate medical assistance—within a day—to prevent ovulation or kill the sperm, thus preventing conception from occurring.)

Christian faith teaches that every child is to be treated as a blessing, as a gift from God with a right to life, not as a burden. Carrying a baby to term and caring for the child or giving the child over to the care of parents who are more able may require great sacrifice. But God's grace is especially present to those who welcome new life in difficult circumstances—if they are open to that grace. **6**

A Societal Critique

Groups as diverse as the Catholic bishops and feminist pro-lifers point out that being pro-life on the abortion issue means much more than being anti-abortion. These groups say that we cannot cry

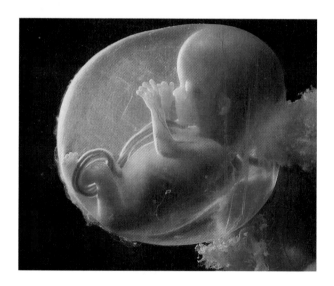

6
React in writing to this statement, proposed by some supporters of the legalized status of abortion:
• I believe abortion is morally wrong, but I wouldn't want to impose my moral beliefs on others.

■
The fetus is a human being sacred to God.
Above: A human fetus at four months

out against abortion but then stand by silently while social structures and attitudes make it harder and harder to welcome a baby into the world. What is needed, they argue, are policies and programs like the following to prevent abortions from happening:

1. flexible school situations
2. freedom from stigma
3. fairness in hiring
4. more "flex time" and part-time job arrangements, maternal and paternal job leaves, jobs that can be done in one's home
5. access to prenatal care and good nutrition for pregnant women, and medical care and nutrition for children, regardless of family income
6. education in responsible family planning
7. help with child care and parenting
8. adequately funded day-care programs
9. attractive adoption alternatives
10. support for learning how to deal responsibly with sexuality

Our whole society needs to put its energies into trying to make the communities in which children are conceived and born more welcoming, supportive places. Instead of seeing unwanted unborn babies as problems to be eliminated, society needs to consider its own anti-life structures and values.

Women who go through abortions are often the victims of these anti-life structures, as are their aborted babies. Pressured by counselors and even by doctors who see abortion as the only "reasonable" alternative, or abandoned by the men who got them pregnant, or desperate as to how to cope when they have no resources, these women endure the trauma of an abortion in the hope that their problems will be solved. Certain problems are "solved" in the short term by abortion. But bigger, deeper problems remain.

First of all, a baby's life has been destroyed. And many of these women go through years, even a lifetime, of grief and remorse for what they have allowed to be done to themselves and their babies. Women who have suffered from abortions need the compassion, not the judgment, of others. **7**

Birth Control

The belief that human life is a precious gift from God also pervades the Catholic church's teaching on birth control.

Two Purposes of Sexual Intercourse

In the Christian vision of sexuality and marriage, when a man and a woman commit themselves to each other in marriage, they pledge to love not only each other but also any new life that comes from their love. Their union in sexual intercourse has two purposes:

1. **to express their mutual love through the pleasure and joy they give each other**
2. **to create new life**

The Catholic church believes that these two purposes belong together in a sexual relationship and must not be separated. If a marriage lacks either of these—love between the spouses or a willingness to love and care for any children they might conceive—something essential to the meaning of marriage is missing. **8**

7
Write an imaginary dialog between you and someone who argues that the Catholic church cares more about the life of the fetus than the life of the mother. How would you respond to that argument?

8
Do you agree or disagree with this statement?
• The expectation of having and raising children is an essential part of a marriage commitment.
Explain your answer in writing.

One Woman's Story

Here is one woman's account of her attempt to heal spiritually and emotionally after an abortion:

"When I was sixteen I found out that I was pregnant by a thirty year old married man. I didn't find out he was married until I was too much in love with him to care. When my parents found out I was dating this man, they became furious with me. We had a terrible fight which left us, although living together, a great distance apart. Months had passed when I found that I was carrying a child. A child that was pure, beautiful, and most of all, innocent, and a child that this man didn't want any part of, and I didn't have the strength within myself to give birth to.

"I felt as if the only one I could depend on was the man I had already given up friends and family for. So who else could I go to? I didn't trust my parents. They'd throw me out, and then where would I go? Friends couldn't help, the ones I had left, so why tell them? Counsellors only convinced me that I was doing the right thing for me and for the baby. But probably worst of all, I didn't trust in God, who had given me the privilege of caring for one of His children, a child that was innocent, that I gave a sentence to die.

"I had an abortion two months into my pregnancy. It was and still is the most horrible experience I have ever had. I don't say this lightly, because physically I have been through a lot. I have been through several operations . . . and none of that has had the effect on me like killing my child has. I can't find another way to put it. In my mind there are no gentle words for the act.

"I still remember the day they put me on the table, bright lights were shining down on me. I laid there and prayed to the Blessed Mother Mary to understand and help me through this. I heard the machine turn on, the loud, horrible noise. And then I felt a pulling from the inside, almost as if my child were clinging to my womb for protection from this horrible machine that was taking its life.

"When it was over, I felt physically and mentally ill. I went through a period of time that I would wake up in a cold sweat hearing a child, my baby crying. I had horrible nightmares which could only be diluted with alcohol. Now I am twenty-four. It was eight years ago that I had an abortion and I still feel remorse and self-dislike when I look at a child or a pregnant woman.

"The sad part of all this is, I could have had a lot of support. I recently told my parents because I couldn't deal with it alone any more, and they have forgiven me and are trying to help with what they can right now. I still live with them, and if I would have told them, I would be living here with my child. I am presently seeing a psychiatrist and trying to understand why I didn't try harder then.

"I prayed to God to help me find the right words for this letter. These may seem like just words on paper to you, but it's been very real for me. But if only one person can gain something from this letter, then maybe they won't be wondering if their baby was a girl or a boy, and what he or she would look like at the age of eight." (Quoted in Mannion, *Abortion and Healing,* pages 29–33)

A Special Word from Pope John Paul II

I would now like to say a special word to women who have had an abortion. The church is aware of the many factors which may have influenced your decision, and she does not doubt that in many cases it was a painful and even shattering decision. The wound in your heart may not yet have healed. Certainly what happened was and remains terribly wrong. But do not give in to discouragement and do not lose hope. Try rather to understand what happened and face it honestly. If you have not already done so, give yourselves over with humility and trust to repentance. The Father of mercies is ready to give you his forgiveness and his peace in the sacrament of reconciliation. You will come to understand that nothing is definitively lost, and you will also be able to ask forgiveness from your child, who is now living in the Lord. With the friendly and expert help and advice of other people and as a result of your own painful experience, you can be among the most eloquent defenders of everyone's right to life. Through your commitment to life, whether by accepting the birth of other children or by welcoming and caring for those most in need of someone to be close to them, you will become promoters of a new way of looking at human life. (*The Gospel of Life*, number 99)

Natural Family Planning

Of course, the church's belief in these two purposes of sexual intercourse does not mean that every sexual act must result in conception. The Catholic church recognizes that for good reasons, couples may want to space their children or limit the number of children they bring into the world. The church is not opposed to this kind of responsible family planning. But, according to church teaching, the methods used must not try to disrupt the nature of sexual intercourse. Artificial methods (whether contraceptives like hormonal implants, condoms, the diaphragm, spermicidal agents, birth control pills, sterilization, and so on, or abortion-causing devices such as the intrauterine device) do disrupt the natural design of the sex act, so the church disapproves of their use. Some of them also carry very serious health risks, and none of them has proved to be 100 percent effective in preventing pregnancy.

If a couple do want to limit or space the number of children they have, the church advises a method called natural family planning (NFP). This method relies on the couple's attention to various signs that ovulation is about to occur or has occurred in the woman, indicating that she can become pregnant if they have intercourse. The couple must be willing to abstain from intercourse during that fertile period of several days (five or six) each month.

Research by the World Health Organization has shown NFP to be 97 percent effective when the couple does abstain from sex during the time they judge the woman to be fertile. This statistic compares favorably with those for the most effective artificial methods, except for sterilization, which is usually permanent. Keeping track of the woman's fertile period in this way also enables couples to conceive a child when they want this to occur.

Birth Technologies

As discussed earlier in this chapter, some of the contemporary advances in medical technology present society with serious ethical dilemmas. This text will not consider them in detail, but here are brief descriptions of three technologies that affect life's beginnings: amniocentesis, surrogate parenthood, and genetic engineering.

Amniocentesis

The procedure of amniocentesis, done during pregnancy, analyzes cells of the fetus in the womb to discover whether or not the baby has a genetic defect (like Down's syndrome), as well as to determine the gender of the child. Sometimes treatment in the womb can correct a genetic defect once discovered, or at least knowing in advance about the defect can prepare medical staff to treat the newborn child more promptly after birth. This knowledge may also help prepare parents for the arrival of a child with special needs. But sometimes, the discovery of a defect results in the parents' decision to have an abortion. Some persons also opt to abort a baby if the baby is not the sex they prefer.

- How might amniocentesis reinforce the notion that only "perfect" children should be brought into the world?

Surrogate Parenthood

Couples who are unable to conceive a child are faced with difficult choices. They may choose to accept that their marriage will not produce children and use their gifts as nurturers in other ways.

Or they may choose to adopt children, knowing that their parental love and commitment is more important than a genetic relationship to their children.

Technology, however, has added to these choices. Due to a variety of technologies (in vitro, or test tube, fertilization; artificial insemination; and embryo transfers), the option of paying someone to be a "surrogate parent" is increasingly more available to infertile couples. In other words, couples can buy someone else's egg or sperm. They can also pay for the use of another woman's womb—that is, pay the woman to bear the child for them. Obviously, a variety of parental combinations are possible. But whatever the combination, motherhood and fatherhood, or at least the basic biological aspects of them, become commodities for sale. And the creation of new life becomes a mechanical process rather than the fruit of a love relationship, its intended context. **9**

Genetic Engineering

Scientists are now able to alter genetic traits in plants and animals, including mammals, by transplanting genes. New forms of life can even be created, patented, and sold. The ability to change and shape the human gene pool (the whole collection of human gene types) is within the grasp of science.

Although genetic engineering offers hope for treating genetic defects in human beings, it also contains many dangers. Chief among the dangers is the temptation to try to improve the human species by getting rid of undesirable traits and enhancing desirable traits. However, who is to decide which traits are desirable and which are undesirable? An attempt to engineer the perfect human being would have little to do with true human worth in the eyes of God.

- What might today's North American society choose as the traits of a perfect human being?
- If it were possible to manufacture such perfect humans, would it be wise to do so?
- Where in twentieth-century history have you heard of an attempt to create an ideal, "master" race of human beings? What happened?

Through our human, sexual nature, we have been given the task of cocreating new life with God. If we have reverence for human life, we will treat that responsibility as a sacred trust and regard the natural processes that enable us to bring forth life as sacred.

In the same way, reverence for human life extends to honoring the sacredness of life at its end.

For Review

- What is the Catholic church's position on abortion?
- Give five examples of the types of policies and programs that can prevent abortions.
- In the Christian vision, what are the two purposes of sexual intercourse?
- What is the Catholic church's teaching on artificial contraception?
- Briefly describe the potential for harm that accompanies amniocentesis, surrogate parenthood, and genetic engineering.

9
List some potential hazards of society's letting the creation of new life become merely a mechanical process, a commodity for sale.

The Hazards of Seeking Perfection

The quest for perfection may seem like a noble and worthwhile endeavor. But, as people say, there are two sides to every issue. In other words, seeking perfection may not be all it is cracked up to be. The following gives a striking illustration.

Molecular biologist Lewis Thomas was once asked if molecular biologists could have achieved the innumerable variations of life on earth if they had been in charge of creating the first DNA molecules, the basic building blocks of heredity. He answered:

"We would have made one fatal mistake: our molecule would have been perfect. Given enough time, we would have figured out how to do this, nucleotides, enzymes, and all to make flawless, exact copies, but it would have never occurred to us, thinking as we do, that the thing had to be able to make errors. The capacity to blunder slightly is the real marvel of DNA. Without this special attribute, we would still be anaerobic bacteria." (Quoted in Birch and Cobb, *The Liberation of Life,* page 266)

Above: A computer model of a double helix, the structural arrangement of the strands that make up a DNA (deoxyribonucleic acid) molecule

At Life's End

Contemporary society is grappling with a number of issues concerning life's end, particularly euthanasia and suicide.

Euthanasia

The term *euthanasia* originally meant "easy death," or a peaceful death without suffering. People today sometimes refer to it as "mercy killing." When the Catholic church speaks of **euthanasia**, it means a specific act or omission done intentionally to directly cause death in a patient, thus relieving the person of all suffering.

Tough Decisions

Consider the following cases, and for each one try to decide whether the actions of the individuals can be called "euthanasia" in the sense of the church's definition:

1. Brad, age sixteen, lies in a hospital bed in a coma following a car accident. He is on a respirator because his breathing has stopped. The doctors tell Brad's parents that his coma is irreversible (he will not recover from it) and that he is in a persistent vegetative state (he has no cerebral brain activity; only involuntary bodily functions remain). Without the respirator, he would not be alive. After a lot of anguish, Brad's parents ask that the respirator be removed, and the doctor does so. Shortly after, Brad dies.

2. Marge, who is married and has three grown children, is dying after a two-year battle with cancer. Her family loves her deeply and cannot stand to see her suffering. Lately, she has been in a lot of pain and does not even recognize her family any-

more. They remember that she said many times throughout her long illness, "If I ever get really bad, just tell the doctor to put me out of my misery. I'd rather not live that way." She even wrote this down on paper so her wishes would be clear. Marge's doctor had also discussed Marge's wishes with her earlier, and now he just needs to know that the family agrees. Reluctantly, the family members call on the doctor to do whatever is needed to end their mother's life. Thus, he gives Marge an injection that ends her life painlessly.

3. Grandpa Fred has been living with his granddaughter Kristin and her husband and two kids for a year. He is totally dependent on them because he has Alzheimer's disease, a progressive, incurable brain disease that causes loss of memory and intellectual functioning, and eventually loss of physical functioning and death. Having Grandpa Fred live with them has been a great strain on the family, especially because he needs to be watched all the time. And the doctors say he could go on another three or four years like this. One day, Fred develops a high fever and a terrible cough. Kristin has seen pneumonia before, and this seems like pneumonia. If she gets Fred to the doctor, she knows that treatment with antibiotics will probably save his life. If she just keeps him at home and doesn't call the doctor, he may die. She decides to keep him at home, and within two days, Fred dies of pneumonia.

4. Flora, a thirty-five-year-old single woman, is in the hospital in the last stages of cancer resulting from AIDS. She has had a lot of pain, but her doctor has done a good job of controlling it through morphine injections. Flora has been able to visit with her family and say all her good-byes. Now, because the pain is increasing, the doctor realizes he will have to increase the dosage of morphine a

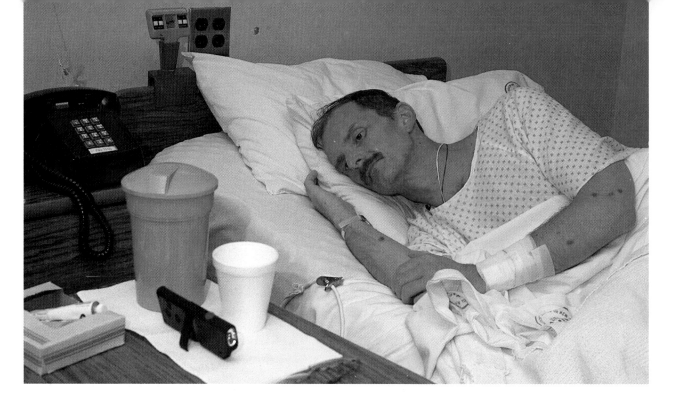

little. He knows this may shorten her life by a few days, because morphine slows breathing in a person as weak as Flora. But the doctor feels it is worth giving Flora the amount of painkiller needed to keep her comfortable. The next day Flora dies peacefully, with her family around her.

These hypothetical cases depict only a few of the many situations in which the issue of euthanasia might arise. And, of course, in real situations many more factors and circumstances would have to be considered. Yet based on what we do know about these cases, we can make some tentative judgments about them, using as a guide the teaching of the Catholic church, in particular the 1980 Vatican *Declaration on Euthanasia.*

The church has declared that euthanasia is not morally permissible. However, according to church teaching, the cases described here are not all instances of euthanasia. Cases 2 and 3 are examples of euthanasia; cases 1 and 4 are something else. Let's look at why this is so. **10**

Killing Versus Letting Go

The church teaches that we may never intentionally and directly take the life of someone in order to relieve that person of suffering. However, this does not mean that we must prolong life using whatever means are possible, no matter what the condition of the patient. The church steers a middle course between two extreme positions:

1. Physical human life must be prolonged at all costs. Staying alive is the most important value.
2. Physical human life should be ended when it becomes frustrating, burdensome, or useless.

Neither of these positions fits the church's perspective on human life. In the Catholic vision, physical life is a precious gift to be cherished and made fruitful. And Catholics believe that fruitfulness can happen in the midst of suffering or even in an apparently pointless existence. Euthanasia is wrong even though the person's life seems miserable to us, or even if a person has asked to have his or her life ended. **11**

■
Catholics believe that life has meaning and value even in the midst of terrible suffering.
Above: A man hospitalized with AIDS at Saint Vincent's Hospital, New York

10
Do you agree that cases 2 and 3 are examples of euthanasia but 1 and 4 are not? Before reading the explanations in the text, explain in writing your reasons for agreeing or disagreeing.

11
Give an example in writing of how good can come out of suffering or even out of an apparently pointless existence.

Proportionate treatment. However, the Catholic church teaches that we are not obligated to accept or continue medical treatment that is disproportionate (out of proportion) to the good that can be done. Obviously, wise judgment (the first cardinal virtue) is essential to figuring out whether a treatment is proportionate or disproportionate to the good that can be accomplished. This involves weighing the burdens of a particular treatment against its benefits for the sick person, given her or his condition. Refusing treatment for someone you are responsible for—or withdrawing it once it has been started—is not considered euthanasia if the treatment would lay more burden on the sick person than benefit. The burden could be the discomfort, complexity, lack of availability, or expense of the treatment. The benefit would be the expected helpfulness of the treatment, given the condition of the patient. Weighing the burdens and benefits of treatment with a respirator, one might responsibly decide to refuse or withdraw treatment, as was done in the first case. Case 1, about Brad, is an example of letting the dying person go naturally, not killing.

The use of painkillers. What about Flora, the woman with AIDS, in case 4? By giving the higher dose of painkiller, the doctor probably did hasten the death of the dying patient. Is that not euthanasia? The church would say no, because to be considered euthanasia, an action or omission must intentionally and directly kill the patient. In this case, the doctor increased the dosage of morphine *not* so that the patient would die sooner, but because it was required to keep the patient from suffering cruel pain. Providing for the comfort, care, and support of the dying person is a significant element of reverence for human life. Cancer, not mor-

phine, was the primary cause of the patient's death.

No "right" to end a life. Why would the Catholic church consider cases 2 and 3 instances of euthanasia? Regarding case 2, about Marge, no one has the right to directly end Marge's life by injecting her with a substance intended to kill her. It does not matter that she expressed the wish to be "put out of her misery," because the choice of ending her life is not hers to make, nor any human being's. In this case, human beings are taking life and death into their own hands, and this violates the sacred trust they have been given to cherish life and not to harm it.

An omission that intentionally and directly takes a life. Why is the third case, about Fred, considered an example of euthanasia even though

Above: Catholic teaching states that we are not obligated to accept or continue medical treatment that is out of proportion to the good that can be done by the treatment.

Kristin did not *actively* kill her grandfather but simply omitted to take him to the doctor to receive treatment for his pneumonia? Here both the principles of proportionate treatment and intention and directness apply. First of all, Fred's primary disease—Alzheimer's—has not pushed him closer to death. Even though his mental functioning is limited, he is relatively healthy and is still capable of experiencing life, joy, and sorrow. The possibilities of Fred responding favorably to hospitalization and treatment with antibiotics for his pneumonia are high. The treatment would not be too burdensome considering the likely benefits it would bring to his health. And Kristin realizes that without treatment, her grandfather will probably die. So by deciding not to obtain medical care for her grandfather, Kristin intentionally and directly causes his death. Her omission can be considered euthanasia.

Decisions about what treatments a person in a given condition ought to have are not always as clear-cut as in the previous cases. Sometimes there are no obvious, morally correct answers. This is why the ability to discern and weigh factors carefully and sincerely is so necessary when we are dealing with issues of life and death.

Suicide

As this discussion has shown, "letting life go" when the time has come to let it go is not the same as intentionally and directly causing death. Taking one's own life, **suicide**, is morally wrong because of all that has been said thus far about the sacredness of life and the responsibility to cherish that life until the natural processes take their course and death comes.

Support and Hope Needed

A person who commits suicide, though, cannot be morally judged by the survivors, who do not know all the physical or psychological pressures the person was under. Persons who say they want to die may have lost all hope that life has any meaning or value, but their wishes or threats to end it all are really signs that they are desperate for love and support to get through an extremely difficult time in their life. All of us need to become more sensitive to persons we rub shoulders with every day who, unknown to us, may not want to go on living. The intervention of a concerned friend, family member, pastor, or professional care giver can make the crucial difference in turning around the despair in a suicidal person and helping him or her to see that life is always worth living. **12**

■
Above: We need to become more sensitive to persons who, unknown to us, may not want to go on living.

12
In writing, describe how support from family and friends could make a positive difference for someone who is considering suicide.

The Nazi Doctors

Most people today do not realize that physicians, scientists, and medical technology made possible much of the horror of the Holocaust by the Nazis in the 1930s and 1940s.

Medical and scientific involvement in the killing of millions of innocent people under the Nazis began with a simple acceptance by German doctors of a thesis presented in a 1920 scientific paper, *On the Destruction of Life Unworthy to Be Lived.* The thesis they agreed with was this: "Not granting release by gentle death to the incurable who long for it; this is no longer sympathy, but rather its opposite."

Beginning with euthanasia for the terminally ill, the Nazi doctors moved on to euthanasia for the chronically ill and psychiatrically disturbed. Finally, they participated in the state's "race hygiene" program to eliminate all undesirables—Jews, Poles, and gypsies among them.

Philosopher Patrick Derr has written on the Nazi doctors' complicity in the Holocaust as a warning to contemporary doctors who want to push the limits of their role as healers and caregivers. Here he comments:

No matter how pure the sympathetic motives of any physician who does not want to see patients suffer a long and painful death, physicians who freely agree to help with a little killing will not long be able to resist society's demand for more and more killing. For there is no limit to the number of social and human problems that can be "solved" by killing. Even today, societies around the world openly practice capital punishment, torture of political dissidents, genocide, and infanticide. ("Allegiance to the Hippocratic Oath")

The "Right to Die"?

Perhaps you have heard an account of the death of a terminally ill person by suicide. This issue has long been debated in the media and in state legislatures, and in some states, it has even been voted on at the ballot box: Should it be legal for a doctor to assist a person, terminally ill or not, to commit suicide? Advocates of legalizing "assisted suicide" claim that everyone has the "right to die," and therefore, helping a person to commit suicide is legitimate. However, by the "right to die," these proponents really mean the right to control the time and manner of one's death.

It is one thing to say we have the right to die naturally, peacefully, and with dignity. It is quite another to say we have a right to take our own life—or to have someone else do it—when and how we decide.

Heart-rending stories are told of a spouse or a doctor who helps a person commit suicide because she or he has a dreaded illness, and we may be sympathetic to the individual's plight. Often the patient has been in great pain or wants to avoid a slow, difficult dying process, and this adds to our sympathy. Yet, the right to die never means the right to end one's own life. As said many times in this chapter, God is ultimately the author of life and death, not humans. Suicide, especially assisted suicide, is another way of trying to "play God."

Other compelling reasons not to legalize assisted suicide are these:

- With proper medical care, pain can usually be controlled for terminally ill patients so that their fears of dying in agony can be alleviated.
- Examining the problem from the patient's perspective can improve the situation the patient is in: get pain under control, bring in the loving support of family and friends, finance health care in such a way that people do not have to go bankrupt during an illness.

Pressure to Die?

One of the dangers of legalizing assisted suicide, and euthanasia as well, is the possibility that in that social climate, the pressure—subtle and not-so-subtle—on a person to choose these practices would begin to build. Suicide and euthanasia would not really be "voluntary," as advocates claim. These practices could gradually become socially expected behaviors for persons who are no longer "contributing" to society. Especially vulnerable to this pressure would be people who already feel useless, or that they are a burden to their families, or that their care is costing too much. The danger of making suicide and euthanasia morally and legally acceptable is that it is highly likely that at least some individuals would come to be regarded as "disposable"—not worth having around. The prospect of evolving into that kind of society is frightening and ought to serve as a warning to those who advocate for the "right to die" by suicide or euthanasia. **13**

For Review

- What does the Catholic church mean by euthanasia? Is it ever morally permissible?
- What two extreme positions do not fit the church's perspective on human life?
- What does the church say about using proportionate treatment in an illness?
- In what sense do we not have the "right to die"? In what sense do we have this right?
- What grave danger is involved in making euthanasia and assisted suicide legal?

13
List some categories of people who might feel pressured toward suicide or euthanasia if these practices were to become acceptable and even expected in a society.

Between Life's Edges

The Seamless Garment

Thus far this chapter has focused on issues of reverencing human life at its most fragile and vulnerable times. We have seen that our cherishing the lives of unborn babies must be matched by our holding as sacred the lives of terminally ill persons. Cardinal Joseph Bernardin expresses why society needs to be vigilant of the right to life at its beginnings and its endings:

"If we become insensitive to the beginning of life and condone abortion or if we become careless about the end of life and justify euthanasia, we have no reason to believe that there will be much respect for life in between." (Quoted in Vanderhaar and Kownacki, *Way of Peace,* page 25)

In the rest of this chapter, we turn our focus to the in-between stages of life.

The Catholic church's consistent ethic of life teaches that the virtue of reverence for human life spans the whole spectrum of life, including all the many stages of life between its edges. What Cardinal Bernardin is getting at in the previous quote is that issues of how every person is treated—at all the life stages—are woven together in a "seamless garment." Like the garment that legend says Jesus wore, these issues are all of one piece.

Thus, people who hold all human life as sacred are very concerned about prisoners on death row; homeless men, women, and children; slumdwellers starving in Third World cities; citizens of another nation defined as "the enemy" by our government; drivers and passengers on the highway; as well as the persons they come in contact with every day at home, school, or work.

Being consistent in our commitment to life means struggling *against* those social, political, and economic policies and structures that threaten the dignity and sacredness of human life and working *for* those that make it possible to live a truly human existence. In addition to those already discussed in this chapter, three other issues that today threaten the sacredness of human life are **capital punishment**, **modern warfare**, and **recklessly endangering human life**.

The Death Penalty

The United States is one of only two Western industrialized nations in which capital punishment is still legal. According to a ruling by the U.S. Supreme Court, the death penalty can be broadly applied: that is, depending on the crime committed, even juveniles and mentally retarded people can be punished by death. Public support for legal murder is strong: 79 percent of the people surveyed in a 1988 nationwide Gallup poll believed that the death penalty should be applied in the case of murder, and that support has remained steady throughout the 1990s.

Effective?

The death penalty is "effective" in that it rids society of some of its more dangerous criminals. However, most supporters of capital punishment claim it does more than that: they say it deters potential criminals from committing crimes, and it reinforces law and order. Furthermore, supporters claim that the death penalty saves taxpayers the years of expense of keeping a criminal in prison for life.

The facts, however, do not support these claims. Murder rates are actually lower in the states where

the death penalty is illegal. And capital punishment is more expensive. Because of court costs that extend over years of legal appeals, carrying out a death sentence is almost three times more expensive than holding a person in prison for life.

Even more alarming is the finding that those given the death penalty are disproportionately poor and black. In addition, even though almost half of the victims of murder in the United States are black, 90 percent of those on death row are there for killing whites. Someone who murders a white person is more likely to incur the death penalty than someone who murders a black person.

Christian?

Sr. Helen Prejean, an active opponent of the death penalty, approaches the controversy from two sides. She has been the spiritual adviser for convicted killers on death row, and has witnessed their executions. She has also met, counseled, and prayed with the families of murder victims.

Patrick Sonnier was on death row in a Louisiana prison, convicted of murdering two teenagers, when Sister Helen became his adviser. Sonnier, she found, was a vulnerable man who had made grave mistakes for which he deserved to be punished, but Sister Helen could see no value in putting him to death. She also got to know Lloyd LeBlanc, the father of one of Sonnier's victims. Sister Helen reports:

Lloyd LeBlanc is an extraordinary man. When the sheriff had brought him out to the cane field, he had knelt by the body of his slain son, prayed the Our Father, and said, "Whoever did this, I forgive them." ("Should Killers Live? Or Die?")

Like Sister Helen, LeBlanc could see no purpose in Sonnier's death. He says:

"On every side I was pressured to support Sonnier's execution, but I didn't want to see a man's life taken. Life is the good Lord's to give and to take, not ours." ("Should Killers Live? Or Die?")

Such radical forgiveness is characteristic of Catholic teaching on the death penalty. Sister Helen asks a question that points to the basis of Catholic teaching:

In no way do I condone the torture and murder of [Sonnier's victims]. But neither can I condone the practice of torture and killing by government officials. Are there not some nonnegotiable human rights that belong to the guilty as well as to the innocent? ("Should Killers Live? Or Die?")

Pope John Paul II provides an emphatic response: "Not even a murderer loses his personal dignity, and God himself pledges to guarantee this" (*The Gospel of Life,* number 9). Public authorities have a dual responsibility: to punish criminals and to ensure public safety, "while at the same time offering the offender an incentive and help to change his or her behavior and be rehabilitated."

■
Lloyd LeBlanc, whose son was murdered, says, "Life is the good Lord's to give and take, not ours."
Above: Indiana's electric chair

For these goals to be achieved, the pope says, the punishment given must be carefully chosen. Capital punishment, the most extreme form, may be used only if public safety cannot be guaranteed without it. The pope notes that due to the quality of the penal system, it is all but impossible to justify the need to put a criminal to death (number 56).

The Catholic church's rejection of capital punishment is linked to its opposition to abortion and euthanasia. These cases share the same basic principle: all human life, without exception, has God-given worth and dignity and must be treated with respect and reverence.

Modern Warfare

Huge Arsenals, Regional Conflicts

The period of history following World War II is often referred to as the Cold War period. Two military superpowers—the United States and the Soviet Union—dominated the international scene. With few exceptions, less powerful nations aligned themselves with one or the other of the superpowers. Though avoiding direct military confrontation, tension between the United States and the Soviet Union grew as each built huge arsenals of nuclear and conventional (nonnuclear) weapons. Smaller nations, too, built arsenals consisting of conventional, chemical, and biological weapons, supplied by one of the superpowers.

The Cold War ended in the early 1990s with the collapse of the Soviet Union, leaving the world with just one major military power. Since then, nuclear arsenals have been reduced, but conventional arsenals have grown throughout the world. The United States has been the primary supplier of new weapons, exporting $31 billion worth to 140 nations in 1993. The availability of weapons fuels regional conflicts around the globe. Ironically, it also increases the chance that when U.S. military forces are sent to intervene in such conflicts, they will come up against weapons supplied by their own government.

Massive Destruction: A Crime Against God and Humankind

Modern warfare, regional or global, inevitably inflicts massive suffering and death. Today's conventional weapons can be as destructive as the early nuclear bombs, making it harder to identify the distinction between the two categories of weapons. Warfare is often aimed at areas where crucial supplies are produced and stored, and these are usually near population centers. Water supplies and other systems essential for maintaining a population (roads, bridges, electricity, fuel) are targeted. Modern warfare therefore tends to kill massive numbers of civilians, or noncombatants.

The Catholic church firmly opposes the use of *any* weapons that inflict massive destruction. In the *Pastoral Constitution on the Church in the Modern World,* the Vatican II bishops declared: "Any act of war aimed indiscriminately at the destruction of entire cities or of extensive areas along with their population is a crime against God and man himself. It merits unequivocal and unhesitating condemnation" (number 80). **14**

Catholics and War

Catholic approaches to the problem of war can be summarized by two categories of thought:

Just-war theory. Official church teaching holds that war can be justified only if it satisfies certain limited and strict conditions set forth in the **just-war theory.** One important condition is referred to as proportionality: the damage to be inflicted must

---

14
List some examples of acts of war in this century that would fall under the condemnation of Vatican Council II.

not be disproportionate to the good to be accomplished by the war. In other words, the harm to be done must not outweigh the good.

Many Catholics, including some bishops, question whether *any* modern war, nuclear or conventional, could be called "just" under the conditions set by the just-war theory. In particular, they point out that modern war inevitably devastates the earth and kills masses of civilians and therefore cannot satisfy the condition of proportionality. Even conflicts that are intended to be very limited are tremendously dangerous, with a great risk of escalation to wide-scale massive warfare. **15**

Pacifism. Other Catholics hold a **pacifist** position: they believe that according to Jesus' teachings and example, and the practice of the church in its first two centuries, Christians are called to renounce all war, modern or otherwise. They advocate creative and nonviolent methods of resolving conflict and resisting evil and aggression. **16**

Toward an International Order

In their 1983 pastoral letter *The Challenge of Peace,* the U.S. bishops endorsed nonviolent means of dealing with world conflicts. Following the tradition of popes since the 1940s, the bishops affirmed that humankind must pursue the building and strengthening of an international order, such as the United Nations, that can regulate conflicts between nations and look after the common good. Ten years later, in a world that had undergone great change, the U.S. bishops issued the statement *The Harvest of Justice Is Sown in Peace.* In this document they outlined the elements of international peace:

- *Structures of peace.* Peace is not achieved simply by proclaiming peaceful ideals. It also requires building structures of peace.
- *Regional and global institutions.* Citizens and leaders should support political and legal institutions, especially the United Nations.
- *Human rights.* Human rights should be promoted and defended.
- *Sustainable development.* Sustainable development will help preserve the environment and diminish poverty.
- *Respect and dialog.* Conflicts based in nationalism or ethnic, racial, and religious differences must be eliminated through respect and dialog.
- *Reduced military spending.* Nuclear proliferation must be stopped, and worldwide military spending should be significantly reduced.
- *A vocation to peacemaking.* The people and leaders of the United States must commit themselves to the vocation of peacemaking.

- Think of a conflict between nations that leads to war. With reference to the U.S. bishops' elements of international peace, how might the conflict be resolved peacefully?

Recklessly Endangering Human Life

The issues discussed in this chapter for the most part may seem far removed from your everyday life. We seldom face the decision of what to do about an unwanted pregnancy or how to treat a terminally ill person or whether to go to war. However, one decision we may have to face daily says volumes about whether we do or do not reverence human life. That is the decision of how we drive a vehicle.

For most of us, a car is the most powerful tool that we will ever operate, and it needs to be treated, in one theologian's words, as "a potentially unguided missile of one or two tons, equipped with

---

15
Do you agree or disagree with this statement?
- Modern warfare, whether nuclear or otherwise, inevitably inflicts more harm than it produces good.

Explain your response in writing.

16
According to your understanding of the Gospels, did Jesus call his followers to renounce all war? Give your answer in writing, using references from the Gospels.

A Just War?

The just-war theory, first proposed in the fifth century by church theologians, offers a set of principles that greatly restrict the circumstances under which a war can be considered justifiable. Eight conditions must be met in order for a war to be considered just:

1. **It must be declared by a legitimate authority.** That is, only the rightful leaders of a country have the right to involve their people in the suffering and hardship of war.

2. **It must be a last resort.** Every other attempt to resolve the conflict or injustice must have been tried and failed before war can be justly declared.

3. **It must be waged only to resist a grave injustice.** Careful consideration must be given to the word *grave*. Modern warfare is far more destructive than that of previous times. So an injustice that justified a war a hundred years ago might not be a grave enough cause today.

4. **The means used to win a war must be moral.** This principle has to do with the way in which a war is actually conducted. A number of rules of warfare set forth in international law offer guidance to countries in this matter.

5. **It must be terminated as soon as justice (not victory) is secured.** Once the injustice that brought about the war is set right, the hostilities must end.

6. **Its terms for peace must be fair.** Otherwise the peace treaty itself becomes an act of war, an act of violence and injustice.

7. **War cannot be waged unless there is a reasonable assurance of success.** Just as an individual has no right to squander money or throw away his or her life uselessly, no nation has the right to engage in futile military operations.

8. **The principle of proportionality must be observed.** There must be a proportion between the injustice suffered and the amount of force used to vindicate that injustice. Modern warfare is enormously more destructive than warfare of the fifth century, when the just-war theory was first proposed. Serious doubt exists as to whether the damage caused by modern warfare could ever be considered proportionate to the good that it accomplishes.

■
Above: Modern warfare is enormously more destructive than warfare of the fifth century, when the just-war theory was proposed.

combustible material." Driving under the influence of alcohol or other drugs is like taking a loaded gun and cocking the trigger. According to *Seventeen* magazine, alcohol is involved in half of the highway deaths in the United States each year—about twenty-three thousand deaths due to drinking and driving. Drunk driving is the leading killer of people ages fifteen to twenty-four.

To drive under the influence of alcohol or other drugs, or to allow someone else to do so, shows a terrible disregard for life. Reverence for human life—our own life and the lives of others—requires that if we have made the mistake of becoming under the influence at a time when we need to drive, we admit our limitations and ask someone else who is capable to drive. Too many people, dealing with the fact that they are responsible for the loss of someone's life, wish *after the accident* that they had been willing to swallow their pride and refuse to drive *before the accident*. **17**

- If a person driving under the influence of alcohol or other drugs causes another person's death in a fatal car accident, how much moral blame does that person have?

For Review

- Is the death penalty "effective"?
- What is the position of Pope John Paul II on the death penalty?
- What factors give modern warfare—conventional or nuclear—its potential to inflict massive destruction?
- What did the Second Vatican Council condemn?
- Which one of the just-war criteria do many people believe could not be met by any modern war?
- What is a Christian pacifist position?
- List and describe four of the elements of international peace outlined by the U.S. bishops.
- What does reverence for human life mean with respect to drinking and driving?

Above: Alcohol is involved in half of the highway deaths in the United States each year.

17

Suppose you are out with a friend who wants to drive while under the influence of alcohol or other drugs. Write down an imaginary conversation between the two of you in which you try to stop the person from driving.

For the Love of Life

The Christian vision affirms that life—human and nonhuman, at all stages—is a wonderful gift of great goodness. Life comes from God and is meant to be cherished as sacred. But as Asher learned from his father in the opening story of this chapter, death is part of life.

Christians, however, believe that God, through the Resurrection of Jesus, has revealed to us that death is not the last word; life is. Even God's creation reflects this basic truth: Death is a necessary part of the continuation of life. And so, part of reverencing the fullness of life means letting life go when the right time comes, so that new life might come forth.

In Mary Oliver's poem "In Blackwater Woods," the dying that occurs in nature every autumn offers material for reflection on the cycles of life, and particularly on how to cherish all the people, places, and events we have loved:

Look, the trees
are turning
their own bodies
into pillars

of light,
are giving off the rich
fragrance of cinnamon
and fulfillment,

the long tapers
of cattails
are bursting and floating away over
the blue shoulders

of the ponds,
and every pond,
no matter what its
name is, is

nameless now.
Every year
everything
I have ever learned

in my lifetime
leads back to this: the fires
and the black river of loss
whose other side

is salvation,
whose meaning
none of us will ever know.
To live in this world

you must be able
to do three things:
to love what is mortal;
to hold it

against your bones knowing
your own life depends on it;
and, when the time comes to let it go,
to let it go. **18**

18
Describe in writing a person, a place, or a part of your life that you loved dearly but eventually had to let go of.

Peacemaking: Handling Conflict with Creativity

To Speak Up or Not to Speak Up

To begin the study of the virtue of peacemaking, reflect on this story of a personal conflict:

Ellie would do anything to see Jared, but he was six hours away by car. Jared had wanted to play hockey, and the college with the best program that he could get into was in another state. So, reluctantly, in September Ellie had waved him off, consoling herself with the knowledge that they had promised each other they would continue their relationship. October rolled by, and they still had not seen each other. With no car or bus service, six hours away was like six days.

Despite frequent phone calls, Ellie was becoming anxious that she and Jared were growing apart. So when Adrianne offered to drive Ellie up to the college for the first hockey game and spend the weekend, Ellie thought that she had just died and gone to heaven. "You are a lifesaver!" she exclaimed over the phone.

"Well, sure, ya dope. What do you think best friends are for? Besides, I may want to go to school there next year."

When Ellie called Jared, to her delight he sounded as excited as she was. He began telling her all the things he would line up for them to do, and Ellie was about to jump out of her skin.

From then on, Ellie couldn't keep her mind on anything else. She kept going over the plans, anticipating how great it would be to spend a whole weekend with Jared.

All day that Friday, Ellie was bubbling with excitement. At lunch she was so wrapped up in telling her friends everything Jared had lined up for them to do, that she didn't notice how quiet Adrianne had been the whole time.

"See you at 3:30 at my house, Adrianne," Ellie called out as she headed off to her sixth-period class.

Sitting out on the front porch, bags packed and ready to go, Ellie's eyes were glued to the street watching for the first sign of Adrianne's little red car. Adrianne's never late for anything, thought Ellie. She probably had to get gas. She'll be here any minute, I'm sure. But still, the further past 3:30 the time went, the longer each minute seemed.

By 4:15, there was still no sign of Adrianne, so Ellie went in to give her a call. "Hi, Adrianne? This is Ellie. Is everything all right with your car? Should I call Jared and tell him we're going to be late?"

"Oh . . . hi, Ellie. I was just going to call you. Uh, I've got some bad news. I won't be able to go this weekend. I've been meaning to say something all week, but . . . well, Philip asked me to the homecoming dance tomorrow night. You know I've been dying to go out with him for months. I just had to say yes. Ellie, I know I should have said something earlier, but I knew how excited you were about seeing Jared this weekend. I was scared to say anything. I didn't want to hurt you. I hope you're not mad at me."

"Oh, no, Adrianne. It's no big deal. . . . Besides, Jared will be home in three weeks for Thanksgiving. I'll see him then. Just have a great time tomorrow night. I am *really* happy for you. . . ."

Ellie put the phone down and began to cry.

After crying for fifteen minutes, Ellie pulled herself together enough to call Jared. Somehow she managed to tell Jared she wasn't coming and why.

"Cripes, Ellie, that was really rotten. I can't believe Adrianne never said anything to you earlier. What a jerk! I hope you told her off."

"I couldn't do that, Jared. She's my best friend."

"If I were you, Ellie, I'd get myself a new best friend."

For the next week, a struggle raged inside Ellie. Each time a feeling of anger toward Adrianne came to the surface, she would say to herself, Stop making such a big deal over this. Of course Adrianne had the right to go to the homecoming dance with Philip. I shouldn't be so selfish. And she was just too scared to tell me. But no matter how hard Ellie tried to talk herself out of it and act like nothing was wrong, the resentment she felt toward Adrianne would not go away.

After two weeks, Ellie came to the conclusion that she had to say something to Adrianne; she couldn't stand the phoniness that had crept into their friendship. They had been friends too long for it to come to this.

At first she felt really stupid bringing this up two weeks after the fact. Also, she and Adrianne had never once had an argument with each other. Ellie worried that Adrianne might even lash back, but she figured that couldn't be any worse than walking around with all this anger inside her.

Ellie spotted Adrianne walking home from school that afternoon. Nervously, she ran to catch up with her. "Adrianne, I've gotta talk with you."

"Sure, El. What's up?"

"I wish I hadn't waited so long. . . . I was really a mess when I found out we weren't going to Jared's. And it wasn't just that I was sad not to see Jared. It was that I felt so let down and hurt by you, like I didn't matter. I wish you would have told me right away. . . ." **1**

Above: Talking things out is essential for resolving conflict.

1
In writing, tell how you would handle a situation like Ellie's.

"Blessed Are the Peacemakers"

To consider how to handle conflicts like Ellie and Adrianne's in a Christian way, it makes sense to listen to Jesus' advice.

Turn the Other Cheek?

Several of Jesus' most memorable and startling teachings focus on how to deal with conflict situations. For example, consider these words from the Sermon on the Mount:

"But I say to you, Do not resist an evildoer. But if anyone strikes you on the right cheek, turn the other also; and if anyone wants to sue you and take your coat, give your cloak as well; and if anyone forces you to go one mile, go also the second mile. . . .

"You have heard that it was said, 'You shall love your neighbor and hate your enemy.' But I say to you, Love your enemies and pray for those who persecute you." (Matthew 5:39–44, NRSV)

Christians have long wondered about the meaning of those words, and about what Jesus really expected of us when he proclaimed, "'Blessed are the peacemakers, / for they will be called children of God'" (Matthew 5:9). In response to Jesus' teaching and example, most Christians in the first two to three centuries after Jesus' death and Resurrection took a pacifist position, refusing to bear arms or fight in war. Later, most Christians adopted the just-war theory, which allowed participation in war if the war met certain highly restricted conditions (see page 267). Some Christians, however, retained a belief in pacifism as the authentic meaning of Jesus' teaching.

At the level of personal conflict, Jesus' words also apply. But what do they mean? **2**

What Jesus Did *Not* Mean

Jesus' teachings about loving our enemies and turning the other cheek have been greatly misunderstood over the years by people who have assumed that Jesus was telling us to be passive and compliant in the face of injustice—to "give up, shut up, and put up" with attacks on us or wrongs done to us.

Even today, many people are confused about what Jesus meant in those teachings from the Sermon on the Mount. Some assume that Jesus wanted Christians to be sweet and submissive, to allow themselves to be walked on like doormats. Or they think that Christians are supposed to avoid conflict at all costs. Certainly these kinds of thoughts must have been what kept Ellie from saying something sooner to Adrianne about how upset and angry she was.

2
Before reading on, write down what you think Jesus meant in saying that when someone strikes you on one cheek, you should turn and offer the other cheek.

■
Above: Some people assume that loving your enemy means being sweet and submissive, avoiding conflict at all costs by masking true feelings.

The Civil Rights Movement: Resistance with Love

The great hero of the nonviolent U.S. civil rights movement, Martin Luther King Jr., believed in the depths of his being that love, not hate, was the only force that could truly overcome evil. The campaign to win the recognition of basic rights for blacks, inspired by the teachings in the Sermon on the Mount, involved the refusal to obey unjust segregation laws and participation in strikes, boycotts, and symbolic actions like marches.

Throughout the years of the campaign, King always respected the dignity and freedom of the oppressors and urged his fellow resisters to do so also. Before a nonviolent demonstration, King or other movement leaders would lead the demonstrators as they prayed, read the Bible, sang spirituals, and talked about the love that God had for the police who were about to spray them with fire hoses and turn vicious dogs on them; for the people who would throw rocks and bottles at them; and for those who had burned their homes, bombed their churches, even killed some of them and their children.

So when the hostile police and members of angry mobs in the South looked into the faces of the demonstrators from King's Southern Christian Leadership Conference, they saw passionately determined, self-respecting people filled with love for the enemy. The demonstrators were inviting the crowds to recognize the humanity of them all, black and white alike.

Here are King's words on the uselessness of countering violence with more violence:

"The ultimate weakness of violence is that it is a descending spiral, begetting the very thing it seeks to destroy. . . . Returning violence for violence multiplies violence, adding deeper darkness to a night already devoid of stars. Darkness cannot drive out darkness; only light can do that. Hate cannot drive out hate; only love can do that." (Quoted in *Peacemaking*, page 126)

■
Civil rights demonstrators invited the crowds to recognize the humanity of them all, black and white alike. *Above:* Demonstrators take refuge in a doorway as firefighters blast them with a fire hose to break up a 1963 civil rights demonstration in Birmingham, Alabama.

What Jesus *Did* Mean

When we look at the whole of Jesus' life and message, though, it becomes clearer that the teachings on loving your enemy were not counseling us to be passive in the face of an enemy doing harm to us. Jesus himself was anything but passive. He stood up to powerful, self-righteous religious leaders over issues of justice and truth.

Jesus also did *not* want his followers to avoid conflict, agreeing with everything and everyone around them in order to "keep the peace." That complacent, don't-rock-the-boat kind of peace is what Jesus was referring to when he said, "'Do not suppose that my mission on earth is to spread peace. My mission is to spread, not peace, but division'" (Matthew 10:34). Jesus wanted his followers to be fully engaged in life, struggling against evil, sticking out their necks and causing trouble, even division, when needed to bring about God's Reign on earth—just as he did during his own ministry. **3**

If Jesus was not urging passivity among his followers, how are we to understand the words "'If anyone strikes you on the right cheek, turn the other also'" (Matthew 5:39, NRSV) and "'Love your enemies'" (Matthew 5:44, NRSV)? Jesus is pointing to an attitude of the heart that must characterize our dealings with people who are hurting or threatening us. He is saying that we overcome evil not by lashing back with more evil and malice, but by responding with creative love.

Conflict: A Natural Part of Life

Life is filled with conflict. Conflict, however, is not necessarily something bad to be avoided. Many of the situations of conflict we face are an inevitable part of human, and all of nature's, existence. We all have varying interests, needs, and wants; and sometimes they clash. That was the case in the story of Ellie's conflict with Adrianne. Even when we are not being bad or selfish we run into conflict—just because we are different.

Not running away from conflict—facing it—is a lot different than looking for it out of meanness or hostility. Facing a conflict requires us to make use of something very human in us—our creative energies. By dealing constructively and nonviolently with conflict, we become more creative, more fully human.

3

Give a one-paragraph example of how following the Gospel can lead a person into conflict with others.

■

Above: A peace activist stands as a nonviolent witness at an anti-war demonstration.

"We will go before God to be judged, and God will ask us, 'Where are your wounds?' And we will say, 'We have no wounds.' And God will ask, 'Was nothing worth fighting for?'" (Quoted in *Peacemaking*, page 26)

- What kinds of things are worth fighting for in a nonviolent way?

This discussion of what Jesus did and did not mean by telling his followers to "love your enemies" brings us to the point of defining Christian peacemaking. The virtue of **peacemaking** is the ability to try to resolve the inevitable conflicts of life in a creative, loving way. With peacemaking, it is easy to see how interconnected all the moral virtues discussed in this course are. Peacemaking would not be possible without these virtues:

- wise judgment
- justice
- courage
- wholeness
- honesty
- respect for persons
- compassion
- respect for creation
- reverence for human life **4**

The creative peacemaking that Jesus calls us to is needed in personal conflicts as well as in conflicts in the wider world.

However, even conflict handled constructively does not always turn out well for us. Reflect on how Jesus confronted the scribes and the Pharisees with their hypocrisy on the occasions when they tried to trap him or when they attacked others unjustly and arrogantly. As a result of these confrontations, Jesus was crucified. Likewise, nonviolent campaigns for justice in the twentieth century at times have actually caused conflict and have resulted in injury, imprisonment, and even death for some of the resisters. But Jesus and his nonviolent followers were willing to accept the cost of standing for something. Their nonviolent stance was not motivated by fear of conflict but supported by courage in the midst of conflict.

From the decades-long movement of nonviolent resistance to apartheid in South Africa comes a story told by a movement leader. It speaks of the necessity for Christians to stand for something with their life and to take the consequences:

For Review

- What moral advice on conflict was Jesus giving when he said we must love our enemies and turn the other cheek if struck? What advice was he not giving?
- Define the virtue of peacemaking.

■
Above: We run into conflict partly because we are all different.

4
For each of the moral virtues studied earlier in this course, explain in a sentence how that virtue relates to peacemaking.

Personal Peacemaking

Creative Strategies

With this understanding of peacemaking in mind, let us consider some strategies for dealing with person-to-person conflicts.

1. Acknowledge Your Own Feelings

Before you even try to do or say anything about a personal conflict, get in touch with how you are feeling. If you think you have been wronged by another person, chances are you feel angry or hurt, and you need to acknowledge that to yourself and not bury it.

Is it okay to feel angry at another person? Believing that anger is not acceptable for nice people or Christians, some persons stuff their anger away or convince themselves that they have nothing to be upset about or just sit on their anger and let it chew at their insides. Repressing your feelings is not healthy, and ultimately it does nothing to resolve a conflict.

If you are still wondering whether it is Christian to be angry, consider these words of Saint Paul to the Christian community in the ancient city of Ephesus:

So then, putting away falsehood, let all of us speak the truth to our neighbors, for we are members of one another. Be angry but do not sin; do not let the sun go down on your anger, and do not make room for the devil. (Ephesians 4:25–27, NRSV)

In other words, being angry is not itself sinful. Anger tells the other person, "I'm hurt or insulted or scared." But if we let anger eat away at us (let the "sun go down" on our anger), we are opening the door to hostility—the desire to hurt, insult, or scare the person with whom we are angry. Hostility, especially if acted upon, can be called sinful and will only lead to persisting problems in the relationship.

2. State What Is Bothering You Without Attacking

Taking Saint Paul's advice, go to the person with whom you are having the conflict and get things out in the open. If you feel hot about the conflict, first take time to cool down so that you will not attack the other person with sarcasm, insults, or a tone of disrespect.

You will have a more straightforward, nonhostile tone if you say what is bothering you using "I" statements rather than "you" statements. For instance, here is one brother speaking to another, using both kinds of statements:

Above: When we find ourselves in a conflict, we need to get in touch with how we are feeling and acknowledge, not bury, our feelings.

- *"You" statement.* "What did you do a dumb thing like *that* for? First you take my tape player without asking me. Then you sit on it on the bus! Get a brain."
- *"I" statement.* "I'm really mad about my tape player. I wanted to use it when I went running, but I couldn't find it. Now it's broken and I can't use it, and fixing it will cost more than buying a new one."

"I" statements convey how the speaker is reacting to the situation. "You" statements, on the other hand, attack the other person by becoming accusatory. "You" statements usually make the other person hostile and defensive, which only escalates the conflict. **5**

3. Be Sincere in Listening to the Other Person

Find out the other person's point of view on the conflict. Listen respectfully and empathetically. Let the person know you understood what he or she said. For instance:

- "Yeah, I can see you felt like you *had* to come up with a tape player for the bus trip, with Lisa expecting you to have it and you wanting to sit with her and all. And I wasn't at home to ask. You must have almost died when you sat on it!"

4. Do Not Retaliate

Some people will be hypersensitive to your criticism or statement of your negative feelings no matter how well you say it. Resist the impulse to retaliate with a personal attack if the other person gets defensive and attacks you. The situation will just get worse. Refrain from saying this:

- "Look, I'm trying to be nice about this, but you seem to think the world owes you everything you want and you can just rip me off anytime you feel like it. You know, you're turning into a real sponge."

Instead, try something like this:

- "Hey, I'm just asking that you try to see things from my side. How would you feel if it had been your tape player?"

5. Be Flexible, but Hang in There

Be willing to see things in a different way if the other person presents a good case for his or her own point of view. However, if you are still convinced your point is valid and the other person does not hear your perspective, hang in there and restate it until you have made yourself clear. For instance:

- "Sure, I realize it was an accident, and I know you don't have the money to pay for another tape player. But I still think in fairness you owe me a new one."

6. Think of Creative Approaches

Try to get both of you involved in coming up with fresh approaches to the problem. Consider lots of suggestions, even some that seem a bit crazy. Such thinking often contains the seeds of a great insight. For instance:

- "Maybe that *could* work out. I wouldn't mind not doing my paper route for a month or so, and that'll give you a chance to earn enough money to replace my tape player."

7. Agree on Something You Can Both Live With

Finally, settle together on how you will resolve the conflict, and create some way for both of you to check later to see that it is working. For instance:

5
Think of a hypothetical situation in which you are upset with someone. Compose two versions of a statement about how you are feeling: a "you" statement and an "I" statement. Which one sounds more likely to be accepted by the other person?

Parents and Curfews: Finding a Creative Approach

Working out a conflict with a parent takes creativity on both sides. Here is an example of how a conflict over a curfew requires creative approaches. It is from an article written by a mother and daughter team:

Let's say you're having a discussion with your mother about how late you ought to be able to stay out on weekend nights. You've already expressed your irritation that your curfew is an hour earlier than any of your friends', and how this messes up the social activities of your whole group. You've listened and really tried to appreciate your mother's point of view that she worries about your safety when you're out late at night, and she doesn't really feel comfortable going to sleep until you're home. However, she can't sleep in the next morning like you, because she has to get up with the younger kids.

You might suggest that you could call home at a reasonable hour to let your mother know where you are, what your plans are for the rest of the evening, and how you're getting home. That might relieve some of her anxiety. Your mother might suggest that you could get up with your younger brother and sister on Saturday or Sunday morning, or babysit them for a while in the afternoon so she could take a nap. One of you might suggest a compromise: come home early Friday night, stay out later Saturday. Or maybe your mother is even convinced by your levelheaded approach to this problem that you're more mature than she realized, and she really doesn't need to worry about you staying out an hour later.

Whatever possible solutions you arrive at, you need to think each of them through, considering pros and cons. And finally, together, you need to choose a solution. (Engelhardt and Engelhardt, "How to Fight F.A.I.R.")

Above: If both persons listen and take a creative, problem-solving approach, a parent and a teenager can resolve conflict.

- "All right. So by the first of February you should have enough saved from my paper route. I'll check with you in a couple of weeks to see how the money's coming, okay?" **6**

8. If These Strategies Do Not Work, Look for Help

Helpful as these strategies might be, they are not foolproof. In some situations, our attempts to be honest and our willingness to negotiate are met with unreasonableness and resistance. Perhaps the creative thing to do when this happens is to find someone to act as a referee, someone who would be able to come at it from an outside perspective. In a situation like the tape player example, another family member might be able to help. In more serious cases, help is available from people like pastors, teachers, school counselors, and therapists.

Now go back to the story that opened this chapter. As the story ended, Ellie was just beginning to talk about the conflict with Adrianne. In terms of the strategies just presented, Ellie has gotten to strategy 2, "State what is bothering you without attacking."

- How well did Ellie follow the first two strategies? **7**

Love My Enemy?

In a conflict, it helps to know the techniques and approaches that are most likely to work. Yet Jesus tells us to do far more than use smart strategies. Jesus tells us to make those strategies a matter of the heart. His most challenging call to us is to love our enemy.

Love the Sinner, Not the Sin

Loving those with whom we are in conflict, however, does not mean that we approve of everything they do. We must love the sinner, not the sin.

In fact, we may never feel warm and comfortable around an enemy or want to become buddies. But Jesus challenges us to love at a deeper level than liking. He calls us to search for the divine spark in each person—that which is of God and which is therefore most human. Finding and loving this core of goodness, buried though it may be under hurtful behavior, we may eventually come to like the person—but not necessarily.

Seeing the Humanity of the Enemy

When we love our enemy, we try to see the person as another human being who, like us, has strengths and weaknesses, pressures and needs, and a history that has shaped the way she or he is today. Understanding this does not excuse the person of doing wrong to us, if she or he did so, but it does help us to see the person in a different light—closer to God's light.

If we see the other person as a human being known intimately and cherished by God, chances are that our way of communicating will be different. We will probably be less fearful, less hostile, and more genuinely concerned about finding a resolution to the conflict than about defeating our enemy. We may even come to change our mind about whether this person really is our enemy after all.

By seeing the humanity of the other person, we are also challenging him or her to recognize *our* humanity and treat us with respect.

6
Consider an actual situation in which your interests were in conflict with another person's. Generate a list of possible solutions that both of you probably could have lived with.

7
Write your own version of how the rest of Ellie's conversation with Adrianne might go if Ellie is able to use all the strategies suggested above.

A Meditation on Love for an Enemy

Here is a meditative way to love an enemy from your heart. Try it sometime when you have some quiet moments.

First, get yourself relaxed and comfortable, and take some deep breaths. Read the meditation to yourself, pausing and closing your eyes to reflect as needed.

Think of someone whom you have real differences or problems with—someone you might consider an enemy. . . . Jesus said to love your enemy, but it's really hard with this person. . . . How can you love this person?

Recall a situation where you were with this person and you had negative feelings about what was happening. . . . What was going on? . . . Try to get in touch with whatever feelings you had then. . . .

Now hold this person in your awareness. Picture him or her sitting or standing alone. . . . Imagine a beautiful light radiating from inside this person and engulfing him or her. . . . That light is the love of God.

Even if you can't feel love for this person, realize that God is surrounding this person with love. . . .

Now imagine that you enter the picture and join the other person. Imagine that this wonderful light is also surrounding you. . . . It is penetrating both of you, soaking into you, and it feels warm and good. . . .

Jesus now comes on the scene. . . . He talks to you and to the other person. . . . Spend a

few minutes listening to what Jesus has to say to each of you. . . . Then just sit or stand there quietly, both of you, in his presence.

When you have opened your eyes, you can end this time of meditation with a prayer for the other person and for yourself. Pray that God's love and light might penetrate to the core of each of you. Pray that God's love will transform you and the other person in the ways you each need most. Pray that God's love will surround both of you the next time you are together.

Forgiveness: Seventy Times Seven Times

Loving our enemy includes forgiving our enemy. In a Gospel incident, Jesus tells us to be generous with our forgiveness:

Peter came up and asked [Jesus], "Lord, when my brother wrongs me, how often must I forgive him? Seven times?" "No," Jesus replied, "not seven times; I say, seventy times seven times." (Matthew 18:21–22)

In Jesus' day, "seventy times seven times" meant an unlimited number of times.

Again, it is important to clarify what it means to forgive. Forgiveness does not mean that we patch things up with the other person and forget the wrong ever happened—"forgive and forget." And it does not mean that we let the person take no responsibility for the wrongdoing. The parents of a boy killed in an accident by a drunk driver may forgive the driver, but they will never forget the terrible crime. Having a spirit of forgiveness, too,

does not necessarily mean they should advocate that the driver get off the hook legally.

Forgiveness, instead, is the decision to truly let go of the vengeful spirit we have toward the one who has wronged us, a spirit that can hurt us more than it can hurt the other person. Sometimes, all we can do to forgive is to turn over the situation to God, asking God to take away the hatred and bitterness in our heart. That act of turning to God is itself graced and can be the beginning of forgiveness. **8**

For Review

- List the eight strategies for dealing with person-to-person conflicts.
- What is the difference between a "you" statement and an "I" statement?
- In what way are we to love our enemy?
- What is forgiveness?

■
Above: A vengeful spirit toward one who has wronged us can hurt us more than it can hurt the other person.

8
Have you ever held on tightly to vengeful feelings toward someone who wronged you? If so, reflect on how your own vengeful spirit adversely affected you, and write down your reflections.

World Peacemaking

Organizations for Justice and Peace

Pope Paul VI showed the link between efforts for justice and efforts for peace in this way: "'If you want peace, work for justice'" (quoted in *Peacemaking,* page 23).

Violence among humans in a family, in a community, in a society, or between nations is usually the bitter fruit of systems of injustice. Thus, working for justice at all levels is a requirement of peacemaking. The concerns discussed in chapters 6, 10, 12, and 13 are all related to justice. Reviewing those chapters might be a good way to focus on an area of justice that needs work.

Numerous organizations that work on issues of international justice and peace need the support and enthusiasm of young people. Many of them are specifically geared to students, or they have student chapters or offer lower membership fees for students. Bread for the World, Pax Christi, Amnesty International, JustLife, the Fellowship of Reconciliation, Students for Social Responsibility, and Global Education Associates are among hundreds of such groups. **9**

Images of the Enemy as Brothers and Sisters

Because most soldiers have a hard time killing people with whom they feel they have a lot in common, part of the training for war is to picture the enemy as less than human. This makes it easier to bomb their villages or shoot them—as required by the war—or even to kill civilians, with whom the military supposedly is not engaged in combat.

In wartime or during a buildup to war, a country's mass media typically portray the enemy nation's citizens or its leaders in a dehumanizing way—sinister and satanic, or ridiculous and laughable. Most people in a society tend to go along with these portrayals of the enemy. This phenomenon also occurs at the level of intergroup conflict, for instance, between races, between gangs, and even between cliques in a school.

Christians can take the lead in challenging stereotyped, less-than-human images of enemy groups, nations, or leaders. Called to be peacemakers, Christians ought to constantly remind their fellow citizens that those with whom we have a bitter conflict are still our brothers and sisters and deserve to be treated with respect.

Jobs and Careers That Promote Justice and Peace

One of the best places to help create a just and peaceful world is in the jobs or careers you choose in your lifetime. Here are some questions to ask yourself about the work you do now or will do in the future:

1. What is the primary goal of the work I do? Overall, does it foster life or harm life, or is it a mixed bag?
2. What kinds of activities does the company I work for get involved in? What is its mission, what means are used to accomplish that mission, and does accomplishing it make the world a better place?
3. Does this company treat its employees and its customers or clients fairly? How can I make my voice heard on issues of company fairness?

9
Interview a person involved in a justice or peace organization. Find out about the work of the organization, why the person joined, and why he or she continues to stay involved.

Pax Christi: Peace and Youth

Ned Smith and Andy Petonak are members of the Pax Christi Youth Forum. In October 1993, one year before the unjustly overthrown president of Haiti, Jean-Bertrand Aristide, was restored to power, Ned and Andy visited Haiti. They were part of a Pax Christi peace delegation providing an international presence in that small nation riddled with the violence of an illegal military government. They met people who had been persecuted because they desired social justice. They listened to stories about supporters of democracy who had been made victims of murder, rape, terrorism, and economic oppression. And they encountered a nonviolent democratic resistance movement made up largely of young, courageous, and faith-filled people.

"For us," wrote Ned and Andy, "the experience with the courageous people of Haiti was an encounter with the divine" ("Pax Christi Youth in Haiti").

Sharing Peace

The Latin words *pax Christi* mean "the peace of Christ," and they are the name of a fifty-year-old international Catholic organization devoted to creating a world that reflects Christ's peace. Pax Christi is present in more than twenty countries on four continents. The U.S. section, founded in 1972, has twelve thousand members. Through the Pax Christi Youth Forum, the vision of Christ's peace is promoted on college campuses and in high schools throughout the nation.

In New York City, Youth Forum members shared peace during the 1994 Christmas season by passing out pamphlets to one thousand shoppers at FAO Schwarz, the ultimate toy store. The pamphlets encouraged buyers to purchase toys that emphasize education, cooperation, and justice, rather than those that promote violence. It even listed suggestions, broken down by age-group, to help shoppers make their choices.

Prayer, Study, Action

Pax Christi student groups are involved in a variety of issues from the local to international levels. Any Pax Christi activity has three vital components—prayer, study, and action.

Prayer. Spirituality is at the heart of the Pax Christi movement. Prayer is a chance to talk with and listen to God, and to understand and pursue faith.

Study. It is necessary to study and understand world conditions if work for justice and peace is to be fruitful.

Action. Actions—such as letter-writing campaigns, vigils, and civil disobedience—are considered to be "love enacted." Pax Christi actions are always nonviolent. Violent actions are devoid of meaning and spirituality.

The Pax Christi Youth Forum provides a national voice for young people who desire to make Christ's peace a reality both close to home and around the world. This voice responds compassionately to the evils that damage society, but it also celebrates life's joys.

For information about starting a Pax Christi student group, contact Pax Christi USA, 348 East Tenth Street, Erie, PA 16503-1110; phone 814-453-4955.

Taking a hard look at how you spend about half of your waking hours as an adult can be challenging and risky. But it can lead to the creation of businesses that care about justice. For instance:

The Anawim Fund (*anawim* means "poor of God" in Hebrew) in Davenport, Iowa, is an alternative investment fund. It pools the resources of religious organizations and makes loans to organizations and companies that serve basic human needs and have fair management, hiring, and wage policies.

Says director Pat Miner: "We try to meet two goals: to help alleviate poverty by fostering economic democracy and independence and to provide socially responsible investments for our members." (Adapted from Humphrey, "Can the Common Good Improve a Company's Bottom Line?")

- Describe how you might use the LISTEN process to help determine a career path that does not ultimately harm life.

Participating in War: A Matter of Conscience

Christians have an obligation to reflect seriously on the possibility of their involvement in a war.

During the Vietnam war, hundreds of thousands of young men were drafted into the army. Of those hundreds of thousands, a significant number of young men from different religious traditions, including many Catholics, reached the conclusion that they could not in good conscience participate in the war.

Legal Options

In the United States, what are a young man's legal options in the event of a draft, or military conscription?

1. He can voluntarily enlist in one of the military branches and take whatever assignment they give him.

■
Christians must keep uppermost in their mind the reality that the "enemy" is our sister and our brother in the human family.

Above, left: An Iraqi woman walks past a building in the center of Baghdad, Iraq, that was destroyed by allied planes in the 1991 Persian Gulf war.

Above, right: Urban graffiti and a homeless man's presence on a U.S. city street together make a powerful statement.

2. He can be drafted into the army and work in whatever assignment the army decides for him.

3. He can try to find out if he qualifies for any of the possible deferments or exemptions offered at the time. For instance, he may have a medical problem that would make him ineligible for the draft.

4. He can file a claim as a *conscientious objector within the military.* This means that though he is not in principle opposed to all war, he himself could not in good conscience kill anyone. If he wins the claim, he can be assigned to a noncombat unit, such as a medic unit or a chaplain's office.

5. He can file a claim as a *conscientious objector with nonmilitary status.* He has the right under U.S. law not to participate in war at all if he is a pacifist, that is, if he is convinced that all war is wrong. He must be able to support this claim with evidence of his moral conviction on religious or philosophical grounds. If he wins the claim, he will be expected to serve his country for two years in some nonmilitary work, for instance, in a human services agency that is approved by the government. **10**

The Catholic Church's Teaching

From a Catholic perspective, a young man drafted into war would still be bound to follow his conscience during the conduct of the war itself, even refusing orders if he judges them to be immoral. Speaking on this obligation, Pope John XXIII in his encyclical *Peace on Earth* said, "We must obey God rather than men."

The Catholic hierarchy also asserts that Catholics have the right to claim **conscientious objector status**, whether of the military or nonmilitary type. The teachings of Jesus in the Sermon on the Mount are sufficient evidence to support a pacifist position on religious grounds. In addition, the U.S. bishops have asked for a change in the draft law to allow for *selective conscientious objection*—the right to refuse to serve in a war that one considers unjust, even though one is not a pacifist.

Current U.S. law requires that men register for the draft at age eighteen. If a man intends in the event of an actual draft to file a claim as a conscientious objector (C.O.), he should indicate that on his registration form by writing, "I am a C.O." across the form. A draft board is more likely to take a later C.O. claim seriously if the man can demonstrate a history of moral conviction on this matter.

• How might a young man go through the LISTEN process to decide on his own response to a draft?

For Review

• What did Pope Paul VI say about the relationship between peace and justice?
• Why does training for war involve picturing the enemy in a dehumanizing way?
• What does it mean to be a conscientious objector on the draft? What is the Catholic church's position on conscientious objection?

10
If you know of someone who was a conscientious objector during the Vietnam war, interview that person. Find out how he arrived at his beliefs about war and what kinds of experiences he had as a C.O. Write up the results of your interview.

A Parable of Peacemaking

A childhood incident with a cat, recalled by a woman, provides a fitting parable with which to end this study of the virtue of peacemaking:

In our family, when we meet someone who seems particularly difficult, we recall an old cat that lived in our neighborhood when I was in sixth grade. The lady next door warned us to stay away from it. She said it was wild and would attack anyone who came near.

My sister and I regarded this admonition as a challenge and immediately set about trying to cultivate a friendship with the cat. Eventually we succeeded in getting within arm's length of the pitiful, emaciated creature.

Its terrified eyes seemed to signify a need for help, rather than an intent to harm, but it wouldn't eat any of the food we offered. It would sniff, make deep guttural sounds, and gaze at us with a desperate look.

Our soft, coaxing words slowly built up enough trust so that one day we were able to touch and then carefully gather the gaunt creature into our arms.

Upon close examination, we discovered something clamped in a corner of the cat's jaw, so it was unable to open its mouth. With the help of Mother, we determined that the cat's upper and lower teeth were embedded in a chicken bone. By working carefully, Mother was able to free its jaw. The poor cat seemed to understand we were trying to help and tolerated the efforts. It gave us a look of gratitude, stretched its mouth and tongue, shifted its jaws, and then turned to the dish of food.

That "wild" cat became a friend—still a little wary, but in no way did it ever lash out or harm us.

So today when we encounter a person who seems unfriendly, we try to see if there's a "chicken bone" that can be removed. (Quinlan, "In the Family")

- How might one see if there is a "chicken bone" that can be removed from an unfriendly or difficult person?
- At the level of personal peacemaking, how does this parable illustrate Jesus' teaching "Love your enemy"?
- At the level of peacemaking among groups and nations, how does this parable illustrate Pope Paul VI's words "If you want peace, work for justice"?

What Kind of Person . . . ?

The first chapter of this course posed the major moral question that each one of us has to answer for ourselves: What kind of person am I becoming, and what kind of person do I want to become? **11**

This course has presented a Christian framework for answering that question. Jesus' life gives the Christian a model of the kind of character she or he can aspire to develop. Thus, Jesus' life points to the kind of destiny that is possible for us. The virtues of Jesus' life can be the virtues of *our* life. The destiny of Jesus' life—the joy and glory of the Resurrection—can be *our* destiny. But in order for us to achieve our life's destiny, we must always be open to God's grace at work in us, for we cannot become who we were meant to be without help from God.

Jesus' words of farewell to his disciples at the Last Supper are also addressed to you. They sum up the Christian moral vision, and so they serve well as the parting words of this course:

"As the Father loves me,
so I also love you.
Remain in my love.
If you keep my commandments,
you will remain in my love,
just as I have kept my Father's commandments
and remain in his love.
I have told you this
so that my joy might be in you
and your joy might be complete.
This is my commandment:
love one another
as I love you."

(John 15:9–12)

11
The above question was first posed in chapter 1 of this course. How would you answer it now that you have completed this course?

Index

Italic numbers are references to photos or illustrations.

A

abortion, 247, 249–251; capital punishment and, 265; of defective fetuses, 112, 254; humiliation avoided by, 146; respect for life and, 263; rising rate of, 175
Abraham, 31, 125
abstinence, 64, 173–177
abuse: of bodies, 168, 170; of children, 118, 201, 202, 204–205; of land, 231; manipulation and, 200; of women, 201, 203. *See also* violence
accused woman parable, 95, 97, 198
action movies, 137
active listening, 78, 278
actual sin, 66
Acuna, Irma, 41
Adam, 31, 66, 230
addiction. *See* alcoholism; compulsive behavior; drug addiction
adolescent morality, 14
adoption, 146, 255
Adult Children of Alcoholics (organization), 36, 57
adult companionship, 54–55
adultery, 95
adult morality. *See* mature morality
Adventures of Huckleberry Finn, The (Twain), 86–87
advertising, 77, 165. *See also* mass media
affirmation, 117
affluence, 125–126
African Americans, 212, 264. *See also* civil rights movement; slavery

aged people, 202, 210–211, 237
agribusiness farms, 232
agricultural workers, 132
AIDS (acquired immunodeficiency syndrome): in babies, *225;* chastity and, 174; family acceptance of, 33–34; final stages of, 257–258, 259; Garden Project and, 237
airplane maintenance records, 190
air pollution, 59, *233–234,* 240
Alanon (organization), 57
Alaska, 47–48
Alateen (organization), 36
Alcoholics Anonymous (organization), 24, 41, 57
alcoholism: beginnings of, 159; blindness and, 41; in families, 35, 85; relapse into, 219; treatment for, 21, 24
alcohol use: arrests for, 193; casual sex and, 161, 162; domestic violence and, 202; fatal, 172–173; lying about, 66–67; reasons for, 160; statistics on, 161. *See also* drunk driving
Ali, Irene and Khalif, *225*
Alzheimer's disease, 257, 260
"Amazing Grace" (Newton), 70
Ambrose, Bishop, 22
Amnesty International (organization), 130
amniocentesis, 249, 254
Amos, Book of, 111
anabolic steroids, 170
Anawim Fund, 285
Anderson, Marian, 211
anger, 272, 277
animal genes, 248
anorexia nervosa, 170

antibiotics, 247, 257, 260
anxiety. *See* fear
apartheid, *52,* 127, 276
apathy, 29
Apollo 17 spacecraft, *239*
Appalachia, 121
Argentina, 62
Aristide, Jean-Bertrand, 284
Aristotle, 58
arrests, 193. *See also* prisoners
artificial birth control, 175, 249
artificial intimacy, 176
"assisted suicide," 262
Atlanta, 121
atmospheric pollution, 59, *233–234,* 240
atomic. *See* nuclear . . .
attitudes, 103
Augustine of Hippo, Saint, *22*
automobiles: accidents with, 138, 150, 161; brakes of, 181; drunk driving of, 43, 161, 268, 282; emissions from, 99; nature observed from, 236; reckless driving of, 58, 136, 266, 268; waste oil from, 98–99

B

babies, *174,* 175, *225*
Babylon, 187
Baghdad (Iraq), *285*
baseball, 212
basketball, 167, 209–210
battered women, 201, 203
beachcombing, 227
Beatitudes, 61, 62, 145. *See also* Sermon on the Mount
Beirne, Shawn M., *106*
Beowulf, 135
Bernardin, Cardinal Joseph, 64, 263

Bible, 31, 32, 35, 111, 230. *See also* Gospels; Jewish Law
Big Brothers (organization), 24
biological activity, 237–238
Birch, Charles, 256
Birmingham (Alabama), *274*
birth control, 175, 249, 254
Birthright (organization), 148
birth technologies, 249, 254–255
bishops, 250–251, 265, 266. *See also* Catholic church; United States Catholic bishops
black Americans. *See* African Americans
Black Panthers (organization), 222
Blair, Walter, 87
bodily abuse, 168, 170. *See also* injuries
Body of Christ, 131, 227
bonding, 175–176
book mutilation, 122–123
Border Agricultural Workers (organization), 132
boredom, 140, 148
Boston, 121, 212, 224–225
Boston City Year Program (organization), 121
Brimner, Larry Dane, 212–213
British colonialism, 62, 102
British Navy, 69
British soldiers, *151*
Brothers and Sisters to Us (USCC), 209
Buddhist ethics, 15
Buddhist monks, 242
bulimia, 155, 170, 177
bus boycott (Montgomery, 1956), 133
businesses: "damage control" by, 189; distributive justice and, 125, 127; employees of, 129; Family and Medical Leave Act and, 132; illegal aliens and, 207; justice issues and, 283, 285; "merger mania" of, 122; sexual harassment in, 143; smog control and, 240; stealing from, 181; unsafe practices of, 190

C

Calcutta (India), 36
California, 64, 121
Campaign for Human Development (CHD) (organization), 132
Campus Life, 55
Campus Outreach Opportunity League, 121
cancer, 165, 193, 242, 257–258, 259
"Canticle of the Sun" (Francis of Assisi), 238
capital punishment, 263–265
carbon, *233,* 234
cardinal virtues, 43–44, 45, 93
careers. See *work*
Carey, Mrs., 219
caring adults, 54–55
casinos, 165
casual sex. *See* premarital sex
Catholic Charities (organization), 148
Catholic church: on abortion, 250; on birth control, 251; Campaign for Human Development and, 132; on civil laws, 60; on conscience, 85; on death penalty, 264–265; on distributive justice, 126; on draft, 286; on euthanasia, 257, 258, 259; human rights and, 113; life ethic of, 245, *246,* 247, 263; on marriage, 174; moral support from, 55; sacraments of, 72, 226, 253; teachings of, 63–65; on weapons of mass destruction, 265. *See also* bishops; local parishes
Catholic Worker, The, 119
Catholic Worker Movement, 23, 36, 119
Central Intelligence Agency (CIA), 189
Centro de los Trabajadores Agrícolas Fronterizos (facility), 132
cerebral palsy, 212

Challenge of Peace, The (NCCB), 266
Chanukah, 169
character, 17–18, 20, 94
Charo of the Barrio, 42
chastity, 64, 173–177
cheating, 58, 189–190
chemical plants, 12
Chesterton, G. K., 198
Chez Panisse (restaurant), 237
Chicago, 222–223
children: abuse of, 118, 201, 202, 204–205; care of, 59, 107, 175, *225,* 227; cultural value of, 12–13; death penalty and, 263; Family and Medical Leave Act on, 132; gifts to, 169; injuries to, 148; learning by, 85; love-deprived, 35–36; lying to, 191, 193; morality of, 13; obligations of, 118; thrival needs of, *174;* wise woman and, 96. *See also* families
choices. *See* decisions
Christ House (Washington, D.C.), 219–220, 224
Christian Testament, 32. *See also* Gospels
Christ in the Breadline (Eichenberg), *216*
Christmas, 169, 284
Christopher News Notes, 36, 43, 182, 203, 212, 240
Churches Acting Together for Change and Hope (CATCH), 132
cigarettes, 165
civil disobedience, 60, 62, 102, 242. *See also* nonviolence
civil duties, 119
civil laws, 58, 59–60
civil rights movement: in Chicago, 222; focus of, 138; Higgins and, 223; love in, *274;* in Montgomery, 133; Sermon on the Mount and, 62
classical philosophy, 58
climatic change, 233–234

Cobb, John B., 256
Cold War, 265
Coleridge, Samuel Taylor, 107
Coles, Robert, 23
college students: credit purchases by, 168; disabled, 138, 150; housing for, 194–195; moral development of, 24; prospective, 192; public vandalism and, 122–123
comas, 257
commission, sins of, 110, 166
commitment, 139, 176–177
common good, 119; civil law and, 59; distributive justice and, 125, 129; education and, 128; everyday service to, 120; harm to, 122–123; individual character and, 20, 131. See also goodness
communication, 78, 181, 192, 278
communion of saints, 55–57
community service, 121, 129, 130, 226
companies. See businesses
compassion, 44, 109, 193, 214–227
competitiveness, 16
compulsive behavior, 159–160, 163–166, 200. See also alcoholism; drug addiction
concentration camps, 193. See also internment camps
confession, 179
conflicting goods, 103–104, 107
conflict resolution, 44, 102, 266, 270–287
conscience, 60, 85–90, 93, 95, 135
conscientious objector status, 286
consistent ethic of life, 247, 263. See also reverence for human life
consumerism, 16, 169
Context, 188
contour strips, 231
contraception, 175, 249

Corinthians, First Letter to the, 43, 227
corporal works of mercy, 216
corporations. See businesses
counseling, 54–55, 206
courage, 10, 44, 104, 134–153, 276
cowardice, 137, 142
creation: allegory of, 30, 31; damage to, 59; goodness of, 20, 112; respect for, 44, 228–243; stewardship of, 230–231, 240–241, 243. See also ecological justice
creativity, 89, 275, 278
credit purchases, 168
criminals, 264. See also prisoners
culture, 12–13, 145
curfews, 279

D

date rape, 204, 249
dating, 11, 145, 202
Day, Dorothy, 22–23, 36
Dean, Sylvester, 219–220
death: accidental, 161, 268; artificial causes of, 257–262; communion of saints and, 55, 57; imminent, 32, 193; inevitability of, 245, 269; of Jesus, 246; medical definition of, 247; of organisms, 234, 238; overcoming, 153; risk of, 146–147. See also life-and-death decisions; Resurrection, Jesus'
death penalty, 263–265
debating, 184–185
debts, 116, 168, 169
deception. See lying; self-deception
decisions: chain reactions of, 19; character development and, 17, 94; freedom for making, 31, 52, 250; grace and, 65; life-and-death, 101–102, 106–107; misguided, 18; moral, 11–12, 74–91, 94; self-esteem and, 24

Declaration on Euthanasia (Sacred Congregation for the Doctrine of Faith), 258
delayed gratification, 169
De Mello, Anthony, 33, 75, 138, 227
depression, 160, 215
Derr, Patrick, 261
desert hermits, 45
desertification, 234
destiny, 17
Detroit Amnesty group, 130
developing countries, 126
dialog, 266
dignity. See human dignity
direct abortion, 250
disabled people, 120, 124, 138, 150, 211–212
discrimination. See prejudice
disease, 132. See also under specific diseases
distributive justice, 114, 125–129
divorce, 54–55, 191, 193
DNA, 256
domestic violence, 201–202
Doolittle, Robert, 210–211, 224, 226
Douglass, Frederick, 67
Down's syndrome, 112, 249, 254
draft (conscription), 285–286
drinking. See alcohol use
driving. See automobiles
drug addiction, 35, 41, 159, 166
drug houses, 132
drug use, 160, 161, 166, 202, 268
drunk driving, 43, 161, 268, 282
drunkenness. See alcoholism

E

earth. See creation
Eastern Europe, 62
eating disorders, 155, 170, 177
Ecclesiastes, Book of, 157
ecological justice, 114, 115, 129, 229, 232, 240, 243. See also creation

economic injustice, 125–127

Economic Justice for All (NCCB), 110, 113

education: deprivation of, 112, 114; private, 128; public, 128–129, 132; survival and, 103–104, 146; undocumented aliens and, 64

Eichenberg, Fritz, *216*

elderly people, 202, 210–211, 237

electric chair, *264*

elephants, 112

El Salvador, 62, 147, 151

Emancipation Proclamation, 60

emotional abuse, 202

emotions, 186, 187, 272, 277

empathy, 198

employment. *See* work

end and means, 58, *59*, 102, 103

endurance, 137

enemies, 273, 275, 280–281

energy sources, 99–100

Engelhardt, Lisa and Emily, 279

environmental crises, 99, 240

environmental projects, 229, 240. *See also* ecological justice

Ephesians, Letter to the, 277

epic literature, 135

errors, 21–24, 177, 256

ethnic slurs, 208–209

Eucharist, 72, *73*

Europe, 249

euthanasia, 257–260, 261, 262, 263, 265

Eve, 31, 66, 230

excessive guilt, 89, 131

Exodus story, 31

exploitation. *See* abuse

extracurricular activities, 104–105

Ezekiel, Book of, 216

F

failure, 140–141, 189

faith, 41, 42, 43, 52, 133. *See also* trust

faith communities, 55, 72, 132

faithfulness, 133

Fall, the, 31, 66

false motives, 105, 185, 186

families: abuse in, 118, 201–202; communication in, 53; love deprivation in, 35–36; moral values in, 85; premarital sex issue and, 79; vacations of, 144. *See also* children; marriage; parents

Family and Medical Leave Act (FMLA), 132

family farms, 132, 232

family planning, 175, 249, 254

FAO Schwarz, 284

farmworkers, 132

fear: absence of, 137; creativity and, 89; divine love and, 153; integrity and, 10; lying and, 182; overcoming, 138, 148–151; prejudice and, 210, 211; sources of, 140–141, 143–147

federal government, U.S., 99, 242. *See also* government

feelings, 186, 187, 272, 277

Fellowship of Reconciliation (organization), 62

feminists, 250–251

fertility research, 247

fetuses, 247, 250, 254. *See also* abortion

financial deals, 116–117

financial institutions, 99, 100, 132

financial obligations, 116, 168, 169

financial security, 143. *See also* wealth

firefighters, *274*

fire metaphors, 171–172

fishing industry, 123

football, 183–185

forgiveness: for drunk drivers, 43, 282; for enemies, 282; of God, 89, 215; for murder, 223, 264

fortitude. *See* courage

fossil fuels, 99, 100, 234

foster children, *225*

Fourqurean, Mary Patricia Barth, 174

France, 193

Franciscan friars, 242

Francis of Assisi, Saint, 198, 238

freedom: of choice, 31, 52, 250; from compulsions, 159, 165–166; injustice and, 131; of speech, 60; truth and, 180, 181

friendship: candor in, 65; compassionate, 215; feared loss of, 140; genuine, 53, 200; gossip and, 181; integrity and, 10; in marriage, 163; physical intimacy and, 176; shared feelings and, 186; wonder in, 235. *See also* peer pressure; personal relationships

frustration, 202

full humanness, 20; breadth of, 29; call to, 40; creation and, 238; of Jesus, 27, 32; negative reinforcement and, 67; poor decisions and, 84; virtues and, 44. *See also* wholeness

future generations, 124, 133

G

Gallup polls, 263

gambling, 165

Gandhi, Mohandas K., 62, *102*, 242

Garden of Eden, 31, 230

Garden Project, *237*

Genesis, Book of, 30, 31, 230

genetic engineering, 247–248, 254, 255

Germany, 60, 189, 193, 261

"get-all-you-can" mentality, 123

gift giving, 169

global climatic change, 233–234

global economy, 125–127

global environmental crisis, 99, 240

global peacemaking, 266, 283–286

God: creation of. *See* creation; crime against, 265; faith in, 41, 42, 43, 52, 133; forgiveness of, 89, 215; full humanness and, 44; grace of. *See* grace; heart given by, 216; help from, 81–82; human life span and, 245–246, 248, 262; image of, 30–31; injustice and, 131, 133; Israelites and, 31; law of. *See* Jewish Law; love for, 50; love of. *See* love of God; prayer to. *See* prayer; reconciliation with, 71; Reign of. *See* Reign of God; sexuality and, 162, 163; submission to, 282; suffering and, 217; unplanned pregnancy and, 250, 252; will of, 90; wrong decisions and, 84; *See also* Holy Spirit; Jesus Christ

Goetcheus, Janelle, 219–*220, 224*

Golden Rule, 15, 58, 198–199

goodness: courage and, 137, 138, 151; of creation, 20, 112; defined, 18, 20; denial of, 31, 89; divine perception of, 33; morality and, 12; respect for, 197, 198; social justice and, 119; triumph of, 42, 131, 153. *See also* common good; conflicting goods

good Samaritan parable, 109, *110*

Gospel of Life, The (John Paul II), 247, 253, 264–265

Gospels, 42, 63, 65, 147, 221. *See also under individual Gospels*

gossip, 181

government: common good and, 129; distributive justice and, 125, 127; executions by, 263–265; facts concealed by, 188; just-war theory on, 267; landowners and, 119; laws of, 58, 59–60; public policy and, 99–100, 188; smog control and, 240; U.S., 99, 242

grace, 51–52, 288; compassion and, 222; in daily life, 65; freedom through, 166; injustice overcome by, 131; rejection of, 66; respect and, 213; in sacraments, 72; sin overcome by, 69, 73; theological virtues and, 41; unplanned pregnancy and, 250

graffiti, *285*

great commandment of love, 38, 61, 110, 115

Great Depression, *216*

Greenwich Village (New York City), 23

grocery sacks, 240

Gudorf, Christine, 206

guilt: cheating and, 190; excessive, 89, 131; lying and, 179, 182; manipulation and, 200; unwarranted, 87; warranted, 86

gypsies, 261

H

habits, 17

Haiti, 62, 284

Halpern, Sue, 169

Hanukkah, 169

happiness, 21, 159, 160

Harding, Vincent, 56, 133

Harney, Corbin, 242

Harvest of Justice Is Sown in Peace, The (NCCB), 266

Hassidic tradition, 32

health care, 64, 127, 219–220, 224, 257–260

Hebrew Scriptures, 31, 111. *See also* Jewish Law

Hecker, Mrs., 37–38

helping professions, 64

hemorrhaging woman story, 156

Henning, Doug, 94

hermits, 45

heroes, 57

Heyward, Carter, 96

Higgins, Mrs., 222–223

Himalayan Mountains, 138

Hinduism, 15

Hiroshima (Japan), 242

Hispanic people, 207

Hitler, Adolf, 58, 60

holidays, 169

Hollyday, Joyce, 219–220, 224

Holocaust, 189, 261

Holy Spirit, 65. *See also* God; Jesus Christ

homeless people, *285;* Catholic Worker Movement and, 23; Garden Project and, 237; Missionaries of Charity and, 36; in Washington, D.C., *218, 219–220. See also* marginalized people; poverty

honesty, 44, 85, 165, 166, 178–195

hope, 42, 43, 133, 153, 260

horror movies, 149, 150

human dignity: common good and, 125; economic security and, 113, 126; medical technology and, 248; rights and, 114; threats to, 263

human gene pool, 255

human realization. *See* full humanness

human rights. *See* rights

humiliation, 89, 145–146, 205

humility, 78, 230

Humphrey, Kelly Norton, 285

hypergymnasia, 170

hypocrisy, 95, 97, 276

I

idealism, 14

identity formation, 175

illiteracy, 112, 114

illness, 132. *See also under specific diseases*

imagination, 198

immigrants, 64, 207

impulsiveness, 168

"In Blackwater Woods" (Oliver), 269

incest, 250
independence, 47–48, 49
India, 62
Indian Home Rule (Gandhi), 102
indirect abortion, 250
individualism, 48, 49
individual justice, 114, 116–118
industrialized countries, 126
industries. *See* businesses
infants. *See* babies
infertility, 247
injuries, 146, 148. *See also* abuse
injustice: avoidance as, 109–110,
    127; domestic violence and,
    202; economic, 125–127;
    response to, 131, 133, 273;
    warfare and, 267. *See also*
    justice
inner reality, 81
instant gratification, 169
integrity. *See* honesty
interconnections, 233
interdependence, 48, 49, 73
intergroup conflict, 283
international. *See* global . . .
internment camps, 212–213. *See
    also* concentration camps
interviews, 141, 149, 193
intimacy, 80, 176. *See also*
    sexuality
intuitive decisions, 82
Isaiah, Book of, 111, 243
Islam, 15
"isms." *See* prejudice
Israelites. *See* Jewish people
"I" statements, 277–278
ivory, 112

J

Jairus, 156
Japan, 240, 242
Japanese Americans, 212–213
Jean, Sister, 37–38
Jeremiah, Book of, 31, 111
Jerusalem, 187
Jesuits, 147

Jesus Christ: adulterous woman
    and, 95, 97; Body of, 131, 227;
    compassion of, 221, 224;
    courage of, 150–151, 276;
    creation and, 232; disreputable
    people and, 27–29, 197–198; on
    distributive injustice, 125; on
    enemies, 273, 275, 281; faith-
    fulness of, 177; farewell of, 288;
    on forgiveness, 282; full hu-
    manness of, 27, 32; on great
    commandment of love, 38–39;
    Higgins and, 223; imitation of,
    40, 138; Jewish Law and, 88;
    life loved by, 246; love-deprived
    people and, 36; martyrs for,
    147; moral vision of, 25; needy
    people and, 217, 220; pacifism
    and, 266, 273, 286; parables of,
    109; on persecution, 145; on
    Reign of God, 38–39, 243; on
    responsibility, 119; Resurrection
    of, 42, 153, 269, 288; on self-
    destruction, 200; Simon the
    Pharisee and, 27–29; sin over-
    come by, 69; teachings of,
    61–63; truth and, 180, 188;
    unconventional wisdom of,
    97–98; virtues of, 44, 288;
    wholeness of, 156, 158; on wise
    judgment, 93. *See also* God;
    Holy Spirit
Jewish Law, 15, 31, 88, 95,
    231–232. *See also* Bible; great
    commandment of love; Hebrew
    Scriptures; Ten Commandments
Jewish people: captivity of, 187;
    divine calls to, 31; "final solu-
    tion" for, 189, 261; Hassidic
    tradition of, 32; legal discrimi-
    nation against, 60; Samaritans
    and, 109
Jewish prayer shawls *(tallit)*, 242
job interviews, 141, 149, 193
jobs. *See* work
John, First Letter of, 33, 43
John, Gospel of, 95, 97, 180, 221,
    288

John Paul II, Pope, 64, 126, 247,
    253, 264–265
John XXIII, Pope, 113, 286
journal writing, 186
Jubilee year, 232
judgment day, 217
judicial decisions, 75
justice, 44, 108–133, 135; non-
    violent campaigns for, 276;
    peacemaking and, 283; respect
    and, 197; social, 114, 119–124,
    125, 129, 133. *See also* injustice
Justice in the Marketplace (John
    Paul II), 126
just-war theory, 265–266, 267,
    273

K

kindness, 194–195. *See also* love
King, Martin Luther, Jr., 222;
    heroism of, 135; in Mont-
    gomery, 133; on nonviolence,
    274; Sermon on the Mount
    and, 62; *A Testament of Hope*,
    142
*King Arthur and the Knights of
    the Round Table*, 135
Kownacki, Mary Lou, 263
Kozol, Jonathan, 112, 114
Ku Klux Klan, 222

L

Lake Superior, 229
landowners, 119
land stewardship, 231–232
Land Stewardship Project, 132
last judgment, 217
law. *See* civil laws; Jewish Law;
    natural law
lax conscience, 87–88
Lazarus parable, 125, 126, 127
LeBlanc, Lloyd, 264
legalistic conscience, 88–89
legalized gambling, 165
Lenora, Sister, 220

letters of recommendation, 192
Letters to a Young Poet (Rilke), 51
life-and-death decisions, 101–102, 106–107
life cycle, 238
life stages, 13–14
Lima (Peru), 42
Lincoln, Abraham, 135
Lipkis, Andy, 240
listening, 78, 278
LISTEN process, 78–84, 90, 91; abortion decisions and, 249; abuse victims and, 206; career choice and, 285; cheating and, 190; college careers and, 138; conscience and, 85, 95; creation and, 234, 243; draft and, 286; family problems and, 118; motives and, 105; oil disposal problem and, 99; poor advice and, 143; self-destructive behavior and, 160; self-honesty and, 185; vacation decisions and, 144
literacy, 112, 114
Little Rock (Arkansas), 54
local ecosystems, 234
local parishes, 55, 72, 132
loneliness, 9
Lord of the Rings, The (Tolkien), 135–136
Los Angeles, 240
lotteries, 165
love: Beatitudes on, 61; call to, 32; centrality of, 43; in civil rights movement, *274;* deprivation of, 35–36; for enemies, 280, 281; great commandment of, 38, 61, 110, 115; habits of, 43–44, 45, 93; justice and, 110; kindness and, 194–195; mistaken notions of, 29; Reign of God and, 39; response to, 37–38; truthfulness and, 194; unconditional, 33–34, 50, 89, 112

love of God: challenge of, 43; for creation, 232; for enemies, 281; human compassion and, 220; inclusivity of, 28, 197–198, 213; love deprivation and, 35–36; permanence of, 153; unconditionality of, 33–34, 50, 89, 112
Luke, Gospel of, 27–29, 63, 109, 119, 125, 156, 221
lying, 66–67; bondage of, 181–182; decisions about, 12; family examples of, 85; to parents, 179; rationalization as, 105; tight squeezes and, 188–189; unreality and, 181; "white," 191–192, 193

M

Madaras, Lynda, 176–177
Maddox, Peggy, 240
Madison Square Garden (New York City), 153
magic, 94
magisterium, 63–65
Maguire, Daniel C., 123
Manalapan (New Jersey), 212
Mandela, Nelson, 52
Manichaeanism, 22
Manila (Philippines), 36
manipulation, 200. *See also* abuse
Mannion, Michael T., 252
marginalized people, 64. *See also* homeless people; poverty
Mark, Gospel of, 38, 88, 150–151, 221
marriage: bonding in, 175; boredom in, 140; commitment in, 139, 176–177; sexuality in, 162–163, 176–177, 251. *See also* families
Martin, Melody, 208
martyrs, 147, 151
Mary, Virgin, 252
Maryknoll lay missioners, *213*
massive destruction, 265

mass media: peer values and, 14; physical imagery in, 170; sexual exploitation in, 205; social values and, 16; violence in, 202; wartime propaganda in, 283. *See also* advertising; movies
materialism, 16, 169. *See also* wealth
Matthew, Gospel of, 39, 88, 200, 217, 221, 232, 243, 275, 282. *See also* Beatitudes; Golden Rule; Sermon on the Mount
mature morality: civil laws and, 59; development of, 21–25, 45; independence and, 47; inner nature of, 13–14; long-term thinking and, 80; self-honesty and, 186; sin and, 66; Ten Commandments and, 61
Maurin, Peter, 23, 36, 119
McKibben, Bill, 169
meals, 206. *See also* soup kitchens
Medicaid, 127
medical care, 64, 127, 219–220, 224, 257–260
medical doctors. *See* physicians
medical emergencies, 101–102
medical exemptions, 286
medical technologies, 247–248, 249, 254–255, 261
Medicare, 127
meditation, 281
Mellan, Olivia, 169
men, 175, 204, 205, *218,* 285–286
Mendez, Rudy, 207
mentally retarded people, 212, 263. *See also* Down's syndrome
mercy, 44, 109, 193, 214–227
"mercy killing," 257–260, 261, 262, 263, 265
"merger mania," 122
Messiah. *See* Jesus Christ
Mexicans, 207
migrant workers, 132

military draft, 285–286
military troops, 147, *151*, 283
military weapons, 242, 265, 266
Milwaukee 9 to 5 (project), 132
Miner, Pat, 285
minimum-wage laws, 127
Minnesota, 121, 132
Missionaries of Charity (organization), 36
mistakes, 21–24, 177, 256
misunderstanding, 144
modern warfare, 263, 265–266, 267
Mogopa (South Africa), 52
money. *See* financial . . .
Monica, Saint, 22
monks, 45, 242
Montgomery (Alabama), 133
moral decisions, 11–12, 74–91, 94
moral virtues, 43–44, 45, 93
morphine, 257–258
Morris, Frank and Elizabeth, 43
mortal sin, 68
Mosaic law. *See* Jewish Law
Moses, 31
Mothers Against Drunk Driving (organization), 43
motives, 104–105
Mount Sinai, 40
movies, 137, 149, 150
murder, 223, 263–264
My Name Is Asher Lev (Potok), 245
Mystical Body of Christ, 131, 227

N

Nagasaki (Japan), 242
National Catholic Reporter, 41, 225, 265
National Conference of Catholic Bishops (NCCB). *See* United States Catholic bishops
"National Conference of Catholic Bishops President's Statement on Immigration Debate," 64

Native Americans, 124, 133, 242
natural family planning, 254
natural law, 59
natural world. *See* creation
Nazis, 189, 193, 261
needs, 167
negative reinforcement, 67
Netherlands, 193
networking, 233
Nevada Desert Experience program, 242
Nevada Test Site, 242
Newman, Cardinal John Henry, 97
New Mexico, 75, 132
newspaper advertising, 165
Newton, John, 69, 70
New York City, 23, 153, 284
New York Times, 116
Nicaragua, 62
niceness, 29
nonhuman creation, 112, 114, 229
nonviolence, 246, *275,* 276, 284. *See also* civil disobedience; pacifism
North America: addictive behavior in, 165; Catholicism in, 23; coastal fishing in, 123; environmental projects in, 240; fuel consumption in, 100; "perfection" concept in, 255; rugged individualism in, 48; social values in, 16
North Shore University Hospital (Long Island, New York), 225
nuclear fuels, 99–100
nuclear radiation, 189
nuclear weapons, 242, 265, 266

O

Odyssey, The (Homer), 135
older people, 202, 210–211, 237
Oliver, Mary, 269
omission, sins of, 66, 67–68, 110, 127
On the Destruction of Life Unworthy to Be Lived, 261

Operation Brown Bags, 240
Operation Civic Serve, 121
oral cancer, 165
orchestras, 133
order, 167
organ transplants, 247
original sin, 31, 66
overspending, 16, 169
ovulation, 250, 254
ozone layer, 59, 233, 241

P

"pacification program," 189
pacifism, 266, 273, 286. *See also* nonviolence
Paderewski, Ignace Jan, 51
pain, 215, 217, 221–222
pain control, 257–258, 259, 262
Paiva, Kathleen M., 139
paper sacks, 240
parables, 63, 109. *See also under individual parables*
paralysis, 138
parents: care by, 59, 174, 175; curfews and, 279; divorce of, 54–55, 191, 193; drug problems of, 161; foster, *225;* independence from, 47; injured children and, 148; love deprivation by, 35–36, 54; lying to, 179; moral teaching by, 85; obedience to, 13; obligations of, 118; opinions of, 53; surrogate, 248, 254–255
Parents Anonymous (organization), 206
parish churches, 55, 72, 132
passionate living, 171–172
passivity, 82, 137, 273
Pastoral Constitution on the Church in the Modern World (Vatican Council II), 265
patience, 137
Paul, Saint, 43, 66, 153, 227, 277
Paul VI, Pope, 110, 153, 287
Pax Christi USA (organization), 62

Pax Christi Youth Forum, 284
peacemaking, 44, 102, 266, 270–287
Peacemaking: Day by Day, 274, 276, 283
Peace on Earth (John XXIII), 113, 286
peace organizations, 62, 283
peace treaties, 267
Pearl Harbor (Hawaii), 212
peer pressure, 9, 14, 162, 166
peer rejection, 222
persecution, 145
Persian Gulf war, *285*
personal character, 17–18, 20, 94
personal identity, 175
personal independence, 47–48, 49
personal needs, 167
personal peacemaking, 277–282
personal power, 31, 131
personal relationships: courage and, 137; grace and, 65; honesty and, 181; justice in, 114, 116–118; moral maturity and, 48–49; parables on, 63; reconciliation in, 71–72; sin and, 66–68. *See also* dating; friendship; intimacy; marriage
personal rights. *See* rights
personal sin, 66–67
Peter, Saint, 151
Petonak, Andy, 284
pets, 236
Pharisees: hypocrisy of, 95, 97, 276; legalism of, 88, 151; spite of, 27
Philippines, 36, 62
philosophy, 58
physical injuries, 146, 148. *See also* bodily abuse
physical intimacy, 176. *See also* sexuality
physicians: abortion and, 251; euthanasia and, 257–258, 259, 260, 261; preparation of, 149, 150

pilgrims, 138
Planned Parenthood (organization), 249
planning, 149
plants, 236
Plato, 22
pleasure, 159
Plutarch, 81
pneumonia, 257, 260
Poland, 62, 135
Poles, 261
police, 206
political prisoners, 130
political process, 129
pollution: atmospheric, 59, *233*–234, 240; land, 231; water, 12, 99
popes, 266. *See also under individual popes*
pornography, 205–206
possessions. *See* materialism; wealth
Potok, Chaim, 245
poverty: in Boston, 224, 226; death penalty and, 264; domestic violence and, 202; in Lima, 42; in Little Rock, 54; marginalization and, 64; racism and, 209; self-help resistance to, 132, 285; in United States, 125–126; unplanned pregnancy and, 249; in Venezuela, *113. See also* homeless people
power, 31, 131
prayer, 50–51, 81–82; civil disobedience and, 242; for courage, 152; for enemies, 281; feelings expressed in, 186, 187; of Jesus, 150–151; neglect of, 66; Pax Christi movement and, 284; with saints, 57
pregnancy prevention, 175, 249, 254
pregnant teenagers, 146, 148, 161, 174, 175

Prejean, Sister Helen, 264
prejudice, 16, 67; defined, 208; disabled persons and, 211–212; reduction of, 210, 212–213. *See also* apartheid; racism; sexism
premarital abstinence, 64, 173–177
premarital sex, 159, 173; decision making about, 75–82, 84, 85; hazards of, 175–176; intoxication and, 161, 162; reasons for, 160, 162
premature bonding, 175–176
priests, 72
prisoners, 130, 218–219, 237. *See also* arrests; criminals
privacy rights, 250
private businesses. *See* businesses
private education, 128
pro-choice philosophy, 250–251
pro-life philosophy, 247, 263
prophets, 31, 111, 234
proportionality, 58, 259, 265–266, 267
Proposition 187 (California), 64
prudence, 44, 92–107, 135
Psalms, Book of, 187, 194, 230, 232
puberty, 175, 176–177
public education, 128–129, 132
public funds, 132
public policy, 99–100, 188
public roads, 119
public vandalism, 122–123

Q

"quick fix" mentality, 16
Quinlan, Betty, 287

R

Rachel and Her Children (Kozol), 112, 114
racism, 208–209, 222, 274. *See also* apartheid; prejudice
rape, 198, 204, 249, 250

Rapien, Mary Lynne, 90
rationalizations, 105, 185, 186
Reading (Massachusetts), 224
reckless driving, 58, 136, 266, 268
reckless endangerment, 263, 266, 268
recommendations, 192
reconciliation, 71–72, 253
recycling, *241*
Reese, Pee Wee, 212
reflection, 84
regional conflicts, 265
Reign of God, 38–39, 232; Beatitudes and, 61; communion of saints and, 55; creation and, 243; faith and, 41; hope in, 42; opposition to, 275
relatedness. *See* personal relationships
religions, 15, 20, 58, 62
rent strike (Chicago, 1966), 222–223
respect: affirmation and, 117; for creation, 44, 228–243; international peace and, 266; for persons, 44, 196–213, 263
respirators, 257, 259
responsibility, 31
Resurrection, Jesus', 42, 153, 269, 288
retaliation, 278
reverence for human life, 12–13, 44, 244–269
Rhein, Alice, 130
Rhode Island Rape Crisis Center, 204
riches. *See* wealth
rights, 112; categories of, 114; civil law and, 59; international peace and, 266; majority desires and, 119–120; respect as, 197
"right to die," 262
Rilke, Rainer Maria, 51
risks, 97, 136
Roach, Archbishop John R., 64
roads, 119

Robinson, Jackie, 212
Roe versus Wade (1973), 249
Rogers, Keith, 242
Romans, Book of, 66, 131, 153
romantic relationships, 11, 145, 202
Romero, Archbishop Oscar, 147
Roosevelt, Eleanor, 147
rugged individualism, 48, 49
rumors, 181
Ryan, Dick, 225

S

Sabbaths, 88, 231–232
sacraments, 72, 226, 253
sacrifice, 119, 123
Saint John the Evangelist Church (Boston), 224, 226
saints, 55–57, 198. *See also under individual saints*
Saint Vincent's Hospital (New York), *258*
Salvador, 62, 147, 151
salvation, 109
Samaritan Inn (Washington, D.C.), 220
Samaritans, 109
San Francisco, *124*, 218–219
San Francisco County, 237
Sarah, 31
Saray, Abd al-Qahhar, 130
savings and loan industry, 99, 100
Schwartzberg, Dr., 55
science, 235. *See also* medical technologies
scribes, 95, 97, 151, 276
seasons, 238
segregation. *See* apartheid; racism
selective conscientious objection, 286
self-caring, 167
self-deception, 163–165, 185, 186, 190
self-destructive behavior, 159–160, 200. *See also* alcoholism; compulsive behavior; drug addiction; vices

self-esteem: gossip and, 181; love deprivation and, 36; moral development and, 24–25; negative reinforcement and, 67; physical aspects of, 168, 170; prejudice and, 210
self-help projects, 124, 132, 285
self-honesty, 183–185, 186
selfishness, 123
self-knowledge, 81
self-restraint, 155, 156, 165, 166, 171–172
self-sacrifice, 119, 123
senior citizens, 202, 210–211, 237
Sermon on the Mount, 39, 61–62, 93, 273, 274, 275, 286. *See also* Beatitudes
sexism, 67, 209–210
sexual abstinence, 64, 173–177
sexual abuse, 198, 202, 204–206, 249, 250
sexual harassment, 143
sexuality, 81, 162–163, 176–177, 251. *See also* family planning; intimacy; pornography; premarital sex
shame, 89, 145–146, 205
Shoshone Native Americans, 242
Simon the Pharisee, 27–29, 198
sin: anger and, 277; of commission, 110, 166; defined, 31; grace and, 69, 73; insensitivity to, 87–88; Jesus and, 32; of omission, 66, 67–68, 110, 127; Sacrament of Reconciliation and, 72. *See also* injustice
Sinai Covenant, 40
Sin Fronteras Organizing Project, 132
single mothers, 175. *See also* pregnant teenagers
Six Nations Iroquois Confederacy (organization), 124
slander, 181
slavery, 60, 69, 86–87, 135
slums, *113*, 222–223

Smith, Ned, 284
smog, 240
smokeless tobacco, 165
Sneed, Cathrine, *237*
Snelling Company, 207
social communication, 181
Social Concerns Bulletin, 127
social justice, 114, 119–124, 125, 129, 133
social problems, 64, 103, 172
Social Security, 127
social sin, 66, 67–68
social values, 14, 16
soil erosion, *231*
Sojourners, 52, 56, 133, 219–220, 224
solar power, *100*
soldiers, 147, *151*, 283
Solidarity movement (Poland), 135
Sonnier, Patrick, 264
soup kitchens, 218–219, 224, 226, 237
South Africa, *52*, 127, 276
Southern Christian Leadership Conference (organization), 274
Soviet Union, 265
Soweto (South Africa), *52*
spiritual works of mercy, 216
sports, *141*, 170
stealing, 179, 181
stereotypes, 207–208, 209, 210, 211, 283
sterilization, 254
steroids, 170
stewardship, 230–231, 240–*241*, 243
St. Francis of Assisi (Chesterton), 198
Stillwater (Minnesota), 132
Storytelling (Lane), 32
Straight (rehabilitation program), 166
Strangers and Guests (NCCB), 231
suffering, 215, 217, 221–222

suicide, 260, 262; attempted, 41; averting of, 106–107; contemplated, 215; intoxication and, 161; permanence of, 24
"sunshine units," 189
support organizations, 57, 206, 224
surrogate parenthood, 248, 254–255
survival rights, 114
sustainable development, 266
Sweetwater (Texas), 240
symphony orchestras, 133

T

tallit, 242
Taoism, 15
Teacher, 202
television advertising, 77, 165
temperance. *See* wholeness
Temple Beth Shalom (Manalapan, New Jersey), 212
Ten Commandments, 38, 40, 61
Teresa, Mother, 36, 198
terminal illness, 257–260, 262
Testament of Hope, A (King), 142
Texas, 132, 240
Thailand, 242
theft, 179, 181
theological virtues, 40–43, 45, 93. *See also* faith; hope; love
Thomas, Lewis, 256
Thoreau, Henry David, 16
"thrival" rights, 114, 118
"tight-squeeze" situations, 188–189
tobacco, 165
Tolkien, J. R. R., 135–136
toys, 284
transplanted organs, 247
Tree Corps (organization), 237
Tree People (organization), 240
Truitt, Don, 51
trust, 179, 181, 190, 204. *See also* faith

truth, 180, 188, 190, 192–193, 194–195. *See also* honesty
Tubman, Harriet, 135
Tutu, Archbishop Desmond, *52*, 127
Twain, Mark, 86–87

U

ultraviolet light, 59
unconditional love, 33–34, 50, 89, 112
unconventional wisdom, 97–98
Underground Railroad, 135
undocumented immigrants, 64, 207
United Farm Workers (union), 242
United Nations, 113, 249, 266
United States: abortions in, 249; capital punishment in, 263–264; civil rights movement in. *See* civil rights movement; domestic violence in, 201–202; draft in, 285–286; holiday celebrations in, 169; incomes in, 125–126, 127; individual justice in, 116; legalized gambling in, 165; military forces of, 265; paper consumption in, 240; peacemaking by, 266
United States Catholic bishops: *Brothers and Sisters to Us,* 209; *The Challenge of Peace,* 266; *Economic Justice for All,* 110, 113; *The Harvest of Justice Is Sown in Peace,* 266; "National Conference of Catholic Bishops President's Statement on Immigration Debate," 64; *Putting Children and Families First,* 132; *Strangers and Guests,* 231. *See also* bishops
United States Catholic Conference (USCC), 126, 132, 209
United States Central Intelligence Agency, 189

United States government, 99, 242

United States Supreme Court, 249, 263

unity, 167

Universal Declaration on Human Rights, 113

universal principles, 15

unmarried mothers, 175. *See also* pregnant teenagers

untruthfulness. *See* lying

unwarranted guilt, 87

usefulness, 200

U.S. News and World Report, 190

V

values, 14, 16

vandalism, 122–123

Vanderhaar, Gerard, 263

Vatican Council II, 265

venereal disease, 174

Venezuela, *113, 213*

venial sin, 68

verbal abuse, 201

vices, 17. *See also* self-destructive behavior

Vietnam war, 189, 242, 285

violence, 16, 102, 150, 201–206. *See also* abuse; murder; rape; war

virtues, 17, 40–44, 45, 93, 94

Voices from the Camps (Brimner), 213

volunteer service, 121, 129, 130, 226

Vuyst, Alex, 124

W

Walden (Thoreau), 16

Walesa, Lech, 135

Wall Street Journal, 175

war, 58, 263, 265–266, 267, 283

warranted guilt, 86

Warren, Robert Penn, 20

water pollution, 12, 99

wealth, 125–126. *See also* financial security; materialism

weapons, 242, 265, 266

Wharton, Paul, 107

"white" lies, 191–192, 193

white-water rafting, 120

wholeness, 44, 154–177. *See also* full humanness

Wilson, Eddie, 37–38

wind power, *100*

wise judgment, 44, 92–107, 135

Witness for Peace (organization), 62

women: childhood abuse of, 205; fertile periods of, 254; prejudice against, 67, 209–210; rape of, 198, 204, 249, 250; violence against, 201, 203. *See also* pregnant teenagers

work: addiction to, 163–165; distributive justice and, 129; justice promotion in, 283, 285; right to, 113; threatened loss of, 143. *See also* job interviews

World Day of Peace (1993), 126

World Health Organization, 254

world religions, 15, 20, 58, 62

World War II, 58, 151, 193, 212

World Youth Day (Denver, 1993), 64

written journals, 186

wrongly formed conscience, 86

Y

You Learn by Living (Roosevelt), 147

"you" statements, 277–278

Youth Update, 45, 55, 90, 139, 279

Youthworker Update, 121, 126, 165, 166, 197–198, 213

Z

Zusya, Rabbi, 32

Acknowledgments (continued)

The scriptural quotations found on pages 109, 111, 125, 153, 157, 217, 221, 227, 230, 232, 243, 273, and 277 are from the New Revised Standard Version of the Bible. Copyright © 1989 by the Division of Christian Education of the National Council of the Churches of Christ in the United States of America. All rights reserved.

The psalm on page 187 is from *Psalms Anew: In Inclusive Language,* compiled by Nancy Schreck and Maureen Leach (Winona, MN: Saint Mary's Press, 1986). Copyright © 1986 by Saint Mary's Press. All rights reserved.

The scriptural quotation found on page 216 is from the New Jerusalem Bible. Copyright © 1985 by Darton, Longman and Todd, London; and Doubleday, a division of Bantam Doubleday Dell Publishing Group, New York.

All other scriptural quotations used in this book are from the New American Bible with Revised New Testament, copyright © 1986 by the Confraternity of Christian Doctrine, Washington, DC; and the New American Bible, copyright © 1970 by the Confraternity of Christian Doctrine. Used with permission. All rights reserved.

The excerpt on page 16 is from *Walden,* by Henry David Thoreau (New York: Grolier, 1969), page 346.

The excerpt on page 23 is reprinted as quoted in *Dorothy Day: A Radical Devotion,* by Robert Coles (Reading, MA: Addison-Wesley Publishing Company, 1987), page 9. Copyright © 1987 by Robert Coles.

The excerpt on page 32 is based on a story from the Hassidic tradition, as told by Rev. Belden C. Lane on an audiotape entitled *Storytelling: The Enchantment of Theology* (Minneapolis: Bethany House Publishers, no date). Used with permission.

The first excerpt on page 33 is from *The Song of the Bird,* by Anthony de Mello (Garden City, NY: Image Books, 1982), pages 67–68. Copyright © 1982 by Anthony de Mello. Used by permission of Doubleday, a division of Bantam Doubleday Dell Publishing Group.

The quote by Mother Teresa on page 36 is from "Little Things Mean a Lot," *Christopher News Notes,* number 323, March 1990. Used with permission.

The excerpt on page 41 is condensed from "Blinded in Suicide Attempt, Woman Rebuilds Life in Faith," by Charlene Scott, *National Catholic Reporter,* 17 June 1988.

The excerpts on page 42 are from *Charo of the Barrio: Lessons in Justice for Youth and Young Adults Leader's Manual* (Saint Columbans, NE: Columban Fathers, 1990), pages 42–44. Copyright © 1990 by the Columban Fathers. Used with permission.

The first excerpt on page 43 is from "Say It with Love," *Christopher News Notes,* number 309, November 1988. Used with permission.

The excerpt on page 45 is reprinted as quoted in "Lent: A Spiritual Workout," by Gloria Hutchinson, *Youth Update,* February 1986.

The excerpt on pages 50–51 is quoted from "Happy to Be Me: The Seven-Day Challenge," *Campus Life,* May–June 1989, page 36. Used with permission.

The first excerpt on page 51 is from *Letters to a Young Poet,* by Rainer Maria Rilke, translated by M. D. Herter Norton (New York: W. W. Norton and Company, 1934), pages 33–34. Copyright © 1934 by W. W. Norton and Company. Used with permission.

The second excerpt on page 51 is adapted from "He Can Enter Our Stage of Life," by Rev. Don Truitt, *Winona Daily News,* 18 February 1990.

The excerpt on page 52 is from "Deeper into God," an interview with Desmond Tutu, *Sojourners,* August–September 1988, page 23. Used with permission.

The first excerpt on page 55 is from "Beyond a Broken Promise," by Gregg Lewis, *Campus Life,* April 1989, page 46. Used with permission.

The second excerpt on page 55 is from "Find Your Place in the Parish," by Robert W. Smith, *Youth Update,* February 1987. Used with permission.

The excerpts on pages 56 and 133 are from "In the Company of the Faithful: Journeying Toward the Promised Land," by Vincent Harding, *Sojourners,* May 1985, pages 16–17. Used with permission.

The first excerpt on page 64 is from "Call for a Consistent Ethic of Life," from Cardinal Joseph Bernardin's 6 December 1983 address at Fordham University in New York, as quoted in *Origins,* December 1983, page 493.

The second excerpt on page 64 is from "NCCB's President's Statement on Immigration Debate," from the U.S. bishops' meeting on Proposition 187, as quoted in *Origins,* 1 December 1994, page 431.

The third excerpt on page 64 is from "Grateful for the Gift: Sexuality, Parents and Teens," by Archbishop John R. Roach, as quoted in *Origins,* 17 March 1988, page 690.

The final excerpt on page 64 is from Pope John Paul II's address on World Youth Day 1993 in Denver, Colorado, as quoted in *Catholic Trends,* 28 August 1993.

The quotation by Frederick Douglass on page 67 is reprinted as quoted in *Overview* 24, number 11, November 1990.

The lyrics to the song "Amazing Grace" on page 70 were written by John Newton (1725–1807).

The excerpts on pages 75, 138, and 227 are from *Taking Flight: A Book of Story Meditations,* by Anthony de Mello (New York: Doubleday, 1988), pages 185–186, 159, and 124, respectively. Copyright © 1988 by Gujarat Sahitya Prakash. Used by permission of Doubleday, a division of Bantam Doubleday Dell Publishing Group.

The idea of moral decision making as being like a blueberry pie, found on page 83, is courtesy of James B. Nelson, professor of Christian ethics at United Theological Seminary in New Brighton, Minnesota.

The excerpt on pages 86–87 is from *The Adventures of Huckleberry Finn,* by Mark Twain (New York: Grolier, 1969), pages 284–285.

The excerpts on page 87 are from *Mark Twain and Huck Finn,* by Walter Blair (Berkeley, CA: University of California Press, 1960), pages 143–144. Copyright © 1960.

The excerpt on page 90 is from "Want to Be Friends?" by Mary Lynne Rapien, *Youth Update,* August 1984. Used with permission.

The excerpt on page 96 is reprinted as quoted from an anonymous author in *Touching Our Strength,* by Carter Heyward (San Francisco: Harper and Row, 1989), page 73. Copyright © 1989 by Carter Heyward. Used with permission of the publisher.

The excerpt on page 97 by Cardinal John Henry Newman is from *The Book of Catholic Quotations* (New York: Farrar, Straus, and Cudahy, 1956), page 918. Copyright © 1956 by Farrar, Straus, and Cudahy.

The excerpt on page 102 is from *Hind Swaraj (Indian Home Rule),* by Mohandas K. Gandhi, 1908.

The excerpt on page 107 is from *Stories and Parables for Preachers and Teachers,* by Paul Wharton (Mahwah, NJ: Paulist Press, 1986), page 35. Copyright © 1986 by Rev. Paul Wharton. Used with permission.

The excerpts on pages 110 and 113 are from *Economic Justice for All,* by the National Conference of Catholic Bishops (NCCB), numbers 39 and 80, 13 November 1986. Published by the *Catholic Telegraph,* newspaper of the Archdiocese of Cincinnati. Used with permission of the Archdiocese of Cincinnati.

The excerpt on page 112 and continued on page 114 is from *Rachel and Her Children: Homeless Families in America,* by Jonathan Kozol (New York: Fawcett Columbine, 1988), pages 102 and 104–106. Copyright © 1988 by Jonathan Kozol. Reprinted by permission of Crown Publishers.

The excerpt on page 116 is by Alexandra Sachs, as quoted in "Metropolitan Diary," *The New York Times,* 20 July 1994, page C2. Copyright © 1994 by The New York Times Company. Reprinted by permission.

The quote by Peter Maurin on page 119 is from "The Aims and Means of the Catholic Worker Movement," *The Catholic Worker,* May 1990, page 5.

The examples of community service on page 121 and the first quote on page 126 are from "A Cup of Cold Water," *Youthworker Update,* April 1989, page 2.

The quote on page 123 is from *The Moral Revolution: A Christian Humanist Vision,* by Daniel C. Maguire (San Francisco: Harper and Row, 1986), page 26. Copyright © 1986 by Daniel C. Maguire.

The excerpt on page 124 is from "Self-help for the Homeless," by Alex Vuyst, *The Humanist,* May–June 1989.

The second excerpt on page 126 is from Pope John Paul II's message for the 1 January 1993 World Day of Peace, as quoted in *Origins,* 24 December 1992, pages 476–477.

The third excerpt on page 126 is from "Special Sensitivity Toward Those in Distress," by Pope John Paul II, *Justice in the Marketplace: Collected Statements of the Vatican and the United States Catholic Bishops on Economic Policy, 1891–1984* (Washington, DC: United States Catholic Conference [USCC], 1985), page 352. Copyright © 1985 by the USCC. All rights reserved.

The quote on page 127 by Archbishop Desmond Tutu was reprinted from *Social Concerns Bulletin* (Diocese of Winona Social Concerns Commission), Winter 1989, page 10.

The excerpt on page 130 is from "A Liberating Flood of Letters," by Alice Rhein, *Christian Science Monitor,* 1 March 1995, no page.

The quote on page 132 is from *Putting Children and Families First: A Challenge for Our Church, Nation, and World,* by the USCC (Washington, DC: USCC, 1992), page 19. Copyright © 1992 by the USCC.

The excerpt on page 139 is from "Lifetime Decisions: How to Shape Your Future," by Kathleen M. Paiva, *Youth Update,* May 1984. Used with permission.

The excerpt by Martin Luther King Jr. on page 142 is from *A Testament of Hope: The Essential Writings of Martin Luther King Jr.,* edited by James Melvin Washington (New York: Harper and Row, 1986), pages 512–513. Copyright © 1986 by Coretta Scott King. Used with permission.

The quote by Eleanor Roosevelt on page 147 is from *You Learn by Living,* 1960, as quoted in *Familiar Quotations,* by John Bartlett, edited by Emily Morison Beck (Boston: Little, Brown and Company, 1980), page 786. Copyright © 1980 by Little, Brown and Company.

The soldier's prayer on page 151 is from *Poems from the Desert,* by members of the British Eighth Army, 1944, as quoted in *Familiar Quotations,* page 925.

The statistics on page 161 are from *Community Update: A Professional Report on Adolescent Chemical Dependency* 5, number 3, November 1988, and *National Survey Results on Drug Use from the Monitoring the Future Study, 1975–1993,* by Lloyd D. Johnston, Patrick M. O'Malley, and Jerald G. Bachman (Rockville, MD: National Institute on Drug Abuse, 1994), pages 6, 8, and 9.

The statistics on page 165 are from "Kids Ante Up for Fun," *Youthworker Update,* November 1989.

The excerpt on page 166 is from "Doing Drugs: Mark and Christy Tell Their Stories," by Lisa Bastian, *Youth Update,* November 1984. Used with permission.

The first excerpt on page 169 is from an interview with Olivia Mellan, as quoted in *Savvy Woman,* May 1990, page 24.

The remaining excerpts on page 169 are from "Hundred Dollar Holidays," by Sue Halpern and Bill McKibben, *Cross Currents,* Fall 1992, pages 365 and 367. Used with permission.

The quote on page 174 is from "Chastity as Shared Strength: An Open Letter to Students," by Mary Patricia Barth Fourqurean, *America,* 6 November 1993, page 11.

The excerpt on page 175 is reprinted as quoted in *Becoming a Man: Basic Information, Guidance, and Attitudes on Sex for Boys,* by William J. Bausch, pages 253–254. Excerpt originally appeared in the *Wall Street Journal,* 11 October 1986, page 26.

The excerpt on pages 176–177 is from *The What's Happening to My Body? Book for Boys,* by Lynda Madaras (New York: Newmarket Press, 1984), page 167. Copyright © 1984, 1988 by Lynda Madaras. Reprinted by permission of Newmarket Press, 18 East 48th Street, New York, NY 10017.

The excerpt on page 182 is from "Honesty Is Still in Style," *Christopher News Notes,* number 308, October 1988. Used with permission.

The quote on page 188 is from *Context,* 1 May 1990, page 4.

The excerpt on page 190 is summarized from "Eastern's Unwitting Safety Lesson," *U.S. News and World Report,* 6 August 1990, page 8.

The excerpt on pages 197–198 is reprinted as quoted in *Youthworker Update,* February 1989, page 8. Used with permission.

The quote about Saint Francis of Assisi on page 198 is from *St. Francis of Assisi,* by Gilbert K. Chesterton (New York: George H. Doran Company, 1924), page 142. Copyright © 1924 by George H. Doran Company.

The abuse statistics on pages 201–202 are from *Infolink,* by the National Victim Center, 1992, volume 1, numbers 14, 5, and 17.

"Reflections of a Battered Wife," on page 203, is from "When Home Is Where the Hurt Is," *Christopher News Notes,* number 326, June 1990. Used with permission.

The excerpt on page 209 is from *Brothers and Sisters to Us: U.S. Bishops' Pastoral Letter on Racism in Our Day* (Washington, DC: USCC, 1979), page 6. Copyright © 1979 by the USCC.

The excerpts on pages 210–211 and the third excerpt on page 224 and continued on 226 are from *Be Alive in Christ,* by Robert Doolittle (Winona, MN: Saint Mary's Press, 1991), pages 91–92 and 81–82. Copyright © 1991 by Saint Mary's Press. All rights reserved.

The excerpts on page 212 are from "Healing the Hate," *Christopher News Notes,* number 327, July–August 1990. Used with permission.

The excerpt on pages 212–213 is from *Voices from the Camps: Internment of Japanese Americans During World War II,* by Larry Dane Brimner (Chicago: Franklin Watts, 1994), page 68. Copyright © 1994 by Larry Dane Brimner.

The excerpt on pages 218–219 is from "Johnny's Holiday," by Jill Keown, *Christian Science Monitor,* 22 December 1988, page 15.

The excerpts on pages 219–220, 220, and the first and second excerpts on 224 are from "Rest for the Weary," by Joyce Hollyday, *Sojourners,* January 1988, pages 18–19, 16, and 19, respectively. Used with permission.

The excerpt on page 225 is from "Foster Parents of Special Breed Emerge to Care for AIDS Infants," by Dick Ryan, *National Catholic Reporter,* 25 May 1990, pages 1 and 10. Reprinted by permission of the *National Catholic Reporter,* P.O. Box 419281, Kansas City, MO 64141.

The excerpt on page 231 is from *Strangers and Guests: Toward Community in the Heartland* (Sioux Falls, SD: Heartland Project, 1980), number 50.

The excerpt on page 236 is from *Dreams Alive: Prayers by Teenagers,* edited by Carl Koch (Winona, MN: Saint Mary's Press, 1991), page 73. Copyright © 1991 by Saint Mary's Press. All rights reserved.

The story on page 237 is based on "These Green Things: Cathrine Sneed and the San Francisco Garden Project," *Orion,* Summer 1994, pages 18–28.

The first excerpt on page 240 is from "What on Earth Can I Do?" *Christopher News Notes,* number 322, February 1990. Used with permission.

The second excerpt on page 240 is from "Operation Brown Bags," by Peggy Maddox, *Holistic Resource Management Newsletter,* number 29, July 1990, page 12. Used with permission.

The account of the Nevada Desert Experience on page 242 is based on "Anti-nuclear Activists Stage Protests" and other news reports by Keith Rogers of the *Las Vegas Review-Journal,* 7–10 August 1995, and private communication with Dr. Arthur Waskow, director of the Shalom Center.

The excerpt on page 245 is from *My Name Is Asher Lev,* by Chaim Potok (New York: Alfred A. Knopf, 1972), pages 156–157. Copyright © 1972 by Chaim Potok. Reprinted by permission of Alfred A. Knopf. British rights applied for.

The quotes on pages 247, 253, and 264–265 are from Pope John Paul II's encyclical *The Gospel of Life,* as quoted in *Origins,* 6 April 1995, numbers 101, 99, and 9 and 56, respectively. Used with permission.

The excerpt on page 252 is from *Abortion and Healing: A Cry to Be Whole,* by Michael T. Mannion (Kansas City, MO: Sheed and Ward, 1986), pages 29–33. Copyright © 1986 by Michael T. Mannion. Used by permission of the publisher.

The excerpt on page 256 was quoted in *The Liberation of Life: From the Cell to the Community,* by Charles Birch and John B. Cobb Jr. (Cambridge, MA: Cambridge University Press, 1981), page 266. Copyright © 1981 by Cambridge University Press.

The excerpt on page 261 is from "Allegiance to the Hippocratic Oath," by Patrick Derr, *Christian Science Monitor,* 19 April 1989, page 18. Used by permission of the author.

The quote on page 263 is from *Way of Peace: A Guide to Nonviolence,* edited by Gerard Vanderhaar and Mary Lou Kownacki (Erie, PA: Pax Christi USA, 1987), page 25. Copyright © 1987 by Pax Christi USA.

The excerpts on pages 264 are from "Should Killers Live? Or Die? The Death-penalty Debate," by Helen Prejean, *Good Housekeeping,* August 1993, pages 94 and 173. Reprinted by permission of the author and the Watkins/Loomis Agency.

The information about modern warfare on page 265 is from "U.S. Emerges as Top Merchant in Global Arms Trade," *National Catholic Reporter,* 17 June 1994, page 28.

The excerpt on page 265 is from *The Documents of Vatican II,* edited by Walter M. Abbott (New York: America Press, 1966), page 294. Copyright © 1966 by America Press.

The quote on page 266 and continued on 268 is from "Catholic Morality Revisited: More to the Morality of the Body Than Sex," by Gerard S. Sloyan, *Professional Approaches for Christian Educators (PACE)* 18, March 1988, page 173.

The just-war theory on page 267 is adapted from *War?* by Timothy McCarthy (Winona, MN: Saint Mary's College Press, 1970), pages 41–69. Copyright © 1970 by Saint Mary's College Press. All rights reserved.

The poem by Mary Oliver on page 269 is from *American Primitive* (Boston: Little, Brown and Company, 1978), pages 82–83. Copyright © 1983 by Mary Oliver. First appeared in *Yankee* magazine. Used by permission of Little, Brown and Company.

The excerpts on pages 274, 276, and 283 are from *Peacemaking: Day by Day,* volume 1 (Erie, PA: Pax Christi USA, 1985), pages 126, 26, and 23, respectively. Copyright © 1985 by Pax Christi USA.

The excerpt on page 279 is from "How to Fight F.A.I.R.," by Lisa and Emily Engelhardt, *Youth Update,* April 1988. Used with permission.

The meditation on page 281 is adapted from an interview with Richard K. Taylor.

The quote on page 284 is from "Pax Christi Youth in Haiti," *The Flame* (Newsletter of the Pax Christi Youth Forum), Spring 1994, page 3.

The excerpt on page 285 is adapted from "Can the Common Good Improve a Company's Bottom Line?" by Kelly Norton Humphrey, *Salt,* September 1994, pages 22–23. Used by permission of *Salt* magazine.

The excerpt on page 287 is from "In the Family," by Betty Quinlan, *Christian Science Monitor,* 21 November 1988.

Photo Credits
Patricia Barry-Levy, ProFiles West: page 118
Mitchell Beazley Publishers: page 136
The Bettmann Archive: pages 22, 36, 52, 60, 142, 147, 151, 264, 274, 285 left
Calvin and Hobbes cartoons by Bill Watterson on pages 19 and 59 are reprinted by permission of Universal Press Syndicate, Kansas City, MO.
Ernesto Cardenal: page 110
Catholic News Service: pages 63, 64
Cleo Freelance Photography: pages 69, 117 right, 139, 157, 227, 260
Columban Fathers: page 42 right
Mimi Cotter, International Stock Photo: page 173
Tomas del Amo, ProFiles West: page 70
Gail Denham: pages 8 right, 11 right, 13 left, 13 right, 50 right, 56, 62, 79 right, 124 top
Michael Douglas, Third Coast Stock: page 199 right
Editorial Development Associates: pages 141 right, 209
Mary Farrell: page 67

J. Patrick Forden: page 237
G. F. Fritz, ProFiles West: pages 238, 248
Habitat for Humanity: page 121
Jack Hamilton: pages 39, 77 right, 104, 120
Tim Haske, ProFiles West: pages 171, 230
Ansel Horn, Impact Visuals: page 258
Gabe Kirchheimer, Impact Visuals: page 111
Land Stewardship Project: page 231
Phil Lauro, ProFiles West: pages 49, 152, 243
Jean-Claude Lejeune: pages 21, 30 left, 30 right, 35 right, 84, 91 right, 101, 117 left, 128, 180, 186, 192, 207 top, 234, 261, 279
Bob Leroy, ProFiles West: page 251
Barry Levy: ProFiles West: pages 54, 164
Maryknoll Fathers: pages 113, 213
Tom Matthews: page 225
Dan McCoy, Rainbow: pages 100 left, 256
Mary Messenger: pages 50 left, 80, 177, 195
Milwaukee Journal Photo: page 23
NASA: page 239
Lennart Nilsson: page 250
Rick Reinhard, Sojourners: page 220
Lisa Rudy, ProFiles West: page 246 right
Allen Russell, ProFiles West: pages 124, 144 right, 161, 174, 184, 191, 205, 273, 275, 288
Saint Francis Medical Center: page 259
Scala, Art Resource, NY: page 102
Mae Scanlan: page 287
James L. Shaffer: pages 11 left, 73, 91 left, 141 left, 144 left, 150, 157 top, 162 right, 165, 201, 207, 268, 272, 276, 285 right
Skjold Photography: pages 8 left, 14, 35 left, 44, 77 left, 158 left, 162 left, 179, 199 left, 246 left, 277, 282
Sojourners: page 218
Paul Spinelli, ProFiles West: page 28
Charles Weber: pages 100 right, 158 right, 208
Doug Wechsler: page 233
Wiley/Wales, ProFiles West: page 241